D1528727

THROUGH
THE EYE OF
A NEEDLE

THROUGH THE EYE OF A NEEDLE

Judeo-Christian Roots of Social Welfare

Edited by
Emily Albu Hanawalt
Carter Lindberg

The Thomas Jefferson University Press
at Northeast Missouri State University
Kirksville, Missouri 63501
1994

Distributed by arrangement with
University Publishing Associates,ᔆᴹ Inc.
4720 Boston Way
Lanham, MD 20706 USA

3 Henrietta Street
London WC2E 8LU England

Library of Congress Cataloging-in-Publication Data

Through the eye of a needle : Judeo-Christian roots of social
welfare / edited by Carter Lindberg and Emily Albu Hanawalt.
p.   cm.
1. Church and social problems—History.   I. Lindberg, Carter.
II. Hanawalt, Emily Albu.
HN31.T457   1993   261.8'3—dc20   93–24819 CIP

ISBN 0–943549–17–5 (cloth : alk. paper)

CONTENTS

Preface   vii

Introduction   1

1. The Ancient Near Eastern Roots of Social Welfare
   PAUL HANSON   7

2. Rich and Poor in the New Testament
   and in Early Christianity
   HOWARD CLARK KEE   29

3. The Holy and the Poor: Models
   from Early Syriac Christianity
   SUSAN ASHBROOK HARVEY   43

4. Byzantium and Social Welfare
   ALEXANDER KAZHDAN   67

5. The Orphanotropheion of Constantinople
   TIMOTHY S. MILLER   83

6. Byzantine Women, Saints' Lives, and Social Welfare
   ALICE–MARY TALBOT   105

7. Hearts Not Purses? Pope Innocent III's Attitude
   to Social Welfare
   BRENDA M. BOLTON   123

8. Religion, the Profit Economy, and Saint Francis
   LESTER K. LITTLE   147

9. Confraternities and Guilds in the Late Middle Ages
   ANDRÉ VAUCHEZ   165

10. The Liturgy after the Liturgy: Welfare
    in the Early Reformation
    CARTER LINDBERG   177

11. Religion and Early Modern Social Welfare
    THOMAS RIIS   193

12. The Long-Term Inheritance of Poverty
    THOMAS RIIS   207

Contributors   213

Bibliography   215

Index of Scripture References   247

Index   249

PREFACE

The dark side of America the beautiful has become increasingly evident in recent years. Perhaps at no time since the Great Depression are the homeless so visible in our cities as they are today. Our newspapers provide editorials and statistics; the former condemn and exhort both "the system" and the victims, and the latter can be unreliable. But regardless of value judgments and numbers beyond comprehension, it is clear that poverty is a growth industry. The lead article in a recent edition of the magazine section of *The Boston Globe* (1 April 1990) sums up the situation in its title: "Whatever Happened To The Common Good? The Spirit Turns Mean in Massachusetts." "America" could be substituted for "Massachusetts" without changing the article.

The question remains: "Whatever Happened To The Common Good?" Or, *mutatis mutandis*, "How Did We Get This Way?" The essays that follow are contributions to an answer. They were first presented in a course titled Religious Roots of Social Welfare offered during the spring semester 1990 at Boston University. The course and the lecture series were not primarily designed to focus on the present situation but rather to identify and analyze the historical religious roots of social welfare. We reasoned that we need a historical context in order to get a perspective on what is near us. Such historical distance may provide freedom from preoccupation with contemporary problem-solving, and thus facilitate judgment and evaluation applicable to the present. With such a context we can judge the relative significance of everything within it and thus evaluate the effects and the resources of the Judeo-Christian heritage for our common good.

The contributions in this volume appear as they were presented with exceptions of minor editing and the inclusion of references to the source materials. We hope that the liveliness of the oral presentations will at least partially shine through the printed words. The contributors, all internationally recognized scholars in their own various fields, were invited to present their perspectives on "Religious Roots of Social Welfare" with the only constraint being the title assigned them. Some chose to share their present research, others to provide overviews of research in the field, and others to argue particular perspectives.

As the subtitle indicates, the emphasis of the lecture series was the religious *roots* of social welfare. Hence apart from occasional references to contemporary issues, there is no effort to describe and analyze modern social welfare theory and praxis. Our goal was to focus on the religious motivations and contributions to the care of the poor which lead into early modern developments of social welfare. For this reason more recent social institutions — such as those developing from seventeenth- and eighteenth-century Pietism, the contributions of the Wesleys, the Inner Mission and the diaconal movement of the nineteenth century, the American Great Awakenings, and the social gospel movements among other fascinating and instructive religious contributions to social welfare—must await another lecture series and its volume.

We are grateful for all whose assistance made the lecture series and this publication possible. The Boston University Humanities Foundation provided the initial seed grant and encouraged us to seek outside funding. A generous grant from the Lilly Endowment provided the necessary financial resources and much more. We also received invaluable support and assistance from the staff of the Endowment, especially from Mr. Fred L. Hofheinz and Sr. Jeanne Knoerle, SP. We acknowledge with pleasure the superb presentations by each and every lecturer; the occasional formal responses to the lectures by our faculty colleagues, Walter Muelder, Simon Parker, Reinhold Schumann, and Abraham Smith; and the lively participation of the students. In addition, we are grateful to Bill Pickel, graduate student in Religion and Literature, for his gracious editorial contributions. Finally, we especially thank Gregory Miller, doctoral candidate in Church History, whose management of the innumerable details and logistics of bringing so many guests to Boston University was indispensable.

Emily Albu Hanawalt
Carter Lindberg

Boston, Massachusetts
Spring 1993

INTRODUCTION

Jesus "exceedingly astonished" his disciples when he stated: "It is easier for a camel to go through the eye of a needle than for a rich man to enter the kingdom of God" (Mark 10:25). He also gave them and their spiritual heirs a point of view, a perspective, on the rich and the poor. Just as children today are amazed that they can view the world around them through a tiny aperture held close to their eye, so the early Christian community viewed their social world anew through the needle's eye.

This new perspective, formed by Hebrew scripture as well as by the words and life of Jesus, contrasted starkly with Greco-Roman values that placed property rights over human rights. Greek vocabulary described political and social status with a mixture of socioeconomic and moral terminology. Words denoting property-owning, rich, fortunate, distinguished, well-born, and influential also connoted the good, the best, the upright. Vocabulary for the lower classes, the poor, the populace had a moral implication weighted toward the bad. As Paul Hanson points out, similar associations of the right and the good with power and wealth were also present in the civilizations of Mesopotamia, Egypt, and Canaan, where the king played a role parallel to God by constituting society through his decrees. The result was a stratified social system that provided privilege to the powerful and wealthy while controlling the poor and disadvantaged as a means for cheap labor.

Aristocratic Romans generally showed disdain for the poor, especially the urban poor, whom they characterized as lazy and slothful. It is true that wealthy individuals supported the public works of the Roman republic, subsidizing aqueducts, roads, new walls, and public buildings. While financing gladiatorial games and spectacles in the circus, they equally provided public baths and the dole of grain and olive oil for all, and they even supported the cleaning of the public latrines. But they performed these duties to win honor and the praise of citizens from their own class; at best they were indifferent to the pain of the poor. Most aristocratic Romans showed little sympathy for any disadvantaged people, with the notable exception of fellow aristocrats who had fallen on hard times. They bolstered these attitudes with the conviction that the gods rewarded the good with wealth and punished the evil or slothful with poverty. The Roman poet Ovid (43 BCE-17 CE) succinctly stated: "Property confers rank." And the Roman statesman Cicero (106-43 BCE) perceived a prime function of the state to be the protection of property rights. "In short, the rights of pri-

1

vate property, and the owners' right to use it as they saw fit, was the back-bone of the Roman legal system."[1]

In contrast to this general attitude, some Roman philosophies fostered care for the commonweal. Stoicism, for example, endorsed the explicit obligation of generosity toward the weak. By the end of the first century CE, the Latin concept of *humanitas* expressed a far broader empathy for the needy than the Greek *philanthropy* ever had. Some have suggested that this represents an extension of the Roman ideal of *pietas* (responsibility) as the boundaries of the Roman world expanded to include a wide range of peoples. Still, Roman society did not seriously question its slave-based economy or reorganize itself to address imbalances. Romans mustered little sympathy, for instance, for miners, whose working conditions were dismal and even life-threatening. They built no public orphanages. In fact, the ancient world utterly failed to create a system of social welfare for the neediest members of society.

The needle's eye saying plainly announces that the values of the biblical world are the reverse of those of the classical world. Echoing throughout the New Testament texts is the refrain of the great reversal: The last shall be first, and the first last; the mighty shall be put down and the lowly exalted; the hungry fed with good things, and the rich sent empty away. The Hebrew prophets do not understand poverty as a consequence of natural causes or fate or destiny, but as a social-ethical phenomenon. God's justice and will are to rescue the poor from their oppressors. That Jesus stands in this tradition is evident in his announcement of his own ministry with the words of Isaiah: "The Spirit of the Lord is upon me because he has anointed me to preach good news to the poor. He has sent me to proclaim release to the captives and recovering of sight to the blind, to set at liberty those who are oppressed, to proclaim the acceptable year of the Lord" (Isa. 61:1-2; Luke 4:18-19).

Western attitudes toward social welfare have their roots in both classical Greco-Roman culture and biblical culture. These roots are so intertwined that one is sometimes mistaken for the other. For example, Russell H. Conwell (1843-1925), who was minister of the Baptist Temple on Broad Street in Philadelphia, and founder and first president of Temple University, raised the money for his college through innumerable presentations of his famous lecture, "Acres of Diamonds." To Conwell, wealth and the gospel were not at all at odds:

[1] Justo Gonzalez, *Faith and Wealth: A History of Early Christian Ideas on the Origin, Significance, and Use of Money* (San Francisco: Harper & Row, 1990), 19. See also A.R. Hands, *Charities and Social Aid in Greece and Rome* (Ithaca: Cornell University Press, 1968).

I say that you ought to get rich, and it is your duty to get rich. How many of my pious brethren say to me, "Do you, a Christian minister, spend your time going up and down the country advising young people to get rich, to get money?" "Yes, of course I do." They say, "Isn't that awful! Why don't you preach the gospel instead of preaching about man's making money?" "Because to make money honestly is to preach the gospel." That is the reason.

Conversely, the poor to Conwell were poor because of their own sins and failures. In a passage reminiscent of the late medieval distinction between the worthy and unworthy poor,[2] Conwell stated:

The number of poor who are to be sympathized with is very small. To sympathize with a man whom God has punished for his sins, thus to help him when God would still continue a just punishment, is to do wrong.... While we should sympathize with God's poor—that is, those who cannot help themselves—let us remember there is not a poor person in the United States who was not made poor by his own shortcomings, or the shortcomings of someone else. It is all wrong to be poor, anyhow.[3]

Western history is replete with such mixing of cultural roots, this mixing often taking the form of a misappropriation of a biblical text in the support of a particular economic or social position. A favorite such text among opponents and critics of social welfare in the early modern period has been Paul's injunction: "If any will not work, let him not eat" (2 Thess. 3:10). But this passage was directed to those in the early Christian community who believed that the end of history was so imminent that they quit their jobs. Thus only when this passage is abstracted from its context and made into a timeless truth can it be made to support the so-called "Protestant ethic" or be used against the unemployed.

The separation of the classical and religious roots of modern social welfare are not, of course, so easily accomplished as the above examples would suggest. Neither can the religious contributions to welfare be easily disentangled from all the other past and present cultural influences operative in a particular context. Nor should they be, for our premise that social welfare has Judeo-Christian roots implies a reciprocal relationship of faith with all aspects of culture.

The development and growth of the religious roots of social welfare are neither univocal nor linear. Christians came to look through the eye of

---

[2] For a discussion of late medieval distinctions of types of poor, cf. Christopher Black, *Italian Confraternities in the Sixteenth Century* (Cambridge: Cambridge University Press, 1989), 137-150.

[3] Russell H. Conwell, *Acres of Diamonds* (Old Tappan, N.J.: Spire Books, 1981), 20–21, 23.

the needle in various ways. The early church was concerned not only that the needle's eye constricted access by the rich to the kingdom of God, but also that it limited access by the church to the rich. Thus theological ingenuity applied itself to widening the eye, providing means for facilitating passage to the other side, and symbiotically linking the rich person to the poor person so that when the latter slipped through the eye he or she could pull the former through as well. Both before and after Clement of Alexandria (c.150-c.215) posed his famous sermon question, "How Is the Rich Person to be Saved?", various answers were given to it.

As Howard C. Kee points out, the process of widening the eye begins already in the New Testament texts. The context for Jesus' famous saying is a young man's question about salvation. In Mark 10:21 and Luke 18:22, Jesus says: "You lack one thing; go, sell what you have, and give to the poor...." The parallel version of the story in Matt. 19:21 reads: "If you would be perfect, go, sell what you possess and give to the poor...." Likewise, the beatitudes are spiritualized from "Blessed are the poor ..." (Luke 6:20) to "Blessed are the poor in spirit ..." (Matt. 5:3). Perfection and spirituality attained by self-denying charity are threads that stretch from the early desert ascetics to Mother Theresa. Such seeming other-worldliness has had astonishing this-worldly consequences for social welfare ranging from the complex of social institutions that developed around the early Syriac ascetics (Susan Ashbrook Harvey) to the foundling institution of Pope Innocent III (Brenda M. Bolton), the development of medieval confraternities as a partial response to marginality (André Vauchez), and the Franciscan development of philanthropy in response to late medieval socioeconomic changes (Lester K. Little).

Philanthropy, in the form of almsgiving, has throughout history been a way to ease one's way through the eye of the needle. Sirach, the Hebrew text so esteemed by the early church that it came to be known as Ecclesiasticus, provided the rationale: "Water extinguishes a blazing fire: so almsgiving atones for sin" (Ecclus. 3:30). Like a red thread woven through the entire fabric of the history of social welfare, this text gave promise not only to the rich but to impious almsgivers that they could squeeze through the eye of the needle. Thus a sermon illustration attributed to Pope Gregory I (✝ 604) describes an adulterer whose fall, at death, into the fire and brimstone pit of devils was arrested by angels who grasped his hands—hands from which he had generously given alms.

Philanthropy in classical society and in Byzantine culture (Alexander Kazhdan) did not imply compassion or concern for the poor but was rather a means for achieving honor, expressing clemency, or investing through contributions in one's own salvation. Nevertheless, philanthropy, perceived as an imperial virtue in Byzantine society, provided an avenue for women to be active in society outside the home (Alice-Mary Talbot), and to contribute personally to the many complex institutions of social welfare that had arisen in the Byzantine empire (Timothy Miller).

Historically and religiously, philanthropy has at times been the means by which the rich serve their own interests, whether these interests be slipping through the eye of the needle into the kingdom of God or perpetuating their own kingdoms of elite education and culture. In an early reversal of the phrase "you can't take it with you," St. Augustine (✝430) stated that the poor will bear to heaven what you give to them on earth.[4]

Augustine's intention was to motivate almsgiving and emphasize the early church's sense of the symbiotic relationship of rich and poor. This view of the mutual interdependence of rich and poor had already been illustrated in the second century by the symbiosis of the vine and the sturdy elm tree. The huge elm itself bears no fruit. And the vine limited to the ground bears only poor fruit that is easily crushed underfoot. But when the elm supports the vine, the vine is able to produce rich fruit for both of them.[5]

Nevertheless, such a perspective could also hinder the religious ideal of the reciprocity of rich and poor if it focused on the utilitarian functions of the poor as receivers of sin-atoning alms and as intercessors for the rich. The most effective bearers of alms to heaven and intercessors with God for the rich were soon perceived to be those who voluntarily embraced poverty as an imitation of Christ. By the Middle Ages the truly needy, the involuntarily poor, were even further marginalized. Their plight was deepened by a series of conjunctions of natural disaster and cultural development. From the fourteenth century into the early modern period, the ranks of the poor swelled due to plague and famine, and urban and economic developments. Widespread poverty and vagabondage led to resentment, fear, and oppression of the poor. We know from the story of Job, whose wife and friends attributed his suffering to past sins, that blaming the victim is not a modern innovation. In the early modern development of the profit economy the day laborer with no social safety net and no reserves for emergencies was always only a step from economic disaster. The able-bodied unemployed were soon affected by the invidious categorization of the poor as lazy and immoral.

[4]"If our possessions are to be carried away, let us transfer them to a place where we shall not lose them. The poor to whom we give alms! With regard to us, what else are they but porters through whom we transfer our goods from earth to heaven? Give away your treasure. Give it to a porter. He will bear to heaven what you give him on earth." *The Fathers of the Christian Church*, vol. 11. (Washington, D.C.: Catholic University Press, 1963), 268. Modern secular equivalents of this perspective are described by Teresa J. Odendahl, *Charity Begins at Home: Generosity and Self-Interest among the Philanthropic Elite* (New York: Basic Books, 1990).

[5] "The Shepherd," *The Ante-Nicene Fathers*, vol. 2 (Grand Rapids: Eerdmans, 1956), 32.

One response was for the poor to organize themselves. These confraternities (André Vauchez), which were widespread in the fourteenth through the sixteenth centuries, provided emergency help to poor members, were a means of their integration into social life, and paid for their funerals. Another response was related to the new theology of the sixteenth-century Reformation (Carter Lindberg). According to the Reformers passage through the eye of the needle was not contingent upon almsgiving but upon the grace of God. Since the poor were no longer viewed as useful objects for the exercise of good works, the theological obstacle to social change was removed. This accelerated the late medieval urban development of poor relief that had frequently been impeded by church control of charitable resources. Cities and towns that accepted the Reformation soon began to establish community chests for relief of the poor, as well as for their education and job training. Another effect of the Reformation was to lengthen the work week by the abolition of many religious holidays (Thomas Riis). These consequences of the Reformation together with Reformation endorsement and acceleration of the late medieval movement toward laicization and rationalization of poor relief led to sharper distinctions between the deserving and undeserving poor.

Nevertheless, there appeared to be arising in the modern industrial world a kind of "culture of poverty." Somehow, once a family had fallen into poverty, it seemed that social and economic forces conspired to make poverty a long-term inheritance. Yet the contemporary American response has largely been to avoid analysis of the socioeconomic and political causes of poverty. Instead we continue to stigmatize and isolate the poor.[6]

In this present context the prophetic recall and proclamation of the memory and ideals of the community and nation (Paul Hanson) are essential if the religious roots of social welfare are to bear fruit. The distillation of the historical western wisdom of this fruit may split many of today's wineskins of social welfare. For the history of welfare in previous centuries which had fewer material resources available than the present makes the clear point that the perennial fundamental issues are those of attitudes and values rather than those of disposable wealth. The presently widely held image of the "welfare queen" and the view that the homeless are so by choice tap into deeply rooted historical biases that not only marginalize the poor but link them to criminality and moral deficiency. The essays in this volume not only uncover these historical roots, but also reveal contributions of the Judeo-Christian tradition to the struggle for social and economic justice for all humankind. The eye of the needle can continue to provide perspective for those willing to look through it.

[6] Cf. Michael B. Katz, *The Undeserving Poor: From the War on Poverty to the War on Welfare* (New York: Pantheon Books, 1990).

CHAPTER 1

THE ANCIENT NEAR EASTERN ROOTS OF SOCIAL WELFARE

PAUL HANSON

The interdependence of a culture's worldview and its value system is a significant motif in each of the chapters in this volume. Consciously or unconsciously, attitudes toward the poor are rooted in a culture's prevailing worldview, which in turn either deters or facilitates specific forms of social welfare. In contrast to the civic and sacral myths of the cultures of the ancient Near East, Israel's self-understanding was rooted in its epic of a historical encounter with God that provided the model for the community's treatment of others. Throughout the Hebrew Bible personal and legal responsibility for the vulnerable was rooted not in timeless myths legitimating the ruler but rather in the oft-recurring clause: "I am Yahweh, who delivered you from the House of Bondage."

A culture's prevailing worldview strongly influences the attitudes adopted by individuals on matters such as social welfare. By worldview[1] we mean the symbolic construction by which a people expresses its shared perspectives and assumptions. A worldview assumes specific form in the laws and institutions that order the society. The actual practice of the population in a viable society will conform reasonably to its laws and institutions and thus be in basic harmony with the overarching worldview.

THE INFLUENCE OF WORLDVIEW ON A CULTURE'S VALUE SYSTEM

In most ancient cultures worldview assumed the form of myth, that is, an account of how the specific culture and its natural habitat originated in the activities of the gods. During biblical times, Israel preferred the genre of epic as carrier of its view of reality and its origins. The more pluralistic and complex a society, the more diffuse is the form in which it describes its worldview.

[1]The nature and function of a society's worldview or, equivalently, symbolic universe is portrayed clearly in Peter Berger and Thomas Luckmann, *The Social Construction of Reality* (Garden City, N.Y.: Doubleday, 1966).

7

In the history of the United States, writers and other would-be myth-makers have experienced great difficulty in giving a unified symbolic form to the nation's fundamental views and values. To conclude from this, however, that our society operates free from the constraints of a shared universe of meaning is misleading. In critical situations certain groups have found and continue to find themselves encountering an undercur-rent of prevailing attitudes that carry daunting force. For example, under-privileged segments of our population find upward mobility encumbered by the widely shared view that they are a service class not entitled to equal opportunity. The chronically unemployed encounter the attitude that their plight is the product of laziness and incompetence. Efforts on behalf of penal reform are frustrated by the bias that inmates constitute a class predisposed to crime by innate moral defects. Such views are no longer explicitly embedded, as they would have been in ancient Babylon, in a myth describing the origins of different classes of gods and humans. Sub-consciously, however, these views carry considerable determinative power in limiting the options available to certain impoverished and disen-franchised groups.

Though our society gives lip service to an ideal of equality, attitudes of discrimination are reinforced by the benefits they offer to those privileged by birth and circumstance. Popular notions like the level of unemploy-ment required for inflation control, the economic imperative against socialized medicine, and mandatory caps on taxation, while not lacking certain analytic warrants, derive their most powerful support from unex-amined attitudes rooted in the prevailing worldview.

Only the considerable influence of worldview on people's thinking can explain the irony implicit in our nation's emphasis on individual rights coexisting free of noticeable tension with the systemic victimization of certain groups denied full access to the laws and social structures of the land. Though some will argue that this miscarriage of justice is merely a result of the imperfections inevitably present in the institutions of any state, I believe that something more basic is involved, namely, a widely assumed distinction in the ontological status of different groups within the society rooted in its dominant worldview.

The ascription of divergent degrees of ontological status to people most satisfactorily explains phenomena in our society such as the follow-ing: the de facto existence of a two-tiered school system in many parts of our country, with suburban children enjoying many educational benefits denied their urban counterparts; a categorically higher rate of unemploy-ment among black males than among white males; a youthful subculture growing up in urban areas so devastated by crime and drug infestation that they resemble war zones. Each of these phenomena involves complex problems that are not aided by naive proposals. Aside from the question of specific programs, however, it seems that another level of question must be raised: To what degree are the persistence of such decay and the inability of the society to marshal its resources in incisive response to it the outgrowth of normative assumptions, that is, worldview?

While officers of the law are charged with narrowing the gap between laws and public practice, even as legislators are obliged to translate the prevailing values of society into binding structures, historians have an opportunity to penetrate to the deeper level of the society's symbol system in the effort to detect elements hospitable to prejudice and partiality in matters of justice and sharing of the commonweal. Such detective work is most effectively conducted within a broadly comparative context capable of providing some critical distance between structures and the observer. Insight gained from this kind of historical study does not translate directly into social change. It can cultivate, however, a more critically informed attitude toward unquestioned assumptions, and can perhaps break the impression that present structures are natural, inevitable, and morally justified.

SOCIAL WELFARE IN MESOPOTAMIA, EGYPT, AND CANAAN

Contrary to popular opinion, the ancient Israelites did not invent social concern for the welfare of the vulnerable persons like the widow and the orphan. Sumerian hymns to Utu, the sun-god,[2] and to Nanshe, goddess of Lagash,[3] extol their just governance and their concern for the widow and the orphan, the poor and the weak.

Shamash, Akkadian counterpart to Utu, is celebrated as the heavenly judge who oversees the execution of justice among humans:

> The unrighteous judge thou dost make to see imprisonment.
> The receiver of the bribe who perverts [justice] thou dost make
>   to bear punishment.
> He who does not accept a bribe [but] intercedes for the weak,
> Is well-pleasing to Shamash [and] enriches [his] life.[4]

The kings of Mesopotamia describe themselves as pious servants of the gods, who accept as one of their solemn responsibilities the administration of justice in imitation of the gods. The connection between the

---

[2]S. N. Kramer, in G. Ernest Wright, ed., *The Bible in the Ancient Near East: Essays in Honor of William Foxwell Albright* (Garden City, N.Y.: Doubleday, 1965), 255.

[3]S. N. Kramer, "'Vox populi' and the Sumerian Literary Documents," *Revue d'assyriologie et d'archéologie orientale* (henceforth cited as RA) 58, 1964, 148–56.

[4]F. J. Stephens, tr., in J. B. Pritchard, ed., *Ancient Near Eastern Texts Relating to the Old Testament* (Princeton: Princeton University Press, 1966), 388; henceforth cited as ANET.

hymnic celebration of divine justice, illustrated above, and the promulgation of royal justice is depicted graphically in the most famous of all law codes from the Land of the Two Rivers: the Hammurabi Code. At its apex Shamash is pictured handing circle and scepter, symbols of order and justice, to the dutiful king.[5]

In setting down laws dealing with domestic, social, and economic matters within his land, Hammurabi was following a well-established tradition with antecedents reaching back at least several centuries into Sumerian times. In this tradition the ancient codes are not systematic codifications of the legal systems of their respective states; rather they represent explication of aspects of common law where the particular king felt he had made important contributions. Urukagina, ruler of Lagash circa 2300 BCE, responded to the exploitation of the poor by palace and temple officials with strict new laws. By these means he

> cleansed the homes of the inhabitants of Lagash of usury, of hoarding, of famine, of theft and of attacks, and instituted their liberty.... [H]e had this declaration sealed by Ningirsu that he would not deliver the widow and the orphan to the rich.[6]

Some two hundred years later Ur-Nammu, founder of the Third Dynasty of Ur, strove to establish justice in his land by normalizing monetary standards and setting up safeguards against the exploitation of the weak:

> The orphan was not delivered up to the rich man; the widow was not delivered up to the mighty man; the man of one shekel was not delivered up to the man of one mina.[7]

The Code of Lipit-Ishtar of Isin, two centuries prior to Hammurabi, and the collection of laws from Eshnunna, only a few decades prior to Hammurabi, addressed similar concerns. None of these collections, however, come close to rivaling the Code of Hammurabi. Not only does the latter contain the most complete collection of law, but its prologue and epilogue give a vivid description of Hammurabi's understanding of his responsibilities vis-à-vis his subjects and his place within the cosmic economy of the gods. That is, Hammurabi's Code depicts both the value system of Babylon and its underlying myth or worldview.

Hammurabi, in the Prologue, declared that he had been appointed by the gods,

---

[5]J. B. Pritchard, *The Ancient Near East in Pictures Relating to the Old Testament* (Princeton: Princeton University Press, 1974), 77.

[6] M. Lambert, "Les 'Réformes' d'Urukagina," RA 50, 1956, 169–84.

[7]J. J. Finkelstein, tr., in ANET, 524, lines 162–68.

to promote the welfare of the people, ...
to cause justice to prevail in the land,
to destroy the wicked and the evil,
that the strong might not oppress the weak....[8]

Hammurabi's reign is described as more than a human enterprise; it is part of the basic order of being. The gods have conferred upon him the "Enlil [chief executive functions of the Sumerian pantheon] functions over mankind," even as they have established the foundations of his city "as firm as heaven and earth." *Enuma elish*, the official myth of Babylon, describes in great detail how the reign of the earthly king stems from the activity of the gods, i.e., how the structures of human society fit into the ordering of reality in its totality. Cosmic order arose out of the theomachy, that is, out of the conflict between two groups of gods that resolved the basic metaphysical polarities through the imposition of structure. Having defeated the main antagonist Tiamat (chaos, salt waters, etc.), Marduk (stormgod, fertile waters, etc.) fashions the universe out of her carcass and creates a society of humans to assume the menial tasks of the gods. At the center of their society is the temple, "a likeness on earth of what he has wrought in heaven"; and it is into the temple storehouses that the products of human effort are to be brought as gifts to the gods. Thereby is established the production and redistribution system of the land, over which the gods establish the earthly king as their regent. Within the overall structure of the universe, therefore, it is the duty of the king to maintain order through the administration of just laws, even as it is the duty of the subjects obediently to uphold what is required of them. Failure on either side threatened to cause not only social chaos but the disfunctionality of the universe, for humans were a humble but essential part of the whole.

In the Epilogue of his Code, Hammurabi summarizes his role as "the beneficent shepherd whose scepter is righteous," who "always governed them in peace," and who wrote his laws "in order that the strong might not oppress the weak, that justice might be dealt the orphan [and] the widow."[9]

The laws themselves indicate that Hammurabi did in fact address issues of justice and fairness such as the dishonest dealings of merchants (e.g., law 94), corruption among judges (e.g., law 5), and the abuses of other officials. Other laws seek to secure the ownership of farmland against the threat of foreclosure arising from misfortunes beyond the control of the farmer (e.g., law 48). In spite of the emphasis placed by the Prologue and Epilogue on protection of vulnerable classes, however, the vast

[8]T. J. Meek, tr., in ANET, 164, lines 27–28, 32–37.
[9]Idem, 178, lines 43, 57–61.

majority of the laws regulate domestic, economic, and social structures on the basis of strict standards of rewards and punishments, and distribute justice not equally across the entire population but according to a descending order of class entitlement, i.e., aristocracy, freeman, commoner, slave.

The social edifice that Hammurabi constructed upon the foundation of earlier models was impressive. Yet a fundamental question arises relative to social welfare. Though laws assuring stability and order are essential to any civilized society, the humaneness of a society also depends on the *quality* of life experienced by the populace as a whole, with the most humble elements providing a key index. It is questionable whether Hammurabi's Code reveals any particular concern for the welfare of vulnerable individuals and groups except to the extent that their impoverishment had a negative impact on the general strength and productivity of the land. Several considerations contribute to this skepticism: (1) the formulations of the Prologue and Epilogue regarding the beneficence of the king vis-à-vis the poor conform to the grandiose, stereotyped rhetoric belonging to the genre of royal pronouncements in the ancient Near East; (2) totally absent from the laws themselves are any elements of parenesis that might give evidence of the ruler's concern for specific aspects of justice in relation to weaker members of his society; (3) even in the narrative framework of the Code, far more space is devoted to cursing successors who choose to ignore the royal commands than to addressing concerns of justice. Though such evidence does not offer a basis for conclusive judgments, we might suggest as the most likely motivation behind Hammurabi's Code the concern for popular support as a prerequisite for the stability of his reign. In a chaotic world such as that occupied by Hammurabi, absolute authority over the populace was deemed necessary. The propagandistic tone of the Prologue and Epilogue fits this interpretation, especially if those scholars are correct who suggest that such inscriptions are addressed as much to the gods whose favor the king curries as to the populace whose support he needs. All of which is not to deny two important facts: (1) a rational ordering of a society that attends to consistency and fairness is not unrelated to concern for justice;[10] (2) the integration of

---

[10]The importance of predictability in the administration of justice comes to expression in the Epilogue:
"Let any oppressed man who has a cause
come into the presence of the statue of me, the king of justice,
and then read carefully my inscribed stela,
and give heed to my precious words,
and may my stela make the case clear to him;
may he understand his cause;
may he set his mind at ease!"

social institutions and common law into the myth of the culture that the Code of Hammurabi seems to foster exemplifies the unified symbolic universe that modern sociologists identify with community stability and that modern American artists and poets search for in vain. As a result, Babylonian society enjoyed the benefit of a clear conceptual foundation or worldview.

Alongside the promulgation of law codes, another practice used by the kings of Mesopotamia from the Old Babylonian Period down to the Neo-Assyrian was the "royal decree" (*simdat sarrim*) issued to "establish emancipation" (*andurarum sakanum*).[11] Occurring at the beginning of a king's reign, such emancipation entailed the release of debt-slaves and the annulment of specific types of debts. Since the enthronement of every new king was understood in terms of divine appointment, the "royal decree" accompanying the king to power should be understood in terms of the reestablishment of the orders of creation for which the king, as regent of the gods, was responsible. In effect, the onset of the reign symbolized a renewal of creation such as was dramatized in the annual ritual celebration of the central myth. It is thus plausible to view the practice of "emancipation" as a means of winning the popular support necessary for a peaceful reign, and of maintaining social and economic stability in the land.

In contrast to the important comparative material from the Mesopotamian realm, the contribution of ancient Egyptian sources to the question of social welfare in ancient Israel is less significant. That is because the cultural connections between Egypt and Israel in antiquity were more tenuous than those between Israel and the Mesopotamian countries. More important is the fact that the Mesopotamian documents dealing with our subject are far more abundant than those that have come to light in the Egyptian realm. It may be true that in ancient Egypt the Pharaoh was identified so closely with divine truth that there was no need to give written form to common law.[12]

---

[11]See N. P. Lemche, "The Manumission of Slaves—The Fallow Year—The Sabbatical Year—The Jobel Year," *Vetus Testamentum* 26 (1976): 38–59; idem, "*Andurarum* and *misarum*: Comments on the Problem of Social Edicts and their Application in the Ancient Near East," *Journal of Near Eastern Studies* 38 (1979): 11–22; S. A. Kaufman, "A Reconstruction of the Social Welfare Systems of Ancient Israel," in W. B. Barrick and J. R. Spencer, eds., *In the Shelter of Elyon: Essays on Ancient Palestinian Life and Literature in Honor of G. W. Ahlstrom*, Journal for the Study of the Old Testament Supplement 31 (Sheffield, England: JSOT Press, 1984), 277–86.

[12]Leon Epzstein, *Social Justice in the Ancient Near East and the People of the Bible* (London: SCM, 1986), 18.

There was, however, a distinct notion of law and custom tracing all the way back to the Old Kingdom. Central to that notion was the concept of *maat*. *Maat* was embodied in the goddess of that name, symbolized in the funerary cult by the balance, characterized by the cosmic order and universal harmony established by the gods from the beginning, and represented by the Pharaoh. Only by conforming to *maat* could individuals and the community hope to prosper. It is therefore not surprising that the most extensive descriptions of *maat* are found in the form of instructions to future leaders such as prince, vizier, and scribe.

What strikes one in the moral system of these instructions is their conservatism and utilitarianism. The good is what brings success, and what brings success is deference to one's superiors, hard work, and dependability. This pragmatic orientation does not prevent the development of a refined definition of professional ethics. In the late third millennium BCE *Instructions of Marikare* we read:

> Do justice and you will endure on earth. Quiet the weeper; do not oppress the widow; do not supplant a man in the property of his father; and impugn no officials in their posts. Be on guard against punishing wrongfully.[13]

A literary genre that ancient Egyptians found fitting to express their conception of *maat* was the tomb inscription. That authors composed such inscriptions to make their case for blessings in the afterlife raises questions about their accuracy, but they do at least describe ideals that individual Egyptians associated with *maat*. Nefer-Seshem Ra, for example, gave this report:

> I have spoken the truth, I have done the truth, I have spoken the good, ... I have saved the wretched from the hand of the violent, ... I have given bread to the hungry, clothing to the naked.... I have buried him who had no son.[14]

This illustrates that the land of the Pharaohs could give noble expression to its sense of goodness and justice. Unfortunately, Egypt's literary legacy has rarely left indication of the concrete social situations being addressed. An exception is Haremheb's decree that arose out of his incisive efforts to restore order and justice after the debacle of Aktenaten's reign. But even this exception corroborates our observations. Haremheb's various reforms are aimed towards the reestablishment of central control over the economy and of royal authority over all subjects within an elabo-

---

[13]John A. Wilson, tr., in ANET, 415.
[14]Epzstein, *Social Justice in Ancient Near East*, 23.

rate bureaucracy reaching from the Pharaoh down to the lowest official. While attention to the elimination of exploitation and corruption, and to the practice of equitable judgment is not absent, it can be seen as an aspect of the overweening concern with stability and centralized control.

This predominant outlook may be accounted for by noting that matters of justice and morality in this Egyptian material are always viewed from the perspective of those in positions of wealth and power. The viewpoint of the lowly and the oppressed is rarely expressed.[15] Equally absent are expressions of inner motivation, feelings of mercy for the weak, or appeals to a sense of solidarity with the poor. The harsh treatment of vulnerable members of the society was countermanded primarily because it abets the breakdown of good order and thus constitutes a threat to the stability and productivity of the land.

The emphasis on stability as well as the pragmatism and elitism of Egyptian moral thought lent themselves to the rigidity and cynicism of the New Kingdom. As increasing amounts of property and wealth were amassed by priesthood and crown, and as an ever larger percentage of the population fell into servitude, expressions of concern for the average person were contradicted by the megalomania of Pharaohs like Ramses II. The myths of Egypt and the social system they informed were incapable of keeping a dynamism alive that could contribute to a deepening of ethical principles. The contribution Egypt had to make to the question of social welfare had been made by the end of the third millennium. What followed was imitation and rigidification abetting exploitation of the masses and a hardening of class discrimination.

When we come to Canaan of the second millennium, we find that evidence of concern for social welfare is even more scanty than was the case in Egypt. This may simply be the result of the accidents of archaeological discovery. The numerous other points of contact between Canaanite culture and the civilizations of Mesopotamia would suggest that also in the realm of social norms were laws and customs similar to those found in the lands of the Tigris and the Euphrates. In the Ugaritic texts from the fourteenth century BCE one finds instead only brief descriptions of the traits of certain legendary figures. Danel, for example,

> sat at the entrance to the gate,
> next to the granary on the threshing floor.
> He judged the cases of widows,
> presided over orphans' hearings.[16]

[15]For an example of life viewed from the perspective of the average citizen, see John A. Wilson, tr., "The Protests of the Eloquent Peasant,"in ANET, 407–10.

[16]Michael David Coogan, ed. and tr., Stories from Ancient Canaan (Philadelphia: Westminster, 1978), 35.

The rebellious son of king Keret, on the other hand, hurls this accusation against his father:

> Listen, Kirta the Noble,
>> listen closely and pay attention:
> as though raiders had raided, you will be driven out,
>> and forced to live in the mountains.
> Weakness has stayed your hand:
>> you do not judge the cases of widows,
>> you do not preside over the hearings of the oppressed;
> you do not drive out those who plunder the poor,
>> you do not feed the orphan before you,
>> the widow behind your back.[17]

These allusions indicate a tradition of the entitlement of the weak and vulnerable to the protection of the king that is akin to that found in Mesopotamia. But there is scant basis to say more.

SOCIAL WELFARE IN ANCIENT ISRAEL

Our brief survey of the lands of Israel's neighbors indicates that the people of Israel did not develop their attitudes towards social welfare in a vacuum. They lived in a world in which ideologies did not respect borders but moved with cultural currents over wide areas. Customs and laws of semi-nomadic peoples in the Middle Bronze Age accordingly were in many respects similar, whether found in the Upper Euphrates or in Canaan. The duty of providing for the welfare of the widow and orphan was ascribed to the king whether he ruled over Babylon or Thebes.

A heightened sensitivity to the bearing of political change on the development of Israel's beliefs and values has come with growth in awareness of the intimate interrelationship between a society's legal conventions and its political organization. The attitudes towards social justice and welfare expressed in the laws, narratives, and confessions of the Bible developed within a complex set of situations and under a diverse array of influences. While efforts at reconstruction of those situations and influences are beset with difficulties relating to both literary and historical problems, questions of social setting are overlooked only at the cost of a hopelessly distorted picture.

The first major factor that must be considered in studying biblical views towards social welfare is the tribal origin of Israel's ancestors. While it is impossible to extract specific historical information from the ancestral stories of Genesis, they fit broadly into the kinship patterns present among the Amorite tribal groups (*amurru*) that migrated from the northwest into

---

[17]Ibid., 73–74.

both Mesopotamia and Canaan in the first half of the second millennium BCE. In contrast to the temple-centered, timeless myth of the great city-states, these groups structured their world in terms of tribal organization and genealogical record-keeping; that is, the ancestral stories of Genesis unfold in the direction of a historical worldview. The stress of the great ancient Near Eastern law codes on order and central royal authority yields to emphasis on divine guidance of the clans in their seasonal peregrinations. The symbolization of reality does not follow the pattern of cosmogonic myths of origin locating temple and palace at the *omphalos mundi*[18] but elaborates on the relationship of the deity to a people, utilizing themes of promise of land, progeny, safety, and oaths of fidelity. The ancestral stories are thus the building blocks of epic and covenant rather than the ingredients of myth and royal authority.

This social-anthropological reconstruction of the tribal prehistory of some of the elements that later comprised early Israel, though vague and speculative in itself, is corroborated in its general features and refined by biblical materials either stemming from or accurately preserving memory of the period of the tribal confederacy, that is, the pre-monarchical period. We shall turn to the laws and customs that fit this category below, but first we shall consider a specific event that seems to have had a decisive influence on the emerging worldview of early Israel.

Israel emerged from the undifferentiated masses of peasants and slaves scattered among the empires of the ancient Near East into the distinctiveness of peoplehood in the escape of a band of slaves from Egypt. The ubiquity of this theme in the oldest biblical sources suggests strongly that Israel's specific consciousness as a people began with the exodus. It does not imply, however, that those entering into the new confederacy of tribes were innocent of all notions of social structure and its relation to ultimate reality. The specific laws and customs that emerged among the tribes, the pervasive hostility towards central authority fueled by fierce loyalty to the clan, and the restless, dynamic view of reality in terms of historical movement under divine guidance were surely present among the *'epiru*, SA-GAZ , and *shasu*, that is, the various unsettled groups that existed along the margins of the great empires. The appellation attached to one of those socially defined groups of outcasts, the *'apiru (habiru)*, they even adopted for themselves. Henceforth Hebrew was not to be a derogatory term but one borne with pride. The experience of escape proved to be a powerful catalyst in forging what departed from Egypt as a "mixed com-

---

[18]Editors' note: On the significance of this symbol of the "navel" or center of the earth for the construction of a symbolic universe see Mircea Eliade, *The Sacred and the Profane: The Nature of Religion* (New York: Harper Torchbooks, 1961) 38, 40, 44–45, 47.

pany" ('*ereb rab*, Ex. 12:38) into an emergent community in search of its particular nature and destiny. Inspired by their encounter with a divine power who demonstrated through their escape solidarity with the weak, the poor, and the enslaved against the tyrant kings of this world, they declared their allegiance: "There is no king but Yahweh."

An epic thus was born that superceded the royal myth as the life-interpreting center of this people. Laws governing social behavior no longer originated in royal decree. They were drawn inferentially from the historical experience of deliverance, as the oft-recurring motive clause within the biblical law collections indicates: "I am Yahweh, who delivered you from the House of Bondage." Not the metaphysics of a static cosmos, but the example of a God present with ordinary people came to serve as a norm for human justice. That norm functioned in the daily life of the people through recitation of the epic, through the function of memory. The Hebrew was obliged to relate to the homeless, the weak, the poor, the widow, and the orphan not in a manner deduced from a timeless myth taught by temple priests but rather drawn from the Hebrews' historical identity: "You shall not oppress the alien, for you know the soul of the alien." Ontologically, then, the Israelite was grounded in the experience of divine grace in deliverance from oppression. Morally, the Israelite was inwardly motivated to act towards other human beings in a manner consistent with the experience of undeserved grace in the consciousness of living in the presence of a just and compassionate God.

Though the moral consciousness conceived in Israel's tribal prehistory and born of the exodus took shape in the individual (as indicated by the personal form of address in the laws and admonitions of the Pentateuch), that consciousness comes to fullest expression as a communal ideal. Israel came to believe that the exodus accomplished a restoration of life within community as God intended it, life in which the wholeness of each individual was safeguarded within the context of shalom. Shalom, the quality of harmony and peace among all members, was believed by Israel to arise where the people called into being by God's deliverance responded in gratitude expressed in worship and in imitation of divine mercy and justice in all of life's activities. Shalom thus differs from the order imposed by the ancient Near Eastern kings for purposes of maximizing royal authority and the productivity of the land. Not a pragmatic means to an end, but the fruits of a community striving to be true to its historical roots by embodying mercy and justice; such was the shalom to which early Israel was committed.

Our observations relating to earliest Israel identify two principles upon which its notion of social welfare was based: (1) a theological principle that located the source of community in divine grace and the norm for human behavior in the nature of the God encountered in the deliverance and empowerment of slaves, and (2) a sociological principle that generated laws and structures from the perspective of a community of equals rather than from the vantage point of the privileged few. Theological monotheism and social egalitarianism set in motion a major revision in social welfare. Injustice and oppression were not treated as threats to the smooth functioning of a hierarchically ordered state, but as an attack on the essence of who this people was, on their *nephesh*, that is, their intrinsic being. The irreducible good was no longer the sacred myth of the temple and the hierarchical ordering of the nation; the irreducible good was the community of shalom, living in covenant relationship with the God of justice and honoring the integrity of each human being. No longer could the king take the alien's wife with impunity. No longer could the bearer of the crown demand the vineyard of the peasant without serious repercussions. Henceforth a radical symbol of justice was set at the heart of the community, the symbol of the God who took up the cause of the poor, the weak, and the oppressed, and judged all humans with impartiality.

While response to the questions of social welfare was thus a matter of the heart rooted in memory, early Israel was not so naive as to believe that all members of the community would be faithful to this lofty ideal. Hence, there is evidence of early efforts to formulate laws as guidelines to life in covenant. This moves us from the level of worldview or symbolic universe, or in Israel's case the epic, to the level of laws and social institutions.

The Book of the Covenant in Exodus 20-24 is a product of the early pre-monarchic period. It is an uneven collection, giving the appearance of a young nation struggling to constitute itself and reaching both into the depths of its unique identity and into the customs prevailing among its neighbors. Some laws merely echo the case laws of the customary royal codes, preserving even the marks of social stratification (e.g., Ex. 21:28–32). Others draw on more humanitarian aspects of those codes (e.g., Ex. 21:1–11).[19] The full force of Israel's unique experience becomes visible, however, in a class of laws enjoining just treatment of vulnerable groups within the society such as widows and orphans, debtors, and aliens, by appeal to the example of the righteous compassion of God.

> If you lend to any of my people with you who is poor, you shall not be to him as a creditor, and you shall not exact interest from him. If ever you take your neighbor's garment in pledge, you shall restore it to him before the sun goes down; for that is his only covering; it is his mantle for his body; in what else shall he sleep? And if he cries to me, I will hear, for I am compassionate. (Ex. 22:25–27)

---

[19]It is of interest that the Hammurabi Code is more progressive in granting release of the debt-slave after three years.

This grounding of law in the nature of the deity encountered in its own history is the unique element in Jewish jurisprudence and the consistent expression of its historical ontology on the level of social structure.

This unique element of rooting ethical behavior in memory recurs in biblical laws, both early and late. A later example is the Levitical law regulating weights and measure:

> You shall do no wrong in judgment, in measures of length or weight or quantity. You shall have just balances, just weights, a just ephah, and a just hin: I am the Lord your God, who brought you out of Egypt. (Lev. 19:35–36)

This tenacious connection with the source of Israel's moral resolve in memory lends the dynamic quality to Hebrew law that is lacking in the cognate cultures.

It would be a mistake to allow the revolutionary breakthrough in social theory that was introduced by early Israelite society to prompt one to adopt an idealized or romantic view of that society. We must again call to mind three levels: worldview, laws and institutions, and practice. Israel's breakthrough occurred on the level of worldview; it had some impact on laws and structures. As the narratives of the Book of Judges indicate, replete as they are with stories of apostasy and intertribal conflict, practice often remained unaffected by the story of gracious deliverance. But we are not searching for Utopia. We are interested in observing and comparing the interplay of worldview, social structures, and behavior in different cultures. In the case of ancient Israel, we have begun to take notice of the impact of worldview on law and practice, and can now add another example.

The Israelites inherited from their neighbors the custom of allowing fields periodically to lie fallow. In their formulation of a law indigenizing this custom, we observe an interesting extension of its application to an important area of social welfare.

> For six years you shall sow your land and gather in its yield; but the seventh year you shall let it rest and lie fallow, that the poor of your people may eat; and what they leave the wild beasts may eat. You shall do likewise with your vineyard, and with your olive orchard. (Ex. 23:10–11)

When evidence of Israelite society in the pre-monarchical period is studied critically, what emerges is not a picture of a utopia but of a struggle between commitment to a transcendent basis for ethics and distractions that are not unfamiliar to moderns. That transcendent basis, moreover, is not an eternal myth revealing immutable verities established by the gods from the beginning, but an epic in which a people experiences the deity drawing it into a historical journey from slavery to shalom. In that journey its beacon is the God revealed in saving acts as the Agent of justice and mercy, even as its norm is the treatment it has received from God now transformed into a model of how it is to treat others. The social model found in early Israel is thus dynamic and open-ended. Within the covenant relationship Israel continues to encounter God in its historical existence and through these encounters it continues to infer lessons about the divine nature and will which must then be applied to changing situations.

THE RECRUDESCENCE OF ELITISM IN THE MONARCHY

We have already noted that Israel's perception of the true and the right is a historical perception. That it is not immune to the ambiguities of history struck Israel powerfully in the last years of the tribal league when the newly emerging people was nearly exterminated by the advance of an intrusive culture, the Philistines. The tribes in the confederacy of Israel had honored their individual autonomy by rejecting centralization under kingship and insisting on reliance on a voluntary militia for defense. But during the time of Samuel that began to crumble under the blows of the professional armies of Philistia. "Appoint for us a king to govern us like all the nations," was the demand put forth by the elders of Israel to Samuel.

Kingship of course was not a neutral category, neither socially, politically, nor ideologically. In the ancient Near East, as we have seen, kingship involved acceptance of the king as mediator (and, from a political perspective, source) of the laws binding on the citizenry. That in turn implied the loss of the very freedom that the Hebrews had won in escaping Egyptian slavery, the freedom to develop a way of life congruent with their historically based identity. Samuel warned them of the price of kingship: the king would take the best of their land, lay claim to their produce, and conscript their sons and daughters. In sum, he warned, "You shall be his slaves." Whereas the earlier generation could repudiate the suggestion of kingship with the categorical assertion, "There is no king in Israel but Yahweh" (paraphrase of Judg. 8:23), the court poet could now extol the divine nature of the king that set him apart from mere mortals (Ps. 45:6–7):

> Thy throne, O God, endures for ever and ever....
> Therefore God, your God, has anointed you
> with the oil of gladness above your fellows.

While there is no gainsaying the fact that monarchy created a centralized force capable of stemming the crushing tide of Philistia, the ideology of monarchy contradicted much that Israel had struggled to develop within the League period. Monarchy introduced an elitist, hierarchical structure of governance in place of a more egalitarian one. Monarchy also brought a major shift on the level of underlying worldview. The events of Israel's epic gave way to allusions of cosmogony and theomachy. A partial description of the sweeping changes thereby introduced include: (1) the land, formerly apportioned to the clans in perpetuity as an inviolable economic trust, became a commodity that could be bought, sold, or even confiscated by the royal house; (2) the populace became a pool for labor corvees and armies; (3) the economy was controlled by an elaborate bureaucracy dependent on whatever taxation was required for court luxuries, building projects, and military operations; (4) the internationalization of trade and the monopolization of farming and industry by an emerging nobility forced commoners into a feudal system as serfs who often amassed huge loans to finance seed and equipment and through foreclosure ended up in bonded slavery. Social stratification and a new set of laws to order the economy threatened to obliterate the revolutionary new concept of human community that had begun to develop in the tribal league. Within this new system, social welfare—for which there was clearly a growing need—was removed from the notion of mutual support within a community of shalom and placed back under the patronage of the king in the role of shepherd of the weak and the poor. Like the hymns of Mesopotamia, the royal psalms could celebrate the beneficence of the king: "In your majesty ride forth victoriously for the cause of truth and to defend the right; let your right hand teach you dread deeds!" (Ps. 45:4). But the jeremiads of the prophets against the corrupt and unjust practices of the new elite classes and the resulting oppression of common people support the skepticism already planted in our minds by the Mesopotamian and Egyptian royal propaganda: the kings were often driven by desires other than the welfare of their subjects!

The sweeping changes introduced by the kingship did not go unchallenged, however. Arising with kingship was a new office in Israel, one refusing cooption or control by the monarch: the office of prophet. Scholarship has provided conclusive proof that the prophets functioned as courageous defenders of the early Yahwistic ideals of community. While accepting monarchy as a historical fact, they deprived it of its mystique by repudiating its mythology and by defending the values associated with the epic and the customs and legal traditions of the League. The ideology of special privilege that entitled some classes to more than others and excused their injustice and callousness was condemned by appeal to the laws of the Book of the Covenant (Amos 2:6-8). The economic system that encouraged the extortion of the commoners' land by the wealthy was denounced by invocation of the divine word (Isa. 5:8-9). The hypocrisy that used religion to defend injustice was repudiated in the name of the God who takes scant notice of kings in demanding justice and compassion (Amos 5:21–24).

The common source of the prophetic social critique in the epic tradition did not give rise to a monolithic response to the relation between religious and civil realms. Elijah seems to have taken a harshly adversarial position towards the monarchy and was remembered as the underlying catalyst of Jehu's bloody coup de grâce. Hosea, though critical of the excesses of the Jehu purge, shared Amos's cynicism in regard to the ways of the kings. Isaiah, on the other hand, sought to draw kingship as an institution into the value system of early Yahwism by advancing a model of the king as a vessel of divine justice and mercy (Isa. 11:3–4):

> His delight shall be in the fear of the Lord.
> He shall not judge by what his eyes see,
> or decide by what his ears hear;
> but with righteousness he shall judge the poor,
> and decide with equity for the meek of the earth.

The integrity of Isaiah's strategy is demonstrated by his actions: he was resolute in his opposition to Ahaz's international policy because he believed it compromised Israel's ultimate reliance on God (Isa. 7-8); he was relentless in striking out at the injustice of the wealthy and the apostasy of many worshippers (Isa. 5:8–23; 1:10–17); and he was supportive of Hezekiah in the period of Assyrian assault because he believed that God had not forsaken the land (Isa. 36–39).

The diversity of approaches taken to issues of justice and social welfare by the prophets indicates that the early Yahwistic tradition was neither subservient to one ideology nor tied to any particular political system. What it contributed was a perspective based on an epic and an accompanying tradition of law and custom. The perspective was theocentric, covenantal, and egalitarian. The tradition of law struggled to translate historical memory into structures of justice and equality. The customs were communal in orientation and fostered the qualities of shalom. In effect, the vision of shalom, of life restored to its God-intended wholeness, was the essence of the message the prophets believed they had received from God. It was the norm against which they were to evaluate, admonish, and judge the civil and sacral realities of their time. This made their messages relevant, dynamic, controversial, and sometimes contradictory. But they were always a humanizing ferment that acted to maintain moral conscience in the land and to restrain political and economic programs of national aggrandizement and economic exploitation with the standards of divine righteousness and compassion. The prophets, more than any other group, sought to maintain the vital interplay between epic, laws and social structures, and practice.

Judged by conventional standards of success, the results of the prophets' efforts were mixed. Jehosophat, Hezekiah, and Josiah all instituted social reforms sensitive to the prophetic message. In the case of Josiah, it is possible to identify the specific literary source of his reform with the core of the Book of Deuteronomy. Deuteronomy thus offers a window through which we can glimpse a prophetically inspired view of social welfare acting as a reforming catalyst within the nation at a given point in history. The old Yahwistic starting point in memory of the past is invoked once again. Remembrance that its life as a people was a gift of divine grace both demanded obedience and bore the promise of life; on the other hand, forgetfulness, ingratitude, and disobedience threatened loss of nationhood and death (Deut. 30:15–20). The motivational power implicit in the appeal to Israel's epic is displayed clearly in the parenesis sections of the Book of Deuteronomy as summarized in the phrase: "Take heed lest you forget the Lord, who brought you out of the land of Egypt" (Deut. 6:12). Applied to the issues of social welfare, the definition of justice inferred from the exodus paradigm is clear and specific. Instances of oppression, impoverishment, and slavery contradict Israel's identity as a redeemed people and threaten its very existence. Because God's justice cannot be compromised, there is no equivocation in the Deuteronomic judgment on poverty: "There will be no poor among you." At the same time, the fact of poverty is not denied, but addressed:

> [T]he poor will never cease out of the land; therefore I command you, You shall open wide your hand to your brother, to the needy and to the poor, in the land. (Deut. 15:11)

The Deuteronomic reform goes beyond this general command to specific laws regulating social welfare. They address two sectors, the private and the public. The specific approach taken in the private sector involves the practice of gleaning. We see its effects both from the side of the benefactor and the recipient:

> When you reap your harvest in your field, and have forgotten a sheaf in the field, you shall not go back to get it; it shall be for the sojourner, the fatherless, and the widow; that the Lord your God may bless you in all the work of your hands. When you beat your olive trees, you shall not go over the boughs again; it shall be for the sojourner, the fatherless, and the widow. When you gather the grapes of your vineyard, you shall not glean it afterward; it shall be for the sojourner, the fatherless, and the widow. You shall remember that you were a slave in the land of Egypt; therefore I command you to do this. (Deut. 24:19–22)

When you go into your neighbor's vineyard, you may eat your fill of grapes, as many as you wish, but you shall not put any in your vessel. When you go into your neighbor's standing grain, you may pluck the ears with your hand, but you shall not put a sickle to your neighbor's standing grain. (Deut. 23:24–25)

The issue of social welfare is addressed to the public sphere in the form of the tithe, the equivalent of today's taxation. The Deuteronomic law regulating the triennial tithe reflects a movement beyond the assumption that voluntary charity meets the needs of the poor. The realism that humans require structures that coerce their charitableness strikes a modern chord:

At the end of every three years you shall bring forth all the tithe of your produce in the same year, and lay it up within your towns; and the Levite, because he has no portion or inheritance with you, and the sojourner, the fatherless, and the widow, who are within your towns, shall come and eat and be filled; that the Lord your God may bless you. (Deut. 14:28–29)

The perennial danger of vulnerable groups being denied full access to the protection of the judicial system is also addressed, once again with the exodus motive clause:

You shall not pervert the justice due to the sojourner or to the fatherless, or take a widow's garment in pledge; but you shall remember that you were a slave in Egypt and the Lord your God redeemed you from there; therefore I command you to do this. (Deut. 24:17–18)

These examples indicate that the goal of a humane society in which the welfare of all members is assured serves as the guiding force behind the entire Deuteronomic program. The foundation of that program is constituted by the traditional Yahwistic theological and moral principles. The recurrent motive clauses point to the source of the entire moral structure of Israel in the God who delivered slaves from their bondage. The righteous and compassionate nature of God revealed in the exodus served as the norm for Israelite society. Even as God was impartial and incorruptible, so too were Israelites to be impartial and incorruptible in the administration of justice; even as God heard the cry of the lowly, and purely out of love gave them freedom and prosperity, so too were Israelites to restore the weak and the impoverished.[20] By locating the source of social justice

---

[20]Moshe Weinfield has correctly observed, "[The Deuteronomic law] is primarily interested in human beings, and above all those whose possibilities of defending themselves are limited." *Deuteronomy and the Deuteronomic School* (Oxford: Oxford University Press, 1972), 243.

and welfare in the heart of a loving God rather than in any specific civic or sacral program, Deuteronomy delivered law from its subservience to the utilitarian aims of leaders and priests, and reestablished the dignity of every human as an irreducible good: "Justice and only justice, you shall follow, that you may live" (Deut. 16:20). At the same time Deuteronomy does not overlook the necessity of introducing laws to take up the cause of the disadvantaged where unaided human generosity fails.

The centering of the Deuteronomic social ethics in a God experienced in the ongoing life of the people combined with a realistic assessment of human limitations accounts both for the progressive nature of the laws themselves and for the eloquence and power of the accompanying parenesis.

Jeremiah similarly takes up the themes of memory of the epic and the egalitarian justice arising therefrom, and envisions the day when Israel's persistence in idolatry and injustice would give way to obedience from the heart (Jer. 31:31–34). Jeremiah stands at the end of the period of Israelite nationhood. During his lifetime the Babylonians conquered the land, destroyed the temple, and exiled the upper tiers of the nation. This tragic conclusion to Israelite history raises the question whether there was any abiding significance in a tradition of justice and a vision of social welfare that failed to secure its own nation from extinction. Was the early Yahwistic tradition and the tradition of prophecy that grew out of it during the period of the monarchy unrealistically utopian after all?

The literature of the exilic and post-exilic periods sheds light on this important question. Briefly stated, it indicates that the tradition and vision not only survived, but survived in a new, more mature form. The destruction of the Davidic state and the national cult tied to it corroborated one of the most emphatic themes of the prophets, namely, that God's justice could neither be contained nor co-opted by human institutions. God's torah of righteous compassion was not destroyed by the demise of its host nation therefore, but in fact was enabled to spread beyond the borders of Israel to other peoples.

The exilic and post-exilic periods thus proved to be times of deepening understanding of the biblical notions of justice and social welfare. Notions that failed to be adopted as official policy by the state like the Jubilee and the transformation of weapons into instruments of peace became objects of intense reflection. Chapters 40–55 of Isaiah, written in exile, present a broadly universal portrait of the envisioned healing of both the realms of nature and of human society. After the Jewish community was reconstituted by the return of considerable numbers from exile, Ezra and Nehemiah set out to reform the economic and religious structures of the community, and their source was once again the torah tradition of God's righteous compassion traced all the way back to the exodus (e.g., Neh. 5:1–13). The loss of nationhood, far from destroying that tradition, thus freed it for application to new settings. Under scribes, rabbis, and apostles, the epic tradition of God's enlisting a people for the cause of impartial justice and creation's healing, and the vision of social welfare that evenhandedly embraced all people lived beyond the demise of one nation and became an important influence in the development of many future nations.

CONTEMPORARY IMPLICATIONS

Drawing contemporary implications from an ancient world is a precarious business that requires ongoing discussion. I shall merely conclude by drawing together the cardinal points that can be extrapolated from this survey of the issue of social welfare in the ancient Near East.

First there is the inextricable connection between the world-structuring myth of a culture and its value system. The symbolic form used by a culture to present itself exercises a powerful influence on its laws and customs. In Mesopotamia, Egypt, and Canaan the myth was cosmogonic, and the king played a role parallel to the creator god by constituting and securing his people through his authoritative decrees. The right and the good was determined from the top down. The result was a stratified social system giving privileged treatment to the powerful and wealthy, and ordering the lives of the poor and disadvantaged as a function of maintaining stability and productivity in the land.

In Israel's pre-monarchical period, an epic of divine deliverance of slaves replaced the myth as the narrative depiction of the world, and the good and the right was patterned after the example of the righteous, compassionate God who treated all humans with impartiality and sought to restore the rights and fortunes of the weak, the impoverished, and the dispossessed. Though early Israelite law addressed many of the same specific areas as had the laws of Mesopotamia and Egypt, the thrust of the law was transformed by the interpretive framework of the epic. Righteous compassion replaced authoritative ordering as the intention of the law. As the story of Tamar in Genesis 38 illustrates, this center of interpretation strongly influenced the function of law in Israel.

The monarchy reintroduced the myth of ordering by the authoritative divine command. Laws and social welfare were drawn back into the concerns of the royal and priestly hierarchy. The prophets arose in defense of the older, egalitarian laws. The result was a history of intense struggle between two different understandings of society's role in social welfare.

Many intermediate links would have to be forged before the implications of Israel's struggle with issues of social welfare could be drawn for our own society. But already the history that we have covered poses certain questions: What is the guiding mythology of our country? How does it influence our attitudes, laws, and treatment of those who do not share fully in the rights and benefits of our society? How is our self-understanding as a people influenced by the particular readings of history that inform our national epic, for example, the displacement and decimation of native American tribes, the forging of a work force out of slaves violently torn from their homelands, the maintenance of a particular theocratic ideal by exclusion of those holding different religious beliefs? Does even that epic of escape from bondage to the new land that we uphold so proudly as our national autobiography contain seeds of the discrimination that divides our nation today between the privileged and the disadvantaged? Is there not a great deal of hypocrisy in our boasting about our honoring of individual rights when our society denies whole classes of individuals the most basic rights of food, shelter, and equal protection under the law?

The critical study of history cannot produce answers on demand to the crucial social crises facing our nation. What it can do, however, is break the myopia that leads us to accept uncritically interpretations of our history which are largely disguised propaganda for one ideology or another. It can also increase our resolve to resist the efforts of those who would co-opt our traditions of justice and social reform for partisan ends —whether from the right or the left—and to hold up paradigms of universal equality as ferment for self-criticism and change. Finally, it can heighten our awareness of the determinative force of the subconscious level of shared views and assumptions that in bygone societies was occupied by a public myth or epic but may now be filled increasingly with self-serving presuppositions and prejudices. If it is true that every viable society needs some sort of shared worldview, we need to begin paying attention to this rather arcane level lest it fall under the control of fanatics and demagogues.

Chapter 2

RICH AND POOR
IN THE NEW TESTAMENT
AND IN EARLY CHRISTIANITY

HOWARD CLARK KEE

Like the Israelite community from which it developed, early Christianity developed attitudes toward wealth and poverty, the rich and the poor, that were rooted in the community's perception of God's activity in history now specified in Jesus. The early Christian context, however, was not ancient Near Eastern kingdoms, but the socioeconomic conditions of Palestine and the wider Roman world. As the Jesus movement spread into this larger realm it attracted people of some wealth and power, and thus was confronted with the question of how to include the wealthy in light of the gospel tradition about how difficult it is for the rich to enter the Kingdom of God. The need for ongoing financial support for the early church further encouraged the adaptation of Jesus' radical teaching about wealth and possessions to the new conditions. Material poverty became rewritten as spiritual poverty. This tension between a radical discipleship that gives up everything and a moderate discipleship of the stewardship of wealth will be seen in the later essays discussing medieval Christian relations to the poor.

Anyone who has ever watched a camel driver in the Middle East try to get his beast simply to get up or down on command, who has heard the animal's vehement objections to change of position, who has seen drivers' forearms from which recalcitrant camels have bit off chunks of flesh, knows how literally preposterous is the proposal attributed to Jesus of getting a camel to crawl through the eye of a needle (Mark 10:25). Presumably, Jesus perceived it as equally problematical that anyone rich would make it into the Kingdom of God. The early Christians did not hear this vivid metaphor as a prohibition against wealthy persons participating in the Jesus movement, but it did pose for them the issue of the terms under which the rich might take part in the common life of God's new people. The answers offered were varied, and they change with the passage of time and the altered circumstances under which the Christian communities lived.

To analyze the attitudes toward wealth and poverty expressed in the gospel tradition and in the other parts of the New Testament demands engagement in two endeavors: (1) examination of the socioeconomic conditions of Palestine and the wider Roman world in the first and early second centuries, and (2) recognition of the changing approach to the question of possessions represented in the literature produced by Christians in this period.

SOCIOECONOMIC CONDITIONS IN FIRST-CENTURY PALESTINE

Anthony Saldarini's insightful analysis of the social and economic conditions in first-century Palestine[1] shows that the population was gathered into two types of communities: villages and (mostly small) cities. Some of these had the major features of cities of the Greco-Roman world: a central *agora*, which served as a marketplace but also was the setting for public gatherings and speeches by individuals with philosophical or religious convictions that they wanted to share and to which they hoped to convert the public. Shrines to traditional deities were there as well, together with baths and theaters. On the edge of the cities were hippodromes where the public could be entertained. In or near the edge of such cities were the opulent houses or extensive villas of the local power figures. Cities of the New Testament period in Palestine which fit this category include Jericho, Caesarea, Scythopolis, Sepphoris, and—though a city of lesser dimensions—Capernaum, where Jesus took up residence (Mark 2:1). We may note in passing that Sepphoris was located less than a half-hour walk down the slope of the Galilean hills from Nazareth, the village where Jesus grew up. Although the subsequent destructions of Jerusalem were so severe that no clear picture can be drawn of that city in the period prior to the Roman invasion in 70 CE, it almost certainly fit into the type we have just sketched. These cities sought to reproduce the hellenistic model of a *polis*, not only in the physical layout and facilities, but in the social organization, whereby the ultimate power (Rome) assigned to the inner core of local prestige and power a role as local council (in Greek, *synedrion*), which was given a remarkable degree of latitude in establishing legal codes and processes to maintain peace and order in a way that was compatible with the empirewide goals of Rome.[2]

---

[1] Anthony J. Saldarini, *Pharisees, Scribes and Sadducees in Palestinian Society* (Wilmington, Del.: Michael Glazier, 1988). Other insightful studies of the region of Galilee in the early centuries of the common era include Martin Goodman, *State and Society in Roman Galilee, AD 132–212* (Totowa, N.J.: Bowman, 1983) and Sean Freyne, *Galilee from Alexander the Great to Hadrian 323 BCE to 135CE* (Wilmington, Del.: Glazier, 1980).

[2] A summary of archaeological evidence of life in the cities of Galilee is provided in Eric M. Meyers and James F. Strange, *Archaeology, the Rabbis and Early Christianity* (Nashville: Abingdon, 1981).

Participation in the *synedrion* was limited to the wealthy and powerful, whom Saldarini and others estimate to have been no more than 1 or 2 percent of the population. Wealth was largely inherited, or in some cases bestowed by Roman authorities as compensation for major favors done to establish, maintain, or regain Roman control. Wealth consisted largely of extensive landholdings, many of them cultivated by tenant farmers, who were obliged to pay to the absentee owners most of the proceeds from production. A most vivid example of this appears in the Parable of the Wicked Tenants (Mark 12:1–12) where those working the vineyard not only refuse to pay the owner his due but kill the agents who come to collect the annual revenue. Precedent, political power, and law enforcement procedures combined to maintain the wealth and prosperity of the elite. Their social base was in the hellenized cities, where social, political, economic, and military power were established. Other Palestinian cities of this type would include Ptolemais, Dor, Ashdod, Ascalon, and Joppa on the Mediterranean coast and Tiberias and Bethsaida-Julias on the Lake of Galilee. Excavations at Tiberias have shown dramatically the extent of the hellenization of this urban center in Galilee during the time of Jesus.

A second type of city lay on major trade routes and shared some of the features of the larger cities. Capernaum, an obvious example, was in an economically strategic location on the main road that brought Mesopotamian wealth to the port of Ptolemais for trans-shipment to major cities of the Roman empire, and it had a remunerative industry of its own: fishing. This introduces for our consideration a different socioeconomic type of person: the local entrepreneur, as represented by the family of fishermen from whom Jesus chose two of his disciples, James and John, who left the family enterprise in the hands of their father and the hired servants (Mark 1:19–20). Similar to a family fishing business was the handcraft work in which Jesus was engaged (Mark 6:3). His designation as a *tekton* is best translated not as "carpenter" but as "craftsman," which could include building in stone or working in metal. In the parallel to this Markan reference to Jesus, Matthew adds the detail that Jesus is the "son of a *tekton*," so it is possible that Jesus was also engaged in family construction work before beginning his public career as a prophet announcing the New Age of God's Rule. We might note in passing that the typical pattern for one with such an occupation as a handworker would have been for Jesus— and perhaps for Joseph as well—to have made their living helping to build or maintain the nearby city of Sepphoris. The economic level of people thus employed would have been roughly equal to that of the tenant farmers. They would have been dependent on the economy as a whole, for which ultimate decision making lay with the Roman power and with the regional elite through whom the imperial control was locally administered.

Another category of social status which figures in the gospel tradition is the client group. These are persons who lacked wealth and power, but who worked with the Roman authorities in ways that were essential for maintenance of imperial control. The best example is the tax collector, who collected taxes and tolls for the Romans, and who obtained this position by bidding on a contract basis. Tax collectors paid a fixed amount to Rome, and they could retain for themselves whatever they could extract beyond their formal obligations to the Roman state. Taxes were collected on goods in transit, as well as in certain markets. Thus the profits of farmers and artisans were grossly reduced through the agency of these local instruments of Roman power. Furthermore, since many of the imported items were ritually impure, tax collectors could not avoid ritual pollution, further discrediting them among the pious. Money lending was another part of the economic configuration, and money lenders were turned to in times of crop failure or other catastrophes. Their financial function served further to concentrate wealth in the hands of the few.

The largest single economic enterprise in Palestine was the temple. The contributions it received from Jews scattered across the world as well as from pious pilgrims who visited it were a major source of income. Sacrifices offered in the temple had to be from approved sources, and the animals had to be properly slaughtered; these activities were supervised by —and were under the economic control of— the priestly establishment. Even monetary offerings had to be made in special temple currency, for which the moneychangers, who were engaged by the priests, charged a fee. While the priesthood was hereditary, the choice of the high priest had lain with the secular powers from the days of the Maccabees in the first century BCE, when approval of the candidate for this post was both sought and granted by the Roman senate. Thus the priestly class was economically similar to its clients: the priests served at the wish of Rome and were regarded as essential to the maintenance of an economically viable and peaceful Palestinian society.

WEALTH AND POVERTY IN THE OLDER LAYERS
OF THE GOSPEL TRADITION

It is remarkable that, from the outset, the circle of Jesus' followers as it is represented in Mark and the Q source cuts across the lines of socioeconomic demarcation which we have traced. Jesus and his followers are from the artisan class near the bottom of the economic scale, as we noted; but among the inner circle of the disciples is a tax collector, known as Matthew or Levi (Mark 2:14; Matt. 9:9). Jesus' association with one so repugnant to most Jews because of collaboration with Roman authorities was not unique or out of character, as shown by the description of Jesus offered by his critics according to the Q tradition (Luke 7:34). There he is charac-terized as "a glutton and a drunkard, a friend of tax collectors and sin-ners." Thus Jesus' defiance of traditional behaviorial standards, of social relationships, and of ritual purity is dramatically evident in his choice of close and continuing association with tax collectors.

The opposition that Jesus encountered, which led to his execution at the hands of the Romans, was comprised of both the elite and the client classes. Among them were the Pharisees, many of whom appear to have served in the client role. This contributed to their wealth and power, although they seem to have sought a kind of private piety and purity through gatherings in homes and public halls where they studied and appropriated the scriptures for personal guidance. Also opposing Jesus were the Sadducees, whose distinctive features as a group are well-nigh impossible to trace, but who can be inferred (from mention of them in the writings of Josephus) to have been a power group—possibly at least some of them with connections to the priesthood. In the coalition that formed to get rid of Jesus, the priests seem to have had a significant role, and the final decision to recommend to the Romans that Jesus be executed was made by the power elite, the *synedrion*. It is important to note that this sociopolitical power group is not the same religious body that in later cen-turies appropriated the name, in semitic transliteration, Sanhedrin, and then sought to legitimate itself by claiming that it had existed before the Common Era. The truly wealthy and the client group saw Jesus and his followers as a common enemy who threatened the social structure of Pal-estinian life. That challenge to the economic order is expressed in both the Q and the Markan traditions.

This challenge to the status quo is most clearly and vividly expressed in the familiar words of Luke 6:20-21: "Blessed are you poor, for yours is the Kingdom of God. Blessed are you that hunger now, for you shall be satisfied. Blessed are you that weep now, for you shall laugh." From what follows in Luke 6:22 and in the Markan and Q tradition as a whole, it is evident that the term "poor" includes not only the economically deprived, but also those who for a variety of reasons are excluded from the main-stream of society. These disqualifications would include non-Jewish ori-gins, physical condition (which would lead to ritual uncleanness), occupation (like the tax collectors), and cultural orientation (like the people from outside Palestine with whom Jesus associated).

Yet the economic factors are important in this stream of the Jesus tra-dition, as is apparent in such sayings as Luke 6:29-30: "From the one who takes away your coat, don't hold back your shirt [or kaftan] as well. Give to everyone who begs from you, and if anyone takes away your goods, don't ask them back again." Material possessions are basically unimpor-tant in view of the imminence of the coming of God's kingdom, and hence there is no point in trying to hold on to them. At the same time, there is a promise of future compensation for present poverty or loss. In the divine reward which will come at the end of the age, compensation will abound: "Lend expecting nothing in return, and your reward will be great, and you will be sons of the Most High; for he is kind to the grateful and the unselfish" (Luke 6:35). This theme is repeated in Luke 6:38: "The measure you give will be the measure you get." God will give you in the new age what you now offer freely to others or what you lose through those who take advantage of you in the present age. There is no denial of the ultimate value of material possessions, but there is a fundamental shift in perspective and priority. The main charge to Jesus' listeners in this tradition is to give priority to generosity and to refuse to be self-destructive. This is effectively stated in the warning against trying to serve two masters: "You cannot serve God and money" (Matt. 6:24).

The model for this behavior and attitude toward possessions is the nature of God's activity in the world. In Luke 12:22–31 there is advice to avoid giving priority to clothing or food, to one's appearance, or to personal security. God will supply all these needs. The sole priority is to seek the coming of God's rule in the world. Then people can rest confident that their basic needs will be met. This freedom from seeking for material possessions is also enjoined upon the disciples in their role as messengers of Jesus and proclaimers of the coming of the end of the age. As they set out on their travels in his behalf they are to rely solely on spontaneously offered food and hospitality, and hence are to carry with them no equipment, supplies, or funds (Luke 9:3; 10:4). God will bring judgment on those who do not receive them or offer support. Their sole task is to proclaim by word and deed (through healings) that "the Kingdom of God has come near" (Luke 10:9).

The fullest statement about wealth and possessions is in Mark 10:17–31. Jesus responds to the question of the rich man who asks what he must do to participate in eternal life by first reminding him in summary form of the Old Testament commandments. On hearing the man claim that he has observed these legal requirements, Jesus articulates the one basic obligation that must be met: to give to the poor all that he possesses. The man leaves discouraged, whereupon Jesus generalizes about the difficulty faced by those who, possessing much of this world's goods, seek to enter the life of the age to come. In answer to the disciples' request for clarification about who can be saved and enter the new life, Jesus says flatly that humanly speaking it is impossible, "but not with God." What is called for is willingness to abandon every ground of human security: home and family, native territories. There will be persecutions for those who choose this route, but there will also be the ultimate reward of life in the age to come. What is essential in this tradition is for the follower of Jesus to perceive that he or she is living at the end of the present age and of its value system. The overwhelming concern is to spread the message as widely as possible before that end occurs. Mark writes in full expectation that during the lifetime of Jesus' original followers this consummation will take place, in which the powers of evil will be finally overcome and the transformation of human life and values will occur in the Kingdom of God (Mark 9:1).[3]

PAUL'S ATTITUDE TOWARD WEALTH

Paul's attitudes toward wealth and poverty were not unlike those of Jesus. Much of the time he worked long and hard to earn his own living (1 Cor. 9:6; 1 Thess. 2:9). According to Acts 18:3, he was an artisan as Jesus was, although his craft was that of a tent maker. Where the communities were more affluent, as was the church in Philippi, Paul was willing to be supported by contributions from the members—which in Philippi were generous and continuing (Phil. 4:15–19). Similarly, in his letter to the Romans he writes that he expects to receive financial support from them during what he hopes will be a brief stay en route to Spain, where he can resume missionary work in virgin territory (Rom. 15:24).

The economic status of the members of the Pauline churches must have varied widely. Generous as the churches of Macedonia were, they were basically a poor segment of society, so that Paul wrote to the Corinthians about the Macedonians, "From the depths of their poverty they have shown themselves lavishly openhanded" (2 Cor. 8:2). Yet he felt that he should call on all the churches in Asia Minor and Greece to contribute to the relief fund for the poor in the church in Jerusalem. Instructions about this fund are given in 1 Cor. 16:1-14 and in Rom. 15:25-27, from which we may infer that there were some people of means who could share in such a common effort of financial support. This inference receives confirmation from the fact that among the earliest supporters of Paul in Corinth were Priscilla and Aquila—apparently mobile, prosperous merchants originally from Rome, who later returned there after extended stays in Corinth and Ephesus. Their home was sufficiently large to serve as the meeting place for the church—or one of the local congregations—in Corinth (1 Cor. 16:19).

The closest that Paul comes to establishing a principle concerning wealth appears in 2 Cor. 8:13-14 where he declares that "there is no question of providing monetary relief [for others] at the cost of hardship to

---

[3]A fuller picture of the community and its perspectives which lie behind the Gospel of Mark are set forth in Howard Clark Kee, *Community of the New Age* (Philadelphia: Westminster, 1977).

yourselves. It is a question of equality. At the moment your surplus meets the need [of the poor in Jerusalem], but one day your need may be met from their surplus." As in the Jesus tradition, Paul considers what one possesses as no more than a basic necessity for day-to-day existence. Members of the community are to share with others in special need. Paul expected the end of the age to come within his own lifetime (1Thess. 4:17), so that wealth was no more than a factor in the transitional period before the end of the age came. Rich and poor alike had roles to play in the new community of faith, but all would soon move to a new era in which the values of the old age would be left behind.

NEW DIRECTIONS IN THE ATTITUDES TOWARD WEALTH AND POVERTY: MATTHEW, LUKE, AND ACTS

In those detailed modifications by Matthew and Luke of material which came to them from a common source of sayings of Jesus (known to scholars as Q), there are clear indications of changes from the older gospel tradition with respect to early Christian perceptions of rich and poor.[4] This is vividly evident in Matthew's modification of the beatitude about poverty. What is almost certainly the Q version preserved in Luke 6:20, "Blessed are you poor," has become in Matthew a generalization in which poverty is a metaphor: "Blessed are the poor *in spirit*." That this transformation is intended is confirmed by a second change that Matthew has made in the Q tradition, by which "Blessed are you that hunger now" (Luke 6:21) has become, "Blessed are those who hunger and thirst for righteousness." The latter term here is a favorite motif in Matthew, as when (only in Matthew) Jesus is baptized "in order to fulfill all righteousness" (3:15), and when the exhortation to seek God's kingdom (Luke 12:31) becomes an instruction to "seek God's kingdom *and his righteousness*" (6:33). As in the case of the beatitudes, Matthew has toned down the original force of these promises in which present deprivation is contrasted with future divine supply, thereby converting the eschatological pronouncements into timeless moral and religious principles. His community is more interested in enduring rules and guidelines than in the sense of immediacy of the end of the age that is evident in Mark and in the original Q material.

Throughout his gospel, Matthew gives more attention to and adopts a more positive attitude toward wealth. This is evident from the opening chapters where the newborn Jesus is visited by the magi bringing costly gifts: gold, frankincense, and myrrh. He is acclaimed as king and draws down the wrath of the puppet ruler, Herod, who sees in the birth of this

---

[4]A reconstruction of the Q source may be found in Howard Clark kee, *Jesus in History*, 2d ed. (New York: Harcourt, Brace, Jovanovich, 1977).

child a threat to his own position of power and wealth. Only Matthew reports the handsome sum paid to Judas as compensation for his having enabled the military to seize Jesus when the authorities want to charge him as a claimant to royal power. There is in Matthew no negative attitude toward wealth, or even the idea that it is a necessary factor during the time of transition to the new age. Instead, poverty and riches have been transmuted into spiritual values, whereby "poor in spirit" has come to mean trust in God in expectation of eschatological reward.

Luke, on the other hand, continues the older tradition according to which God's primary concern is with the economically poor and the socially deprived or ostracized. We shall note in a moment, however, that the community for which Luke writes probably included people of some wealth and power, so that he is careful to leave a place for the latter within the people of God. Further, he deals directly with issues of wealth and possessions among the members of the community.

Unlike Matthew, Luke not only preserves the earlier form of the beatitude about the blessedness of "you poor" (Luke 6:20), but he also adds a parallel set of woes to the rich and prosperous (6:24-26). Similarly, to the command to love one's enemies he adds the rhetorical question, "And if you lend to those from whom you hope to receive, what credit is that to you? Even sinners lend to sinners, to receive as much again." And in the instruction to love one's enemies, he inserts the command, "Lend, expecting nothing in return" (Luke 6:24-35). To the Q material with its warning against judging others he adds (or preserves from the Q source material which Matthew omits) the promise that the generous will be rewarded: "Give, and it will be given to you; good measure, pressed down, shaken together, running over, will be put into your lap" (Luke 6:38). Clearly the motivation for this generosity is not an abstract principle but the nature of God who showers such benefits on his people. The dynamic behind this is God's transformation of the human heart, as Luke notes, drawing again on the Q tradition: "The good man out of the good treasure of his heart produces good, and the evil man out of his heart produces evil; for out of the abundance of the heart the mouth speaks" (Luke 6:45). Wealth is in these passages a metaphor for inner renewal.

In material which is unique to Luke, however, or which he has radically transformed from his sources, the questions of wealth and poverty are directly addressed. His version of the infancy stories picture the birth of Jesus as taking place in a stable. The visitors are local shepherds, not distinguished foreigners. They bring no gifts. The great hymnic utterance of Mary that precedes his birth, the Magnificat, announces the reversal of fortunes in the new age which he will bring: "He has scattered the proud in the imagination of their hearts, he has put down the mighty from their thrones, and exalted those of low degree; he has filled the hungry with good things, and the rich he has sent empty away" (Luke 1:51-53).

Jesus' first public statement in Luke reports Jesus as claiming to be the fulfillment of the announcement in Isaiah 61 that God will empower by his Spirit his chosen agent for the renewal of his people. Quoting from the prophet, Jesus declares, "The Spirit of the Lord is upon me, because he has anointed me to preach good news to the poor" (Luke 4:18). He then declares, "Today this scripture has been fulfilled in your hearing" (4:21). That the significant factor in the redefining of participation in the covenant people is not literal poverty alone, however, is apparent from the subsequent assignments to the anointed one to "proclaim release to the captives and recovering of sight to the blind and to set at liberty those who are oppressed." In this context "poor" means deprived or denied participation in God's people by physical condition or by social maltreatment. It is the outsiders who now become the insiders in the divinely appointed reversal of human conditions. Luke reports Jesus as drawing a parallel to the work of Elijah and Elisha (Luke 4:25-27), through whom God's renewing grace went out to heal those who were non-Israelites and who were further excluded by reason of social status (the Sidonian widow) or ritual condition (the Syrian leper). In this mode, Luke adds to the story of Jesus' healing the slave of a Roman military officer, found in the Q source (7:1-10), an account of his restoring to life the son of a widow (7:11-17). The marginal—ethnically, ritually, socially—are the chief beneficiaries of God's action through Jesus according to Luke. These are the "poor" in Luke's view.

The Lukan parables fill in further details of the attitude toward wealth. The epitome of generosity and human concern is depicted in the uniquely Lukan parable of the Good Samaritan, whose ethnic and religious origins were despised by pious Jews (10:29-37) but whose personal kindness and financial support of one in need are exemplary. The parable of the Rich Fool (Luke 12:13-21) is preceded by a combined command and principle: "Take heed and beware of all covetousness, for human life does not consist in the abundance of one's possessions." The parable itself vividly makes the point that acquisition of material goods is no guarantee about one's future destiny. To the Q parable of the Great Supper (Luke 14:15-24) Luke has added the details that, once those initially invited to the supper (which symbolizes the joyous gathering of God's people at the end of the age) refused to accept the invitation, it was extended to those in the streets and lanes of the city, "the poor and maimed and blind and lame." Clearly, Luke perceives the role of the community as having a top priority for caring for the poor and others who are marginal to society by reason of their physical, ritual, or moral condition.

There is a dimension of Luke's portrait of the early Christian community which is often overlooked, but which must have had special importance for the Lukan wing of this movement. This is the role of a wealthy group of followers who provide support for Jesus (Luke 8:1-3). Surprisingly, they are all women, and at least one of them is highly connected with the political structure of Galilee in the first century. One of those who provide for Jesus and/or his followers[5] is Joanna, the wife of Chuza, who was the manager of financial and property matters for Herod Antipas, who had been installed by the Romans as tetrarch (provincial ruler) of Galilee in this period. It is this same core of wealthy women supporters of Jesus who are reported by Luke to have observed where Jesus was buried and who prepared the spices and ointments to apply to his corpse as a proper burial (23:55-56). It is they who go to the tomb on Sunday morning and first hear the message that Jesus has been raised from the dead (24:1-9). These details do not seem to be chance additions by Luke to the older gospel tradition, but instead reflect the situation within Luke's community in which there is a vital and continuing role for wealthy women who provide support for the work of the gospel, in addition to their testimony based on their own personal experience of the risen Christ.

In the book of Acts, new social and economic dimensions of the developing Christian community are evident. In Acts 2:44–45 the Jerusalem Christians are pictured as having pooled the resources of all the members, including the sale of all their goods and possessions in order to create a common fund to which all might have access on the basis of need. The condition is neatly summarized in the phrase, "All who believed were together and had all things in common." The description of this communal arrangement is repeated in 4:32-35, with the added detail that houses and land were sold. If this is an accurate representation of what was going on in the community of which Luke was writing this account in Acts, there must have been members of the Palestinian elite who had joined the movement, since they alone would have had houses and lands to sell. If it is only an idealized picture, it is difficult to see what its relevance would have been for impoverished former farm and craft workers. The mirror image of this arrangement of pooled resources is evident in Acts 5, where a couple who retain a portion of their property are divinely punished by death. Again, the point of this story would be important only to those who did have considerable possessions, and were therefore potential violators of what is here pictured as a divinely ordained arrangement of common resources within the community.

This feature of the inclusion of the wealthy and powerful in the Christian community is confirmed in Paul's letters as well as in the later Acts narratives. Among those whose greetings Paul conveys to the church in

---

[5]The oldest and best texts read "provided for *them*," while other ancient manuscripts read "for *him*."

Rome is the city treasurer of Corinth (Rom. 16:23), a position of importance and power in any city, but especially in such a wealthy center of
commerce as Corinth. Among those converted to Christianity according to
Acts are: a court official from Ethiopia; a Roman centurion; a member of
the court of Herod the tetrarch; a wealthy business woman, Lydia, whose
occupation was selling an expensive purple dye; Dionysus of Athens, a
member of the Ariopagites, whom the council charged with overseeing
the cultural and moral life of the city. The historicity of these accounts is of
less importance than the fact that they show the intent—and probably the
achievement—of the early Christians in reaching to the socioeconomic
level of the elite in Roman society across the Mediterranean world. This
seems to have been accomplished to some degree from the early decades
of the church's existence, and to have been a significant factor by the end
of the first century.[6] If the report by Dio in his *Roman History* about Domi-
tian's having condemned to death his relative Domitilla and her husband
on the charge of atheism is correctly interpreted to mean that they had
converted to Christianity and given land for Christian burials in the area
now known as the Catacomb of Domitilla, then by the end of the first century Christianity had penetrated to the imperial family itself."[7]

ATTITUDES TOWARD WEALTH IN THE SECOND-CENTURY CHURCH

In the Didache, or Teaching of the Twelve Apostles, written early in the
second century the instructions concerning wealth are for the most part
merely modest elaborations of the gospel tradition. There is primarily a
call for generosity toward those who are in need (Did. 1:4–6; 4:5), and
there are warnings against greed (Did. 2:6) or love of money (3:5). Similarly, in the Epistle of Barnabas there is a call for Christians to share their
possessions with their neighbors (Barn. 19:8). Another aspect of the teaching of these documents concerning wealth has to do with the financial and
other forms of tangible support to the church leaders. The charge in the
Didache (13:1-7) is closely related to the Q tradition about support for the
itinerant followers of Jesus: the laborer is worthy of his reward (Luke 10:7;
Matt. 10:10). The early second-century document I Tim. 5:18 also echoes
this sentiment. The assumption is that members of the community who
have the means to provide support for their leaders are enjoined to do so.

Two factors from the older tradition are missing, however: there is no
hint of pooling resources, as in Acts, and the radical notion of divesting

---

[6]Discussed in Howard Clark Kee, *Good News to the Ends of the Earth: The Theology of Acts*
(London: SCM; Philadelphia: Trinity Press International, 1990).

[7]A succinct and persuasive assessment of the evidence is offered by Jack Finegan, *Light
from the Ancient Past* (Princeton: Princeton University Press, 1959), 461–64.

oneself of possessions, as in the older gospel tradition, is also absent. Neither Barnabas nor the Didache contains a warning about how difficult it is for the rich to enter the Kingdom of God. The nearest approach to this radical demand is found in several parts of the *Shepherd of Hermas*, which dates from near the middle of the second century, but even here the gospel tradition is used selectively. In Vision 3 of the *Shepherd*, an important feature of the elaborate allegory of the stone tower (which symbolizes the people of God) is the matter of the round stones which do not fit into the structure and are discarded. These are said to be those members of the community who have not only faith but "the riches of this world."
When their wealth is trimmed off, then they become useful to God (Vis. 3.6.5–6). What is involved in cutting off wealth is later described more fully as sharing one's possessions with the poor. This trimming process will enable the rich to fit into the tower which is being built.

Later in the *Shepherd of Hermas* the new community is discussed with direct reference to the gospel tradition about how difficult it is for the rich to enter the Kingdom of God (Similitude 9.20.1–4). The vision of the mountain covered with thorns and thistles represents the rich who are "mixed up with many affairs of business." They find it difficult to identify with the other members of the community because they are afraid that the poor will ask them for financial aid. Yet the vivid image of Mark—the camel going through the needle's eye—is replaced by that of someone walking with naked feet among thistles. This experience is painful and awkward, but not impossible, as is the camel crawling through the needle's eye. The rich must simply repent and make up for lost time and failed opportunities for generosity in the past: "If then they repent and do some good, they will live to God." The radical nature of the demand in the earlier tradition has now been modified and mollified. The rich are not excluded, but a serious demand is placed upon them to share the wealth.

CONCLUSION

What is evident from tracing these lines of change in the early Christian attitude toward wealth and possessions is what we might expect when the outlook of the group shifted from its initial confidence that the present age would end within a generation and that accordingly the major task of Christians was to proclaim the good news about Jesus as widely and quickly as possible. All other values had to be made subordinate to this charge by Jesus. Accordingly, it was initially highly unlikely that any members of the tiny elite of the rich and powerful would renounce their wealth in order to participate in this work which God had launched through Jesus. As decades passed, and the first generation of followers of Jesus began to disappear, the need for some sort of financial support for the leadership and for the ongoing life of the community became more urgent. One attempt to meet these needs seems to have been the pooling of funds depicted in Acts. Other Christian groups were content to insist that the more affluent members of a movement that by the end of the first century had penetrated all layers of society should be generous in sharing their goods with the poor. The radical demands of the older tradition were accordingly toned down. Blessedness was no longer seen as the unique privilege of the financially impoverished but was available to those of modest values and expectations who might be described as "poor in spirit." It is not surprising that a document which shows this kind of adaptation of the radical teaching about wealth and possessions—the Gospel of Matthew—should have found its place at the head of the Christian canon of scripture.

Once those radical demands regarding wealth and possessions had been eased, the way was open to invite and to accommodate within the community people of wealth and power. By the early second century the path was set for the development of the church's relation to economic and political resources. But even so, who would have predicted that by the early fourth century the wealth and power of the emperor would be supporting the church? There is a completely understandable silence in the Christian documents of Constantine's era about the comparison between the rich entering the kingdom and a camel crawling through a needle's eye. Clearly the wealthy are now welcome.

CHAPTER 3

THE HOLY AND THE POOR: MODELS FROM EARLY SYRIAC CHRISTIANITY

SUSAN ASHBROOK HARVEY

To Jesus, radical discipleship—dispossessing oneself for the sake of the poor—took various forms in early Christianity. In early Syriac Christianity there were paradigmatic expressions of this asceticism in the ecclesiastical hierarchy, the solitary ascetic, and the "holy fool." These expressions of personal efforts to imitate Christ are remarkable for their social effectiveness in stimulating care for the poor. Rabbula, bishop of Edessa, and Simeon the Stylite are paradigms of action whose highly visible withdrawals from the world paradoxically stimulated others to develop institutions and activities to benefit the vulnerable of their day. The anonymous "holy fool" or "man of God" was a paradigm whose extreme asceticism identified him not only with Christ but with the homeless, faceless, nameless poor. The bishop and Simeon imitated the ministry of Christ in feeding, clothing, healing, and caring for the destitute; the "holy fool" reminded others that Christ abased himself to dwell in the midst of the anonymous poor.

Recent scholarship has shown great interest in the problem of poverty for the Christian world of Late Antiquity, both in terms of what poverty meant and in terms of how Christianity responded to it.[1] The period is one marked by important social shifts with regard to the meaning of poverty and wealth in this culture. The reduction of the Roman Empire's social structure into two basic classes, the *honestiores* and the *humiliores* —the elite and the humble—solidified a distinction not only of economics but also of legal identity and rights; these distinctions lent a starkness to the

---

[1]By far the most important study is the seminal work of Evelyne Patlagean, *Pauvreté économique et pauvreté sociale à Byzance 4e–7e siècle* (Paris: Mouton, 1977). See also Demetrios J. Constantelos, *Byzantine Philanthropy and Social Welfare* (New Brunswick: Rutgers University Press, 1968); Dimitris Kyrtatas, *The Social Structure of the Early Christian Communities* (London: Verso, 1987), and L. William Countryman, *The Rich Christian in the Church of the Early Empire: Contradictions and Accommodations* (New York: Mellen, 1980). Other material for important classic Christian views and background will be found in the Bibliography of this volume.

gap between rich and poor, and a deceptive air of simplicity to the problem.[2]

From a societal perspective, the meaning of charity itself changed. For the classical world charity had been a way of being rich—of exercising the privilege of one's status and wealth—and a way of carrying out the responsibilities of social relationships, granting beneficence to friends, relations, and fellow citizens.[3] For Christian society, it was a way of being Christian, without giving primary regard to a pre-existing relationship.[4] Charity was no longer the prerogative of a certain social rank: anyone could give alms, and the poor as well as the rich gave to others.[5] Moreover, charity was no longer tied to civic structure. In classical tradition it had served as an action by which one adorned one's city to its greater glory, just as one adorned it with a new building or an exhibition of games.[6] But charity for Christian society was defined by the concrete needs of individuals: food, clothing, shelter, and care for the sick. The city was not the organizing principle of this work; the needy themselves were. Such needs could also cut across the traditional structures of social class to present new social configurations.[7]

This study will take the case of Rabbula, bishop of Edessa from 411/2 to 435/6 and known especially for his work on behalf of the poor, as an entry into the problems of poverty for the late antique world.[8] Although exemplary as models, neither the work of Rabbula nor the city of Edessa were unique in the Christian Roman Empire of the time. But considering their case will allow the delineation of two paradigmatic responses to poverty for Late Antiquity—that of the ecclesiastical hierarchy and that of the ascetic operating outside it (though often in tandem). Further, this consid-

---

[2]See Patlagean, *Pauvreté,* 9–35; Peter Garnsey and Richard Saller, *The Roman Empire: Economy, Society, and Culture* (Berkeley: University of California Press, 1987), 107–25.

[3]Garnsey and Saller, *Roman Empire,* 148–59; Countryman, *Rich Christian,* 105–7; A. R. Hands, *Charity and Social Aid in Greece and Rome* (Ithaca: Cornell University Press, 1968); Peter Garnsey, *Social Status and Legal Privilege in the Roman Empire* (Oxford: Clarendon, 1970).

[4]Patlagean, *Pauvreté,* 9–35, 181–96; Constantelos, *Byzantine Philanthropy,* 3–41.

[5]The model was the gospel story of the widow's mite, Luke 21:1–4. There is a common hagiographical motif of saints who live as beggars, and give from the alms they receive to other beggars. See below for the example of the Man of God in Edessa.

[6]Robin Lane Fox, *Pagans and Christians* (San Francisco: Harper & Row, 1986), 46–63.

[7]Patlagean, *Pauvreté,* 181–96. The distress that the Christian attitude toward charity caused the Emperor Julian is well known: see esp. *The Letters of the Emperor Julian the Apostate,* ed. and tr. W. C. Wright, Loeb Classical Library (New York: Macmillan, 1913), 2:337–39 (Letter 22 [49], To a Priest), and 3:127–29 (Letter 40 [43], To Hecebolius).

[8]The definitive study is Georg G. Blum, *Rabbula von Edessa: Der Christ, der Bischof, der Theologe,* Corpus Scriptorum Christianorum Orientalium 300/ Subsidia 34 (Louvain, 1969). For the city itself, J. B. Segal, *Edessa: The Blessed City* (Oxford: Clarendon, 1970) remains the best overview.

eration will suggest a context for the Syrian understanding of the holy fool, a form of asceticism that emerged in the eastern Roman cities at this time and would come to affect the larger history of Christianity East and West. The connection is not accidental: the response to poverty and the meaning of that response were vividly revealed in the person of the holy fool.

PARADIGMS OF ACTION

For the Christian world east of Antioch during the period of Late Antiquity, the city of Edessa held pride of place. Edessa was called "the Blessed City" because of its legendary ties with the ministry of Jesus and with the missionary activities of the apostle Thomas; and was famous for its martyrs and saints, its great theological school, and the extraordinary richness of its literary heritage. Edessa's glory was at its height in the early fifth century.[9] The tempestuous career of the bishop Rabbula marks that moment of glory like no other for Syrian Christian tradition, and to him many of the great events of the late fourth and fifth centuries have been attributed as if in testimony to the force of his career. Various sources on Rabbula survive to our day. Most important are a long, elegant Syriac hagiography about him, written soon after his death probably by a member of the Edessan clergy;[10] various canons[11] and liturgical texts[12] ascribed to him (some are probably authentic, and the rest are indicative of his spirit at least), though most of his writings are lost;[13] and references to him from other ecclesiastical texts. For most of this study, I will focus on

[9]Segal, *Edessa*.

[10]*Life of Rabbula* was edited by J. J. Overbeck, *S. Ephraemi Syri, Rabulae Episcopi Edesseni, Balaei Aliorumque Opera Selecta* (Oxford: Clarendon, 1865), 159–209, and re-edited by P. Bedjan, *Acta Martyrum et Sanctorum*, vol. 4 (Paris: Harrassowitz, 1894; repr. Hildesheim: Olms, 1968), 396–450. There is a German translation of Overbeck's edition in G. Bickell, "Sämmtliche Prosa-Schriften des Bischofs Rabul von Edessa," in idem, *Ausgewählte Schriften der syrischen Kirchenväter Aphraates, Rabulas und Isaak v. Ninive, Bibliothek der Kirchenväter*, nos. 102–4, 204–5 (Kempten, 1874–76). I have followed Bedjan's edition.

[11]Edited in Overbeck, *Opera Selecta*, 210–21; and in part in Bedjan, *Acta* 4:450–9; Overbeck's edition is translated by R. H. Connolly in "Some Early Rules for Syrian Monks," *Downside Review* 25 (1907): 152–62, 300–6. I have followed the more recent edition and translation of Arthur Vööbus, *Syriac and Arabic Documents Regarding Legislation Relative to Syrian Asceticism*, Papers of the Estonian Theological Society in Exile, Vol. 11 (Stockholm: Etse, 1960), 24–50, 78–86.

[12]Edited in Overbeck, *Opera Selecta*, 245–50, 362–78; and in part in Bedjan, *Acta* 4:469–70; Overbeck's edition is translated by R. H. Connolly, "Some Early Syriac Hymns," *Downside Review* 35 (1916): 146–49.

[13]There are several letters to and from Rabbula, and the sermon he is said to have preached in Constantinople. These are edited in Overbeck, *Opera Selecta*, 222–44; the letters between Cyril and Rabbula, and the sermon, are in Bedjan, *Acta* 4:459–69.

the hagiographical remembrance of this saint, especially as we see it in the *Life of Rabbula*.

The *Life of Rabbula* is a text written with full consciousness of its hagiographical task; but if one reads it with a view to the literary constraints of its genre, it provides a portrait of the bishop that reveals as much about his time through its imagery as it does through the historical information it contains.[14] In the present study I am less concerned with the historicity of actual details than with the picture drawn: how is this saint remembered? What is seen to be significant and why? What did his actions mean to the society that witnessed them?

The *Life* reports that Rabbula was born to a wealthy family in the city of Qenneshrin near Aleppo, son of a pagan father and a Christian mother. Married at his mother's behest to a Christian woman, he was set on the road to a profitable career as a leading nobleman of the region. His conversion to Christianity began when he witnessed a healing miracle performed by a hermit living on one of the family estates; fervent debate with two local bishops provided the necessary intellectual conviction to complete Rabbula's change of heart. He traveled to the Holy Land on pilgrimage to be baptized in the Jordan, and crosses of blood miraculously appeared on his baptismal garments, marking the promise of greatness to come. Then he returned to settle his business affairs: he sold the family lands, distributed the wealth to the poor, freed his slaves, and placed his widowed mother, his wife, and his children in monasteries. Finally, freed of the cares of this world, Rabbula himself entered a monastery and took up an ascetic practice of uncommon severity and fervor.[15]

Such a man would not lead a peaceful life. Soon Rabbula's passion drove him to seek martyrdom by leading a raid of monks to demolish a pagan temple; the pious pagan worshippers, outraged at the desecration, beat him and left him for dead. But the Lord preserved Rabbula for a greater task. When the see of Edessa fell vacant, the bishops sensed that the Holy Spirit was upon this monk. Never a humble man, Rabbula made

---

[14]The *Life* received brutal analysis in terms of its historicity in P. Peeters, "La Vie de Rabbula, Évêque d'Édesse (†7 août 436)," *Recherches de science religieuse*, 18 (1928):170–204. A more sympathetic reading, granting full weight to the issue of literary genre and to the criticisms of Peeters, was given by F. Nau, "Les 'belles actions' de Mar Rabbula, évêque d'Edesse de 412 au 7 août 435 (ou 436)," *Revue de l'histoire des religions* 103 (1931): 97–135. Nau's reading was affirmed by M. Lagrange, "Bulletin: Nouveau Testament," *Revue Biblique* 40 (1931): 121–29, and provided the groundwork for Blum, *Rabbula*, 5–14.

[15]Bedjan, *Acta* 4:397–405. For the problems identifying the key figures with historical persons of the same names, see Peeters, "Vie de Rabbula," 172–76. There is a second account of Rabbula's conversion preserved in the Greek *Life of Alexander Akoimetos;* see *Vie d'Alexandre l'Acémète*, ed. and tr. E. de Stoop, *Patrologia Orientalis*, ed. R. Graffin and F. Nau, Vol. 6 (Paris: Firmin-Didot, 1911), 645–704, at 663–74.

no pretense of protesting his unworthiness for the honor. Instead, as the *Life* tells it, he strode into battle.[16]

Rabbula is credited, and fairly so, with consolidating the Christian church of Edessa. During his episcopacy, Nicene orthodoxy came into control, heresies were suppressed, and paganism was sent spinning into serious decline. To him is attributed the replacement of the "heretical" *Diatessaron* of Tatian by the separated canonical gospels; and the sponsorship of the Peshitta, the authorized Syriac version of the Bible, though it now seems that at best he was responsible only for a revision of part of the Syriac New Testament.[17] Fittingly, the *Life* compares him to the great military kings of ancient Israel, Joshua bar Nun, Josiah, and David, as well as to Moses: the zeal of battle no less than of governing well, characterized Rabbula's term of office.[18]

"Fired by the love of God in his heart,"[19] Rabbula legislated his church into order, writing strict canons for clergy of all levels; and he legislated in similar fashion for monks and nuns, providing some of the earliest institutionalized controls on the flourishing but unregulated Syrian ascetic movement.[20] He took a prominent role in the Christological debates of the time, first supporting the dyophysites and then siding decisively with Cyril of Alexandria.[21] He translated a work by Cyril from Greek into Syriac at that patriarch's own request, and translated other texts, notably hymns and liturgical pieces. He traveled to Constantinople, preached against Nestorius, and brought home generous imperial largesse for his territories. Throughout all of his work, Rabbula was known for his violence as much as for his love towards his people; called "the tyrant of Edessa" by his enemies, he seems to have ruled by fear as much as by efficiency and winning loyalty. Yet love did shine through the vio-

---

[16]Bedjan, *Acta* 4:407-9.

[17]See esp. T. J. Baarda, "The Gospel Text in the Biography of Rabbula," *Vigiliae Christianae* 14 (1960), 102–27; Arthur Vööbus, *Studies in the History of the Gospel Text in Syriac*, Corpus Scriptorum Christianorum Orientalium 128/ Subsidia 3 (Louvain 1951), 1–71; Blum, *Rabbula*, 106–10. The *Diatessaron* was often the only Gospel version used in the Syrian Orient until well into the fifth century. Rabbula's contribution to the Syriac Gospel version seems to have been a revision of the translation of the Gospel of John, no doubt because of its importance for the Christological debates of the time.

[18]Bedjan, *Acta* 4:397, 408, 431.

[19]A constant motif in the *Life*. E.g. Bedjan, *Acta* 4:398, 401, 407, 442.

[20]For the texts, see above n. 10. For the context see, e.g., Sebastian P. Brock, "Early Syrian Asceticism," *Numen* 20 (1973):1–19; =idem, *Syriac Perspectives on Late Antiquity* (London: Variorum, 1984), chap. 1; J. Gribomont, "Le monachisme au sein de l'église en Syrie et en Cappadoce," *Studia Monastica* 7 (1965):7–24; Arthur Vööbus, *History of Asceticism in the Syrian Orient*, Vol. 1, Corpus Scriptorum Christianorum Orientalium 184/ Subsidia 14 and Vol. 2, CSCO 197/ Subsidia 17 (Louvain, 1958).

[21]E.g., Blum, *Rabbula*, 152–208.

lence: the entire city—pagan, Jew, and Christian—was said to have mourned at his death; and some fifteen years later, when the Christological controversy brought riots upon the city, it was to Rabbula that the crowds prayed for intercession.[22]

Despite this array of accomplishments, Rabbula was best known for his work with the poor. If his episcopacy was characterized by a rigorous hand, in charity his extraordinary compassion was displayed. He established a thorough and generous system of care for the needy that extended throughout the territories dependent on Edessa, and possibly even into Palestine. Furthermore, his system was directed both to the laity and to ascetics, those who lived in voluntary poverty. It was this work, tied intimately to his administration of his duties, that led his hagiographer to compare Rabbula to the apostle Paul in Paul's collections for the church in Jerusalem and to the other apostles in their care for the needy. [23]

It is important to understand the comprehensiveness of Rabbula's reforms regarding the practice of charity. Unlike the bishops of Edessa that preceded and followed him, he did not build church buildings, whether cathedrals or monasteries (he may have imposed a ban on such activity) but was content to repair those that were already in place.[24] His successor Ibas, by contrast (and perhaps in direct reaction against the austerities of Rabbula's term), upon taking office undertook a massive building program, opulently adorning the city's churches and constructing an extravagant new cathedral. Ibas, in fact, was to face serious charges of embezzlement and other financial misdoings during his stormy career.[25] Instead of adorning his city with monuments as custom would have it, Rabbula used his office and its considerable resources to adorn the city with good works.

---

[22]Bedjan, *Acta* 4: 421–22 ('and so he was feared while being loved,' p. 422); *Acta* 4:447–48. Rabbula's violent nature is remembered in Michael the Syrian, *Chronicle* XI.9, ed. and tr. J.–B. Chabot, *Chronique de Michel le Syrien* (Paris, 1901; repr. Brussels: Culture et Civilisation, 1963), 2:436; and in *Barhadbsabba ʿArbaya. évêque de Halwan (VIe siècle). Cause de la fondation des écoles*, ed. and tr. A. Scher, *Patrologia Orientalis* 4 (Paris 1907): at 380–1.The report of Count Chareas regarding the riots is given among the Acts of the Second Council of Ephesus in 449, ed. and tr. J. Flemming, "Akten der ephesinischen Synode vom 449 Syrisch," *Abhandlungen der Königlichen Gesellschaft der Wissenschaften zu Göttingen*. Philologisch-Historische Klasse, n.f. 15 (Berlin: Weidmannsche, 1917), esp. 14–26.

[23]See Blum, *Rabbula*, 71–81; Bedjan, *Acta* 4:441, 446.

[24]Bedjan, *Acta* 4:429. The *Chronicle of Edessa* records that he turned a synagogue into a church: *Chron. Ed.*, LI, ed. and tr. I. Guidi in *Chronica Minora*, Corpus Scriptorum Christianorum Orientalium 1/1, pp. 1–13, and 2/2, pp. 1–11 (Paris 1903).

[25]*Chronicle of Edessa* LIX records the building of the church; for Ibas' conduct in office, his building program, and his demise, see Segal, *Edessa*, 93–95, 130–33. For the charges against Ibas, see Flemming, "Akten," 15–55.

Rabbula made no change in his ascetic practice when he entered the episcopacy. He was particularly noted for his habit of fasting regularly, and for rigidly maintaining retreat time for solitary prayer in a hut in Edessa; each year, moreover, he withdrew periodically to his former monastery near Qenneshrin for a total of forty days of solitude. His table laid with earthenware dishes and wooden cutlery as well as his threadbare robes were appropriate to a monastic setting rather than a bishop's palace. Rabbula "diligently enfolded the harsh labors of his monastic life into his episcopacy," and his legislation forced the same austerity on his clergy, whatever their rank. These were strictly forbidden to make any profits from their work, for example by charging for their services, or requiring interest on church loans. He directed his clerical staff to live as he did, so that unlike clergy who enjoyed the lavish grandeur of other cosmopolitan churches, Rabbula's men could be recognized by their haggard appearance, their faces "anointed with pallor." Because of his personal poverty, Rabbula evoked an increase in voluntary gifts to the church of Edessa, acquiring bounty through his own self-denial. He distributed the gifts people brought him to the sick and afflicted in the city hospice (the *xeno-docheion*), and to the needy who dwelt as hermits or in monasteries.[26]

The *Life* reports that each year Rabbula distributed 7,000 darics to the poor, apart from that which he supplied to those who worked in his service (clerics and domestics of the Edessan church) and those registered for welfare.[27] "From the love of the poor which he possessed in his soul," he renovated a hospital that had barely functioned before, granting it the annual revenues of certain church properties which amounted to 1,000 denarii per year. Under his direction, the hospital became notable for its cleanliness, pleasant beds, and clean garments for the patients, and for the attentiveness shown to the sick by the deacons assigned to work there. He founded a hospital for women run by deaconesses and the Daughters of the Covenant, built with stones from four "violently ruined" pagan temples.[28] Further, Rabbula took over supervision of the leper colony that had grown up outside the city. He placed it under the care of "honest deacons," and himself came often, "in word and in deed giving rest to their souls," exhorting, comforting, and kissing their "decaying bodies." Not least in his work was the granting of dignity to those denied it by society. He attended to widows and orphans, and seems to have lent money to

---

[26]Bedjan, *Acta* 4:420–25; "Rules for the Clergy," 5, 6, 9, in Vööbus, *Documents*, 37–38.

[27]I take this as the meaning of "those inscribed in the city": Bedjan, *Acta* 4:429.

[28]Ibid., 443–44. A Syrian tradition, the Sons and Daughters of the Covenant (Bnay and Bnat Qyomo) were consecrated laity under vows of celibacy and poverty in the service of the church. See esp. G. Nedungatt, "The Covenanters of the Early Syriac-speaking Church," *Orientalia Christiana Periodica* 39 (1973): 191–215, 419–44.

floundering businesses, specifically to the goldsmiths. For the poor outside the city, he established a special category of deacon whose job it was to oversee the distribution of aid in towns and villages (in each place staying "with honest people"). These deacons operated throughout the districts under Edessa's jurisdiction, and sometimes beyond. [29]

How did Rabbula pay for this? At one point he declared, "Whatever the church possesses, she inherits for the sustenance of orphans, widows, and the needy."[30] Edessa was a wealthy city; its church had considerable assets both in treasure (gold, silver, jewels, and other precious goods) and in revenues from landholdings, and the austerities of Rabbula's ecclesiastical administration must certainly have freed additional income.[31] But Rabbula's operations seem to have exceeded the limits of his coffers, and he supplemented the church's income in three primary ways. First he sold off church treasure, replacing gold and silver sacred vessels with pottery ones as he declared, "Lovely sacred vessels of silver and gold are in no way useful for the glory of God, but the Spirit is pleased with pure hearts."[32] The radical nature of this action may be sensed from the shocked response that greeted the bishop Acacios of Amida ten years later, when he sold church treasure to ransom seven thousand captives of war who were dying of starvation.[33] Second, Rabbula took the inheritance of the clergy, who were required by canon law to bequeath their wealth to the church upon their deaths; and third, he obtained largesse from the imperial court and (apparently) from the coffers of other great nobles and perhaps even other churches of the eastern empire.[34]

When his final illness struck and he perceived his end, Rabbula commanded one last spree of almsgiving. Although it was July, he ordered that the bounty he distributed every January should be given out at once. He sent alms to the monasteries throughout all his territories and into Pal-

[29]Bedjan, *Acta* 4:444-46.

[30]Ibid., 429.

[31]On the wealth of Edessa's church, see Segal, *Edessa*, 132–33.

[32]Bedjan, *Acta* 4:410-1.

[33]Socrates, *Ecclesiastical History*, VII.21; ed. J. Bidez and G. C. Hanson, *Die griechischen christlichen Schriftsteller der ersten drei Jahrhunderte* 50 (Berlin, 1960). This event took place in 421/2. Acacios justified his action by saying, "Our God, my brethren, needs neither dishes nor cups; for he neither eats, nor drinks, nor is in want of anything. Since, then, by the liberality of its faithful members the church possesses many vessels both of gold and silver, it behooves us to sell them, that by the money thus raised we may be able to redeem the prisoners, and also supply them with food." Trans. A. C. Zenos, *Select Library of Nicene and Post-Nicene Fathers* 2d Series, Vol. 2 (New York: 1890; repr. Grand Rapids: Eerdmans, 1979), 164.

[34]"Rules for the Clergy," canon 40, in Vööbus, *Documents*, 46; Bedjan, Acta 4:438–40. See the discussion in Nau, "Belles Actions," 122–26, where he suggests a connection with Alexandria in this regard.

estine; to all the clergy and Sons and Daughters of the Covenant under his jurisdiction; to the poor, widows, and lepers in all his villages and in Edessa; and he remitted all his loans. After his death the relic of his body became a source of almsgiving when, at his funeral, the sick were healed, the healthy were helped, demons were expelled, the distressed were comforted, the poor were provided for, and the rich were enriched. His mourners named him "Father of Orphans" and "Brother of the Poor."[35] It is noteworthy that when the people of Edessa rioted in 449 against the bishop Ibas, their charges were partly over his Christological stance and partly over what they saw as the abuse of church funds. The people accused him not merely of plundering the church, but of taking "what belongs to the poor."[36]

Rabbula's work has been justly compared to that of Basil of Caesarea in Cappadocia, with his extensive hospital/hospice/monastery complex; to John Chrysostom and his vigorous championing of the poor in Antioch and in Constantinople; and to the later work of John the Almsgiver in Alexandria, whose massive works of charity at the turn of the seventh century may well have been unparalleled in the late antique period.[37] All these bishops had as their primary agenda the use of their considerable financial and political authority to address the problems of the poor. Rabbula's work is distinct from that of these others, however, by its extension into a further realm, for he explicitly included among its recipients the ascetics and monastics of his jurisdiction.

---

[35]Bedjan, *Acta* 4:446-49.

[36]In the report of Count Chaereas given at the second Council of Ephesus; Flemming, "Akten," 180-26, esp. 18.

[37]The work of these bishops is discussed at length in Constantelos, *Byzantine Philanthropy*; see e.g. Gregory of Nazianzus, *Oration 43* ("On St. Basil the Great"), secs. 34–36, 61–63, ed. J. P. Migne, *Patrologiae cursus completus... Series Graeca* (hereafter *Patrologia Graeca*) Vol. 36 (Paris: Garnier and Migne, 1865), tr. L. P. McCauley, in *St. Gregory Nazianzen and St. Ambrose: Funeral Orations*, Fathers of the Church 22 (New York: Fathers of the Church, Inc., 1953), 27–99; Basil, *Long Rules*, Questions 3, 7, 9, 38–40, ed. Migne, *Patrologia Graeca* Vol. 31, cols. 889–1052, trans. M. M. Wagner, *Saint Basil, Ascetical Works*, Fathers of the Church 9 (New York, 1950); John Chrysostom, *Homily 12 On First Timothy*, ed. Migne, *Patrologia Graeca* Vol. 62, cols. 501–662, tr. Philip Schaff, *Select Library of Nicene and Post-Nicene Fathers*, 1st Series (New York: Christian Literature Co., 1889; repr. Grand Rapids: Eerdmans, 1979) 13: 444–48, and *Homilies on Lazarus*, ed. Migne, *Patrologia Graeca*, Vol. 48, cols. 963–1054, trans. Catherine P. Roth, *St. John Chrysostom: On Wealth and Poverty* (Crestwood: St. Vladimir's Seminary Press, 1984); *Life of St. John the Almsgiver*, ed. Heinrich Gelzer, *Leontios' von Neapolis Leben des Heiligen Johannes des Barmherzigen Erzbishofs von Alexandrien*, Sammlung ausgewählter kirchen- und dogmengeschichtlicher Quellenschriften, Heft 5 (Leipzig, 1893), trans. Elizabeth Dawes and Norman Baynes, *Three Byzantine Saints* (London: Mowbrays, 1977), 195–270.

Rabbula's canons are notable for the severe controls they place on the economic activities of monasteries.[38] The fifth century was a boom-time for monasticism across the empire. Already in the later fourth century, monasteries had been able to amass great wealth of their own, apart from the churches to which they were beholden. Some of this derived from gifts and bequests, but it is clear that by the late fourth century monasteries in Egypt and Cappadocia were also running sophisticated business enterprises as well—a situation that had its roots in the value placed on self-sufficiency and on work as part of the ascetic vocation.[39] The Syrian Orient shows evidence of the same trends during the fifth century, though there this evidence is most often associated with those great monasteries that were centers of pilgrimage.[40] Some fifth-century Syriac ascetic writers lament the prosperity of the monasteries, and see this as a danger to the principles of the ascetic life, despite the fact that Syrian monasteries, like those of Cappadocia, played important roles in food distribution and care of the sick.[41]

Rabbula's legislation strictly curtailed any possibility of economic growth for monastic communities and severely limited their standard of living, a move that would seem to indicate concern about monastic wealth. This legislation also created a situation wherein the distribution of wealth as a responsibility of the Edessan church was centralized back into the hands of the bishop; that is, monasteries themselves could not claim the authority to acquire and give out money or goods. The change enhanced Rabbula's own power, and we cannot discount this as a motive for such an autocratic leader.[42] But our sources may also indicate the reverse situation. The *Life of Rabbula*'s constant emphasis on Rabbula's

[38]"The Rules of Rabbula for the Monks," ed. and tr. in Vööbus, *Documents*, 24–33; these seem to incorporate some earlier material. The "Rules Attributed to Rabbula," in Vööbus, *Documents*, 78-86 are probably later.

[39]E.g., Hans Lietzmann, *A History of the Early Church*, Vol. IV, *The Era of the Church Fathers*, trans. Bertram L. Woolf (London: Lutterworth, 1961); Derwas J. Chitty, *The Desert a City* (London: Mowbrays, 1966; repr. 1977); James E. Goehring, "The World Engaged: The Social and Economic World of Early Egyptian Monasticism," in *Studies in Antiquity and Christianity: Essays in Honor of James M. Robinson*, ed. J. E. Goehring, J. Sanders, and C. Hedrick (Sonoma, Calif.: Polebridge, 1990), Vol. 2.

[40]The most spectacular case is Qal'at Sim'an, the monastic complex that housed the relic of Simeon the Stylite's pillar. See G. Tchalenko, *Villages Antiques de la Syrie du Nord* (Paris: P. Guethner, 1953), 1:227–76. For the phenomenon on a more local level, see now Andrew Palmer, *Monk and Mason on the Tigris Frontier: The Early History of Tur ᶜAbdin*, University of Cambridge Oriental Publications 39 (Cambridge: Cambridge University Press, 1990).

[41]Vööbus, *History of Asceticism*, Vol. 2, CSCO 197/ Sub. 17, 140–58.

[42]On the powers of the Edessan bishops see Segal, *Edessa*, 127–36; Rabbula was among the most autocratic. In this he followed an older tradition, more common in the early church, in which the bishop had sole authority for the distribution of funds in his jurisdiction; see Countryman, *Rich Christian*, 160–62, for the example of Cyprian of Carthage. What is striking about Rabbula's control of monastic finances is that generally monasteries took care of their own situation.

gifts to monastics and "unattached" ascetics as part of his program of almsgiving, and his repeated canons requiring financial ministry to these people as well as to the lay poor may testify that in his time a substantial number of Syrian ascetics continued the ancient Syrian tradition of living in absolute poverty, to the point of requiring care by others in order to survive.[43] Certainly, the *Life of Rabbula* attributes his concern to his "exalted love for the holy poor"[44]—seeing it as a response to genuine need and not an effort to reestablish the integrity of holy poverty.

The extant canons of Rabbula indicate how these programs operated at the village level as well as in the city, and the integration of clergy, monastics, and laity that Rabbula effected for these efforts.[45] The clergy were required to fast, pray, "take care of the poor and demand justice for the oppressed" (canon 11); they were required to care for all the poor who came to them, especially the consecrated lay ascetics, the Sons and Daughters of the Covenant (canon 12). If the parish clergy could not afford care for the Sons and Daughters of the Covenant, they were to inform the bishop so that the Edessan church could give aid, "so that because of their need they may not be compelled to do something that is not suitable" (canon 19). Every parish was required to have a house "in which the poor, that come there, shall rest" (canon 16). All parishioners were exhorted to live simply and to distribute goods to the poor (canon 24), but the clergy were also forbidden "to require by force" that people give to the poor (canon 8). Moreover, the social hierarchy was to be respected only as far as was necessary: "Hold all the lords of the villages in the honor that is owed to them, but do not be favorable to them and oppress the poor" (canon 34, slightly altered).

In her work on poverty in Late Antiquity, Evelyne Patlagean has made a distinction between the poor as subjects of the (state) law (persons bound by legal limits in their actions, responsibilities, and rights) and the poor as objects of the (Christian) law (persons dependent on the initiative and compassion of others for their care), leading to the formation of establishments for these services, especially as run by the church. She has further noted that the problem of poverty has two aspects for any society. It is a social problem because of the economic needs of the poor, and it is a political problem because of the arrangements necessary to provide care.[46] The political problem is seen in the economic position of privilege granted to the church by the state in order to provide that care, and the

[43]Chronicled in Vööbus, *History of Asceticism*, Vol. 1.

[44]Bedjan, *Acta* 4:441.

[45]"The Rules of Rabbula for the Clergy and the Qeiama," ed. and tr. in Vööbus, *Documents*, 34–50. Citations by canon number are given in the text.

[46]E. Patlagean, "La Pauvreté à Byzance au Temps de Justinien: Les Origines d'un modèle politique," in idem, *Structure sociale, famille, chrétienté à Byzance, IVe-XIe siècles* (London: Variorum, 1981), chap. 1; and idem, *Pauvreté*, 1–72.

resulting delicate tension in church-state relations. The social problem is apparent, for example, in the charges that the bishop Ibas had stolen from the poor.[47]

The situation we see in Edessa under Rabbula's leadership highlights Professor Patlagean's model first by presenting the poor almost exclusively as objects of the law—persons with nothing to contribute to the society, and no resources or recourse of their own; and second, by highlighting the dependence of the state on the church for the running of programs that adequately addressed the needs of the poor and suffering.[48] The problem in the late antique system, as characterized by the experience of Edessa, is that too much depended on the church leadership at any given moment. Thus Rabbula developed a system that functioned efficiently and with considerable social depth; his successor Ibas had a different mode of operation and a different set of priorities. Though the system functioned with continuity, both by law and by common societal agreement,[49] it was also highly vulnerable to the whims of those in power.

Nonetheless, the work of the church on behalf of the poor had another center of operation. The ascetics, the holy men and women, operating sometimes on their own, sometimes through monastic communities, and sometimes in conjunction with the church hierarchy, had as their particular charge the care of the needy.[50] An ascetic career often began with an act of almsgiving, and often in the very manner of Rabbula's. The scene described in his *Life* is stereotypical in early Christian literature: when saints convert to Christianity in hagiography, the first thing they do is to give their wealth to the poor.[51]

In Syriac the word for alms, *zedqto*, means "alms, as the right or due of God or of our neighbor"; the word is derived from the root *zdq*, "to be

[47]Flemming, "Akten," 18.

[48]The sick and disabled are automatically included in the category of the poor, as persons unable to provide for themselves. Cf. Mollat, *The Poor in the Middle Ages*, 5–6, on the close correspondence between economic and biological aspects of poverty.

[49]See Patlagean, *Pauvreté*, 181-97 for the strength of this tradition and its long-term impact on the Byzantine world.

[50]The seminal work has been Peter Brown, "The Rise and Function of the Holy Man in Late Antiquity," in idem, *Society and the Holy in Late Antiquity* (Berkeley: University of California, 1982), 103–52; and "The Saint as Exemplar in Late Antiquity," *Representations* 1 (1983): 1–25. For the development of Syrian tradition specifically in this regard, see Susan Ashbrook Harvey, *Asceticism and Society in Crisis: John of Ephesus and the "Lives of the Eastern Saints"* (Berkeley: University of California, 1990).

[51]The classic model is St. Antony of Egypt; see *Life of Antony*, secs. 2–3, ed. Migne, *Patrologia Graeca*, Vol. 26, cols. 837–976; trans. Robert C. Gregg, *Athanasius: The Life of Antony and the Letter to Marcellinus* (New York: Paulist Press, 1980).

right; to justify; to judge right[eously]."[52] The term is directly related to the Hebraic concept of righteous action and justice, particularly articulated by the great prophets of ancient Israel.[53] The Greek term for almsgiving, ἐλεημοσύνη, is derived from ἐλεήμον, the concept of pity and mercy.[54] These two traditions stand behind the Christian understanding of charity: almsgiving as a righteous action, and almsgiving as an act of mercy. They are not mutually exclusive concepts, but the nuance in Syriac has bearing on the ascetic imagery of early Syrian spirituality: the same word can mean "righteousness" and "almsgiving," and in the *Life of Rabbula* such word play is frequent.[55]

Rabbula, like many of the great bishops of his time, was first and foremost an ascetic—a holy man. As we have seen, his asceticism defined his episcopacy. The connection was crucial in the eyes of the people: even while alive, they sought pieces of his clothing for relics, and at his burial great care was necessary to prevent the dismemberment of his body for the same purpose.[56] At all times in Christian history ascetics have enacted powerful symbolic imagery that charges their physical discipline with particular meanings.[57] The Syrian ascetic tradition, emerging with the first beginnings of Syrian Christianity, was marked from its inception by commitment to service in the church community, and particularly by care for the poor.[58] In his role as holy man, quite apart from his position as bishop, Rabbula enacted a well-established tradition.

No more famous example existed than Simeon the Stylite, whose career was contemporary with Rabbula's. Simeon passed forty years on a sixty-foot high pillar in the wilderness beyond Antioch. Standing unsheltered midway between heaven and earth, suffering the physical trials of exposure to the elements compounded by fasting, vigils, and a grueling prayer regime, Simeon conducted an extensive welfare program of his own from his pillar. Pilgrims flocked to his site, around which a huge monastic complex developed to tend to the crowds; they came from the

---

[52]Robert Payne Smith, *Thesaurus Syriacus* (Oxford: Clarendon, 1879–1901, *Supplement* by Jessie Payne Smith [Mrs. Margoliouth], 1927; repr. Hildesheim: Olms, 1981), vol. 1, cols. 110–11.

[53]Countryman, *Rich Christian*, 103–5; Richard A. Horsley and John S. Hanson, *Bandits, Prophets, and Messiahs: Popular Movements in the Time of Jesus* (San Francisco: Harper & Row, 1985), 135–89.

[54]G. W. H. Lampe, ed., *A Patristic Greek Lexicon* (Oxford: Clarendon, 1961), 447–48.

[55]E.g., Bedjan, *Acta* 4:403.

[56]Ibid., 425, 449.

[57]For Late Antiquity see, above all, Peter Brown, *The Body and Society: Men, Women, and Sexual Renunciation in Early Christianity* (New York: Columbia University Press, 1988).

[58]Gribomont, "Le monachisme au sein de l'église en Syrie et en Cappadoce"; Vööbus, *History of Asceticism*, 2:360–87.

whole of the Christian world, from every social class and station in life. They brought their sick and suffering, their tax problems, civil disputes, questions of government policy, family problems, legal tangles. Simeon healed, judged, distributed food and water during famine and drought, preached, exhorted, and worked on behalf of the poor, every day. His contributions to society were concretely constructive, and belie the apparent "uselessness" of leading a life of brutal self-mortification. But like Rabbula, although he is a striking case, Simeon was not unique in the work that he did for those in need. He is an example of how the ascetic filled the role of holy man or woman as the one who acted on behalf of the needy.[59]

Simeon's ascetic vocation was understood in various ways by the Christian world of his time. For the fifth-century Syrian community, however, Simeon was above all a prophet in the most traditional sense. He acted out the symbolism of his prophetic message in physically shocking ways, in order to rouse people to their senses, just as the Old Testament prophets had done. And like those prophets, his primary task was to be the champion of the oppressed—the righteous judge, the one who speaks out against injustice. Thus the Syriac Life of Simeon the Stylite, written by his disciples in the 470s, describes how Simeon began his holy vocation on behalf of the poor. No less than the prophet Elijah himself appeared to the young ascetic, and delivered him this charge:

> "Be not afraid and be not affrighted, but be strong and valiant and brave, and of mortal man be not afraid. But rather above everything have care for the poor and the oppressed, and rebuke the oppressors and the rich. For lo, the Lord is thy helper, and there is no one who will harm or hurt thee."... But Simeon, the Blessed One, was greatly astounded at this vision, while he thought and pondered, "Who are those poor about whom the command was given? The cripples who go about begging? The oppressed? Or those who live in monasteries, who for the sake of God left their people and their possessions, and rest upon the hope of our Lord?" And when he had been many days thinking and pondering about this vision, while he stood and prayed there appeared to him St. Elijah a second time in the chariot of fire. And he drew

[59]See Susan Ashbrook Harvey, "The Sense of a Stylite: Perspectives on Simeon the Elder," Vigiliae Christianae 42 (1988): 376–94; H. J. W. Drijvers, "Spätantike Parallelen zur altchristlichen Heiligenverehrung unter besonderer Berüchsichtigung des syrischen Stylitenkultus," Göttingen Orientforschungen 1, Reihe, Syriaca 17 (1978): 77–113; Theodoret of Cyrrhos referred to the crowds as "a human sea": History of the Monks of Syria, 26.11. Théodoret de Cyr. Histoire des Moines de Syrie, ed. and tr. P. Canivet and A. Leroy-Molinghen, Sources Chrétiennes 234 and 257 (Paris: Cerf, 1977–79); also tr. R. M. Price, A History of the Monks of Syria by Theodoret of Cyrrhus (Kalamazoo: Cistercian, 1985); and Brown, "Holy Man."

near and stood before the saint and answered and said to him, "On what account is thy mind disquieted? Concerning that which I commanded about the poor? Thou shalt care equally therefore for all people, for the poor, and the injured and the monks who dwell upon the hope of our Lord. Have a care also for the priests, the churches, and the laws of God which are established, and see that no one treat with contempt or despise the commands of the priest. Deliver the oppressed from their oppressors, rescue the burdened from those who crush them, and uphold the rights of orphans and widows. Be not afraid and do not tremble and do not be terrified, neither before kings or judges. Do not show favoritism to the rich. But openly rebuke them, because they are not able to harm thee."[60]

This passage is perhaps the most important we have about Simeon and the meaning of his vocation, but it could equally well be used to explain the work of Rabbula. Indeed, the *Life of Rabbula* stresses the motif of Rabbula enacting the "justice of God" (*cinuto d'alloho*), and states repeatedly that Rabbula performed God's work "in word and in deed." With these images, he is brought into the focus of the prophetic model that provides a more overt, overarching theme for the Syriac *Life of Simeon*.

Exact contemporaries, Simeon and Rabbula mark the two paradigms of ministry to the poor in the late antique Syrian Orient. Both are ascetics, pursuing severe private practice: they renounced all worldly ties and mortified their flesh of all worldly comforts. Both conducted highly visible public careers, one inside the church structure (literally: inside the city) and one outside it (literally: outside the city). Precisely because of what they had given up, the public believed Rabbula and Simeon capable of genuine giving and provided them the means for that giving. Having given up food (or, the normal food of a normal life), these ascetics could be trusted to give food fairly and justly: to provide for those in need and, even further, to distribute it in times of famine. Having given up their own bodies, they could minister to the bodies of others—to the sick and the disabled: Simeon performed healings, Rabbula built hospitals. Having given up any wealth or livelihood of their own, they could be trusted to provide livelihood to others: to distribute wealth. Having given up secular careers, they could be trusted to judge fairly and with justice, and to represent those who had no voice. Rabbula did these things—performed these righteous acts: gave alms—with the resources placed at his disposal by his

---

[60]Bedjan, *Acta* 4:572–73; here trans. Lent, "Simeon Stylites," 152–53.

ecclesiastical office. Simeon did these things—performed these righteous acts: prophesied—with the resources of others; he spoke, and people did what he told them to do.

Though it is unlikely they ever met, the work of Rabbula and the work of Simeon stood in close correlation.[61] Official ecclesiastical operations (such as Rabbula's) were protected from suffering too greatly at the hands of corrupt bishops by the prophetic presence of the holy man or woman (such as Simeon), the ascetic who performed the work of the church outside the church structure. And so the poor could be served. Bishop and saint provided the two paradigms of ministry to the poor for late antique society.

PARADIGMS OF MEANING

While we can be certain of some of Rabbula's work, the man himself is shrouded in legend. Significantly, much of that legend revolves around Rabbula's work for the poor. If legends fail to give facts as we might like them, they do not fail to give serious statements on the meaning of memories. The particular way in which Rabbula is remembered in relation to the poor has much to tell us about poverty and the response to the poor in early Syrian Christianity.

In the *Life of Rabbula*, almsgiving plays a key role in the story long before Rabbula gains the see at Edessa. Rabbula gave alms at the moment of his conversion from paganism and again while walking to his baptism. Most importantly, when he returned to Qenneshrin and began the dismantling of his estates, "his gold and silver and everything he possessed he distributed to the needy, until his almsgiving was extended even as far as the holy men and poor of Edessa, which he thus prepared prophetically to receive his inheritance ... betrothing [Edessa] to him with the pledge of his alms, because her wedding guests were the poor."[62] An exact parallel is drawn later when Rabbula accepts the office of bishop: his first action after his consecration was the selling of church treasure for alms.[63] Almsgiving defines both turning points in Rabbula's life, and it also defines his career. It is this extension of the almsgiving motif that contrasts with the classic models. Cyprian of Carthage divested himself of some of his

---

[61]The language and imagery used in *Life of Rabbula* to describe his early ascetic suffering and his death are used for the same scenes about Simeon in *Homily on Simeon the Stylite* by the sixth-century Syriac writer Jacob of Serug. Cf. *Life of Rabbula* at Bedjan, *Acta* 4:406 and 447–48, with Jacob's *Homily on Simeon*, ed. Bedjan, *Acta* 4:650–65, esp. 651–53 and 664–65. Jacob's Homily is now translated by Susan Ashbrook Harvey, in Vincent A. Wimbush, ed., *Asceticism in Greco-Roman Antiquity: A Sourcebook* (Philadelphia: Fortress, 1990), 15–28.

[62]Bedjan, *Acta* 4:401–3. The passage deliberately recalls the wedding feast parables, esp. Luke 14:16–24.

[63]Ibid., 4:410–11.

wealth when he converted, but seems to have kept some back for his own security; Antony of Egypt gave his away simply to get rid of it.[64] For Rabbula, the redistribution of wealth is the story of his whole life as a Christian. But the extension runs further. So powerful a model did Rabbula present that even his name evoked the same response in others: "For as soon as his friends heard the sweet name of Rabbula, his love was kindled in their hearts and their love was fervent, and they gave alms. And the recipient rejoiced and the giver was helped and God was glorified, while the labor of our father Rabbula was preserved because of this."[65]

The hagiographer speaks of Rabbula's almsgiving as betrothal to his city. By the late fourth century, the motif of the bishop as the spouse of his church was gaining popularity.[66] But what might it mean to have this standard image confirmed by almsgiving? Rabbula's legend was enhanced by his appearance in another fifth-century Syriac text about Edessa, the story of the anonymous Man of God.

The *Life of the Man of God*[67] is a story about humility. We do not know his name. The unnamed son of an unnamed noble Roman family, as a young boy this "instrument chosen by God" showed no interest in the distinguished affairs of his parents' household, much to their dismay. At his parents' bidding, schoolmates, household slaves, and young serving girls all contrived to initiate the saint "with his humble custom" into the ways of the world, but to no avail. At last his parents arranged a wedding for him. On the first day of the feast, not even having met the bride, the Man of God slipped out, climbed aboard a ship bound for Syria, and made his way to Edessa. There he settled as a beggar.

The Man of God's vocation was this: he lived the life of a street person among the poor in the vicinity of the church, fasting and praying. He accepted money from almsgivers, but most of it he gave to the other poor. And there he stayed, for "he was not separated from the poor in his dwell-

---

[64]See Countryman, *Rich Christian*, 184–88; *Life of Antony*, secs. 2–3.

[65]Bedjan, *Acta* 4:442.

[66]The motif of bishop as spouse of his church was given concrete force when connected with canonical rulings, such as Canon 15 of the council of Nicea, forbidding clergy, especially bishops, from serving more than one city. Ephrem Syrus is the first Syriac writer to explore this image in depth, and it had become increasingly prevalent by the time of Rabbula's vita. See R. Murray, *Symbols of Church and Kingdom: A Study of Early Syriac Tradition* (Cambridge: Cambridge University Press, 1975), 150–54.

[67]Ed. and tr. in Arthur Amiaud, *La Légende Syriaque de Saint Alexis l'homme de Dieu* (Paris, 1889). See H. J. W. Drijvers, "Die Legende des Heiligen Alexius und der Typus des Gottesmannes im syrischen Christentum," in Margot Schmidt and C. F. Geyer, eds., *Typus, Symbol, Allegories bie den östlichen Vätern und ihren Parallelen im Mittelalter* (Regensburg, 1982), 187–217 (=Drijvers, *East of Antioch: Studies in Early Syriac Christianity* [London: Variorum, 1984], chap 5); and the discussion in Harvey, *Asceticism and Society*, 18–21.

ing place. And when night arrived, then all of the poor slept where he was with them, while he stood standing in the form of the cross against a wall or a pillar and praying."[68] He told no one his story. Meantime, his family had undertaken a search for him, in the course of which the servants even made inquiries in Edessa. The saint recognized them as they passed by the church, but they "did not even think of him, not even quickly... for how could they know a man who was clothed in the rags of shame and beggary?"[69] And so they went away.

After a time, the caretaker (*paramonarios*) of the church discovered his nightly practice of cruciform prayer and pressed him, "Who are you, and what is your work?" Gesturing to the poor who lay sleeping around them, the saint answered, "Ask those in front of you, and from them you will learn who I am and whence I am, for I am one of them."[70] Finally, vowed to silence, the caretaker extracted his story. He begged to become his disciple, but the saint held to his singular vocation. Thenceforth, the caretaker watched over him secretly while undertaking a vocation of private, severe askesis, becoming a prayer presence on the model of his chosen master: a disciple unrecognized as such.

When the saint fell ill, the caretaker convinced him with difficulty that he should move to the public hospice (*xenodocheion*), where he tended him himself. One day when the caretaker was delayed in coming, the saint died. The workers took him to the cemetery for poor strangers and buried him, anonymous in death as in life. When the caretaker arrived to find the saint gone, he rushed weeping to the bishop Rabbula, begging that the body be taken back and with proper honor laid "in a known place" to be granted due veneration.[71] But at the burial site no body could be found, only the rags in which the saint had lain.

Awestruck, Bishop Rabbula undertook an oath to serve the poor and destitute in the city, marveling, "For who knows but that there are many like this holy man who seek abasement, and they are great in themselves in God's eyes. And they are not known to the people because of their

---

[68]Ibid., p. [8]. Early Syriac literature frequently refers to cruciform prayer from as early as the second century, but does not describe it as the imitation of the crucifixion much before the seventh century; instead, cruciform prayer seems to be seen as a stance of supplication and of victory over Satan, imaging Christ's ascension from the cross into glory. Compare the *Odes of Solomon*, ed. and tr. James H. Charlesworth, 2d ed. (Chico, Calif.: Scholars Press, 1982), e.g. Odes 21, 37, 42; and the excellent study by Brian McNeil, "The Odes of Solomon and the Suffering of Christ," *Symposium Syriacum 1976, Orientalia Christiana Analecta* 205 (Rome: Pont. Institutum Studiorum Orientalium, 1978), 31–38. The crucifixion is not mentioned in the *Odes*, nor is it mentioned here in the *Life of the Man of God*.

[69]Amiaud, *Légende syriaque* [8], [9].

[70]Ibid., [10].

[71]Ibid., [12].

humiliation."[72] According to this text, it was now that Rabbula's campaigns began, both in Edessa and beyond, "[bringing] to perfection the love of strangers." As for the caretaker, he undertook to tell the saint's story. But so well did he understand his master's work that even this action was done in humility: himself anonymous, he gives us a saint with no teachings, no miracles, no body, no tomb, and no name.[73]

In the story the Man of God manifests a true humility: he denounces no one, not even those sent to tempt him, not even the women. His chosen asceticism is private in its exercise, but he himself remains public. Rather than withdraw from the world he takes up the harsh consequences of its condition, the destitution of a city, "For I am one of them." He lives among men and women, with no preaching against the sins of the flesh or the evils of the world. He shows no disrespect for society, or for those who live in it, whatever their gender or position in life. He performs no works. He is simply there. The story is luminous with the presence of Christ, which the saint evokes in both his way of life and his way of death. Indeed, so transparent is the simplicity of our text that one might read it as allegory: here is the *imitatio Christi*, just so.[74] The only named character is the bishop Rabbula, whose legacy on behalf of the poor is here justified.

But the timing of the story is important. Set in the years of Rabbula's office and written probably between 470 and 475, the time when the disciples of Simeon the Stylite penned his Syriac hagiography, this story seems discordant. It does not fit with the patterns noted above for Rabbula's work in office, or Simeon's outside it.

Rabbula's efforts to create a just society—one in which the poor, voluntary or involuntary, were properly cared for—are inseparable from his efforts to establish an orderly, unified, and orthodox Christian church. To accomplish this goal, Rabbula legislated the proper place and conduct of the different parts of the church (clerical, religious, lay), standardized the church's sacred texts, organized a welfare system that provided services for the needy, and centralized authority into the hands of the bishop. Establishing a just society meant establishing order: putting everyone in the proper place. Thus the Rabbula canons include rules that tightly mon-

---

[72]Ibid., [13].

[73]The story of the Man of God passed into Greek and thereby into Latin, eventually to be found in every Christian language of the medieval world east and west. In its later form the saint is named Alexis the Man of God, and the story acquires numerous extravagant additions. See the discussion in Amiaud, *Légende Syriaque*, xxviii–lxxix; and, e.g., A. G. Elliott, *The Vie de Saint Alexis in the Twelfth and Thirteenth Centuries: An Edition and Commentary*, North Carolina Studies in the Romance Languages and Literatures 221 (Chapel Hill: University of North Carolina Press, 1983).

[74]This is stressed in Drijvers, "Legende des Heiligen Alexius."

itor the clergy, monks, and nuns in their contact with the laity: there should be little if any direct contact between these groups, no contact between the sexes, distinct dress to allow visual discrimination, and careful vigilance on the part of chaperones.[75] The boundaries of religious life in an urban context (city or village) required careful demarcation if they were to be effective.

Simeon, like Rabbula, also represented a vocational life sharply demarcated from the world of the laity. Simeon's physical separation from society—on his pillar, in the wilderness, sixty feet in the air—was an essential ingredient of the work he did on society's behalf. Furthermore, because of the extremity of Simeon's physical location, he required a personal following to put his work into effect as well as to take care of him. Thus his separation was twofold: first by where he actually was, and second by a community of followers that mediated between the saint and the pilgrims seeking his aid.

In both situations the holy element is unambiguously separated from the ordinary; people can see and tangibly know that separation. This is the essential meaning of the word "holy" or "sacred": that which is set apart.[76] The stark radicality of the Man of God's vocation stands out: he does not separate himself physically from the laity nor from women; indeed, in the text this refusal to separate himself is named as the culmination of his ascetic regime.[77] He does not mark himself off by clothing, conduct, or chaperone; he allows no personal following, rejecting the caretaker's request for discipleship, and leaving no body for relics. He is invisible as a holy man.

Even in terms of Syriac ascetic literature, the story of the Man of God is missing some surprising things for a fifth-century text. There are no contrived extremities in this saint's ascetic practice: no pillars, iron chains, or years of confinement in small, narrow boxes. More striking is the absence of the standard Syriac ascetic vocabulary of the time. This emphasized the

[75]"Rules of Rabbula for the Monks," canons 1–3, 7–8; "Rules of Rabbula for the Clergy and Qeiama," canons 2, 4, 10, 15, 18, 22, 37, 38.

[76]The parameters of this discussion for modern theorists of religion were laid by Emile Durkheim, *The Elementary Forms of the Religious Life*, tr. J. W. Swain (1915; repr. New York: The Free Press [Macmillan], 1965), Bk. 1.1 and Bk. 3; Rudolph Otto, *The Idea of the Holy*, tr. J. W. Harvey (Oxford: Oxford University Press, 1923; 2d ed. 1950); and Mircea Eliade, *The Sacred and the Profane: The Nature of Religion*, tr. W. R. Trask (New York: Harcourt Brace Jovanovich, 1959).

[77]Cf. Gregory of Nyssa's *Life of Macrina*, where considerable emphasis is placed on Macrina and her mother, Emmelia, eating at the same table and living in the same quarters with the other nuns, including their servants. *Vita S. Macrinae*, ed. Virginia W. Callahan, in *Gregorii Nysseni Opera*, ed. Werner Jaeger, Vol. 8.1: *Opera Ascetica* (Leiden: Brill, 1952), 347–414; trans. Virginia W. Callahan, *Saint Gregory of Nyssa: Ascetical Works*, Fathers of the Church 58 (Washington: Catholic University of America, 1967), 161–91.

saint as an *ihidoyo*,[78] a "single one," a person single-hearted in devotion to God in a sense that parallels the absolute separation we noted earlier. Rather, the Man of God's ascetic practice required that "he was not separated from the poor."

What, then, is the nature of this saint? The caretaker asks him, "Who are you, and what is your work?" Arthur Amiaud has commented that if not for the miraculous ending to the story—the disappearance of the body—there would be no reason for this story to survive.[79] But the second question of the caretaker is compelling, "What is your work?" What indeed?

Literarily, the Man of God's story is twinned to that of the bishop Rabbula. Historicity is not the point. In the text the work of these two saints is shown to be not merely interwoven, but actually interdependent.[80] The anonymous saint performed the work of God by his presence alone. The caretaker perceived that the holy was there, where the Man of God himself was. For this reason, he wanted the body moved to "a known place." But the Man of God was in no known place, just as he was no known person. He was indistinguishable from those with whom he dwelt. He sanctified the city, the world, from within its very core. The result was that works were performed, but by others—the bishop Rabbula and the caretaker who took up the same role as the Man of God himself. The presence of the anonymous prayer life (the caretaker) continues to sanctify works on behalf of the needy (Rabbula). Herein lay the real work of the saint.[81]

The Man of God was part of an ascetic vocation emerging in the eastern Roman Empire around the time of Rabbula's career.[82] Taking their cue

[78]For the background, see, e.g., Murray, *Symbols of Church and Kingdom*, 12-16.

[79]Amiaud, *Légende Syriaque*, xlvii.

[80]For a similar pattern of twinned stories—of one saint who leads a purely contemplative life and one who leads a life of service, each validating the work of the other—see the accounts by the sixth-century Syriac writer John of Ephesus, of the monks Thomas and Stephen and the sisters Mary and Euphemia: *John of Ephesus, Lives of the Eastern Saints*, ed. and tr. E. W. Brooks, *Patrologia Orientalis* 17–19 (Paris, 1923-25), chaps. 12, 13, at *Patrologia Orientalis* 17:166–213. The pattern is a major theme of John's.

[81]A measure of this work may be seen to this day in the Roman Catholic order of the Alexian Brothers. First a society that emerged during the Black Death in fourteenth-century Europe, these brothers took as their work the care of the sick and the burial of the dead. In 1469, the Holy See raised them to a religious order, and the monks took Alexius the Man of God as their patron saint. Still widespread in Europe, the Alexian Brothers founded the first of their many hospitals in the United States in Chicago, Illinois, in 1866; see *New Catholic Encyclopedia* (1967) 1:306–307.

[82]"Fous pour le Christ," *Dictionnaire de Spiritualité: ascétique et mystique, doctrine et histoire*, ed. E. Mioni, D. Stiernon, et al. (Paris, 1937–), Vol. 5, cols. 752–70 (I. Spidlik and F. Vandenbroucke); John Saward, *Perfect Fools: Folly for Christ's Sake in Catholic and Orthodox Spirituality* (Oxford: Oxford University, 1980).

from 1 Cor. 4:10, these were the ascetics who became "fools for Christ's sake," and by their apparent life of folly acquired great sanctity. Certain features of the Fools are especially noteworthy. They were an urban phenomenon. They emerged at times of complacency and political stability, when the Christian community had come to take its place for granted. Their behavior was profoundly disturbing: they reversed the accepted order of society, whether secular or religious.[83] Their companions were society's outcasts: the homeless, the street people, prostitutes, drunks. Despised by the world as lunatics or debauched bums, they received the scorn and abuse of the world into their bodies: the image of the Suffering Servant of Isaiah 53, or the mocked and tortured Christ of the crucifixion. Eventually they became known for who they were, those who truly bore the crucifixion in their bodies. It was another form of prophetic behavior.

The Man of God represents a moderate version of this phenomenon. His story is early for a Fool's: the vocation came into prominence in the sixth century with the great Syrian saint Simeon Salos of Emesa.[84] The Man of God's story may be its earliest expression in Syrian tradition, and it is no accident that it emerges contemporaneously with the glorious careers of Rabbula, Simeon the Stylite, and the heyday of the Edessan church. The social location of this text is not to be taken lightly. The story holds key images for understanding its origins.

Like all hagiography, the *Life of the Man of God* is framed with scenes reminiscent of gospel episodes: the Garden at Gethsemane, the empty tomb.[85] But the religious understanding behind this text goes deeper than the usual use of gospel parallels. A profound appropriation of early Syriac Christology is present in the story. This text uses two different terms for the poor. For most of the story the term *meskine* is used, meaning the "poor, wretched, needy."[86] But at the story's end, when Rabbula and the

---

[83]See the fine study by A. Y. Syrkin, "On the Behavior of the 'Fool for Christ's Sake,'" *History of Religions* 22 (1982), 150–71.

[84]The first appearance of the motif in Greek literature is in Palladios, *Lausiac History*, ch. 39, the story of a nun pretending madness and abused by the sisters of her convent. *The Lausiac History of Palladius*, ed. and tr. Cuthbert Butler (Cambridge: Cambridge University Press, 1898-1904), 2 vols.; also tr. in *Palladius: The Lausiac History*, tr. Robert T. Meyer, Ancient Christian Writers 34 (New York: Newman, 1964). The report of Simeon Salos is given in Evagrios Scholasticos, *Ecclesiastical History* 4.34, ed. J. Bidez and L. Parmentier, *The Ecclesiastical History of Evagrius with the Scholia* (London: 1898; repr. New York/Amsterdam: A.M. Hakkert, 1979); tr. A.-J. Festubière, "Evagre, *Histoire Ecclésiastique*," *Bizantion* 45 (1975): 187–417.

[85]In general, see Evelyne Patlagean, "À Byzance: ancienne hagiographie et histoire sociale," *Annales: économies, sociétés, et civilisations* 23 (1968), 106–26 [tr. "Ancient Byzantine Hagiography and Social History," in Stephen Wilson, ed., *Saints and their Cults: Studies in Religious Sociology, Folklore, and History* (Cambridge: Cambridge University Press, 1983), 101–21.] For the Man of God, the point is stressed in Drijvers, "Legende des Heiligen Alexius."

[86]Payne Smith, *Thesaurus Syriacus*, vol. 2, col. 285.

caretaker seek the Man of God in vain and finally identify his vocation for what it was, the Man of God is called by another term, *aksnoyo*, literally "a stranger"; and the poor themselves are called *aksnoye*, "strangers."[87] This term is sometimes used to refer to the poor, but it also carries an undertone of ascetic terminology. Living as a stranger—wandering homeless and alone—was one prominent form of Syrian ascetic vocation. The Man of God was indeed a stranger; Rabbula's recognition speech echoes the verse from the prologue of the Gospel of John: "the world knew him not" (John 1:10).

This identification with the model of Christ is enhanced by another line in our text. The Man of God is described as "clothed in the rags of shame and beggary."[88] The term for clothed, *lbish*, is the word used almost exclusively in early Syriac Christology to describe the incarnation. For early Syriac writers, Christ had "put on (*lbesh*) the body" or "was clothed (*lbish*) in flesh."[89] The Man of God "put on" the condition of the poor, even as God himself "put on" the human condition. He literally became what the poor are: homeless, faceless, and nameless. In fact, the terminology that appears most often in this text is that based around the root *mkek*, to humble oneself. The Man of God is repeatedly called *mkiko*, the humble one, and his condition repeatedly referred to as *makikuto*, humility. No other concept is so present in the vocabulary of this story. This is the terminology of the passage in the Christological hymn in Phil. 2:8: "he humbled himself, and was obedient unto death."[90]

The story of the Man of God represents a profound understanding of the imitation of Christ, with a different emphasis than either the bishop Rabbula or the holy man Simeon the Stylite represented. They imitated the ministry of Christ: feeding the hungry, clothing the naked, healing the sick. The Man of God, by contrast, was shown to conform himself to the gospel model in a most intimate sense; he put on himself the human condition at its most helpless and hopeless: "He humbled himself and was obedient unto death." The imitation of Christ for the early church involved devotion to the model Christ had offered—not the imitation of

---

[87]Ibid., vol. 1, col. 188. The term drives from the Greek ξένος.

[88]Amiaud, *Légende Syriaque*, p. [9]. Compare the *Life of Rabbula*, Bedjan, *Acta* 4:445: "[Rabbula] put the commandment of his Lord on himself like a garment."

[89]See Sebastian P. Brock, "Clothing Metaphors as a Means of Theological Expression in Syriac Tradition," in Schmidt, *Typus, Symbol, Allegorie*, 11–38. It is worth nothing that the body Christ "puts on" in Syriac is always generic, never gender-specific.

[90]For the social implications of this passage, see Stanley K. Stowers, "Friends and Enemies in the Politics of Heaven: Reading Theology in Philippians," in Jouette Bassler, ed., *Pauline Theology* (Philadelphia: Fortress Press, 1991), vol. 1.

the Son of God himself (which would be an act of sinful pride), but conformity to the pattern his life and death laid before the believer.[91]That imitation could take various forms. In the Man of God, we are reminded that abasement (humility) is the fundamental life to which Christ called the faithful.

The ascetic Rabbula, soon to be bishop, betrothed himself to Edessa when he gave alms to her poor. In Syriac spirituality, asceticism is often referred to simply as betrothal to Christ: the marriage of one's body and soul to the divine.[92] The Holy Fool as personified by the Man of God represents not only the prophet, but a reminder of the incarnate Lord himself, present in the midst of the anonymous poor. And the act of almsgiving on the part of Rabbula represents more than a righteous act. In the eyes of the society that witnessed his work and wrote these texts, Rabbula's almsgiving was nothing less than the act of marriage to God himself, the God who summoned "the poor and maimed and blind and lame" to be his wedding guests (Luke 14:21).

[91]For an important treatment of this issue, see Robin Darling Young, "Recent Interpretations of Early Christian Asceticism," The Thomist 54 (1990): 123–40. I am grateful to Dana Miller for discussion on this point.

[92]E.g., Murray, Symbols of Church and Kingdom, 131–42.

CHAPTER 4

BYZANTIUM AND SOCIAL WELFARE

ALEXANDER KAZHDAN

The theory and praxis of Byzantine Christian social welfare are explored in this essay on Byzantine philanthropy. That concept was complex and not exactly the same as our own. Roman state generosity was directed not to the poor but to the citizen. In contrast, the institutional and personal philanthropy of the Byzantine church was more oriented to the poor and was motivated by obedience to biblical mandates and by eschatological expectation of reward. Charitable activity both imitated Christ and his saints, and was a form of giving to Christ himself through the poor. This latter spiritual interpretation of almsgiving became a fundamental motivational theme in both Byzantine and medieval Western Christianity. In the words of Chrysostom, almsgiving will "buy paradise for as little as you want."

In his useful monograph devoted to Byzantine social welfare, Professor Demetrios Constantelos draws attention to the Byzantine self-perception as a nation that excelled in philanthropy over all other states. He cited five testimonies supplied by five authors who belonged to different periods (Theophylaktos Simokatta, Photios, Nicholas Mystikos, John Kantakouzenos, and Alexios Makrembolites), all of whom emphasize that the nation of the Rhomaioi, which we call Byzantium, stood above all others in *philanthropia*. As Constantelos put it, the empire was "a state devoted to philanthropy." He claimed, furthermore, that "the Byzantines were much concerned with rather practical virtues: justice, social action, practical philanthropy, and humanitarian works in general."[1] The question arises, however, whether the Greek φιλανθρωπία is truly synonymous with the English "philanthropy," a word that sounds so much like its Greek source and means "efforts to promote human welfare"; in other words, can we interpret the Greek *philanthropia* to mean social welfare?

Much has been written about the term *philanthropia* in classical antiquity, in the Roman empire, and in early Christendom. I do not intend to

---

[1]D. J. Constantelos, *Byzantine Philanthropy and Social Welfare* (New Brunswick, N.J.: Rutgers University Press, 1968), IX-XI, 61.

attack the problem anew or even give a comprehensive bibliography.[2] If we summarize the previous observations—and this was done in part by Constantelos himself—we may conclude that the Greek *philanthropia* (a) was very close to the concepts of clemency and mercy; (b) was considered as the attribute of gods (later God), rulers, and civilized citizens; and (c) denoted general benevolence (including forgiveness) that could imply "practical philanthropy" but by no means coincided with it. This ancient concept of philanthropy survived in Byzantium.[3]

Perceived theologically, *philanthropia* is divine love toward humanity expressed by God in making man in the divine image, in giving his First-Born to death, in admonishing wrongdoers, and even in punishing sinners out of fatherly *philanthropia*. In the sphere of political life, *philanthropia* was primarily "the caesar's clemency," usually juxtaposed with such qualities as *epieikeia* (benevolence) and *praotes* (mildness); in the vocabulary of a fourth-century rhetorician, Themistios, for instance, *philanthropia* is linked with piety, justice, and gentleness, and it makes the ruler "divine."[4] When the Christian concept of *agape* (love) was introduced, it became interchangeable with *philanthropia*.

Following in the same vein, later Byzantine texts use the term *philanthropia* without loading it with a specific sense of practical philanthropy. In an eighth-century legal text, the *Ekloge*, the term emerges only once, in the title, and is void of any welfare connotation: the title (or lemma) proclaims as the legislators' goal the improvement of Justinianian laws in the direction of clemency, gentleness, or kindness (εἰς τὸ φιλανθρωπότερον).[5] Even more evocative is the phrasing of the 111th novel (statute) of Leo VI (886-912) that treated the case of a man married to a mad wife. "No one is so relentless (ἀφιλάνθρωπος) that he would confine a person with a beast even for a short time; how will the *philanthropia* of law allow a person's eternal confinement with a maniac spouse?"[6] And in accordance with this princi-

---

[2]See, e.g., R. le Déaut, "Philanthropia dans la littérature grecque jusqu'au Nouveau Testament, Tite III.4, Mélanges Eu. Tisserant, vol. 1, Studi e testi 231 (Vatican: Biblioteca Apostolica Vaticana, 1964), 255–94; J. de Romilly, *La douceur dans la pensée grecque* (Paris: Belles Lettres, 1979); H. J. Bell, "Philanthropia in the Papyri of the Roman Period," *Hommage à J. Bidez et à F. Cumont* (Brussels: Latomus, 1948), 31–37; G. Downey, "Philanthropis in Religion and Statecraft in the Fourth Century after Christ," *Historia* 4 (1955): 199-208; J. Kabiersch, *Untersuchungen zum Begriff der Philanthropia bei dem Kaiser Julian* (Wiesbaden: Marrassowitz, 1960); H. Hunger, *Prooimion* (Vienna: Böhlau, 1964), 143–53.

[3]H. Hunger, *Philanthropia—Eine griechische Wortprägung auf dem Wege von Aischylos bis Theodoros Metochites* (Graz, Vienna: Österreichische Akademie der Wissenschaften, 1969).

[4]Kabiersch, *Untersuchungen*, 8–12.

[5]*Ecloga. Das Gesetzbuch Leons III. und Konstantinos' V.*, ed. L. Burgmann (Frankfurt a.M.: Löwenklau-gesellschaft, 1983), 160. See T. E. Gregory, "The Ekloga of Leo III and the Concept of Philanthropia," *Byzantina* 7 (1975): 278–87.

[6]P. Noailles and A. Dain, *Les Novelles de Léon VI le Sage* (Paris: les Belles Lettres, 1944),363.

ple of kind and gentle law (that comes within the general concept of Byzantine *oikonomia*), Leo VI permitted divorce from the mad spouse.

It now becomes clear that in the five works cited by Constantelos those authors were writing not about welfare but, in harmony with Byzantine terminology, about the general principle of clemency. Thus Nicholas Mystikos, in letter 102 (not 82 as in Constantelos) praises the race of the Rhomaioi for their *philanthropia* and *epieikeia*, "mercy and benevolence" as it is rendered by editors; and he continues: "How was it reasonable that those whose mercy (*philanthropia*) is commonly attested ... should have acted so mercilessly, (ἐνεργηθῆναι πράξεις ἀφιλανθρώπους)?"[7] Alexios Makrembolites also links *philanthropia* and gentleness (ἡμερότης), and Simokatta contrasts *philanthropia* and wrath.[8] Even more remote from the idea of welfare is the passage in Photios' letter 98 (olim 218) sent from exile to emperor Basil I (867-886). Photios complains about the severe conditions he is enduring, and he asks the emperor to show his benevolence (*epieikeia*) and mercy (*philanthropia*). "We are not demanding," says Photius, "the [patriarchal] throne, glory, well-being, or comfort but only that which is given even the prisoners, which is not refused the captives, which barbarians kindly confer (φιλανθρωπευόνται) upon the fettered." And he concludes, "This I am asking from the emperor, and namely [the emperor] of the most merciful (φιλανθρωπότατος) nation of Rhomaioi."[9]

Finally let us consider the passage from the *History* of John Kantakouzenos.[10] Here *philanthropia* emerges in the context of philanthropic institutions since Kantakouzenos characterizes monasteries and hospices as "a wonderful creation of the Rhomaioi exuding manifold *philanthropia*." Nothing, however, prevents us from interpreting this phrase in a general sense of mercy; monasteries and other institutions performed acts of clemency and gentleness.

The Greek word *philanthropia* was used by Byzantine authors first and foremost in a general ethical sense to mean clemency, mercy, kindness, and so on. For the concept of welfare other terms were employed—*eleemo-*

[7]Nicholas I Patriarch of Constantinople, *Letters*, ed. R. J. H. Jenkins and L. G. Westerink (Washington, D.C.: Dumbarton Oaks Center for Byzantine Studies, 1973), 374.

[8]A. Papadopoulos-Kerameus, *Analekta Hierosolymitikes stachyologias*, vol. 1 (St. Petersburg: B. Kirschbaum, 1891), 146 (In an Italian translation it is rendered: "alla bontà ed alla mitezza dei Romani"; see E. V. Maltese, "Una fonte bizantina per la storia dei rapporti tra Costantinopoli e Genova alla meta del XIV sec.: il 'Logos Historikos' de Alessio Macrembolite," *Sicietà savonese di storia patria. Atti e memorie* 14 (1980): 62); Theophylactus Simocatta. *Historiae*, ed. D. de Boor (Leipzig, 1887), 42.

[9]Photius, *Epistulae et Amphilochia*, vol. 1, ed. B. Laourdas and L. G. Westerink (Leipzig, Teubner, 1983),136.

[10]Joannes Cantacuzenus, *Historiae*, vol. 3, ed. L. Schopen (Bonn, 1832), 227 (not p. 223 as indicated in Constantelos).

syne (alms, charity), *euergesia* (well-doing), and simpler, more specific words: *doreai, diadoseis* (grants).

Byzantium did create various philanthropic institutions, and the description of their structure and administration is the strongest part of Constantelos' book. It is even plausible to surmise, together with him, that the system of philanthropic institutions was more highly developed in Byzantium than in the Western medieval world. Westerners seem to have been interested in the Byzantine organization of welfare. At any rate, several ninth-century glossaries survive which give Greek names of welfare institutions and Latin explanations of them. Six terms form this list: *xenodochium, ptochotrophium, nosochomium, orphanotrophium, gerontochomium, brephotrophium.*[11] All these terms are well known from Greek documents, and Latin explanations of them can be traced back, probably, to Julian Antecessor, a Constantinopolitan jurist of the sixth century. What matters, however, is the interest of Carolingian compilers in the Byzantine philanthropic nomenclature.

Here I am not dealing with the institutions,[12] but will concentrate on three questions about the so-called theory of welfare: Who were the administrators of welfare in Byzantium? Who were the recipients (subjects) of welfare? What was the goal of welfare?

Three categories of administrators or agents of Byzantine philanthropy can be distinguished: the emperor or state; the church, monasteries, and ecclesiastical institutions; and private persons. In the pagan Roman empire, it was the state (personified by the emperor) that exercised the function of supporting the poor (whoever was encompassed by this category). The state tended to restrict private activity in distribution of a dole because it menaced the social order, especially in the provinces.[13] Largess was the duty and right of the state although it could be delegated

[11]B. M. Kaczynski, "Some St. Gall Glosses on Greek Philanthropic Nomenclature," *Speculum* 58 (1983): 1010f.; *Greek in the Carolingian Age. The St. Gall Manuscripts* (Cambridge, Mass.: Medieval Academy of America, 1988), 61.

[12]After Constantelos' book was published, several new works were issued, mainly on Byzantine hospitals, such as T. S. Miller, *The Birth of the Hospital in the Byzantine Empire* (Baltimore: Johns Hopkins University Press, 1985); U. B. Birchler-Argyros, "Byzantinische Spitalgeschichte: Ein Überblick," *Historia hospitalium, Zeitschrift der Deutschen Gesellschaft für Krankenhausgeschichte* 15 (1983–85): 51-80; E. Kislinger, "Der Pantokrator-Xenon, ein trügerisches Ideal?" *JÖB* 37 (1987): 173–79; M. Zivojinović, "Bolnica Kralja Milutinau Carigradu," *ZRVI* 16 (1975): 105–17; C. Cupane and E. Kislinger, "Xenon und Xenodocheion im spätbyzantinischen Roman,"*JÖB* 36 (1986): 201–6; T. S. Miller, "The Sampson Hospital of Constantinople," *Byzantinische Forschungen* 15 (1990): 101–35; A. Moutzale, "Nosokomeia kai koinophele idrymata sto Byzantio," *Byzantinai meletai* 2 (1990): 231–36.

[13]G. Krüger, "Die Fürsorgetätigkeit der vorkonstantinischen Kirchen," *ZSavSt. Kanon, Abt.* 24 (1935): 134f.

to individual representatives of the state bureaucracy. Since the very beginning of its existence, the Christian church defied this principle and entrusted individual communities (local churches) with the obligation to assist the needy. Gradually the role of the church in charitable activity increased. It is well known that Julian (361-363) ascribed the success of Christianity to the extent of ecclesiastical almsgiving and tried to impose a similar duty upon pagan temples. On the other hand, the state largess shrank, at any rate after Justinian I (d. 565). In the seventh century the program of free games was curtailed, provincial hippodromes decreased in number if they did not disappear, and in 618, after the Persian conquest of Egypt, the free distribution of bread was cancelled. Patriarch Nikephorus I (806–815) relates in his *Chronicle* that there was a famine in the earlyyears of the reign of Herakleios (610-641) since Egypt stopped supplying grain.[14] The seventh-century *Paschal Chronicle* is more specific: recipients of "the state bread" (κτήτορες τῶν πολιτικῶν ἄρτων) were required to pay three gold coins for each loaf, and that thereafter, in August of the sixth indiction (i.e. in 618), the distribution of the *artoi politikoi* was completely suspended.[15] The *Basilika*, however, in the late ninth century mentions the state bread as an existing benefit; but this is one of the many cases when this law book preserves rules that were in fact nullified and obsolete.[16]

An episode in the history of ecclesiastical philanthropy that has attracted special attention from scholars is Patriarch Athanasios' establishment of "soup kitchens" to feed the poor of the capital during the famine of 1306–1307.[17] His biographer reports that Athanasios even opened the warehouses of the rich and gave bread to the needy. The

[14]Nicephorus, *Opuscula historica*, ed. C. de Boor (Leipzig, 1870), 12.

[15]*Chronicon paschale*, ed. L. Dindorf, vol. 1 (Bonn, 1832), 711.

[16]B. Kübler in *Real-Encyhclopädie der classischen Altertumswissenschaft*, Halbband (1949): col. 606f.

[17]These dates should be interpreted with caution. Our information originates almost exclusively from Athanasios' correspondence and from his Vita and evidently bears a personal and hagiographical tinge. Furthermore, Athanasios was an exceptional politician, whereas his imperial counterpart, Andronikos II (1282–1328), was a timid man. Their relations might be atypical of Byzantium, with the patriarch acquiring unusual power. Nevertheless, the episode shows that the church possessed substantial resources and experience in the sphere of welfare.

patriarch set up the grain commission to reinstitute state control over the supply of Constantinople.[18]

Probably more important than this dramatic episode is the administrative structure of Byzantine welfare. It was based on institutions organized and administered together by the state and church; *orphanotrophoi, xenodochoi,* and *gerokomoi* (caretakers, respectively, of orphans, strangers, and the aged) were officials of double allegiance.

But replacement (albeit partial) of the Late Roman state welfare system by ecclesiastical philanthropy was accompanied by a salient sociopsychological change. The Late Roman recipients of state benefits had acted as if they were entitled to games and bread; the state was obliged to provide them with food and entertainment. When the administration of philanthropy shifted from the state to the church, the citizens' right to assistance was replaced by begging for alms. The church's welfare activity was not a "constitutionally" prescribed obligation but a voluntary "grace," an example of good works (as in 1 Pet. 2:12), a realization of piety and high moral standards, and so on. This sociopsychological shift became more obvious as the private sector (an undesirable element in the Roman empire) was summoned to participate in philanthropy.

Private persons in Byzantium participated in charity and were encouraged to do this by biblical indoctrination and hagiographical example. Giving to the poor and distributing property among the poor form a regular element of hagiographical literature. The classical example of generosity is Philaretos the Merciful (d. 702), who was always ready to share with the needy everything he possessed—often to the detriment of his family.[19] When taking the monastic vow, the saints customarily left their property behind; Michael Maleinos (d. 961) is said to have distributed all his liquid assets among the poor while he transferred the ownership of his fixed assets to his brother Constantine.[20] Theodore of Edessa (ninth century) acted differently—he gave an unspecified portion of his inheritance to his

[18]A. Laiou, "The Provisioning of Constantinople during the Winter of 1306-1307," *Byzantion* 37 (1967): 106f.; A.-M. M. Talbot, "The Patriarch Athansius (1289-1293, 1303-1309) and the Church," *DOP* 27 (1973): 13f.; D. J. Constantelos, "Life and Social Welfare Activity of Patriarch Athanasios (1289-1293, 1303-1309) of Constantinople," *Theologia* 46 (1975): 620–22; N. D. Barabanov, "Konstantinopol'skij patriarch Afanasij I o nedugach vizantijskogo obščestva na rubeže XIII-XIV vv.," *Antičnaia drevnost' i srednie veka* 15 (1978): 54f.; J. L. Boojamra, "Social Thought and Reforms of Athanasios of Constantinople (1289-1293, 1303-1309), *Byzantion* 55 (1985): 350f. This list is far from being comprehensive.

[19]*BHG* 1511z-1512a. On this Vita, P. Giannopoulos, "Paratereseis sto 'Bio tou hagiou Philaretou,'" *Byzantina* 13 no. 1 (1985): 487–503; S. V. Poljakova, "Fol'klornyj sjužet o ščastlivom glupce v nekotorych pamjatnikach agiografii VIII v.," *VizVrem* 34 (1973): 130–36.

[20]*BHG* 1295, ed. L. Petit, "Vie de saint Michel Maléinos suivie du traité ascétique de Basile Maléinos," *ROrChr* 7 (1902): 588.

sister; the rest, consisting of both fields and precious metals, he distributed among the poor.[21] We could be suspicious of philanthropy as a hagiographical topos, but these data are confirmed by wills, whose clauses describe both the emancipation of slaves and distribution (διανομή) among the poor.[22]

Hagiography unquestionably demanded the exercise of charity by its saintly heroes. Hagiography, however, also attests a hostile attitude toward almsgiving that existed in a certain milieu of Byzantine society. Many a saint, in his or her passion for performing charity, encountered stubborn resistance from parents, husbands, or teachers who did not desire to give alms. Hagiographers vividly depict conflicts that arose because of these differing attitudes. Saints were forced to act secretly, even to steal from the household. A tenth-century saint, Thomais of Lesbos, is said to have had an unlucky marriage: her husband, Stephen, did not assist her in her acts of philanthropy; on the contrary, he disapproved of her behavior and even beat her, so that she suffered "for the poor."[23]

Hagiographical anti-heroes might be a literary invention created to emphasize the virtue of the saint, but again the hagiographical topos of anti-philanthropic sentiment finds confirmation in other genres of Byzantine literature. This critical approach emerges sometimes in satirical attire, as in a poem of Ptochoprodromos (twelfth century), who portrayed a henpecked husband whose wife is so involved in charitable activity that he is completely neglected. When he becomes hungry, his only means of getting food is to come to his own house disguised as a beggar; he is then welcomed and fed.[24] This critical sentiment also found serious theological treatment, as by Symeon the Theologian (d. 1022?). Certainly, he repeats the traditional formula calling for the distribution of goods among the poor, but more frequently he stresses that the riddance of property by itself cannot secure a person's salvation. "Tell me," says Symeon, "what shall we gain if we distribute all our belongings among the poor without restraining ourselves from evil, without developing hatred toward sin?"[25] He refuses to acknowledge the merits of those who, frightened by the menace of future punishments or hoping "to receive a hundred times as much" (Mark 10:30) or in sympathy with the calamities of humankind, give little of their means or even all they have to people in trouble and in

[21]*BHG* 1744, ed. I. Pomjalovskij, *Zitie iže vo sviatych otca našego Feodora archiepiskopa Edesskogo* (St. Petersburg, 1892), 7.

[22]For instance, P. Lemerle, *Cinq études sur le XIe siècle byzantin* (Paris: CNRS, 1977), 28.

[23]*BHG* 2454, ed. *AASS* Novembris 4: 236f.

[24]D. C. Hesseling and H. Pernot, *Poéemes prodromiques en grec vulgaire* (Amsterdam: Joh. Müller, 1910), no. 1.

[25]Syméon le Nouveau Théologien, *Catéchés*, ed. B. Krivochéine (Paris: Editions du Cerf, 1963–65), vol. 1, no. 5.

need, and therefore are considered merciful (ἐλεήμονες) as if they had fed Christ or performed a deed deserving a reward.[26] He knows the point of the Sermon on the Mount (Matthew 5–7)—"How blest are those who show mercy"—but Symeon asks who those *eleemones* are. Are they those who gave money and fed the poor? Not at all; but rather those who are poor for the sake of him who became poor for our sake (cf. 2 Cor. 8:9), those who have nothing to give but who remember the poor and widows and orphans and infirm, those who come to see them and shed warm tears for them.[27] Symeon cites the example of Mary of Egypt (dates of life uncertain), who has never fed the hungry or given a drink to the thirsty or clad the naked or visited prisoners or gathered aliens, and nevertheless is listed among the saints.[28] "Do not think, O my brother, that God is so powerless that he is unable to feed the poor and therefore commands us to perform charity."[29]

In the same vein, Nicholas Kataskepenos (first half of the twelfth century), author of the Vita of Cyril Phileotes, draws a strict line between the *agape* toward a neighbor and the *agape* toward God. "The passionate *agape*," emphasizes Kataskepenos, the cause of all good, can become the cause of incalculable evil if it is not used properly.[30] Thus in some circles of Byzantine society charity was viewed with reservations, as an activity that might prevent the complete self-subjugation of persons to God.

The recipients of charity in the Byzantine world were the poor and the ecclesiastical institutions. In hagiographical texts and in sermons the poor often appear linked with orphans, widows, prisoners, the hungry, and the thirsty—but does this rhetorical phrasing actually identify the Byzantine poor with the truly needy?

The Byzantines had several terms to denote the poor: πένης, πτωχός, ἄπορος, ἀκτήμων, καλυβιώτης. Some scholars have tried to draw a distinction between these terms, but I think it is impossible to expect much from Byzantine terminology that was usually vague and imprecise.[31] Probably *aktemon* and *kalybiotes* had more restricted or specific meanings, but *penes*, *ptochos*, and *aporos* can be rendered indiscriminately as "the poor." However, what did the Byzantines understand by "the poor"?

[26]Ibid., vol. 2, no. 9.

[27]Ibid., vol. 3, no. 31.

[28]Ibid., vol. 2, no. 9.

[29]Ibid., vol. 2, no. 9. See A. Kazhdan, "Predvaritel'nye zamečanija o mirovozzrenii vizantijskogo mistika X–XI vv. Simeona," *BS* 23 (1967): 12.

[30]*La vie de saint Cyrille le Philéote moine byzantin*, ed. E. Sargologos (Brussels: Société des Bollandistes, 1964), 241.

[31]M. Ja. Sjuzjumov, "O ponjatii 'trudjaščijsja' v Vizantii," *VizVem* 33 (1972): 3–6; E. Patlagean, *Pauvreté économique et pauvreté sociale á Byzance* (Paris, Mouton, 1977), 25–35. A list of terms, with an attempt at categorization, is given by P. A. Yannopoulos, *La société profane dans l'Empire byzantin des VIIe. VIIIe et IXe siècles* (Louvain: Université de Louvain, 1975), 191.

The author of a fourteenth-century dialogue, Alexios Makrembolites, clearly contrasts the rich parasites—gamblers, voluptuaries, greedy people, disrupters of civic order—with the *penetes* who are "the tillers of the soil, the builders of houses and merchant ships, and the craftsmen."[32] The *penetes* and *ptochoi* in the tenth-century agrarian legislation were peasants, contrasted with the "powerful," and P. Lemerle suggests that these terms be translated as "weak" rather than "poor."[33] Byzantine legislative texts distinguish the poor from the rich. According to the *Ekloge* both the *aporos* (bk. 17, par.11) and the *penes* (par. 29) had to undergo flogging, whereas the rich person paid a fine for a similar crime. However, the distinction between the rich and the "poor" was set relatively high. Both the *Procheiron* (issued in 907 [?]; bk. 27, par. 22) and the *Basilika* (60: 34.10) define the poor as having less than 50 nomismata—a substantial sum if we consider that a worker's annual salary was between six and nine nomismata and the price of a horse was about twelve nomismata.[34]

Now the question arises: who were those weak or poor who were entitled to receive state, ecclesiastical, or private allowances? Were they the real needy only, or was the concept of the welfare recipient broader than that of the needy?

The recipients of state welfare were not selected on the basis of actual poverty. For one thing, only citizens were entitled to receive the *artoi politikoi*. For another, the *Codex Theodosianus* (XIV. 17.1) prescribes that *annonae*, the right to the bread rations in Constantinople, "should follow the houses." The law issued by Arkadios and Honorius in 396 emphasizes this connection between house ownership and bread distribution. Addressing the city prefect, the emperors wrote: "If you learn that any persons do not have houses in this city, you shall order that they shall be deprived of the new *annonae*.... For if any person should neglect to show his affection for the city by the construction of a house, it is not right that he should thoroughly enjoy its advantages" (*Cod. Theod.* XIV. 17.13). The law of Valentinian I and Valens of 369 solemnly proclaimed that the bread was assigned to the populace of Constantinople and to their successors "if they have no means of subsistence from any other source" (*Cod. Theod.*

---

[32]I. Sevčenko, *Society and Intellectual Life in Late Byzantium* (London: Variorum Reprints, 1981), pt. 6I, p. 210, and commentary, p. 201 f.

[33]P. Lemerle, *The Agrarian History of Byzantium* (Galway: Galway University Press, 1979), 95f.

[34]On Byzantine prices, see G. Ostrogorsky, "Löhne und Preise in Byzanz," *BZ* 32 (1932): 293–333; M. Kaplan, *Les hommes et la terre à Byzance du VIe au XIe siècle* (Paris: Publications de la Sorbonne, 1992), 470–81; P. Schreiner, *Texte zur spätbyzantinischen Finanz- und Wirtschaftsgeschichte in Handschriften der Bibliotheca Vatticana* (Vatican: Bibliopteca apostolica Vaticana, 1991): 372–81.

XIV. 17.7, 8); but it is hard to imagine that Constantinopolitan home-
owners were indigent, especially when Palatines, soldiers, and the members of the *scholae* were also among the recipients of the civic bread (*Cod.
Theod*. XIV. 17.7, 8). Furthermore, when describing the exceeding generosity of St. Olympias (d. 408), her hagiographer reports that she conferred
upon the church, via the agency of John Chrysostom, "all her estates
located in various provinces as well as the *politikoi artoi* which belonged to
her."[35] One of the richest landowners in the empire, St. Olympias was
entitled to sundry bread rations that she could dispense according to her
will.

Thus the Late Roman state donations were not necessarily directed
toward the actual needy; they were rather, so to speak, citizen-oriented.
The remnants of such an attitude can be traced in the ninth-century law
book, *Epanagoge*, which assigned the quaestor the function of limiting the
stay of aliens in Constantinople and sending the beggars and indigents to
public work.[36] Albeit restricted, the privileges of the denizens of Constantinople had to be protected.

A well-known example concerns the poet called pseudo-Prodromos,
who retreated to the Mangana monastery of St. George. He persistently
begged Emperor Manuel I (1143-1180) to provide him with an *adelphaton*
(fellowship) to this institution, which he received after cutting his way
through much red tape.[37] The identity of the author of the so-called Mangana poems is obscure, and his identification with Theodore Prodromos
(and Ptochoprodromos) is still under discussion, but whoever he was, he
was not a common street beggar, but a man with certain means and connections. His *adelphaton* in the monastery of St. George was not a simple
shelter for a man starving and freezing in the porticoes of Constantinople;
rather, it was a privilege conferred upon a member of the middle class.

On a grander scale, one of the magnificent gestures of state charity
was the order of Romanos I Lekapenos (920-944) to discharge all the debts
of the citizens of Constantinople. A chronicler writes that nineteen *kente-
naria* were spent and that all the contracts were burnt in front of the

[35]Jean Chrysostome, *Lettres á Olympias*, 2d ed., ed. A. M. Malingrey (Paris: Editions du
Cerf, 1968): 420; vita of Olympias, par. 7.4–6 (*BHG* 1374).
[36]K. E. Zachariä von Lingenthal, *Geschichte des griechisch-römischen Rechts* (Aalen in
Würtemburg,: Verlag Scientia, 1955), 368; J. B. Bury, *The Imperial Administrative System in the
Ninth Century* (London: H. Frowde, 1911), 74.
[37]S. D. Papadimitriu, *Feodor Prodrom* (Odessa, 1905), 28–33; S. Bernardinello, in The-
odori Prodromi *De Manganis* (Padova: Liviana editrice, 1972), 3–5; M. J. Kyriakis, "Poor Poets
and Starving Literati in Twelfth Century Byzantium," *Byzantion* 44 (1974): 291–300; A. Kam-
bylis, "Die Wehklagen eines alternden und kränkelnden Dichters,"*Philophronema: Festschrift
für M. Sicherl zum 75. Geburtstag* (Paderborn: F. Schöningh, 1990): 171–95.

Chalke, the solemn entrance of the Great Palace.[38] Significantly, this act of mercy concerned not only the needy but everyone in debt—"the rich, the high-ranked, the *ptochoi*, and the *penetes*."

The Byzantines continued to believe that it was not only the poor who deserved the grants of state generosity. The eleventh-century historian Michael Attaleiates praises Emperor Nikephoros III Botaneiates (1078-1081) for his lavish donations. The emperor gave rich endowments of land, distributed estates and gold, freed the plebs and the nobility from debts, and gave generous pay and bonuses to the army. Even the poor became wealthy, as they received lavishly from those who had been rewarded by the emperor. The aristocratic writer Nikephoros Bryennios, husband of the imperial princess and historian Anna Komnene, acknowledged the generosity of Nikephoros III, but his evaluation of this generosity differs drastically from that of Attaleiates. The magnanimity of the emperor, Bryennios wrote, exceeded the bounds of good sense and produced considerable confusion.[39]

Even more striking is the distinction between the principles developed in the speech of Justin II (565-578) to Tiberius (recorded by Simokatta and Theophanes and variously paraphrased by many later historians) and the concepts stated by Kekaumenos, an eleventh-century figure. Justin II is said to have recommended that his successor protect the property of the rich and also provide for the needs of the poor. Kekaumenos, on the other hand, restricts this all-embracing philanthropy. He thinks that the emperor must show generosity not indiscriminately but only to those who deserve it.[40]

Thus the recipients of state philanthropy were not first and foremost the poor. Byzantine ethics encouraged the emperor to give, but the grants were directed in the Late Roman empire to the citizens and through the next centuries to the powerful rather than to the needy—or at any rate not only to the needy. The emperor was called to give to the deserving and to support equally the rich and the poor.

But did Byzantine society exercise real care about the *ptochoi*, the poor in their sense of the word (i.e. the lower- income citizens)? If we set aside the emotional cases recounted by hagiographers and turn to prosaic documents, we can observe a strange phenomenon that forces us to question the idea of ubiquitous Byzantine philanthropy. A number of *praktika* (fiscal records) from the fourteenth century include peasants who held no

[38]*Theophanes Continuatus*, ed. I. Bekker (Bonn, 1838), 429.
[39]A. Kazhdan and S. Franklin, *Studies on Byzantine Literature of the Eleventh and Twelfth Centuries* (Cambridge and Paris: Cambridge University Press and Editions de la Maison des Sciences de l'Homme, 1984), 29f.
[40]Ibid., 26f.

property but nonetheless paid taxes.[41] Moreover, the rate of taxation of the poor peasants was heavier than that of their well-to-do neighbors.[42] And it was the powerful, not the peasantry, who were granted tax exemption, the so-called *exkousseia*.[43]

Ecclesiastical and private charity was evidently more oriented toward the poor, even though the ambiguity of the Byzantine idea of poverty leaves the question open to interpretation. Certainly, we can always find examples of assistance received by the members of the lower social stratum, including old slaves, but was it a system of welfare or spontaneous help that intervened when an individual suffered from physical or economic weakness (disease, for instance, or loss of a horse) or when the whole population was struck by calamity (such as famine or earthquake)? We know about various charitable institutions in Byzantium, but we do not know to whom they were available or who had access to hostels and hospitals operated by the church.

Leontios of Neapolis, the hagiographer of the seventh century, records an attempt to establish in Alexandria a regular system of welfare administered by the church. He writes that Patriarch John the Merciful (or Almsgiver; 610–19) sent officials all over the city to make a list "of all his lords." The officials could not grasp the meaning of the patriarch's words, but he explained that he was proclaiming as lords and companions (συγκροτηταί) those whom they call *ptochoi* and beggars (ἐπαίται).[44] The entire list contained more than 7,500 persons.

Again we face a difficult problem: who were these *ptochoi* and *epaitai*?- Were all of them actually destitute, or were some of them the poor according to Byzantine standards (i.e., possessing less than 50 gold coins)? To what extent could professional beggars be considered as destitute?

The data concerning money that professional beggars could collect are scarce and come to us from unreliable, hagiographical sources. The same Leontios of Neapolis mentions that the monk Bitalios, who earned daily a keration (12 folleis) spent one folleron on food.[45] The same ratio is

[41]A. E. Laiou-Thomadakis, *Peasant Society in the Late Byzantine Empire* (Princeton: Princeton University Press, 1977), 180.

[42]G. Ostrogorsky, *Pour l'histoire de la féodalité byzantine* (Brussels: Institut de Philologie et d'Histoire Orientales et Slaves, 1954): 337.

[43]G. Ostrogorsky, "Pour l'histoire de l'immunité à Byzance," *Byzantion* 28 (1958): 165–254.

[44]*BHG* 886, Leontios von Neapolis, *Leben des Heiligen Johannes des Barmherzigen Erzbischofs von Alexandrien*, ed. H. Gelzer (Freiburg i.B., Leipzig, 1893), 8–9, reproduced in Léontios de Néapolis, *Vie de Syméon le Fou et Vie de Jean de Chypre* , ed. A. J. Festugière (Paris: P. Geuthner, 1974), 347f. Cf. Constantelos, *Byzantine Philanthropy*, 74.

[45]Leontios, *Leben des Heiligen Johannes des Barmherzigen*, 70; Festugière, ed.*Leben des Heiligen Johannes*, 387.

given for the earnings of beggars. In the narrations of abba Daniel of Sketis (d. after 576), the beggar Mark is said to have received every day 100 oboloi, of which he allegedly spent ten on food.[46] The legendary saint, Andrew the Fool (whose Vita was probably written in the tenth century), collected daily 20, 30, or even more lepta (also called folera and oboloi); for his food he spent only two folleis.[47] Whatever kind of coins these denominations represent, the hagiographers assume that the beggar collected much more than an individual needed for sustenance.

The church was also a recipient of charity. The stream of alms was supposed to rain upon the *ptochoi* through an intermediary; instead of giving directly to the poor, the emperors and private individuals donated their assets to ecclesiastical institutions charged with distributing this aid among the needy in the form of money, goods, clothing, services, and so on. Several serious problems arose from this practice.

First, there was the troubling concept of ecclesiastical and especially monastic property. Was the church or the monastery only a vehicle for transferring charity to the poor, or was it supposed to accumulate property that originated from donations, transactions, and the labor of the monastic community? This is not the place to discuss in detail the problem of ecclesiastical or monastic property. Only some general observations may be made. Probably, until the tenth century, the Byzantine church had no extensive estates or regular income. It sustained itself either by the work of monks or by occasional grants, such as imperial *solemnia* in money and in kind. Emperor Nikephoros I Phokas (963-969), a friend of monks and a man closely connected with St. Athanasios of Athos, still tried to prevent the growth of monastic estates. His attempts failed, however. Since we possess primarily monastic archives, our vision of the growing monastic landownership must be lopsided; but it did grow, at least to the end of the fourteenth century, when the political danger required confiscation of a certain part of monastic lands for military purposes.

Second, this constant ecclesiastical and monastic involvement in business led to the distortion of the *aktemosyne*, the freedom from property, that was considered one of the monastic virtues. A pamphlet written in the twelfth century by Eustathios of Thessalonike, *On the Improvement of*

---

[46] A. P. Rudakov, *Očerki vizantijskoj kul'tury po dannym grečeskoj agiografii* (Moscow, 1917), 107.

[47] PG 111: 656A, 656C. On the system of coinage in the Vita, see C. Mango, "The Life of St. Andrew the Fool Reconsidered," *Rivista di studi bizantini e slavi* 2 (1982): 301f. I do not share Mango's view on the lepta of the Vita as copper coins of five nummi, but this disagreement does not affect the subject of this chapter.

Monastic Life, is surely a caricature;[48] but the hunting for property became a substantial element in many a monastic establishment. A considerable section of extant monastic documents is devoted to land litigations. Moreover, in contradiction to the idea of *aktemosyne,* Byzantine monks administered a certain amount of private means (with the excuse that it was necessary to have money for individual almsgiving)[49] and had the right to draw individual wills.[50]

Third, the involvement in material life could distort the morality of a few church administrators, as is attested by Symeon Metaphrastes' late tenth-century additions to the Vita of St. Sampson, which reveal various wrongdoings in the hospital of St. Sampson that necessitated the saint's intervention to heal the abuses by evil officials.[51]

We must now ask why, despite all these drawbacks, Byzantine society clung to this system of funneling charity to the poor through ecclesiastical administration. The explanation is, at least in part, that the foundation of churches and philanthropic institutions was a sort of material investment.[52] We would have searched in vain for such a clue in hagiographical texts or in preambles to monastic typica, but Byzantine historians are more sober and critical. When Nikephoritzes, a powerful favorite of Emperor Michael VII (1071-1078), acquired the Hebdomon monastery of St. John the Theologian, the emperor provided John with land and lavish income. On the pretext of supporting his monastery, say the historians, Nikephoritzes accumulated enormous wealth.[53] The question of *charistikion,* the private administration of monastic and philanthropic institutions, was hotly discussed by Byzantine ideologues of the eleventh and twelfth centuries. Quite naturally, church leaders condemned secular con-

---

[48]Eustathii, *Opuscula,* ed. Th. L. F. Tafel (Frankfurt a.M, 1832), 214–67. German translation by Tafel, in Eustathius, *Betrachtungen über die Verbesserung des Mönchswesens* (Berlin, 1847). A partial Russian translation by V. G. Vasil'evskij, "Materjaly dija vnutrennej istorii Vizantijskogo gosudarstva *Zurnal Ministerstva Harodnogo* Prosveščenija 202 (1879): 433–38. On this pamphlet, see Kazhdan and Franklin, *Studies on Byzantine Literature,* 150–54.

[49]The problem was discussed in the monastery of Mount Galesios in the eleventh century, and St. Lazaros reluctantly tolerated this custom. *BHG* 979, ed. *AASS Novembris* 3:566 A-D.

[50]A. Kazhdan, "Vizantijskij monastyr' XI–XII vv. kak social'naja gruppa," *VizVrem* 31 (1971): 58f.

[51]Rudakov, *Očerki vizantijskoj kul'tury,* 97. On the xenon of St. Sampson, see Constantelos, *Byzantine Philanthropy,* 191–96; Miller, *Birth of the Hospital,* 80–85, and other works cited in n. 12.

[52]C. Mango, *Byzantine Architecture* (New York: N. N. Abrams, 1976), 28. See also, J. Ph. Thomas, *Private Religious Foundations in the Byzantine Empire* (Washington D.C.: Dumbarton Oaks Research Library and Collection, 1987).

[53]Michaelis Attaliotae, *Historia,* ed. I. Bekker (Bonn, 1853), 201. *He synecheia tes Chronographias tou Ioannou Skylitse,* ed. Eu. Tsolakes (Thessalonike: Hetaireia Makedonikon Spoudon, 1968), 162.

trol over church establishments, but such authors as Michael Psellos and Eustathios of Thessalonike emphasized the beneficial role played by *charistikarioi*, who developed monastic estates and liberated monks from material concerns.[54]

We can also hypothesize that social welfare served as a safety valve to regulate the dismay and dejection of the populace, especially at the time of general calamities. But it would be misleading to emphasize the material roots of philanthropy and to deny the existence of "disinterested piety" (in the words of Cyril Mango). The cardinal interests and concerns of a medieval society lay often beyond worldly wealth and the struggle for earthly privileges. Two major spiritual issues motivated Christian charity: Christian tradition and eschatological expectation.[55] Almsgiving (ἐλεημοσύνη), modest, without a flourish of trumpets, was recommended by the Scripture (Matt. 6:2–4), and church fathers insistently stressed the divine origin of *eleemosyne*. "Almsgiving," says John Chrysostom, "is a craft whose workshop is set up in heaven and where the master is not a man but God."[56] Charity was an activity that everyone was supposed to perform in imitation of Christ and his saints, and on the other hand, giving to the poor (or to the church) amounted to giving to Christ.

The eschatological expectation of reward for almsgiving was rendered, in a brief and simple (probably even simplistic) form, by John Chrysostom who describes almsgiving as an inexpensive and convenient way to reach paradise. "You just stay at home, and a *penes* comes to sell you paradise; he says 'Give me bread and take paradise, give me an old dress and take the Kingdom of Heaven' ... and you buy paradise for as little as you want."[57]

In summary, the Byzantine idea of philanthropy was a complex concept. Not only did the Greek word *philanthropia* (clemency) *not* coincide with modern philanthropy, but the recipients of Byzantine charity were different from those who claim welfare in modern times. The Roman state generosity was directed not toward the poor but rather toward the citizen. The Byzantines partially replaced this system with ecclesiastical and private charity that was oriented toward the poor. We do not know, however, the precise meanings of such Byzantine terms such as *ptochos* and *penes*. At any rate, there seems not to have been a systematic organization of welfare later than the era of Alexandrian patriarch John the Merciful. After that,

[54]Thomas, *Private Religious Foundations*, 167–213. On Eustathios ("A reactionary clergyman," in the words of Thomas, idem, 227), see Kazhdan and Franklin, *Studies on Byzantine Literature*, 153f.

[55]M. Puzicha, *Cristus peregrinus* (Münster: Aschendorff, 1979), 138, 175–77.

[56]*PG* 58: 522.

[57]*PG* 64: 436D.

our scanty sources tell us about occasional help that reached its peak in times of national calamity. Accordingly, the right to "bread and circuses" was replaced by begging for help. The motivation for charity was complex and included both material reasons and spiritual virtues—Christ-imitating piety and the expectation of admission to the Heavenly Kingdom.

CHAPTER 5

THE ORPHANOTROPHEION
OF CONSTANTINOPLE

TIMOTHY S. MILLER

The most prominent institution for social welfare in the Byzantine Empire was the great orphanage of Constantinople. It served for nine hundred years as a center of Greek education in music, grammar, and literature as well as a major shelter for orphans. The origin of this orphanage is clouded by lack of sources, but it is clear that by the mid-fifth century it controlled substantial assets that provided revenues to support the sustenance and education of the orphans. The legal and economic power of this institution occasionally attracted rapacious administrators; but Byzantines believed that the spirit of charity exemplified by the orphanage made Constantinople a truly Christian city.

From the painstaking work of such scholars as Demetrios Constantelos, Raymond Janin, and Robert Wolf, historians of Byzantine civilization and those interested in the religious roots of social welfare have come to appreciate how numerous were East Roman charitable institutions and how sophisticated their operations.[1] The Byzantine state, the Orthodox Church, the monastic movement, and wealthy individuals worked together to provide *xenones* (hospitals), *gerokomeia* (rest homes), *xenodocheia* (hospices), and *ptocheia* (shelters for the poor) for the needy citizens of Constantinople, Thessalonica, Nicea, and other towns and even villages of the empire. Among these many philanthropic foundations, however, the Orphanotropheion, the great orphanage of Constantinople, held first place. As early as the mid-fifth century, its director, called the *orphanotrophos*, played a leading role in ecclesiastical politics. As head of the Orphanotropheion in 472, the priest Akakios had achieved such renown that he was selected as patriarch of the capital city. That same year, Emperor Leo I

---

[1]Demetrios J. Constantelos, *Byzantine Philanthropy and Social Welfare* (New Brunswick, N.J.: Rutgers University Press, 1968); Raymond Janin, *La géographie ecclésiastique de l'empire byzantin, première partie: Le siège de Constantinople et le patriarchat oecuménique: Les églises et les monastères*, 2d ed. (Paris: Institut français d'Etudes byzantines, 1969), 550–69; Robert Wolf, *Gesundheitswesen und Wohltätigkeit im Spiegel der byzantinischen Klostertypika*, Miscellanea byzantina Monacensia, 28 (Munich: Institut für Byzantinistik und neugriechische Philologie, 1983).

83

granted to the orphanage the same financial and legal privileges which he and his predecessors had bestowed upon the chief ecclesiastical institution of the Eastern Empire, the patriarchal church of Hagia Sophia.[2]

Through the many centuries of the East Roman Empire, the Orphanotropheion never ceased to serve the people of Constantinople. Between 650 and 800, when traditional urban institutions of the capital city—the great public baths, the famous chariot races, and even many of the schools—were slowly disappearing, the Orphanotropheion continued to function. Two of its directors during these years, Andrew of Crete and Nikephoros (later patriarch of Constantinople), even entered the small circle of significant literary figures of the period. During the ninth century, the office of *orphanotrophos* attained a place among the high ranks of the Byzantine bureaucracy. The orphanage and its estates now belonged to the state and came to enjoy new privileges. By the eleventh century, the Orphanotropheion had become such a powerful government agency that one of its directors, John the Paphlagonian, was able to use its resources to control imperial policy as the de facto prime minister under Michael IV (1034-43).[3]

Although the Orphanotropheion became a powerful institution first within the Constantinopolitan church and then within the secular government of the empire, historians have made little progress in understanding how the orphan home functioned and why it became so important.[4] Byzantine chronicles, legal sources, oratorical pieces, and hagiographical works frequently refer to the Orphanotropheion, but no text has survived which describes its organization, finances, or daily operations. By contrast, the *typikon* of Emperor John II Komnenos (1118-43) contains detailed information about the *xenon* (hospital) attached to the famous Pantokrator

[2]Timothy S. Miller, *The Birth of the Hospital in the Byzantine Empire*, The Henry E. Sigerist Supplements to the Bulletin of the History of Medicine, 10 (Baltimore: Johns Hopkins University Press, 1985), 89–140; *The Syria Chronicle known as that of Zachariah of Mitylene*, 4, trans. F. J. Hamilton and E. W. Brooks (London, 1899), 79–80; *The Ecclesiastical History of Evagrios with the Scholia*, 2, ed. J. Bidez and L. Parmentier (London, 1898), 63; *Codex Justinianus*, 1.3,34(35), ed. Paul Krüger, *Corpus iuris civilis*, vol. 2 (Berlin, 1929), 23.

[3]For Andrew of Crete, see *Vita Sancti Andreae*, ed. Athanasios Papadopoulos-Kerameus, *Analekta hierosolymitikes stachyologias* (St. Petersburg, 1898), 5:169–79; for Nikephoros, see *Ignatii vita Sancti Nicephori archiepiscopi Constantinopolitan*, ed. Carolus de Boor, Nicephor: archiepiscopi Constantinopolitani apuscula historica (Leipzig: Teubner, 1880), 152. For general history, see George Ostrogorsky, *History of the Byzantine State* (New Brunswick, N.J.: Rutgers University Press, 1969), 323–26; Raymond Janin, "Un ministre byzantin: Jean l'Orphanotrophe," *Echos d'Orient* 30 (1929): 431–43.

[4]R. Guilland, "Études su l'histoire administrative de l'empire byzantin: l'orphanotrophe," *Revue des Études Byzantines* 23 (1965): 205–21 provides a review of the sources which refer to the Orphanotropheion or the *orphanotrophoi*, but he does not try to describe how the orphanage functioned. See also Constantelos, *Philanthropy*, 241–58.

Monastery. This invaluable document has enabled researchers to study closely the structure and function of the philanthropic hospitals offering medical care to citizens of medieval Constantinople and to residents of other large Byzantine towns. From the information in the *typikon*, historians have been able not only to draw a detailed picture of Byzantine hospital physicians and their support staff of nurses and servants, but also to provide a complete description of hospital facilities for patients.[5] As no such document exists for the Orphanotropheion, almost nothing is known about its teaching staff, its disciplinarians, and its service personnel, or about its facilities for housing and feeding the children in its care.

Nevertheless, it is still possible to collate the many references to the orphanage found in a variety of sources and thereby to extract some details regarding the story of its early development and the services it came to provide. Extant sources reveal where the Orphanotropheion was located in Constantinople, who established it, and approximately when it began its operations. Byzantine sources also reveal that the orphan home supported a school for the children which became an important center of Greek Christian music and of Hellenic culture in general. Indeed, the Orphanotropheion was one of the few urban institutions in Constantinople to survive the time of troubles that descended upon the Byzantine Empire during the seventh century. Though primarily a philanthropic institution, the orphanage also acted as an institutional shelter that helped preserve Greek grammar and important selections of Greek literature from the upheavals of the early Middle Ages and to hand down the treasures of Hellenic culture to later generations.[6] Because the Orphanotropheion came to possess great estates and to enjoy special judicial powers, the position of the *orphanotrophos* (director) evolved into that of a magistrate who judged cases regarding wills and property disputes.

The Orphanotropheion functioned, then, as a center of Byzantine music, as a school helping to preserve and expand the influence of Greek and Christian culture, and as a court administering medieval Roman Law. An examination of the Orphanotropheion's varied activities not only reveals new aspects of Byzantine philanthropic activities but also provides valuable insights concerning East Roman civilization in general.

Where was the Orphanotropheion located? Two reliable narrative histories provide the answer. One was written by the historian Joseph Genesios during the reign of Constantine VII (913-59). In describing the

---

[5]"Le typikon du Christ Sauveur Pantocrator," ed. Paul Gautier, *Revue des Études Byzantines* 32 (1974): 1–145. For interpretations of the contents of the *typikon*, see Miller, *Birth of the Hospital*, 12–29, 141–66; and Wolf, *Gesundheitswesen*, 134–99.

[6]For the role of Byzantine hospitals in preserving Greek culture in the period 650–800, see Miller, *Birth of the Hospital*, 171–75, 215–16.

overthrow of Emperor Michael I (811-13), Genesios mentions a secret meeting between Michael's advisor Theodotos and the future Emperor Leo V (813-20). These two men met in the church of the Orphanotropheion, which according to Genesios' account stood on the acropolis of Constantinople.[7] The twelfth-century writer, Anna Komnena, confirms Genesios' statement. In her laudatory biography of her father, Emperor Alexios I (1081-1118), Anna includes the most complete extant description of the Orphanotropheion, an institution which her father rescued from financial ruin following the Turkish seizure of estates in Asia Minor. Alexios provided it with new estates in Thrace and Macedonia and also enlarged its complex of buildings. In her highly rhetorical description Anna mentions that the Orphanotropheion was located on the city's acropolis, a hill overlooking the Bosporus.[8]

Constantinople's acropolis was in fact the space which the ancient Byzantium had occupied, the old pagan city which Constantine the Great had expanded and made his New Rome. As Cyril Mango has emphasized, Constantine and subsequent East Roman emperors did not build extensively on the old acropolis. It remained a place of crumbling pagan temples until at least the sixth century. On the north side of the acropolis, however, Byzantine ruins have been found, ruins which show signs of reconstruction under the Komnenoi emperors. Mango has identified these remains as those of the Orphanotropheion which Alexios I Komnenos remodeled ca. 1100. An inscription found on a column capital near these ruins seems to confirm Mango's identification; it reads Δημητρίου ὀρφανοτρόφου.[9]

Who founded the Orphanotropheion? Emperor Leo I provided the key to answering this question when he issued a law in 472 concerning the rights and privileges of the orphanage and its director. In this law, Leo states that the present *orphanotrophos*, the priest Nikon, would exercise certain rights as would all men in the future who would assume the directorship of the orphanage, an office created by "Zotikos of blessed memory."[10] The emperor's words indicate that a man named Zotikos, deceased some-

[7]*Josephi Genesii regum libri quattuor*, ed. A. Lesmueller-Werner and I. Thurn (Berlin: DeGruyter, 1978), 8–9.

[8] Anne Comnène, *Alexiade*, XV.7, ed. Bernard Leib (Paris: Belles Lettres, 1945), 3:214–15.

[9] See Cyril Mango, *Le développement urbain de Constantinople (IVe–VIIe siècles)* Travaux et Memoires de Centre de recherche d'histoire et civilisation de Byzance, 2 (Paris: De Boccard, 1985; 2d ed. 1990), 33–34 and 34 n. 6; *Parastaseis syntomoi chronikai*, ed. Averil Cameron and Judith Herrin, *Constantinople in the Early Eighth Century: Parastaseis syntomoi chronikai* (Leiden: Brill, 1984), 162.

[10]*Codex Justinianus*, 1.3.34(35): *Corpus iuris civilis*, 2:23.

time prior to 472, had been the first *orphanotrophos* and, presumably, had founded the orphanage of Constantinople.

In subsequent centuries, the name of Zotikos was always associated with the office of *orphanotrophos*. The Church of Jerusalem came to celebrate the memory of Saint Zotikos on 31 December. The Georgian version of the Jerusalem lectionary, dating from the eighth century, identified Zotikos as the sustainer of orphans. The several tenth- and eleventh-century redactions of the *synaxarion* of the Great Church of Constantinople refer to Zotikos as priest and *orphanotrophos*; a tenth-century version of the *Patria Constantinopolis* stated that Zotikos was the first to assume control of the Orphanotropheion in Constantinople; and a novel of Emperor Herakleios (610-641) identified the home for orphans in Constantinople specifically as the Orphanotropheion of Zotikos.[11]

Although Byzantine sources are unanimous in identifying Zotikos as the first *orphanotrophos* in Constantinople and as the blessed founder of the capital's orphanage, no sources provide precise information.[12] One confronts difficulties even in determining the century in which Zotikos lived. For example, the tenth-century *Patria Constantinopolis* includes two contradictory accounts. According to the first account, Emperor Justin II (565-78) and his wife Sophia actually founded the Orphanotropheion and then entrusted its management to Zotikos. According to the second account, Zotikos had lived and worked in Constantinople under Emperor Constantius (337-361).[13] The law of Leo I, however, offers reliable evidence that Zotikos had lived sometime before 472 and thus could not have served under Emperor Justin II. This law and a subsequent novel of Justinian (no. 131; issued in 545) prove that the Orphanotropheion had been operating long before Justin II became emperor in 565.[14]

According to the reliable chronicler Theophanes (early ninth century), Justin II and Sophia did add to the Orphanotropheion by building a large church dedicated to Saint Paul, which they located within the precincts of the orphanage. Apparently, the tenth-century *Patria*'s first account confused the facts and credited Justin II and his wife with establishing the

[11]See the study of Zotikos by Michel Aubineau, "Zoticos de Constantinople, Nourricier des pauvres et serviteur des lépreux," *Analecta Bollandiana* 93 (1975): 92–95; *Patria Constantinopolis III*, ed. Theodor Preger, *Scriptores originum Constantinopolitanarum* (Leipzig: Teubner, 1907), 2:235; *Nov.* 4 (Herakleios), ed. Georgios A. Rhalles and Michael Potles, *Syntagma ton theon kai hieron kanonon* (Athens, 1855), 5:240.

[12]See the text of one version of the *Vita Sancti Zotici*, ed. Michel Aubineau, "Zoticos de Constantinople," 71–85, but many of the details in the vita are purely legendary (ibid., 95–108).

[13]*Patria Constantinopolis III*, cf. paras. 47, 48 (Preger, *Scriptores*, 2:235).

[14]Leo I's law, *Codex Justinianus*, 1.3.34(35): *Corpus iuris civilis*, 2:22; Justinian's law, *Nov.* 131.15, ed. Rudolf Schoell and William Kroll (Berlin, 1928), *Corpus iuris civilis*, 3:664.

entire orphanage complex when, in fact, they had only built a church for the institution's use. One is moved to reject the first account of the *Patria* and to accept, tentatively, the second account identifying Zotikos as a contemporary of Emperor Constantius.[15]

Extant sources from the fourth and fifth centuries offer additional information concerning the religious and political conditions of the mid-fourth century, details which strengthen the case that Zotikos opened his refuge for orphans during the reign of Constantius. According to the fifth-century church historian Sozomenos, Makedonios, bishop of Constantinople from 340 to 348 and again from 350 to 360, promoted a sweeping program of social welfare in this growing city. He was moved to philanthropic action by the pious Marathonios, one of the deacons of the Church of Constantinople.[16] Marathonios embraced an ascetic life-style he had learned from the renowned monastic leader Eustathios, who had lived in Constantinople sometime before 357. Eustathios and other monastic leaders of Anatolia had developed a form of urban asceticism which demanded ascetic self-sacrifice in the service of others rather than flight from society and retreat into the desert wilderness. After Eustathios became bishop of Sebasteia in Lesser Armenia, he founded a monastic community at the gate of the town, a community whose members devoted themselves not to contemplation and continuous prayer, but, rather, to the ceaseless chores of caring for lepers and other disabled and abandoned people.[17]

Inspired by the teaching of Eustathios, Marathonios organized loose-knit communities of Anatolian ascetics in Constantinople. With the support of Bishop Makedonios, Marathonios employed these urban monks to aid the poor and sick from the city's streets and byways. This program of social welfare was popular among the people of the capital, and when in 360 Emperor Constantius deposed Makedonios for his interpretation of Arian theology, a crowd of people from the city followed their former

---

[15]Cf. *Theophanis chronographia*, ed. Carolus de Boor, (Leipzig: Teubner, 1883), 1:244, and *Patria Constantinopolis III*, paras. 47, 48 (Preger, *Scriptores* 2:235).

[16]*Sozomenus: Kirchengeschichte*, IV.27.4–5, ed. Joseph Bidez, Griechische Christlichen Schriftsteller, 50 (Berlin: Akademie Verlag, 1960), 184.

[17]For the Anatolian monastic movement see Gilbert Dagron, "Les moines et la ville: Le monachisme à Constantinople jusqu' au concile de Chalcédoine (451)," *Travaux et Mémoires* 4 (1970): 229–76, and Miller, *Birth of the Hospital*, 76–85. For Eustathios' philanthropic institution see Epiphanios, *Panarion*, 75.1, ed. Karl Holl, Griechische Christlichen Schriftsteller, 37 (Leipzig: Akademie Verlag, 1933), 333.

bishop beyond the walls and continuously hailed him as "the lover of the poor."[18]

Although Makedonios and his deacon Marathonios were beloved for their philanthropic activities during the fourth century, they later were remembered as heretics. Makedonios, Marathonios, Eustathios of Sebasteia, and many of the other Anatolian ascetic leaders—including Basil of Cappadocia, later one of the champions of Nicean orthodoxy—rejected the Nicean Creed and its key trinitarian formula *homoousios*, (which holds that God the Father and God the Son are of the same substance). They accepted instead the formula *homoiousios* (that God the Father and God the Son are of similar substance), a position close to, but distinct from that of Nicea. The orthodox Niceans branded this *homoiousios* creed as heretical and classed its adherents among the various Arian sects. As a result, Marathonios and Makedonios were eventually considered heretics, and the ascetic movement they had organized and its vigorous social welfare programs were viewed with suspicion.[19] When supporters of the Nicean Creed finally regained control of the episcopal office in Constantinople under Emperor Theodosios (380), the new Nicean bishop, Gregory of Nazianz, tried to win over the followers of Makedonios from their *homoiousios* creed. But even while attacking their beliefs, Gregory hailed these so-called Macedonians for their love of the poor, the sick, and the strangers. He also commended them for their ascetic lifestyle, which still adhered to the rules established by Marathonios.[20]

Gregory of Nazianz also praised the Macedonians for their interest in singing and holding all-night vigils. In fact, an emphasis on antiphonal singing had marked the Anatolian ascetics since they first emerged as a movement in the middle of the fourth century. Basil of Cappadocia emphasized the importance not only of the urban monks' philanthropic activities but also of their fervent singing. As late as the mid-fifth century the followers of Makedonios continued their singing tradition. Influenced by his Macedonian uncle and a Bythinian community of Macedonian nuns, the future saint Auxentios developed a love for choral music and all-night vigils.[21]

---

[18]See Dagron, "Les moines et la ville," 246–52; Miller, *Birth of the Hospital*, 78–80; *Vie des saints Notaires, Analecta Bollandiana* 64 (1946): 170. See especially Gilbert Dagron, *Naissance d'une Capitale* (Paris: Presses Universitaires de France, 1974), 440.

[19]Dagron, *Naissance*, 436–42; Miller, *Birth of the Hospital*, 76–88. For Basil's attraction to Eustathios' ascetic ideals see Ep. 223, in *Saint Basil: Letters*, tr. Roy J. Deferrari and Martin R. MacGuire, Loeb (Cambridge, Mass.: Harvard University Press, 1961), 3:292–98.

[20]Gregorius Nazianzus, *Oratio 41: In Pentecosten* (PG, 36, 440).

[21]Regarding Gregory's comments, see ibid., 440. Ep. 207, *Basil: Letter*, 3:184–86; Soz.: *Kirchengeschichte*, VII.21.6–8 (p. 334); *Vita Sancti Auxentili* (PG, 114, 1380).

With regard to the Orphanotropheion of Saint Zotikos, an early reference to it in the Syrian chronicle of Zachariah of Mitylene reveals that the people of Constantinople associated the institution with choral singing. While Gennadios held the patriarchal office (458-472), the priest Akakios served as director of Zotikos' orphanage. Zachariah added that during Akakios' tenure as head of the institution the people of Constantinople often visited the Orphanotropheion to hear the children sing, and Akakios' brother, Timokletos, composed hymns especially for the orphans to sing.[22]

Comparing Makedonios' movement in Constantinople with the information collected about Saint Zotikos and his orphanage indicates that Zotikos founded his home for orphans as part of Makedonios' philanthropic program during the reign of Constantius (337-361). First, Makedonios served as bishop of Constantinople while Constantius held the imperial office. Makedonios was also the first Christian leader to organize a system of social welfare in the capital city. Second, the only plausible story about Zotikos in subsequent Byzantine sources holds that he, too, lived during Constantius' reign. Also, it is clear that Zotikos was involved in social welfare, given the fact that he established the Orphanotropheion on the old acropolis of Constantinople and also founded a leprosarium outside of the city on the Galata Hill.[23] Third, the ascetic movement associated with Makedonios' philanthropic activities won renown for its emphasis on choral singing, as did Zotikos' orphanage.

For centuries Zotikos' Orphanotropheion continued to train a children's choir. When the daughter of a prominent official of Emperor Theophilos (829-842) fell gravely ill, her father summoned a chorus to soothe the dying girl with hymns sung "according to the custom of the Orphanotropheion."[24] Apparently, in the ninth century the orphanage choir was still known for a distinctive style of choral singing. In the late ninth and tenth centuries the orphanage choir frequently participated in imperial ceremonies. On the Feast of the Epiphany the emperor customarily held a great banquet to which he invited the Patriarch of Constantinople, the *synkellos*, ten metropolitans of the empire, and most of the clergy from Hagia Sophia, a total of 216 guests. During this festival meal, one of the *domestikoi* of Hagia Sophia led in the orphans who then sang hymns in the

---

[22]Zachariah of Mitylene, IV.11 (pp. 79–80).

[23]*The *Vita Sancti Zotici*, in fact, only describes Zotikos' founding of the leprosarium. See "Zoticos de Constantinople," 71–84 and the brief summary in the *Synaxarium Constantinopolis*, in *Synaxarium ecclesiae Constantinopolitanae e codice Sirmodiano nunc Berolinensi adiectis Synxariis selectis*, ed. Hippolyte Delehaye, *Acta Sanctorum. Propylaeum ad acta sanctorum Novembris* (Brussels, 1902), 359–62.

[24]*Vita Sancti Antonii*, in *Pravoslavnij Palestinskij Sbornik* 19 no. 3 (1907): 211–12.

antiphonal manner, perhaps a relic of the antiphonal singing popularized by Makedonios and the other fourth-century Anatolian ascetic leaders. On the feast of the Purification (2 February) the orphanage choir stood on benches to the right of the great door in the narthex of Hagia Sophia and greeted the emperor with prayers and traditional acclamations. On the feast of the Annunciation (25 March) the orphans participated in a similar manner.[25]

One of the greatest of Byzantine hymnists, Andrew of Crete, served as director of the Orphanotropheion. Andrew was born ca. 660 in Damascus, by that time under Umayyad rule. When he came of age, he journeyed to Jerusalem and joined the monks of the Church of the Resurrection, a community descended from Anatolian urban monks who had come to the Holy City in the fifth century.[26] Here Andrew led an austere life of self-sacrifice and philanthropic labor. He fed the poor, sheltered the orphans, and defended the oppressed. In 685 the patriarch of the Holy City sent Andrew to Constantinople to represent the views of the Jerusalem church concerning the decrees of the Sixth Ecumenical Council (681). After reaching the Byzantine capital, Andrew decided to stay in the empire. At first, he turned to the contemplative life of withdrawal from the world, but he eventually returned to the practice of active charity. He became a deacon of Hagia Sophia and earned such a reputation for piety that Emperor Justinian II (685-699) appointed him director of the Orphanotropheion.

Andrew found the resources of the orphanage nearly depleted, not a surprising situation given the constant warfare of the seventh century and the great loss of territory which the East Roman Empire had suffered during these years. Andrew's careful management of the Orphanotropheion, however, restored its financial stability. As a result of his successful stewardship of the Orphanotropheion and of another philanthropic foundation, the Eugenios Diakonia, he eventually was appointed archbishop of Gortyna in Crete.

During his life, Andrew of Crete wrote many hymns for Orthodox liturgical services. In fact, he contributed to developing and popularizing a new form of liturgical music called a canon. Among the many pieces of

---

[25]See *Kleterologion of Philotheos (Le Traité de Philothée)*, ed. Nicolas Oikonomides, *Les listes de préséance byzantines des IXe et Xe siècles* (Paris: CNRS, 1972), 185–86; *Le livre des Cérémonies*, I:36(27), ed. Albert Vogt (Paris: Belles Lettres, 1935), 1:139–40, 153.

[26]This short sketch of Andrew's life is taken from the vita composed by Niketas, *Vita Sancti Andreae*, 169–79; the Jerusalem *spoudaioi* are discussed in Miller, *Birth of the Hospital*, 122–32, esp. 125, 130. The Anatolian ascetic movement was established at the Church of the Anastasis as early as the mid-fifth century. See the *Vita Sancti Theodosii (Lebensnachrichten über den heiligen Theodosios von Kyrillos aus Skythopolis)* in *Der heilige Theodosios: Schriften des Theodoros und Kyrillos*, ed. Hermann Usener (Leipzig, 1890), 105–6.

music he composed, his penitential hymn for Holy Week, called the Great Canon, is the most famous. Nowhere did his biographer Niketas mention that Andrew had turned to composing hymns while director of the Orphanotropheion, though it is not unreasonable to assume that he took an active interest in its choral traditions.[27]

The relationship between the Orphanotropheion and choral singing does not end in Constantinople; it can be traced from the new capital of Constantine westward to Old Rome. In describing the pontificate of Sergius II (844-847), the *Liber Pontificalis* mentions that the pope repaired the *schola cantorum*, which had formerly been called the *orphanotropheum* (Latin spelling).[28] Probably during the seventh or early eighth century when clerics of Greek origin dominated the Roman Church, one of the popes had established an orphanage modeled on the Orphanotropheion in Constantinople and adopted the program of musical training. Teaching good choral singing became such a dominant activity of the Roman *orphanotropheum* that people began calling it the school of singers.

Singing—the public performances, but especially the rigorous training required for good choral music—formed a significant part of the educational program for the children of the Orphanotropheion, but the institution surely offered a general education as well, schooling to prepare the children for a productive life in society. In one of his edicts concerning the orphanage, Emperor Leo I declared that those who supervised the minors at the institution had the obligation not only to feed the children but also to instruct them "with fatherly affection."[29] Unfortunately, no source before the twelfth century provides any evidence concerning the educational curriculum of at the Orphanotropheion.

To his *Long Rules* for the monastic life, however, Basil, the great theologian and bishop of Caesarea (370-379), added a fascinating section on the school the monks of his mastery were to maintain.[30] Basil's views on education, classical pagan literature, and even on aspects of Roman Law came to exert tremendous influence on Byzantine thought and practice in later years. No doubt the section of his *Long Rules* concerning the monastic school at Caesarea was used by subsequent generations as a guideline for

---

[27]For a brief discussion of Andrew's musical compositions see E. Wellesz, "Byzantine Music and Liturgy," *The Cambridge Medieval History*, IV: *The Byzantine Empire, Part 2: Government, Church and Civilization* (Cambridge: Cambridge University Press, 1967), 148–49.

[28]*Le Liber Pontificalis: Texte, introduction et commentaire*, ed. L. Duchesne (Paris, 1892), 2:86, 92.

[29]*Codex Justinianus*, I.3.31(32): *Corpus iuris civilis*, 2:22.

[30]*Regulae fusius tractatae. Interrogatio* 15 (PG, 31, 952–57).

the education of children.[31] Basil at first had associated himself closely with Eustathios of Sebasteia and his Anatolian ascetic movement.[32] Since Zotikos' Orphanotropheion also had its roots in Eustathian asceticism as it was interpreted by Marathonios and Makedonios, it is likely that Basil's monastic rules came to influence educational practices at the orphanage.

Basil's monastery school accepted both orphan students and those with parents still living. More surprising, it accepted both boys and girls. As no Byzantine sources mention the sex of the children at the Orphanotropheion, one cannot tell whether Basil's custom was followed in this respect. Of course, Basil required that the boys and girls have separate facilities and receive different training, but he laid even greater emphasis on separating the younger children from the older. They were to live in different facilities, eat apart, sleep, study, and work separately. The two age groups were to come together only at prayer time. Basil thus established a lower and upper schools for children. He also advised that a few of the more responsible and mature among the older students be selected to supervise groups of younger students. An eleventh-century lead seal of the Orphanotropheion probably belonged to a student officer, similar to Basil's monitors. The seal bears the inscription "the first of the students of the Orphanotropheion."[33]

Basil also made recommendations about what to teach and how to teach. He preferred that grammar lessons use names from the sacred scriptures. He also wanted students to learn of the marvelous deeds of ancient Greek history, but not the pagan myths. Finally, he suggested that students study intently the Book of Proverbs as a guide for ethical behavior. Although Basil did not exclude classical Greek literature from his monastic school, he assumed that biblical and Christian literature would form the backbone of the children's curriculum.

With regard to teaching methods, Basil recommended that the children participate in contests to test their knowledge of biblical stories and of ancient Greek literature and history. The students loved these contests and would study more diligently to prepare for them. Basil also prescribed that the student monitors frequently interrogate the younger stu-

---

[31]Basil believed, for example, that it was immoral to prefer one child over the others in writing one's testament. See *Homilia VIII. Hexaemeron*, in *Basile de Césarée: Homélies sur l'hexaéméron*, ed. S. Giet, Sources Chrétiennes, 26 (Paris: Cerf, 1968), 459–61. This view eventually shaped the rules of Byzantine inheritance.

[32]Ep. 223, *Basil: Letters*, 3:292–98.

[33]Gustave Schlumberges, *Sigillographie de l'empire byzantin* (Paris, 1884), 379: πρώτη μαφητῶν σθράγις ὀρθανοτροφίου. For reasons of meter the line has been altered to read "the first seal of the students," but the meaning is clearly "the seal of the first of the students." I thank Dr. John Nesbitt of the Byzantine Studies Center, Dumbarton Oaks, Washington, D.C., for interpreting this seal.

dents about their secret thoughts. By such questioning, the boys and girls would come to see the silliness of many of their fantasies and would learn to avoid them.

From the fifth through the early twelfth century, Byzantine sources provide only one clue concerning education at the Orphanotropheion. The tenth-century *Book of Ceremonies* describes a court ritual on the Wednesday of Easter Week in which the *orphanotrophos* introduced to the emperor twelve newly baptized persons, six of them adults and six orphaned children.[34] Possibly the *orphanotrophos* presented these newly initiated Christians because they had received religious training at the orphanage. Perhaps they were orphan captives and adult barbarian refugees from frontier provinces, barbarians or Moslems who had accepted the Christian faith. By the twelfth century, the Orphanotropheion surely did provide catechetical instruction to non-Christian refugees, as we shall see below.

In 1081, Alexios I Komnenos seized the throne of the East Roman Empire. By combining military skill with cunning diplomacy, he managed to save the Byzantine state from Seljuks, Pechenegs, and crusaders. Three nearly contemporary observers—his own daughter Anna, the perceptive historian John Zonaras, and the ascetic Cyril Phileotis—considered the emperor's renovation of the Orphanotropheion among his outstanding deeds. In the biography that she wrote in honor of her father, Anna Komnena devotes an entire chapter to praise of the splendid philanthropic institution he had refurbished and thereby provided the most detailed description of the Orphanotropheion found in extant Byzantine sources. She mentions the new estates the emperor donated to the orphanage, the novel philanthropic services he devised, and the monastic communities he added to the orphanage complex. In the course of her laudatory description, she also includes some valuable observations about the orphan school.[35]

According to Anna, Emperor Alexios had turned the orphanage into a school where the children studied Greek grammar (elementary subjects) and the *enkyklios paideia* (a well-rounded secondary education in Greek literature). On any given day one could see students from diverse lands surrounding the teachers of the Orphanotropheion: "a Latin [from the West] pursuing his education, a Scythian [from the North] learning the Greek language, a Roman [i.e. a Byzantine Greek] studying Greek literature, and an uneducated Greek [a student from the Greek peninsula?] learning his

---

[34]*Le Livre de Cérémonies* I.21(12), 1:82.
[35]Anne Comnène, *Alexiade*, XV.7, 3:213–18.

language properly." A thirteenth-century chronicler stated that the foreigners at the orphanage were in fact captives taken in Alexios' many battles.[36]

Anna also mentions two methods that the students used in their studies. Some puzzled over grammatical questions. Were these students perhaps engaged in contests similar to those recommended by Basil of Cappadocia? Other students were busy copying *schede*. These were short essays on diverse themes which Byzantine teachers composed to illustrate for their students particular points of grammar, orthography, or meter. The historian Zonaras observed that Alexios not only allowed resident orphans to attend the school of the Orphanotropheion, but he also admitted children of living parents too poor to afford to pay a regular teacher.[37]

According to the Vita composed by Nicholas Kataskepenos, Saint Cyril Phileotis also praised Alexios for having restored the Orphanotropheion on one occasion when the emperor came to him for spiritual help in governing the empire. In the course of their discussion, the saint hailed Alexios for his imperial *philanthropia*, especially for his efforts on behalf of the orphanage. Through this newly renovated institution, Cyril knew that the emperor had assisted those who were hungry and thirsty, but Alexios' greatest service was aiding those who hungered spiritually. Cyril then explained to Alexios that these spiritually hungry people were the Christians whom the victorious emperor had brought back to Constantinople from his raids against the Seljuk Turks in Asia Minor. Some of these refugees had already abandoned Christianity and had begun to learn "the works of paganism (Islam)." The younger refugees and captives Alexios assigned to the Orphanotropheion, where they were reintroduced to the tenets of the Christian faith. In the course of their conversation Cyril also mentioned that the Orphanotropheion brought many captive pagans from different languages to the saving waters of Baptism. Especially common among these catechumens were Scythians, a class of students whom Anna Komnena had also mentioned in her description of the multilingual student body at the orphanage.[38] Perhaps these Scythians were Pechenegs whom Alexios had decisively defeated some years earlier in the Balkans.[39]

---

[36]See ibid., XV.7.9 (3:217–18); *Anonymou synopsis chronike*, in *Mesaionike bibliotheke*, ed. K. A. Sathas (Paris, 1894), 7:177.

[37]See Anne Comnène, *Alexiade*, XV.7, 9 (3:218); for a description of a *schede* see Giuseppe Schirò, "La schedografia a Bisanzio nei sec. XI–XII e la scuola dei ss. XL martiri," *Bollettino della Badia greca de Grottaferrata*, n.s. 3 (1949):11–29. *Ioannis Zonarae Annales*, ed. Maurice Pindar and Theodor Büttner-Wobst, *Corpus Scriptorum Historiae Byzantinae* (Bonn, 1897), 3:744–45.

[38]*La vie de saint Cyrille le Philéote, moine byzantin*, ed. Étienne Sargologos, Subsidia Hagiographica, 39 (Brussels: Société des Bollandistes, 1964), 225–31.

[39]Robert Browning, *The Byzantine Empire* (London: Weidenfeld and Nicolson, 1980), 119–20.

Throughout the twelfth century the Orphanotropheion continued to serve as an important educational institution in Constantinople. Theodore Prodromos, one of the most prominent literary figures of the Comnenian period, worked at the orphanage, probably as a teacher. A high-ranking professor (*didaskalos*) of the Patriarchal School, Constantine Stilbes, began his career lecturing on the Gospels in the Orphanotropheion where he worked for twelve years. According to one of his obscure remarks, however, he seems never to have made enough money while teaching there.[40]

Robert Browning has carefully studied the educational institutions of twelfth-century Constantinople and has linked the Orphanotropheion with a system of instruction under the supervision of the patriarch of Constantinople. Several men who eventually held the highest patriarchal professorships—the *didaskalos* of the Psalter, the *didaskalos* of the Apostle (i.e., of the Epistles), and the *didaskalos* of the Gospels—began their careers as instructors at the Orphanotropheion. This was the case with Constantine Stilbes who, after his twelve years of humble service at the orphanage, was appointed *didaskalos* of the Apostle.[41]

Beginning with the sack of Constantinople by the soldiers of the Fourth Crusade (1204), the Latin occupation of the Byzantine capital brought disaster to the churches and philanthropic institutions of the city and its surrounding territory. Some institutions such as the Sampson Xenon suffered severe damage at the hands of the marauding crusaders themselves; others died a slow death, cut off from the estates of Asia Minor and Western Thrace which had supported their operations. Even in the mid-fourteenth century, long after Emperor Michael VIII Palaeologos had restored Constantinople to Byzantine rule, many churches, monasteries, and charitable foundations still lay in ruins.[42]

When Michael Palaeologos regained Constantinople, he found the Orphanotropheion no longer in operation. Whether it had been destroyed during the sack of 1204 or had perished from lack of funds under Latin

---

[40]For Prodromos see *Michel Italikos: Lettres et discours*, ed. Paul Gautier, Archives de l'orient chrétien, 14 (Paris: Institut français d'études byzantines, 1972), 61; *Costantino Stilbes: La prolusione del Maestro dell' Apostolo*, ed. Lia Raffaella Cresci, Letteratura e civiltà bizantina, 2 (Messina, 1987), 48.

[41]Robert Browning, "The Patriarchal School at Constantinople in the Twelfth Century," *Byzantion* 32 (1962): 167–76; 33 (1963): 22, 26. For additional information on the school at the Orphanotropheion see Sophia Mengiali-Falangas, "L'Ecole Saint-Paul de l'orphelinat à Constantinople: Bref aperçu sur son statut et son histoire," *Revue des Etudes Byzantines* 49 (1991): 237–46.

[42]For the fate of the Sampson Xenon see Timothy S. Miller, "The Sampson Hospital of Constantinople," *Byzantinische Forschungen*: 15 (1990): 128–35;*Actus du Lavra*, III: *de 1329 á 1500*, ed. Paul Lemerle et al., Archives de l'Athos, 10 (Paris: P. Lethielleux, 1979), no. 123, 20–26.

administration cannot be determined from extant sources. According to the historian George Pachymeres, Michael VIII decided to restore a part of the Orphanotropheion. Within its ancient precincts, he set up a new school of grammar and provided salaries for teachers and stipends for students. He also established suitable prizes to offer as rewards for those students who excelled in their studies. Michael appointed the learned Holobolos both head of this new school and official court orator.[43]

From Pachymeres' brief account, it seems that Emperor Michael did not reestablish an orphanage with facilities to feed and house homeless children. Rather, he opened a school for indigent children, apparently without any facilities to board the students at the institution. Although the title of *orphanotrophos* reappeared in the Palaeologan government, there is little evidence that the court official who held this archaic office had any relationship with the emperor's school. In fact, by the mid-fourteenth century, *orphanotrophos* had become a purely honorific title and no longer indicated a specific function related to the care of orphans or even to the supervision of a subsidized school. Apparently, Zotikos' famous orphanage no longer existed.[44]

For nine hundred years the Orphanotropheion was a center of Greek *paideia* in Constantinople. Besides serving as a school of music, grammar, and Hellenic literature, it also developed into an important economic institution. As the manager of the orphanage's own estates and as the legal guardian of the children in his care, the director of the Orphanotropheion came to control large tracts of land throughout the empire. Over the years, the *orphanotrophos* evolved into a leading figure, first within the ecclesiastical structure of Constantinople and then within the ranks of the state bureaucracy. By the tenth and eleventh centuries, he had become a powerful financial and judicial official of the Byzantine state.

Lack of sources prevents any study of the early Orphanotropheion's endowment or its legal privileges. It is impossible to ascertain what rights Zotikos and his early successors exercised, although the leading role of Akakios as *orphanotrophos* under the patriarch Gennadios (458-472) indicates that by the mid-fifth century the Orphanotropheion already controlled substantial assets. The legislation of Emperor Leo I, issued in 472, provides the first specific evidence concerning the orphanage's resources and the privileges of its director. By that time the institution owned a complex of properties whose revenues supported the sustenance and educa-

---

[43]See *Georgii Pachymeris de Michaele et Andronico Palaeologo libri XIII*, ed. Immanuel Bekker, *Corpus Scriptorum Historiae Byzantinae* (Bonn, 1835), IV.14, 1:282–84.

[44]Guilland, "Études: l'orphanotrophe," 214–16; *Pseudo-Kodinos: Traité des Offices: Introduction, texte, et traduction*, ed. Jean Verpeaux (Paris: CNRS, 1966), 184.

tion of the orphans. To increase the yield of these properties Leo himself and his predecessors had granted the orphanage various legal and financial privileges. Not only did the *orphanotrophos* supervise the children's home, but he also controlled several other philanthropic institutions, monastic foundations, and public churches in and around Constantinople. Leo confirmed that this entire complex of properties and ecclesiastical institutions was subject to the then present *orphanotrophos* Nikon and to all who succeeded him in his office. The emperor also extended to the Orphanotropheion and its dependencies all the rights and privileges which the patriarchal church of Hagia Sophia had enjoyed in the past and would receive in the future. In 545 Emperor Justinian confirmed the many grants and privileges which Leo had bestowed upon the Orphanotropheion.[45]

Justinian's successor, Justin II (565-578), also favored the Orphanotropheion. In addition to providing the magnificent Church of Saint Paul for the orphanage complex, he also gave it imperial estates generating an annual income of 443 *noumismata*. To collect the revenues in kind from its far-flung possessions, the Orphanotropheion maintained agents who shipped grain and other commodities back to Constantinople.[46]

The invasions of the seventh century and the subsequent loss of imperial territory deprived the Orphanotropheion of many of its properties and seriously diminished its annual revenues. But as shown, Andrew of Crete managed to restore its financial stability in the early eighth century. And, according to the ninth-century chronicler Theophanes, the Orphanotropheion suffered an even greater financial disaster at the hands of Emperor Nikephoros I (802-811). Theophanes claimed that, to increase the government's revenues, Nikephoros had revoked some of the orphanage's tax exemptions. Even worse, he confiscated its most valuable estates. There is no evidence, however, that Nikephoros' policies diminished the Orphanotropheion's resources. Theophanes seems to have misrepresented Nikephoros' program. The emperor had not deprived the orphanage of any lands; rather, he had transformed the entire institution from an independent ecclesiastical foundation into an imperial state agency, a process which could be called state confiscation, but which did not deprive the institution of resources essential to its operations.[47]

---

[45]One cannot rely on the testimony of the *Vita Sancti Zotici*, 71–85 regarding details on imperial grants to Zotikos' charitable activities. Regarding the influence of Akakios as *orphanotrophos* see *Zachariah of Mitylene*, IV.11, pp. 79–80; see also *Codex Justinianus*, I.3.34(35): *Corpus iuris civilis*, 2:23; and *Novellae*, 131.15; *Corpus iuris civilis*, 3:664..

[46]*Theophanis chronographia*, 1:244; see also the reference to Justin II's grant in one of the novels of the late ninth or early tenth century, attributed to Leo VI, *Les Novelles de Léon VI le Sage*, ed. P. Noailles and A. Dain (Paris: Belles Lettres, 1944), 377–78; and *Chronicon paschale*, ed. Ludwig Dindorf, *Corpus Scriptorum Historiae Byzantinae* (Bonn; W. Weber, 1832), 721–23.

As a result of Nikephoros' reforms, the orphanage director became a government officer. Before the ninth century, the head of the orphan home had always been considered among the ecclesiastical hierarchy, but in 842 a roster of secular state bureaucrats listed him as an imperial official.[48] The *orphanotrophos* appeared on this roster as one of the government financial supervisors, after the *sakellarios* (state treasurer), the various *logothetes*, and the *chartoularioi* of the financial bureaus.[49] The *Kleterologion of Philotheos*, a more detailed list of state officials drawn up in 899, added a short description of the subordinates whom the *orphanotrophos* supervised. This staff included *chartoularioi* (scribes with legal training) who directly managed the funds of the orphanage proper, *chartoularioi* who controlled the funds of the leprosarium (also founded by Zotikos), the *arkarios* (general treasurer), and *kouratores* (managers) of the individual estates belonging to the orphanage.[50]

The Orphanotropheion thus became a powerful department of the imperial government. As its director, the Paphlagonian eunuch John wielded great influence in the government of Emperor Romanos III (1028-34) and was able to secure the imperial throne for his younger brother Michael. Continuing to serve as *orphanotrophos* under the new emperor Michael IV (1034-43), John in fact directed imperial policy and also enriched his family by despoiling the resources of the Orphanotropheion. His mismanagement was partly responsible for impoverishing the orphanage to the point where it had ceased to function just prior to the reconstruction program of Alexios I.[51]

The power of the *orphanotrophos* rested on his management of the vast resources belonging to the orphanage and its subsidiary institutions, but his influence also rested on the extraordinary legal powers which over the years he came to possess. In an edict of 472, Emperor Leo I granted the *orphanotrophos* the right to serve as guardian (*tutor* in Latin) for all the children in the orphanage under the age of fourteen and to serve as curator for all those over fourteen but under twenty-five. Leo required that the *orpha-*

[47]See *Vita Sancti Andreae*, 174; *Theophanis chronographia*, 1:486–87; see the comments of John Philip Thomas, *Private Religious Foundations in the Byzantine Empire*, Dumbarton Oaks Studies, 24 (Washington, D.C.: Dumbarton Oaks, 1987), 129.

[48]Justinian classed *orphanotrophoi* together with bishops, *oikonomoi* of churches, and *xenodochoi* as ecclesiastical officials; see *Theophanis chronographia*, 1:176.

[49]See the *Taktikon Uspenskii (842–843)* , in *Préséance*, 51.

[50]*Kleterologion of Philotheos (Traité de Philothée)*, in *Préséance*, 123.

[51]*Georgii Cedreni historiarum compendium*, ed. Immanuel Bekker, *Corpus Scriptorum Historiae Byzantinae* (Bonn, 1839), 2:503–4; Constantelos, *Philanthropy*, 256. *Zonarae annales*, 744, states that the Orphanotropheion had ceased to function before Alexios began his restoration project. How much of this was due to mismanagement or to Turkish invasions is not clear; see below, p. 103.

notrophos of Constantinople accept the property of his wards in the presence of the magistrate of the census, an officer of the Urban Prefect, so that the director would know the value of the property he had to manage on behalf of each of the orphans. The emperor, however, exempted him from the audits to which ordinary guardians were subjected.[52]

Leo's edict inadvertently reveals an important detail about the orphanage in Constantinople. Although some of the children there might have been homeless waifs who were found wandering the streets of the capital, others obviously had inherited substantial amounts of property. Why did well-to-do orphans not have relatives willing to assume the duties of guardianship? Were the obligations of Roman tutorship becoming too burdensome? Were the extended families breaking down? These are important questions to consider, but answering them would require a far more thorough investigation than is possible in this brief survey. In 545, Emperor Justinian confirmed this edict of Leo's by repeating its provisions in Novel 131.[53]

Just as the legislation of the emperors Leo and Justinian shows that the Orphanotropheion accepted both impoverished street urchins and children with property, one can find the same mix of social classes in Byzantine hospitals.[54] The Sampson Xenon accepted the poverty-stricken sick of Constantinople who had no home where they could rest and recuperate, but it also admitted in the seventh century a prosperous deacon of Hagia Sophia for surgery, and in the tenth century even a member of the emperor's personal retinue.[55] That both rich and poor were able to benefit from Byzantine social welfare institutions distinguishes these agencies sharply from Western charitable institutions, which were shunned as places of degradation by the established nobles, by the rising bourgeoisie, and even by the struggling artisans.[56]

When, in the eighth century, Emperor Leo III revised the laws of Justinian, he substantially increased the role of the *orphanotrophos* in provid-

[52]*Codex Justinianus*, I.3.31(32): *Corpus iuris civilis*, 2:22. For the Roman laws regarding guardianship and the distinctions between *tutor* and *curator* see Max Kaser, *Roman Private Law*, trans. Rolf Dannenbring (Pretoria: University of South Africa, 1980), nos. 62–64.

[53]*Novellae*, 131.15: *Corpus iuris civilis*, 3:664.

[54]Miller, *Birth of the Hospital*, 147–52.

[55]For the deacon of Hagia Sophia at the Sampson Xenon see the *Miracula Sancti Artemii*, ed. Athanasios Papadopoulos-Kerameus, *Varia graeca sacra* (Saint Petersburg, 1909), *miraculum* 21, pp. 25–28. For the *oikeios* of the emperor see the *Vita Sancti Sampsonis* (PG, 115, 301–5).

[56]Henry Sigerist, "An Outline of the Development of the Hospital," *Bulletin of the History of Medicine* 4 (1936):579ff.; Christian Probst, "Das Hospitalwesen im hohen und späten Mittelalter und die geistliche und gesellschaftliche Stellung des Kranken," *Medizin im mittelalterlichen Abendland*, ed. Gerhard Baader and Gundolf Keil, Wege der Forschung, 363 (Darmstadt: Wissenschaftliche Buchgesellschaft, 1982), 260–74.

ing guardians for orphaned children. The laws of Leo I and Justinian had simply recognized the right of the *orphanotrophos* to assume the guardianship of the children who happened to be staying at the orphanage. According to the *Ecloga* of Leo III, however, the head of the orphanage was to assume the guardianship of all orphaned children in Constantinople whose parents had left them property but had failed to designate a guardian by testament. The *Ecloga* seems to have abolished what Roman Law called *tutela legitima*, the duty of the nearest surviving relative of an orphan to assume the guardianship if no testamentary guardian (*tutela testamentaria*) had been designated.[57] Leo III justified this innovation by indicating that in the past ordinary guardians had despoiled the property of the orphans they were supposed to protect. Leo III believed that the director of the orphanage, as a respected cleric, would be more trustworthy.

If it were ever followed, Leo's law would rapidly have filled the Orphanotropheion with wealthy orphans. An expanded version of the *Ecloga* from the ninth century probably reflects how Leo's innovations were put into practice. If the deceased parents had failed to establish a guardian for their children, then within the city of Constantinople, the *orphanotrophos*, assisted by the *scribas*, reviewed the case and assigned a guardian by magisterial decree (what Roman Law had sometimes termed *tutela dativa*).[58] Since the reign of Emperor Theodosios (379-395), the Urban Prefect had been making such determinations in Constantinople; now the *orphanotrophos* assumed this responsibility.[59] If the *orphanotrophos* was unable to find a suitable guardian, he no doubt admitted the child into the orphanage and took over the rights and duties of tutorship himself.

When the Macedonian emperors Basil I and Leo VI (867-912) reformed the Byzantine legal system, they apparently abrogated the *orphanotrophos'* authority to assign guardians. Their legal handbook, the *Prochiron*, did not repeat the titles of the *Ecloga* concerning the powers of the director of the orphanage to appoint and supervise guardians. By the eleventh century, when the famous jurist Eustathios Romaios was commenting on Byzantine laws and legal practice, another judicial officer, the

---

[57]*Ecloga: Das Gesetzbuch Leons III und Konstantinos' V*, ed. Ludwig Burgmann (Frankfurt a.M: Löwenklau, 1986), title 7, p. 198.

[58]*Ecologa privata aucta*, title 8.2, *Jus Graeco-romanum*, ed. P. Zepos and I. Zepos (Athens: G. Phexis and Son, 1930–31), 6:28–29. For the date of the *Ecloga privata aucta* see Peter E. Pieler, "Dreizehntes Kapital: Rechtsliteratur," in Herbert Hunger, *Die hochsprachliche profane Literatur der Byzantiner*, Handbuch der Altertumswissenschaft, 12.5.1–2 (Munich: C.H. Beck, 1978), 2:458–59.

[59]*Theo*. III.17.3, *Theodosiani libri XVI cum constitutionibus Sirmondianis*, ed. Theodor Mommsen (Berlin, 1905), 1:118.

quaistor of the sacred palace, had acquired the power to designate guardians and to monitor how they performed their duties.[60]

Although the eleventh-century *orphanotrophos* had lost his authority over guardians, he continued to function as a magistrate. Serving on the high court of the Hippodrome, this same Eustathios Romaios reviewed a case referred to him by the *orphanotrophos*. It involved a dispute between the Gerokomeion (rest home) of Saint Helias and a particular church over the leasing of some land. In his legal opinion Eustathios pointed out that philanthropic institutions such as this *gerokomeion* possessed different rights and privileges depending upon whether they had been founded by imperial order or by private individuals. Eustathios sent the case back to the *orphanotrophos* for him to determine precisely which privileges the Gerokomeion of Saint Helias enjoyed.[61] From this single case, it is impossible to know exactly the scope of the *orphanotrophos'* jurisdiction. It seems, however, that he had come to exercise primary jurisdiction over disputes involving philanthropic institutions. Since the Orphanotropheion was the most prestigious of the social welfare facilities in Constantinople and its director had been serving as a Roman magistrate since the time of Leo III, this would seem a logical development in the evolution of the office.

During the twelfth century the directors of the orphanage continued to function as imperial magistrates. At least two prominent jurists of the age held the office of *orphanotrophos*. The first, Alexios Aristenos, is best known as one of the greatest of Byzantine canonists. He and Theodore Balsamon composed excellent commentaries on Byzantine ecclesiastical and civil law. Under Emperor Manuel I (1143-1180), Aristenos also served as *nomophylax*, the official who supervised the imperial law school at the Mangana Palace. For a time Aristenos also held the post of *dikaiodotes*, the highest-ranking civil magistrate in the twelfth century. During his distinguished legal career, he was twice appointed *orphanotrophos*.[62]

The second famous jurist was John Belissareotis who served as director of the orphanage at the end of the twelfth century. As a youth Belissareotis had developed a love for the science of law. He abandoned the study of philosophy and natural science to attend the law courts and listen to the debates. He surpassed all others in the field of jurisprudence. According to his encomiast, Niketas Choniates, Belissareotis was appointed *orphanotrophos* both because of his legal brilliance and because of his loving nature.[63]

[60]See *Prochiron* in *Jus Graeco-romanum*, 2:108–228; and *Pira (Peira)*, 16.5, 13; 51.29, *Jus Graeco-romanum*, 4:55, 59, 218.

[61]*Pira*, 15.12. For the legal career of Eustathios Romaios see Günter Weiss, "Hohe Richter in Konstantinopel: Eustathios Romaios und seine Kollegen," *Jahrbuch der österreichischen Byzantinistik* 22 (1973): 120–43.

[62]*George et Dèmètrios Tornikès: Lettres et Discours*, ed, Jean Darrouzès (Paris: CNRS, 1970), 53–56; Theodore Prodromos (PG, 133, 1268).

Choniates praised Belissareotis for having been an excellent manager of the Orphanotropheion. As a result of his good stewardship, Belissareotis had acquired many spiritual children even though he had never married or produced any natural offspring. Choniates then makes an interesting observation. Belissareotis had attained the office of *orphanotrophos* because he had led a blameless life of *philanthropia*. "Such a Man," Choniates claimed, "would not conceive a desire for anything belonging to others." Belissareotis knew well "that the small change taken from those without means (i.e., the orphans) was blown away like chaff by the orphans' sighs and scattered like dust in the summer." To protect the property of the orphans, Belissareotis had fortified the Orphanotropheion and made it an unassailable acropolis.

Choniates' encomium implies that Belissareotis' virtuous behavior was not the norm, and that men who had held this office in the past had, in Niketas' words, "falsified the noble title of *orphanotrophos* and adulterated it." When, in the eleventh century, the scheming eunuch John the Paphlagonian had despoiled the resources of the orphanage to benefit his family, perhaps he had done nothing essentially new; he had only done it on a grander scale. Periodically men had held the office of *orphanotrophos*, men who had procured the position by corruption and then enriched themselves.[64] Choniates' remarks indicate that Byzantine social welfare agencies probably suffered more from immoral administrators than from enemy raids or poor harvests.

When, sometime prior to 1156, Emperor Manuel I appointed Alexios Aristenos *orphanotrophos* for a second time, Theodore Prodromos wrote a speech in honor of this joyous occasion. Aristenos came again to the Orphanotropheion, not as one ready for plunder, but bringing with him a new birth of prosperity for the institution and its beneficiaries. The needy people of Constantinople—the poor, the crippled, the sick, and the orphans—greeted the return of this honest administrator with a greater triumph than the ancient Romans had staged for the victorious Caesar. The orphans from the grammar school hailed Aristenos' arrival with hosannas just as the children of Jerusalem had sung praises to Christ the King. In his speech, Prodromos compared the Orphanotropheion to Mount Sion, the temple citadel of the Holy City, and the virtuous *orphanotrophos* to the Ark of the Covenant containing the true Law of God.[65]

Prodromos' speech is a typical example of Byzantine rhetoric, full of exaggerated classical and biblical allusions. Nevertheless, it offers valu-

---

[63]Niketas Choniates, *Orationes et epistulae*, ed. Jan–Louis van Dietan (Berlin: De Gruyter, 1973), *oratio* 15:147–51.

[64]Ibid., 154–55.

[65]Theodore Prodromos (PG, 133, 1268–71).

able insights. Although Prodromos clearly recognized that rapacious administrators constantly threatened philanthropic institutions such as the great orphanage, still he considered the site of the Orphanotropheion to be Constantinople's Mount Sion. Located on the city's acropolis, overlooking the Bosporos, the Orphanotropheion served as the temple of the New Jerusalem, a repository not of the tablets of the Old Law, but of the New Law of Christ, the living law of love. As a virtuous *orphanotrophos*, Aristenas had wedded the law of Christ to the law of the state and had helped to make Constantinople God's Holy City.[66]

[66]Ibid., col. 1269.

CHAPTER 6

BYZANTINE WOMEN, SAINTS' LIVES, AND SOCIAL WELFARE

ALICE-MARY TALBOT

As the church increasingly took over from the state the responsibility of caring for the needy, Byzantine religious life and philanthropy became inextricably entwined. Women benefited from the church's charitable institutions as both recipients and donors. In the former role, women and girls found refuge and support in homes for widows, hospitals for women, orphanages, and nunneries that took in battered and mentally ill women and prostitutes hoping for a better life. It was as donors, however, that charitable activity provided another dimension for women beyond the traditional search for salvation through aiding the poor. Personal ministry to the needy provided women with a socially acceptable opportunity for leaving the confines of their homes and interacting with people outside their immediate household. Through their active charity roles, some of these women forged a new type of sainthood, that of the holy married woman.

The historian in search of Byzantine women works at a considerable disadvantage, since the sources provide much less information about the female half of the population than about their male counterparts. Narrative histories, written almost exclusively by men, normally ignore the activities of women unless they happen to be empresses or prominent members of the aristocracy. If we turn to hagiography, it soon becomes apparent that far fewer women than men became saints, with the result that there are fewer biographies of female saints. If we look at typika, the foundation documents for monasteries, we discover that only 10 percent of the surviving charters deal with nunneries. There are many reasons for the omission or relative neglect of women in the Byzantine historical sources, but paramount is the fact that women by and large remained at home, bearing children and caring for their families and households, and thus played no role in the political and military events that predominate in narrative texts. Women of the lower classes were more likely to work outside of the house: peasant women tended gardens and helped with other farm chores, while in the cities women worked as artisans and merchants. They, too, however, are largely invisible in the sources.[1]

Nevertheless, there were several arenas outside the home in which women of the upper and middle classes were more active and visible, those of religious observance, philanthropy, and patronage of the arts; the first two of these are the subject of this study. Among the few acceptable reasons for well-bred women to venture forth in public were attendance at church services, visits to religious shrines, and the performance of the charitable activities which were viewed as an expression of love for Christ. Women in Byzantium inherited an equal share of the family fortune, at least in theory, and maintained control of their assets; they thus had the opportunity of spending their money as they chose although, as we shall see, their families sometimes disapproved of their choices. Many of these wealthy women, of both imperial and aristocratic rank, participated in philanthropic activity primarily through the donation of funds for the construction and support of charitable institutions. But there are examples of women who engaged in more direct forms of assistance to the poor and sick, and left the confines of their homes to come into contact with the needy. Thus, their religious and philanthropic activity is a profitable area of research to understand better the lives of Byzantine women.

The women and girls of Byzantium faced many of the same problems as women today: there were orphans, poor widows, battered wives, the mentally ill, the homeless, refugees, the elderly. As now, the nuclear or extended family was the first line of support for women in need, but if there were no relatives or the family was unable or unwilling to provide the needed services, then charitable individuals or state and church institutions stepped in to succor the needy.

PHILANTHROPIC ACTIVITY OF EMPRESSES

Philanthropia (lit. "love for humankind") was viewed as an imperial virtue, and both emperors and empresses were praised by historians and panegyrists and in the preambles to official documents for their concern for their less fortunate subjects. While *philanthropia* was but one of many admirable traits in an emperor, for an empress it was one of the few ways in which she could make an impact on the lives of her subjects.

Thus, many empresses sponsored the construction of charitable institutions, or helped the needy in other ways. Occasionally historians emphasize the fact that a particular empress did not spend her personal fortune on jewels and cosmetics, but instead gave it to the poor. In a few cases where we have the actual records of the donation of property to a

---

[1]For a general survey of women in Byzantium, see A. Laiou, "The Role of Women in Byzantine Society, *JÖB* 31.1 (1981): 233–60.

charitable institution, it is clear that the empresses did indeed hand over substantial lands for the construction and upkeep of the complex.[2] In the fifth century Pulcheria, the sister of Emperor Theodosios II and for a time his regent, is reported to have used her own funds to establish churches, shelters for beggars and the homeless, and monasteries. In the same century the exiled empress Athenais-Eudokia built in Jerusalem countless hospices for pilgrims, the poor, and the elderly.[3] In the sixth century the empress Theodora, the wife of Justinian I, founded a specialized sort of institution, a reformatory for repentant prostitutes. Since she is reported to have been in her youth an actress of scandalous reputation, this seems a most appropriate undertaking for her. The historian Prokopios writes that Theodora realized that these women were not inherently evil, but had been driven to prostitution through poverty. The empress "made what had formerly been a palace into an imposing convent designed to serve as a refuge for women who repented of their past lives, so that there through the occupation which their minds would have with the worship of God and with religion they might be able to cleanse away the sins of their lives in the brothel."[4] Theodora also bought prostitutes from pimps and set them free. In another of his works, the same historian reports that not all prostitutes were eager to enter the "Convent of Repentance," that some were forcibly installed there, and a few were so unhappy that they threw themselves from the building and committed suicide. Supposedly five hundred women were housed in this institution.[5]

One late ninth-century empress, Theophano, even achieved sanctity for her charitable activity and ascetic life-style.[6] She was married to the emperor Leo VI, who did not much care for her, and preferred the company of a mistress. Theophano consoled herself by devoting herself to works of mercy, giving everything away to the poor. According to the

[2]See, e.g., the list of donated properties in the typikon for the Lips nunnery founded by the Empress Theodora Palaiologina: *Deux typica byzantins de l'époque des Paléologues*, ed. H. Delehaye (Brussels: M. Lamertin, 1921), 130–32 (hereafter, Delehaye, *Typica*).

[3]Sozomenos, *Historia ecclesiastica* 9.1.1-10. See also K. Holum, *Theodosian Empresses*, vol. 7 (Berkeley: University of California Press, 1982), 91, 219.

[4]Prokopios of Caesarea, *Buildings*, 1.9.7–8, tr. H. B. Dewing, *Procopius*, vol. 7 (London: Heinemann and Cambridge: Harvard University Press, 1961), 77.

[5]Prokopios of Caesarea, *Secret History* 17.5–6.

[6]There are two vitae of Theophano, one by an anonymous contemporary, the other by Nikephoros Gregoras, *Zwei griechische Texte über die hl. Theophano, die Gemahlin Kaisers Leo VI.*, ed. E. Kurtz (St. Petersburg, 1898). For a French summary of the earlier vita, see G. da Costa-Louillet, "Saints de Constantinople aux VIIIe, IXe et Xe siècles," *Byzantion* 27 (1957): 823–36. The mother of the anonymous hagiographer was herself a woman devoted to charitable service: she bathed and fed poor people at a bath in the Harmatios quarter (*Zwei griechische Texte*, ed. Kurtz, 18). See also G. Majeska, "The Body of St. Theophano the Empress and the Convent of St. Constantine," *Byzantinoslavica* 38 (1977): 14–21, for a discussion of Theophano's cult in later centuries.

doubtlessly exaggerated account of her hagiographer, "Whatever money and property came into her hands she gave away to the poor....She provided the needy with valuable robes, and furnished the livelihood of widows and orphans."[7] She also founded a number of poorhouses, hospitals, and other such institutions, which she generously endowed.[8] She died at a relatively young age, and surprisingly was honored as a saint by her husband who built a funeral chapel to house her tomb. Theophano was the first empress to be sanctified on account of her philanthropy and asceticism; the other empresses of the late eighth and ninth centuries who became saints (Irene and Theodora) were honored for their role in overthrowing iconoclasm and restoring the veneration of images.

It was much less common for the empresses to have direct contact with the needy. One notable exception was Flaccilla, the wife of Theodosios I, in the fourth century, who visited hospitals in Constantinople and personally ministered to the sick. She "brought them the pot, fed them soup, gave them their medicine, broke their bread, served them morsels, and washed the bowl, performing with her own hands all the tasks normally given to servants and handmaids...."[9] In the twelfth century, Irene Doukaina, the wife of Alexios I Komnenos, distributed money to beggars when she accompanied her husband on military campaigns. As reported by her daughter Anna in a panegyrical passage of the *Alexiad*,

> She took what money she had in gold or in other precious metal ...when she left the capital. Afterwards, on the journey, she gave liberally to all beggars, clad in goat-hair cloaks or naked; no one who asked went away empty-handed. And when she arrived at the tent set apart for her and went inside, it was not to lie down at once and rest, but she opened it up and all the mendicants were allowed free access. To such persons she was approachable and showed herself ready to be both seen and heard. Nor was it money alone that she gave to the poor; she also dispensed excellent advice. All who were obviously fit and strong (but preferred to be lazy) were exhorted to work and become active; she urged them not to beg from door to door, but to earn their own keep; not to lose heart because they were neglected.[10]

---

[7]*Zwei griechische Texte*, ed. Kurtz, 14, 29–32.

[8]Ibid., 41.26–27.

[9]Theodoret of Cyrrhus, *Historia Ecclesiastica*, 5.18.2–3; Holum, tr., *Empresses*, 26.

[10]Anna Komnene, *Alexiad*, bk. 12, chap. 3, ed. A. Reifferscheid (Leipzig, 1884), 2:152–53; E.R.A. Sewter, tr., *The Alexiad of Anna Commena* (Baltimore, Md.: Penguin, 1969), 377f.

It should also be noted that when Irene's husband fell ill, she made donations to those who were sick and in prison and asked them to pray for the emperor's recovery; in this case charitable actions were viewed as a way of obtaining God's mercy through giving mercy to the less fortunate.

PHILANTHROPIC ACTIVITY OF WOMEN OF THE ARISTOCRACY AND THE MIDDLE CLASS

The example set by empresses was followed by other women as well, whether wealthy aristocrats, or those of the middle class. Contributions of money and land to needy individuals or to charitable institutions were viewed as a pious act, for which these women would be rewarded by attaining the salvation of their soul. Donation of property seems to have been most common when a woman was about to enter a convent. In Byzantium, women might adopt the monastic habit at almost any stage of life. Many became nuns as teenaged girls; others took monastic vows in middle or old age, after having married and raised a family. These women frequently gave away their entire fortunes upon entering monastic life, distributing some to the poor, and handing over the rest to the monastery. As we shall see later, the donation to the convent could be used for many purposes, depending on its size. A relatively small contribution would be used to support the nun for the rest of her life, and to pay her burial expenses. A larger donation might be used for the maintenance of the convent buildings or be earmarked for distributions of food to the poor. Normally the woman's family supported her decision to enter a convent and give away her property, but occasionally there was resistance. A well-known case is that of Irene Choumnaina, the daughter of Nikephoros Choumnos, an important state minister in the early fourteenth century.[11] She was briefly married to the *despotes* John Palaeologos, one of the younger sons of Andronikos II, but was tragically widowed after only four years of marriage, at the age of sixteen. Somewhat to the dismay of her parents, she decided to restore the double monastery of Christ Philanthropos in Constantinople and retire there as abbess for the rest of her life. Despite her youth, she already controlled sizeable amounts of property; she gave away part of her fortune for poor relief and to ransom prisoners of war, and spent much of the rest on construction of the monastery. Evidently she did retain some of her property, however, and engaged in disputes with her parents over its appropriate disposal.

As in the case of the empresses, women of means usually helped the needy indirectly, through the provision of funds. A rare glimpse into a

[11]For the most complete study of Irene Choumnaina, see A. C. Hero, "Irene-Eulogia Choumnaina Palaiologina, Abbess of the Convent of Philanthropos Soter in Constantinople," *Byzantinische Forschungen* 9 (1985): 119–47.

more "hands-on" form of charitable activity is afforded by the Lives of two female saints, Mary the Younger in the late ninth century and Thomais of Lesbos in the tenth century. The stories of these women are of considerable interest from a number of viewpoints, not least because they reflect a new trend in Byzantine hagiography, the sanctification of relatively ordinary married women, in contrast to the ascetic nuns who were made saints in earlier centuries. The cases of St. Mary and St. Thomais showed that it was possible to achieve sanctity outside the confines of a hermitage or convent, through unusual devotion to the poor as well as patient endurance of adversity.

The biographer of St. Mary the Younger stresses at the beginning of the Vita (692A) that he intends to demonstrate that all sorts of people can find favor with God, whether they be rich or poor, old or young, male or female, married or single: "The course of virtue has been opened not only to men, but also to women."[12] Thus Mary could be blessed even though she was a woman, was married, bore children, and never took monastic vows or worked miracles. To briefly summarize Mary's life: she was a woman of Armenian extraction, who married a military officer named Nikephoros. They first settled in a town in Thrace and then moved to the city of Bizye (in the European part of modern Turkey), and she is sometimes called "Mary of Bizye." Mary was a virtuous soul, who was kind to her servant girls and never raised her voice in anger. She was assiduous in her devotions in the early years of her marriage; since there was no private chapel attached to her house, she went to the local cathedral morning and evening, disregarding bad weather and the distance, and the necessity of fording a stream en route. The hagiographer notes, "she bore the soul of a man in the body of a woman."[13] After the couple settled in Bizye, however, she stopped going to church on a daily basis, so as not to expose herself to the gaze of strange men; instead, she made her prayers at home.

Mary was known for her charitable activities, making donations to poor people and monks. The hagiographer emphasizes that she used her own money for her philanthropy, to such an extent that she left no inheritance for her children. On one occasion she even borrowed money in order to pay the debts of fellow townsmen who had been imprisoned for their inability to pay their taxes. After their release, the men came joyfully to Mary's house to thank her for her generosity. In some ways Mary's life

[12]Her vita is published in *Acta Sanctorum*, Nov. 4: 692–705. See also C. Mango, "The Byzantine Church at Vize (Bizye) in Thrace and St. Mary the Younger," *Zbornik Radova Vizantoloskog Instituta* 11 (1968): 9–13, and R. M. Bartikian, "Razmyslenija o Zitii sv. Marii Novoj," in *Bulgarsko srednevekovie: Moyen âge bulgare: Recueil bulgaro-soviétique rédigé en l'honneur du prof. Ivan Dujčev*, ed. V. Giuzilev, I. Bozilov, et al. (Sofia: Naauka i izkoustvo, 1980), 62–64.

[13]*Acta Sanctorum*, Nov. 4:693C, 694AB.

resembled that of a nun, even though she had taken no vows; she lived ascetically, avoiding meat whenever her husband was away on military campaign. She also endured with resignation the premature deaths of her first two sons. Her quiet life was shattered, however, when her husband's relatives accused her of adultery with a servant and of squandering the family fortune. Nikephoros became infuriated with Mary, and struck her repeatedly; during the beating, she fell and hit her head, suffering serious injury. As his wife lay on her deathbed, Nikephoros realized that she was innocent of the charges made against her, and discovered the astonishing extent of her charity. She had given away all her clothing to the poor, so that there was no clean tunic in which to wrap her body!

Except for her charitable activities and unfortunate death, Mary did not lead an extraordinary life; nonetheless she apparently attracted considerable attention during her lifetime, for we are told that "all the women of Bizye" came to her deathbed. Four months after her death a man possessed by an evil spirit came to the church where Mary was buried, calling upon her to drive out the demon. The archbishop wondered at this, commenting, "She was a fine woman, but she has not been deemed worthy of performing miracles. For God has given the power of miracle-working to pure men and to holy monks and martyrs... but this woman was married to a man ...nor did she accomplish any extraordinary or great deed. How then should she work miracles?"[14]

But the archbishop was wrong; the demoniac was cured, and many other miracles subsequently took place at Mary's tomb. It is not surprising that significant numbers of women came to seek healing at her sarcophagus, some even making long pilgrimages to see the miraculous tomb. Twenty-five years later, when her remains were translated, it was discovered that her body was wondrously preserved, and had suffered no corruption. Then an icon painter had a vision in which Mary urged him to paint her image. So all the elements for sanctification were present: posthumous miracles, uncorrupted body, an icon, and finally a Vita.

Closer analysis of this tale permits a better understanding of Mary's life style and the opposition it aroused in her husband and in-laws. First, the hagiographer notes that when she lived in a small town she went to the cathedral for services because there was no private chapel attached to her house. This implies that among the upper classes it was the norm to have a private chapel, not just for convenience and as a mark of social status, but because it was considered more seemly for the women of the family to worship within the privacy of their homes. Mary, however, had to walk a considerable distance morning and evening to attend services at the cathedral, so that twice a day she was out in public. The hagiographer

---

[14]Ibid., 697CD.

implies this was not customary behavior for women, but that Mary was driven by her great piety to go to church regularly, even though a certain amount of personal hardship was involved. In any case, as a result of her church attendance, Mary had ample opportunity to see for herself local beggars and poor people. Not only did she give money to "the poor and monks," as we are told by the hagiographer, but she also gave away all her clothing. Her in-laws criticized her behavior on two accounts: she was squandering the family fortune and she was suspected of adultery. The first charge reveals that not all Byzantines supported the concept of generous contributions to the poor; most felt that a certain restraint was necessary in order to safeguard the family property. Second, Mary's personal contact with men not related to her made her more liable to accusations of sexual misconduct.

Like Mary the Younger, Thomais of Lesbos was a married woman who became a saint even though she remained in the world and never entered a convent.[15] Thomais lived in the first half of the tenth century, and was the only daughter of a pious, relatively prosperous couple from Lesbos. After her birth, her parents moved to the Bosporus, near Constantinople. At the surprisingly late age of twenty-four, Thomais was married, against her wishes, to a coarse and brutal man named Stephen. He beat her frequently, but she endured patiently the suffering inflicted upon her. She led a pious life, visiting the churches of Constantinople, feeding the poor, and clothing them with garments made from material she wove with her own hands. She wandered around the agora, seeking out homeless people in its dark corners, so that she could pay their debts. Her husband tried to restrict her philanthropic activities and kept close watch over her pocketbook. In contrast to Mary, who performed miracles only after her death, Thomais effected miracles in her lifetime. Particularly noteworthy is her healing of two specifically female complaints: she cured one prostitute who had suffered from a flow of blood for six years, and healed another prostitute who had cancer of the breast. After fourteen miserable years of marriage, Thomais died at age thirty-eight; posthumous miracles occurred at her tomb for forty days following her death. Thomais' hagiographer praised her masculine qualities: "although female by nature, in her virtue and asceticism she greatly exceeded the manliness of men";[16] he also compared her to a martyr because of the abuse she suffered from her husband.

---

[15]Her Vita is published in *Acta Sanctorum*, Nov. 4:234–46. For a summary in French, see Da Costa-Louillet, "Saints de Constantinople," 836–39. An article by A. Laiou, "Hobias tes hagias Thomaidos tes Lesbias," in *Kathemerine zoe sto Byzantio* (Athens: Kentro Byzantinon Ereunon, 1989), appeared after this study was submitted for publication.

[16]*Acta Sanctorum*, Nov. 4:235DE.

Several features of Thomais' life remind us of Mary of Bizye. She frequently left her house to visit churches, and spent a considerable amount of money on food and clothing for the poor. Her husband tried to limit the extent of her charitable activity, and beat her frequently. The hagiographer states explicitly that Stephen was upset by the way his wife was spending the family fortune; left unsaid is whether he also disapproved of his wife's spending time outside the house, and associating with lower echelons of society. The account of Thomais' healing of the two prostitutes is interesting not only because it describes a woman curing diseases characteristic of women, but because it implies that she came into personal contact with prostitutes.

The Vita of a slightly earlier saint, Athanasia of Aegina, who lived in the first part of the ninth century, presents some parallels with the biographies of Mary and Thomais.[17] Athanasia was married not once, but twice, since her first husband was killed in battle a few days after their wedding. During her second marriage, Athanasia led a life devoted to prayer and asceticism, and practiced charity toward all those in need, widows, orphans, wandering monks, even to members of the heretical sect of Athinganoi, who were in dire straits at a time of famine. She gave them not only food but clothing.[18] Unlike Mary and Thomais, however, Athanasia enjoyed good relations with her husband, and even persuaded him to retire to a monastery. Thereupon she, too, was able to take monastic vows, and spent the rest of her life in the seclusion of the convent.

It is now recognized that the Vitae of Mary and Thomais represent a new type of saintly woman in Byzantium.[19] Popular cults developed at the tombs of these married laywomen, who provided attractive role models for the secluded women of the Byzantine Empire. Asceticism in remote hermitages or even retirement to a convent was not an option for many women, but most could identify with Thomais and Mary, emulate their piety and charity, and if necessary, bear with fortitude the miserable existence of a "battered wife." It is possible that the sanctification of Mary and Thomais was prompted by that of the empress Theophano, who died only a few years before Mary of Bizye, for there are definite similarities in

---

[17]L. Carras, "The Life of St. Athanasia of Aegina," in *Maistor: Classical, Byzantine and Renaissance Studies for Robert Browning*, ed. A. Moffatt (Canberra: Australian Association for Byzantine Studies, 1984), 199–224.

[18]Ibid., 213.5

[19]E. Patlagean, "L'histoire de la femme déguisée en moine et l'évolution de la sainteté féminine à Byzance," *Studi medievali*, ser. 3, no. 17 (1976): 620–22, reprinted in *Structure sociale, famille, chrétienté à Byzance* (London: Variorum, 1981), pt. XI; A. Kazhdan, "Hermitic, Cenobitic, and Secular Ideals in Byzantine Hagiography of the Ninth to Twelfth Centuries," *Greek Orthodox Theological Review* 30 (1985): 474f.

their lives. Although the hagiographer of Theophano is silent about the marital discord between the empress and her husband, it is known from other sources, for example, the *Vita Euthymii*, that Leo wanted to divorce her and that he kept a mistress.[20] Theophano was forced to endure patiently rumors and innuendo rather than physical abuse.[21] She devoted herself to pious works, and lived ascetically, although within the confines of a palace instead of a nunnery. It seems clear that in the late ninth and tenth centuries there developed a new type of woman saint, the married woman, who nobly endured an unhappy marriage, found solace in works of charity, and engaged in the prayer, fasting, and night vigils normally associated with monastic life.

CHARITABLE WORK OF DEACONESSES

As we have seen, it was relatively rare for upper-class women personally to provide care for the poor, sick, and elderly; they preferred to donate funds so that others could provide these services. One might well ask who did the actual nursing and ministration to the poor. For much of the Byzantine period the answer seems to be deaconesses. The role of deaconesses in the early church has been much discussed, especially their distinction from the so-called order of widows.[22] It has now been concluded that deaconesses originally played a major role in the baptism of women, at the time when large numbers of adult women were being baptized by immersion. Once the empire was Christianized, however, and infant baptism became the norm, the deaconesses seem to have served primarily as visiting nurses, tending the sick and bathing them. They also acted as social workers, visiting the homes of poor families and reporting to the bishop on the conditions they found. It is assumed that deaconesses worked as nurses and attendants in orphanages, hospitals, poorhouses, and so on. They are last attested in the twelfth century in connection with the vast complex of St. Paul founded by Alexios I Komnenos,[23] but their specific function at this time is not described.

The best-known deaconess is St. Olympias, who lived in the late fourth and early fifth centuries.[24] She was an extremely wealthy young widow who became a supporter of the patriarch John Chrysostom. Her

[20]See P. Karlin-Hayter, *Vita Euthymii Patriarchae CP* (Brussels: Editions de Byzantion, 1970), 37–41, 45.

[21]Vita in *Zwei griechische Texte*, ed. Kurtz, 42.

[22]R. Gryson, *The Ministry of Women in the Early Church* (Collegeville, Minn.: Liturgical Press, 1980), 30–34, 41–43, 75–99. See also C. Vagaggini, "L'ordinazione delle diaconesse nella tradizioine greca e bizantina," *Orientalia Christiana Periodica* 40 (1974): 145–89, and A.G. Martimort, *Les diaconesses. Essai historique* (Rome: C.L.V. Edizioni Liturgiche, 1982).

[23]Anna Komnene, *Alexiad*, bk. 15, chap. 7, ed Reiffescheid, 2:293

biography tells us that "she distributed all of her unlimited and immense wealth and assisted everyone, simply and without distinction." She gave John Chrysostom 10,000 pounds of gold and 20,000 pounds of silver, all her lands in Thrace, Galatia, Cappadocia and Bithynia, as well as houses and baths in Constantinople, a mill, and suburban properties.[25] She was ordained a deaconess and built a monastery right next to the patriarchate. She was joined in this convent by 250 women, including at least three of her relatives who gave all their possessions to the convent and were ordained deaconesses. These deaconesses did not go out of the convent, however, so it seems that not all deaconesses engaged in nursing and similar services. When Chrysostom was exiled from the patriarchate, Olympias as his supporter was banished to Nikomedeia, where she spent the rest of her life. Near the end of the Vita her hagiographer concludes: she "helped ... the beggars, the prisoners, and those in exile; quite simply she distributed her alms over the entire inhabited world. And the blessed Olympias herself burst the supreme limit in her almsgiving and her humility." She devoted herself to "supplying the widows, raising the orphans, shielding the elderly, [and] looking after the weak...."[26]

PHILANTHROPIC INSTITUTIONS

Let us now turn from the individuals who engaged in charitable activities to the principal institutions which provided welfare services to the needy: the orphanages, poorhouses, hospices, hospitals, leprosaria, and old-age homes. For the most part the sources which describe these foundations do not specify whether they were segregated according to sex, but I assume that in many cases they provided for both men and women. One exception would be the rarely attested *cherotropheion*, a home for widows. There are few detailed descriptions of philanthropic institutions; they are usually just mentioned in a list of buildings sponsored by a wealthy imperial or aristocratic patron. Fortunately, the historian Anna Komnene, who wrote a biography of her father Alexios I Komnenos, did include a lengthy passage on the complex which he founded in Constantinople to care for the poor and needy, a veritable "city for the poor" in the vicinity of the Church of St. Paul:

> In a circle were numerous buildings, houses for the poor and ... dwellings for mutilated persons. One could see them coming

[24]A.–M. Malingrey, "Vie d'Olympias," in *Jean Chrysostome: Lettres à Olympias*, 2d ed., ed. A.-M. Malingrey (Paris, Editions du Cerf, 1968), 393–449; Eng. tr. E. A. Clark, *Jerome ,Chrysostom and Friends* (New York: Mellen, 1979), 127–42.

[25]Clark, *Jerome, Chrysostom and Friends*, chap. 5, pp. 130–31.

[26]Ibid., chaps. 13, 15, pp. 137, 139.

there singly, the blind, the lame, people with some other trouble. … The buildings were in a double circle and were two-storeyed, for some of these maimed persons, men and women, live on the upper floor, while others drag themselves along below on the street level. … Each of them, man or woman, dwelt in the house built for them and everything, so far as food or clothing are concerned, was provided for them through the emperor's generosity. …I myself saw an old woman being assisted by a young girl, a blind person being led by the hand by another man who had his sight.… a man who had no hands being aided by the hands of his friends, babies being nursed by foster mothers and the paralyzed being waited on by strong, healthy men.[27]

Evidently people with all sorts of needs were cared for in this complex, and wherever possible they helped each other in whatever way they could.

Sometimes a male monastery might include an institution which provided care for both men and women, such as the hospital of the Pantokrator monastery in Constantinople, described in the typikon of 1136 of its founder, John II Komnenos.[28] The 50-bed hospital, designed for lay patients rather than the monks themselves, included a 12-bed ward specifically assigned to women, and had a female physician on its staff. The same monastery, however, had an old-age home that was strictly limited to men, as was its leprosarium.

HOSPITALS

The Byzantine charitable institution about which the most information survives is the hospital.[29] Since Byzantine hospitals are discussed in another article in this volume,[30] I shall mention only a few points about hospitals specifically designed for women. An early example is found in seventh-century Alexandria, where the patriarch John the Almsgiver was particularly concerned about the plight of refugees from the Arab invasions. He decided to establish seven maternity hospitals of forty beds each where women could give birth and then recuperate for a full week afterwards.[31] We do not know whether the women's ward at the Pantokrator

[27]Anna Komnene, *Alexiad*, bk. 15, chap. 7, ed. Reifferscheid, 21–92; Sewter, tr., *Alexiad of Anna Commena*, 492f.

[28]P. Gautier, ed. "Le typikon du Christ Sauveur Pantocrator," *Revue des études byzantines* 32 (1974): 83–109, with French tr.

[29]The basic work is T. S. Miller, *The Birth of the Hospital in the Byzantine Empire* (Baltimore: Johns Hopkins University Press, 1985).

[30]T. S. Miller, "The Orphanotropheion of Constantinople" (chap. 5 of this work).

monastery was similarly designed for obstetrics or was instead for women with a variety of ailments; since the patients are described as "ill," the latter alternative seems most likely.

The Constantinopolitan convent of Lips, restored in the capital in the late thirteenth century by Dowager Empress Theodora Palaiologina, widow of Michael VIII, also had a small attached twelve-bed hospital, limited to the care of laywomen.[32] This hospital received an endowment that provided funds for the salaries of the hospital staff, as well as food, clothing, firewood, and lamp oil for the patients. The hospital had a surprisingly large staff, twenty in all, to care for twelve patients: three doctors, one assistant, one nurse, one head pharmacist, and two apothecaries, six attendants, one blood-letter, three servants, one cook, and one laundress.

CONVENTS

Nunneries played an important role in helping the less fortunate members of society, especially women. Although convents were not specifically designed as welfare institutions, they did provide all kinds of charitable services. Their philanthropic activities took several forms: the distribution of food, money, and perhaps clothing to poor people who came to beg at the convent gates; the admission to the nunnery of women with a variety of problems; and the provision of services through affiliated institutions such as the hospital at the Lips convent just described.

The foundation charters of nunneries are the best source of information about the charitable donations which they made to the poor, since these documents set forth the rules and regulations for all aspects of life in the convent. It was the custom at most monasteries, male as well as female, to give away food daily at the gates to those in need. This normally consisted of bread plus leftovers from the principal meal of the day. As a fourteenth-century typikon enjoins, "On no account should you store away the leftovers from this daily meal of yours, nor keep them for the next day, but rather you must distribute them to the poor, my brethren in Christ, those who are driven by starvation and harsh and grievous famine to come to your gate every day, and who look to your generosity, so as to be nourished by you with a small morsel of bread and the tiniest bit of food." That this distribution of food was specifically viewed as an act of Christian charity is made clear by the next sentence, "With these small surplus morsels of yours, you will alleviate to a degree their great poverty, with both compassionate mercy and with much gladness, since through

---

[31]*Leontios' von Neapolis, Leben des heiligen Johannes des Barmherzigen*, ed. H. Gelzer (Freiburg-Leipzig, 1893), 13, 18–19.

[32]Delehaye, *Typica*, 134.

them you all but feed Christ, and through them you really welcome Christ, and as a result you do yourselves an even greater favor than you do them."[33] There follows a page of quotations from the Bible stressing the importance of mercy towards the poor. Several typika specify that when a nun died, for forty days following her death her portion of food was to be given to the poor.[34] In the early fourteenth century the patriarch Athanasios I of Constantinople urged all monks and nuns to eat only once a day, and noted that whatever food was saved should be distributed to the needy who were suffering from famine.[35] There are some indications that nuns' cast-off clothing was also donated to the poor.[36] Although the texts are usually not specific on this point, it seems probable that normally both male and female monasteries gave away food to beggars of both sexes, but a few male monasteries discriminated against poor women; the monks of Meteora were not to give food to a woman even if she were dying of hunger.[37] As one typikon for a male monastery ordained, "It is our desire that no one should go away from the gate empty-handed, unless it should be a woman. No distribution must be made to them, not because we despise our fellow human beings, but out of concern lest they cause harm by coming more frequently to the gate and thus become a cause of evil rather than good for the monks within."[38] It should be noted, however, that even those typika of male monasteries which prohibited giving food to poor women on a daily basis did allow women to partake of the general food distribution made on special feast days, such as the Dormition of the Virgin, and days of memorial services, since these occasions occurred only a few times a year.[39]

In addition to the daily donations of food, most monasteries made special distributions on certain important feast days and anniversaries. Thus on the feast day of the patron saint of the monastery, and on other

[33]Typikon for Bebaias Elpidos nunnery, in Delehaye, ed., *Typica*, 68–69.

[34]E.g., ibid., 98–99.

[35]*Les Regestes des actes du patriarcat de Constantinople*. I, *Les actes des patriarches*, 14, *Les regestes de 1208 à 1309*, ed. V. Laurent (Paris: Institut Français d'Etudes Byzantines, 1971), no. 1651 (hereafter, *Reg Patr*).

[36]For example, the typikon for the Lips nunnery provides that the nuns should return their old and worn-out clothes to the storeroom when they receive new garments; Delehaye, ed. *Typica*, 126. It is possible that some of these old clothes were given away, while others were mended; idem, 73. The vita of Irene of Chrisobalanton states expressly that her old habits were donated to poor women; J. O. Rosenquist, *The Life of St. Irene, Abbess of Chrysobalanton* (Stockholm: Almquist & Wiksell, 1986), 48.

[37]N. Bees, "Symbole eis ten historian ton monon ton Meteoron," *Byzantis* 1 (1909): 251.

[38]P. Gautier, "Le typikon de la Théotokos Evergétis," *Revue des études byzantines* 40 (1982): 83, lines 1184–88.

[39]Ibid., 83, lines 1188–91.

major holidays (for example, Christmas, Epiphany, Easter, Pentecost, the feast of the Dormition of Virgin) extra bread, wine, and small coins were handed out at the gate. Likewise on the anniversaries of the deaths of the relatives of the founder of the monastery there were special distributions of bread, wine, and money. The typika of some convents list in great detail the exact amounts to be handed out in commemoration of each family member. These donations were viewed as a method of assuring the spiritual salvation both of the deceased relative and of the nuns who oversaw the distribution of food.

As in so many aspects of Byzantine life, the instructions for these donations reflect a hierarchical pecking order, indicating the importance of each member of the founder's family. For example, the twelfth-century typikon drafted by the empress Irene Doukaina for the convent of the Theotokos Kecharitomene specified that on the death anniversaries of her husband, the emperor Alexios I Komnenos, and herself, ten *modioi* of bread, eight measures of wine, and ten coins be distributed. To commemorate the deaths of their children, five *modioi* of bread were to be distributed and six coins, while most sons-in-law and daughters-in-law merited three *modioi* of bread. Irene listed nineteen different relatives whose death anniversaries were to be commemorated with food distributions, plus nine feast days meriting extra food donations, for a total of twenty-eight days on which more food would be available at the convent gates.[40] Since each monastery would be commemorating the deaths of the founder's family members and the feast days of patron saints on different days, this would mean that a poor person who knew the distribution schedules could plan to move from monastery to monastery to beg. A modern parallel can be found at urban soup kitchens, many of which cannot afford to provide three meals a day, seven days a week. Some serve only during the week, others only on weekends, some only lunch, others only dinner. The needy individual who masters the system can plan to go from one church to another to be assured at least one free meal a day.

PROVISION OF SOCIAL SERVICES WITHIN THE CONVENT

One of the principal ways in which convents provided social services was to offer refuge for girls and women in need, whether they were orphans, poor widows, refugees, the elderly, the mentally ill, or battered wives.[41]

---

[40]P. Gautier, "Le typikon de la Théotokos Kécharitôménè," *Revue des études byzantines* 43 (1985): 109–11, 119–25.

[41]For an analysis of the reasons why women entered convents, see A.-M. Talbot, "Late Byzantine Nuns: By Choice or Necessity?" *Byzantinische Forschungen* 9 (1985): 103–17.

Many of these women actually took vows and became nuns; others lived at the convent as lay pensioners.

We know that nunneries did occasionally take in orphans, although some discouraged the practice because of their concern that the presence of young children might be disruptive to convent life.[42] These girls were cared for and educated, and usually about the age of sixteen were allowed to decide whether they wished to take monastic vows or to leave the convent. Among the younger women who found refuge in convent life were those escaping from unhappy marriages, such as a woman from Thessalonike, who in the fourteenth century became a nun after her husband falsely accused her of adultery and murdered her mother![43] Convents might also provide a refuge for unwed mothers. In a case from fourth-century Egypt a young unmarried woman became pregnant and falsely accused an *anagnostes* (reader) of seducing her. Although he was not the father, he took pity on the woman, agreed to marry her, and then took her to a convent where he begged a deaconess to take care of the woman until the birth of her child.[44]

The largest category of women who took refuge in the convent were widows. In Byzantium it was quite common for women to take monastic vows in middle age, after their children were grown, especially if their husbands predeceased them. Sometimes they entered convents primarily for spiritual reasons; in other cases loneliness and economic factors were the motivation. In the thirteenth century a widow from Thessaly named Zoe was concerned about her future because she had no relatives to look after her in old age. She did have some assets, however, and was admitted to a local convent in exchange for donating her ancestral property, including three vineyards, four fields, a fig tree, and two houses. In return the convent agreed to look after her for the rest of her life, and at the time of her death to arrange for proper burial and commemoration at annual services.[45] Similar arrangements are found in the medieval West. The agreement was a gamble for both parties: if the elderly person died shortly after she entered the monastery, then she had liquidated her assets to little avail; on the other hand, if she lived a long time and required considerable care, then the convent came off second best.

The most vivid description of the care of the elderly within a convent is found in the ninth-century Life of St. Theodora of Thessalonike; it should be noted, however, that the patient was a nun who had spent her

---

[42]See,e.g., typikon for Belbaias Elpidos nunnery, Delehaye, ed., *Typica*, 97–98.

[43]F. Miklosich, J. Müller, *Acta et diplomata graeca medii aevi sacra et profana* (Vienna, 1862): 2:238–40.

[44]*The Lausiac History of Palladius*, ed. C. Butler (repr. Hildesheim: Olms, 1967), 2:165–66

[45]Miklosich and Müller, *Acta*, 4:393–96.

career at the convent, not an "outsider." When Anna, the abbess of The-odora's monastery, retired because of old age (she was supposedly 108), Theodora took Anna's care upon herself, especially after the aged nun fell in the courtyard and broke her hip. She was then bedridden for seven years until her death at the remarkable age of 120. Nursing Anna was a sore trial for Theodora, since the old woman became senile, and cursed and struck the younger nun when she was caring for her. Theodora perse-vered, however, mindful of the injunction, "Child, care for your father in his old age, and do not cause him grief in his lifetime. And if he should lose his senses, have mercy on him and do not dishonor him...."[46]

Many of the widows who turned to convents for assistance were refu-gees or displaced persons, especially in the final centuries of the Byzantine empire when the Turks were inexorably advancing and conquering Byz-antine territory. In the fourteenth century, for example, a woman named Eudokia had been forced by the Turkish conquests to leave her home in Asia Minor and emigrate to Macedonia in Greece. Subsequently, her hus-band died and her two sons were recruited by the Turks in the dreaded child levy for the Janissary troops. Eudokia found herself "deprived of everything; [she] had no relative or any other consolation... [she] wept and lamented the loss of her dear children ... and had no one to help her ... she was in a strange and alien land and had no parents or husband." Therefore, she gave all her possessions to the poor and entered the female part of a double monastery. Note that even this woman, who was in dire straits, realized that there were some people even worse off, and gave away her meager possessions. The story ended happily: Eudokia's two sons (one of whom was to become St. Philotheos the Athonite) escaped from the Turks, and by miraculous coincidence took the monastic habit at the same monastery where their mother was a nun, so that the family was reunited.[47]

The convent also provided a refuge for women afflicted with mental illness; miracle accounts frequently describe the cure of a demoniac by a saint and her subsequent adoption of the monastic habit. One example is a woman named Katenitzina living in Brousa (later Bursa) in the four-teenth century at the time of the Ottoman conquests of northwestern Ana-tolia. She suffered from what is now called Tourette's syndrome, but she

---

[46]Bishop Arsenij, *Zitie i podvigi sv. Feodory Solunskoj* (Jur'ev, 1899), 21–22; E. Kurtz, *Des Klerikers Gregorios Bericht über Leben, Wunderthäten und Translation der hl. Theodora von Thessa-lonich nebst der Metaphrase des Joannes Staurakios* (St. Petersburg, 1902), 21. See also E. Patla-gean, "Theodora de Thessalonique: Une sainte moniale et un culte citadin (IXe–XXe siècle)" in *Culto dei santi, istituzioni e classi sociali in eta preindustriale*, ed. S. P. Gajano, L. Sebastiani (Rome: L'Aguila, 1984), 39–67.

[47]B. Papoulia, "Die Vita des heiligen Philotheos vom Athos," *Südostforschungen* 22 (1963): 274–76.

was thought by her contemporaries to be afflicted with a demon. In the words of the compiler of a miracle collection, "the evil spirit continually lived with her for thirteen whole years and did not cease night and day to shout disgusting and uncouth words through her mouth, a strange sight for those who met with her and a really unpleasant encounter for travellers—sometimes it cursed those who passed by, sometimes it howled like a dog or uttered unintelligible and inarticulate sounds, sometimes it burst out in sardonic laughter, and other times it wept and assumed all sorts of postures." After Brousa fell to the Turks, Katenitzina managed to escape to Constantinople, where she made the rounds of healing shrines, trying to exorcise the demon which tormented her. She finally was cured at the tomb of the saintly patriarch Athanasios, and immediately thereafter entered the convent next to the shrine.[48] She was not only a refugee from the Turks but was recovering from serious mental illness, and she welcomed the opportunity to spend her remaining years as a nun. Another woman, named Tzourakina, who lived in Constantinople some eighty years later, was so seriously afflicted with mental illness that she was incompetent to handle her own affairs. In her case, the patriarch arranged for the sale of her house, and handed over the proceeds to a convent which agreed to look after the woman for the rest of her life.[49]

CONCLUSION

Religious life and philanthropy were inextricably entwined in Byzantium, especially since the church increasingly took over from the state responsibility for care of the needy. Most of the institutions that provided welfare services were directly or indirectly run by the church. The bread dole of Late Antiquity, the distribution of free bread to the people that had been a feature of the Roman Empire, was replaced to a certain extent by daily donations of food at the gates of monasteries. In the case of individuals, the chief motivation for charitable activity was the search for salvation, since the Byzantines believed that in feeding or otherwise aiding poor people they were ministering to Christ himself, and they hoped that as a reward for their acts of mercy God would look mercifully upon them on the Day of Judgment. For women, personal ministry to the needy offered yet another dimension, since it provided them with a socially acceptable opportunity for leaving the confines of their homes and interacting with people outside their immediate households.

[48] A.-M. Talbot, *Faith Healing in Late Byzantium: The Posthumous Miracles of the Patriarch Athanasios I of Constantinople by Theoktistos the Stoudite* (Brookline, Mass.: Hellenic College Press, 1983), 114–20.

[49] H. Hunger, "Zu den restlichen Inedita des Konstantinopler Patriarchatsregisters im cod. Vindob. Hist. gr. 48," *Revue des études byzantines* 24 (1966): 66–68. *Reg Patr*, fasc. 6, ed. J. Darrouzés (Paris: Institut Français d'Etudes Byzantines, 1979), no. 3257.

CHAPTER 7

HEARTS NOT PURSES?
POPE INNOCENT III'S ATTITUDE
TO SOCIAL WELFARE

BRENDA M. BOLTON

Innocent III, one of the most powerful and influential popes in medieval history, took seriously both the theory and the practice of his episcopal responsibilities for the poor, already described in the work of Bishop Rabbula. Innocent's ideas, reflecting the medieval theological and canonical tradition, are set forth in his two short treatises, *Book of Alms* and *In Praise of Charity*. Almsgiving is a medicine of salvation that removes the stain of sin and helps to eradicate the desires of the flesh. The natural and social disasters of the early thirteenth century provided manifold opportunities for Innocent to persevere in modeling his theology of charity. Of Innocent's many charitable activities ranging from feeding the poor to ransoming captives, it was his foundation of the Hospital of the Holy Spirit on the banks of the Tiber that epitomized his aspirations for social welfare in Rome, linking past and present, tradition and innovation, care of body and soul. The Hospital's services ranged from the acceptance of unwanted babies, with no questions asked, to an outreach program to the poor in the streets of the city.

In northern Europe, the twentieth century's last decade began with storms, with devastation, but not with total famine. This type of end-of-century phenomena would have been familiar in the decade of the 1190s, and indeed, was perhaps the main preoccupation as the twelfth century gave way to the thirteenth. Contemporary chroniclers described the suffering caused by a succession of natural calamities from 1194 to 1207, which resulted in a series of bad harvests from the Atlantic to the Apennines.[1] The specter of famine, worse north of the Alps before 1198, had moved south to the Mediterranean by the end of the century and plague

---

[1] *Oeuvres de Rigord et de Guillaume le Breton: Historiens de Philippe Auguste*, ed. H. F. Delaborde, *Recueil des Historiens de la France* 17 (Paris, 1882), 130–41.

followed in its wake.[2] Wolves appeared in inhabited areas where they had not previously been seen and vied with humans for the meager food supplies. In 1202, the Chronicler of the Cistercian Abbey of Fossanova (midway between Rome and Naples) wrote, "In this year, there were great gales, uprooting trees, damaging churches, overturning buildings and wreaking terrible destruction. This year was known to everyone as the year of hunger."[3] This truly disastrous period made a deep impression on contemporaries.

When such disasters occur today, local mayors establish funds to provide and maintain care and welfare for the stricken community. If the disaster is large-scale, national emergencies are declared and international relief agencies rush to the rescue. But what of France in the 1190s or Italy in the early thirteenth century? To whom then might one turn in the hour of need? With whom lay the responsibility of providing succor for the poor and vulnerable, particularly since the disaster was not just one emergency event but a continuous occurrence? Naturally, in the groves of academe and particularly in the University of Paris, there was much intellectual debate, both spiritual and theological, with Peter the Chanter (d. 1197), Robert de Courson (d. 1219), and Stephen Langton (d.1228) well to the fore.[4] A variety of initiatives—which others could take—were put forward.[5] The laity were to be encouraged to perform works of care and welfare.[6] Kings and princes were expected to provide generous gifts, implicit in their double duty to render both justice and charity to their

[2] "1199 ... scilicet fame, gladis et peste," *Auctore ignoti monachi Cisterciensis*. S. M. de Ferraria, ed. A. Guadenzi (Naples, 1888), 33. The following works have been of great value: J. M. Bienvenu, "Pauvreté, misères et charité en Anjou aux XIe et XIIe siècles," in *Moyen Age* 72 (1966): 389-424; ibid. 73 (1967): 5–34, 189–216; M. Mollat, "Pauvres et pauvreté dans le monde médiéval,"*La povertà del secolo xii e Francesco d'Assisi*, Atti del II Convegno Internazionale, Assisi 17-19 ottobre 1974 (Assisi: Societa internazionale di studi francescani, 1975), 81–97; M. Mollat, ed., *Etudes sur l'Histoire de la Pauvreté*, 2 vols. (Paris: Sorbonne, 1974; cited as *Etudes*); M. Mollat, *Les Pauvres au Moyen Age* (Paris: Hachette, 1978); M. Mollat, "Le problème de la pauvreté au XIIe siècle,"*Cahiers de Fanjeaux* 2, (1967): 23–24; M. Mollat, "Hospitalité et assistance au début du XIIIe siècle,"*Poverty in the Middle Ages*, ed. D. Flood (Werl-Westfallen: Dietrich-Coelde, 1975), 37–51.

[3] *Chronicon Fossaenovae Auctore Anonymo ... ad annum MCCXVII* in L.A. Muratori, *Rerum Italicarum Scriptores*, 25 vols. (Milan, 1723-1751), 7 (Milan, 1727): col. 886.

[4] J.W. Baldwin, *Masters, Princes and Merchants: the Social Views of Peter the Chanter and his Circle*, 2 vols. (Princeton: Princeton University Press, 1970); J. Longère, "Pauvreté et richesse chez quelques prédicateurs durant la seconde moitié du XIIe siècle,"in *Etudes*, 1:255–73.

[5] G. Couvreur, *Les Pauvres ont-ils des droits? Recherches sur le vol en cas d'extrême nécessité depuis la "Concordia"de Gratien (1140) jusqu'à Guillaume d'Auxerre (d.1231)* (Rome-Paris: Gregorian University, 1961) and ibid., "Pauvreté et droit des pauvres à la fin du XIIe siècle,"*Recherches et débats du CCIF* 49 (1964): 13-37.

[6] Mollat, "Hospitalité et assistance,"41-42; B. M. Bolton, "The Poverty of the Humiliati," in Flood, *Poverty in the Middle Ages*, 52-59.

subjects.[7] The rich should be induced to give to the poor in time of famine[8] while ecclesiastics, merely stewards of their goods, which belonged to the church, might not only be admonished but actually compelled to distribute alms.[9]

Did any positive results emerge from these high-level discussions? Perhaps not but already, in both rural and urban parishes human need called forth certain practical responses, especially to help those who could so easily fall below subsistence level.[10] Confraternities of like-minded lay people were established for the purpose of supporting those in need, including voluntary acts of manual labor and care for the sick.[11] Indeed, hospital foundations often developed from such spontaneous activities as tending the poor and leprous. Yet in spite of these voluntary initiatives, the chief burden of responsibility in the twelfth century still fell, as in earlier periods, on the church. Monasteries continued to play an important role in hospitality and works of mercy, albeit with an increasingly symbolic rather than strictly practical element.[12] For example, food was distributed in a liturgical ritual to a selected group of the poor. Local priests too could sometimes provide more than just the cure of souls. Julian of Cuenca (d.1207) earned his living by weaving rush baskets, and used all the revenue so gained for charitable works.[13] In such disastrous times, the body needed to be treated and healed before the soul could be attended to. Unfortunately, in the late twelfth century, the bishop in his diocese, who

---

[7] 1195 ... Rex Philippus motus pietate, largiores elemosynas de suo pauperibus erogandas precepit,"*Oeuvres de Rigord*, 132; *Recueil des Actes de Philippe-Auguste*, ed. E. Berger and A.F. Delaborde, (Paris, 1916), esp. 152, 183.

[8] Most famous of all was Theobald IV, Count of Blois and Champagne (c. 1090–1152). See Sermon XXXIX of Jacques de Vitry, *De comite Campaniae Theobaldo et leproso, Analecta Novissima Spicilegii Solesmensis altera continuatio*, ed. J.B. Pitra, (Tusculum, 1888), II, 449; Couvreur, *Les pauvres*, 165–166, 193–97; Baldwin, *Master, Princes and Merchants*, 1:237, 2:255–56; G. Gracco, "Dalla misericordia della cheisa alla misericordia del principe" in *La carità a Milano nei secoli xii-xv*, ed. M.P. Alberzoni and O. Grassi, (Milan: Jaca Book, 1989), 3–46

[9] B. Tierney, *Medieval Poor Law: A Sketch of Canonical Theory and Its Application in England* (Berkeley: University of California Press, 1959); Couvreur, "Les pauvres," 197–202.

[10] Tierney, *Medieval Poor Law*, 9–16.

[11] G. Ferri, "La Romana Fraternitas," in *Archivo della Società Romana di Storia Patria* 36, (1903) 453-466 (cited as *ASRSP*); G. G. Meersseman, *Ordo, Fraternitatis, Confraternite e pieta dei laici nel Medio Evo*, 3 vols. (Rome: Herder, 1977), 1:24–26; J. M. Bienvenu, "Fondations charitables laiques au XIIe siècle. L'exemple de l'Anjou,"in *Etudes* 1:563–69; G. Barone, "Il movimento francescano e la nascita delle confraternite Romana," *Richerche per la Storia Religiosa di Roma* 5 (1984): 71–80.

[12] M. Mollat, "Les moines et les pauvres XIe-XIIe siècles," in *Il monachesimo e la riforma ecclesiastica (1049–1122)* (Milan: Vita e Pensiero, 1971), 193–215.

[13] Julian, Bishop of Cuenca in the province of Toledo (1179-?1208), *Acta Sanctorum*, January II (Venice, 1734), 893–97.

ought to have been playing a key role, was more often than not, was not so doing.[14]

The task before the church ultimately devolved to the one bishop in Christendom who was both unable and unwilling to shirk this responsibility—the Pope. Innocent III, elected January 8, 1198, was later consecrated as bishop of his city on February 22 in that year.[15] At age thirty-seven (possibly the youngest-ever pope), he approached his formidable task with all the vigor and enthusiasm of his relative youth. He himself had witnessed those famine years between 1194 and 1198 while serving in the Curia and set about providing solutions to what others saw as an intractable problem. As a former student of the University of Paris and friend of all those elegant debaters,[16] he was well aware of their concern and theoretical suggestions. Peter the Chanter in particular had the opportunity to inspire him when this great academic was on a personal visit to the Curia in 1196 or 1197.[17] He was also well aware of the more active work of Fulk of Neuilly, Robert de Courson, and Jacques de Vitry[18] in the fields of popular preaching, pastoral care, and genuine caritative acts.

As Bishop of Rome, Innocent III inherited traditional ideas of welfare and its obligations from his predecessors, particularly Gregory the

[14]One model bishop was William le Donjeon, Bishop of Bourges, known as "the Hermit"(November 23, 1200–January 10, 1209), a Cistercian from Charlieu, diocese of Pontigny, *Acta Sanctorum*, January X: 627-81.

[15]*Gesta Innocentii PP III* in *Patrologia Latina* (hereafter *PL*) 214, ed. J.P. Migne, (Paris, 1855), cols. xvii-ccxxviii (cited as *Gesta*) 5: cols. xix-xx; M. Maccarrone, *Studi su Innocenzo III, Italia Sacra*, 17 (Padua: Antenore, 1972); Idem, "La 'cathedra Sancti Petri' nel Medievo: da Simbolo a reliquia," *Revista di Storia della Chiesa in Italia* 39 (1985): 349–47, esp. 427–29.

[16]M. Maccarrone, "Innocenzo III, Prima del Pontificato,"*ASRSP* 66 (1943): 59–134, esp. 93–108; W. Maleczek, *Papst und Kardinalskolleg von 1191 bis 1216*, (Vienna: Österreichen Akademie der Wissenschaften, 1984), 101–4. Cf. Innocent's work of this period, *De Miseria Conditionis Humanae, PL* 217, cols. 701–46, esp. col. 708. "O miserabilis mendicantis condicio. Et si petit, pudore confunditor et si non petit, egestate consumitur."

[17]Maccarrone, "Prima del Pontificato," 71-79; in Baldwin, *Masters, Princes and Merchants*, 1: 317–43, 336, 343; 2:227 n. 191, 2:233 n. 245.

[18]Fulk of Neuilly (d. 1202), see *The Historia Occidentalis of Jacques de Vitry: A Critical Edition*, ed. J. F. Hinnebusch, Spicilegium Friburgense 17 (Fribourg: Fribourg University Press, 1972): 94–101, 273–274; Mollatt, "Hospitalité et assistance," 467–47; Baldwin, *Masters, Princes and Merchants*, 1:19–25, 36–38, 102, 290; M. and C. Dickson, "Le Cardinal Robert de Courçon: Sa vie," in *Archives d'histoire doctrinale et littéraire du moyen âge* 9 (1934): 53–142, Jacques de Vitry (1160/70–1240), was Augustinian canon of St. Nicholas at Oignies (1211–1216), Bishop of Acre (1216–1227), Auxilary Bishop of Liège (1227–1229) , and Cardinal-Bishop of Tusculum (1229–1240); see *Historia Occidentalis* for a critical bibliography of De Vitry.

Great (590-604).[19] An administrative framework had then existed for the time-honored responsibilities of feeding the poor, *miserabiles personae*, and arranging for the welfare of captives and their ransoming. Linked to the care of the indigent and sick was the upkeep of *zenodochia* or hostels for poor strangers and pilgrims arriving in Rome without lodgings.[20] Innocent aimed to revive and update support for such charitable foundations both within Rome and elsewhere. We know from the Pope's anonymous biographer in his Deeds or *Gesta* of his concern for the poor and disadvantaged, repeating Christ's own exhortation to provide alms and charity for those in need.[21] His ideas are set out in two short treatises, the *Libellus de Eleemosyna* (*Book of Alms*) and the *Encomium Charitatis* (*In Praise of Charity*), which apply the tradition of almsgiving to his time.[22]

It will be rewarding to step aside to examine these two works as the basis for Innocent's reasoning on the care of those in need. His *Book of Alms* consists of two short chapters, full of scriptural texts. Almsgiving removes the stain of sin and washes away vice. Almsgiving benefits, liberates, redeems, protects, seeks out, perfects, blesses, justifies and saves. Innocent demonstrates that one who professes faith in Christ Jesus cannot possibly ignore almsgiving but such giving is worthless if there is no real charity of heart. People have to make themselves ready, eager, and suitable to give in the same way as they would prepare for salvation. Fasting is good but almsgiving is better. While fasting, which starves and weakens the body, is a matter for the individual alone, almsgiving is of positive benefit for it restores the bodies of others. Prayer is good but almsgiving is more universal, affecting one's neighbor before ascending to God. Nor should the poverty of the donor ever be an excuse to avoid almsgiving: the value of the widow's mite is one of Innocent's favorite themes[23]

Innocent is completely in accord with the canonists, conceiving almsgiving as an act of justice or of love but never as a matter of sentimental impulse.[24] He is at pains to stress that effective almsgiving needs prac-

---

[19] F. Niederer, "Early Medieval Charity,"in *Church History* 21 (1952): 285–95; J. Richards, *Consul of God: the Life and Times of Gregory the Great* (London: Routledge & Kegan Paul, 1980), 95–97. Cf. PL 217, Sermo XIII, *In Festo S. Gregorii Papae*, cols. 513–22, where Innocent III places charity first amongst his great predecessor's qualities. I am grateful to Conrad Leyser who allowed me to read a draft of his Oxford D. Phil. thesis on Gregory's charitable works.

[20] W. Schonfeld, "Die Zenodochien in Italien und Frankreich im frühen Mittelalter," *Savigny-Zeitschrift* 43 (1922): 1–54.

[21] *Gesta* CXLIII, cxcvi-cc. Cf. *De miseria divitis et pauperis, PL* 217, cols. 708–9.

[22] Ibid., cols. 745–64. In MS Vat Lat 700, *De Eleemosyna* is incorporated into Innocent's Lenten Sermons between fols. 25r and 28v..

[23] Ibid., cols. 747, 748, 749–50, 752–53; see also A. Albani, *Collectionis Bullarum Sacrosanctae Basilicae Vaticanae*, 1: 79, 82.

[24] Couvreur, "Les pauvres,"121–26.

tical organization—well known by our relief agencies today—and sets down four points to be considered: cause, outcome, means, and order.[25]

1. The cause: an urgent need which must be met by an act of charity.

2. The outcome: should be a blessing for all concerned.

3. The means: almsgiving, which should be carried out joyfully. Here Innocent cites St. Paul (2 Cor. 9:7), "God loves a cheerful giver."

4. The order: almsgiving should be performed regularly.

For a work of charity to be a meritorious act pleasing to God it had to be inspired by right intent, the correct attitude to God and to one's neighbor. While St. Augustine defines two kinds of almsgiving—of the heart and of money, Innocent's definition is fuller. For him it becomes a three-fold activity that involves the heart, mouth, and action.[26] Compassion comes from the heart, admonition and encouragement from the mouth, and generosity from actions. Nor is almsgiving ever restricted: alms must be given equally to the good and to the wicked, to the pious and impious, to friend and foe alike. What determines almsgiving is need and opportunity. If at all possible, the circumstances must be weighed and a practical decision made about where and to whom more charitable welfare should be given. In so doing, almsgiving becomes a medicine of salvation against all ills. If one special quality is to be sought in the almsgiver, it is perseverance.[27] Perseverance excludes impatience, eliminates contempt, and fights against obstinacy. Perseverance produces an adult donor of mature habit with no sentimental self-esteem who is the best giver of alms; the spiritual rewards will speak for themselves.

Innocent's *In Praise of Charity* carries further the sentiments of the *Book of Alms* by showing how the spiritual benefits of charitable actions help eradicate the desires of the flesh. The virtue of charity is that it is inseparable from the life of Christ himself, his crucifixion and resurrection, from the love of God the Father, and from the guidance of the Holy Spirit.[28] Yet there are dangers in performing an act of charity when one simply follows one's own wishes and desires in the matter of choice. It is through God's grace that failure will be prevented and the true humility of the virtuous giver ensured. In many ways this brief work by Innocent epitomizes the

---

[25]*PL* 217, cols. 355–56.
[26]Augustine, *City of God* 1:18; *PL* 41, col. 31; cf. *PL* 217, cols. 355–56.
[27]*Pl* 217, cols. 759–62.
[28] Ibid., cols. 761–64.

vita apostolica, the life of the apostles in the Jerusalem community updated to the twelfth century and underpins all his charitable and welfare activities.[29]

Both treatises are deeply serious and thoughtful works, perhaps written in 1202 or 1203 when, as his biographer tells us, Innocent boasted of fulfilling the Lord's work[30] as did the apostles in doing the work of Christ their Savior. The natural disasters of the time were then very much on his mind. In the spring of 1202, after a disastrous winter and little prospect of a harvest to come,[31] the pope, who had been at Anagni, rapidly returned to Rome when he heard of the widespread distress there and began the distribution of alms. This he did in a variety of ways, both organizationally and materially. To those who were too ashamed to beg publicly (perhaps the noble poor who were able to keep such sums safe), he ensured that they received money secretly in sufficient amounts to sustain them for a week at a time. On the other hand, those who begged openly in the streets received sufficient for each day (for they might dissipate anything more than day-to-day handouts). The number of this multitude reduced to such distress exceeded 8,000 of the approximately 30,000 total population.[32] Still more received alms in the form of food in their own homes. Thus the hungry poor were freed from imminent danger, and Innocent could exhort the rich and powerful to follow his example.[33] Here Innocent again shows himself in tune with contemporary canonists who believed that a poor man had a right to the help he received and should not be humiliated in any way.[34] Yet he was not content to leave matters of welfare to his example alone. All bishops and archbishops in the Church were his potential agents.[35]

The letters—and there were many—that Innocent wrote to Berengar II (1190–1212), Archbishop of Narbonne in Languedoc, show clearly the

---

[29] E. W. McDonell, "The *vita apostolica*: Diversity or Dissent?" *Church History* 24 (1955): 15–31; G. Olsen, "The Idea of the *Ecclesia Primitiva* in the Writings of the Twelfth-Century Canonists," *Traditio* 25 (1969): 61–81; M. D. Chenu, *Nature, Man and Society in the Twelfth Century: Essays on New Theological Perspectives in the Latin West*, trans. J. Taylor and L. K. Little, (Chicago: University of Chicago Press, 1968), 239–46.

[30] *Gesta* CXLIII, col. cxcvi. Interea dominus Innocentius, suum jactans in Domino cogitatum, operibus pietatis plenius insistebat.

[31] *Chronicon Fossaenovae* 1202, col. 886.

[32] See *Gesta* CXLIII, cols. cxcvi-cxcix.

[33] One such follower was the Roman nobleman Peter of Parenzo, who gave secretly to the poor when he visited them by night. See S. Pietro Parenzo, *La legenda scritta dal Maestro Giovanni, Canonico di Orvieto*, A. Natalini, ed., Lateranum NS 2 (Rome, 1936): 157.

[34] B. Tierney, "The Decretists and the Deserving Poor," *Comparative Studies in Society and History* I (1958-59): 360–73.

[35] December 5, 1198. *Die Register Innocenz III.*, eds. O. Hageneeder and A. Haidacher, (Graz-H. Böhlaus Nachf., 1964), nos. 445, 668; *PL* 214, cols. 421–22; B. M. Bolton, "*Via ascetica*: a papal quandary," *Studies in Church History* 22 (1985): 161–91, esp. 175–76.

pope's view of the way in which a late-twelfth-century bishop should function.[36] Had not Gratian himself said that a bishop ought to be solicitous and vigilant concerning the defense of the poor and the relief of the oppressed? Charity, generosity, concern for the welfare of his flock, integrity and honesty in the handling of tithes and alms were just some of the necessary qualities of a bishop. Berengar failed spectacularly to match up! In Innocent's eyes he was the worst of offenders—where his heart should have been, there was instead a purse![37] The Pope's letter of 1200 could not have been more scathing in its condemnation. The natural disasters of the age now seemed to be reflected in the religious disasters afflicting the Church of Narbonne. The depths of adversity were marked there both literally and metaphorically by a weeping and shedding of tears.[38] In the darkness of that province, gold had ceased to shine and bright colors lost their hue. Clergy were afflicted with every variety of misery; people saw bishops as no more than a laughing stock, and the church as a whole, the bride of Christ, was held in contempt and utter derision.[39] Fertile ground indeed for the seeds of heresy!

The cause of all this evil was the Archbishop of Narbonne himself. "He it is whose god is money, who lives by avarice and greed and by extorting money from those who sought his services as archbishop."[40] Had he not quite openly charged the Bishop of Maguelonne 50 shillings for his consecration? What Berengar himself had so freely accepted, he was unwilling to pass on to others in the same way. Such a man, says Innocent, has his heart where his treasure is and loves the sight of gold better than the sun. He is far more concerned with the glory of money than the glory of God. In the ten years since Berengar's election, in the shadow of his great predecessors, the Archbishops of Narbonne, he had not once carried out a visitation of his province nor even of his own parish. Pastoral care for the welfare of his flock had been replaced totally by greed. The pope's order to convene a council was met with contempt.

---

[36] K. Pennington, *Pope and Bishops in the Thirteenth Century: The Papal Monarchy in the Twelfth and Thirteenth Centuries* (Philadelphia: University of Pennsylvania Press, 1984), 48–51; C. Morris, *The Papal Monarchy: The Western Church from 1050-1250* (Oxford: Clarendon Press, 1989), 434.

[37] Cujus mens pecuniae avida ... qui habens cor suum ubi est thesaurus suus. See Jacques de Vitry, *Historia Occidentalis*, 78–79. *PL* 214, cols. 902–5. Cf. P. Baumann, "The Deadliest Sin: Warnings against Avarice and Usury on Romanesque Capitals in Auvergne,"*Church History* 59 (1990): 7–18.

[38] *PL* 214, col. 903.

[39] Ibid., col. 904.

[40] Ibid., col. 905. Cujus Deus nummus est et gloria in confusione ejus ... a Magalonensis episcopo pro consecratione sua, solidos[*sic*] quengentos exegit.

Berengar feared neither God nor the Holy See and made no attempt to fulfil the papal mandate.[41]

Further letters reveal Innocent's continuing concern that the bishops in the province of Narbonne still followed their archbishop in their lack of care for the welfare of their flocks. In June 1203, Innocent wrote that the church of Narbonne was still in a state of dereliction.[42] The poor were seeking bread but it was not being broken for them. They died and no one cared. Clearly Berengar was still inactive. On 29 January 1204, Innocent wrote once more in even sterner terms. He reminded the Archbishop that the highest place in God's house was reserved for the gospel injunction to charity.[43] He implored Berengar to feed his sheep before he fed himself. Hunger is still in the land and the poor seek bread, both for the body and the spirit. We have no known reaction from Berengar who was perhaps too old and set in his ways either to understand the message or to wish to implement it. The curse of the miser is very strong![44]

By June 1204, Innocent states that the Church of Narbonne had now been without pastoral care for thirteen years.[45] Heresy was spreading because of Berengar's negligence. That hospitality which was expected from a bishop was not forthcoming, nor were alms being given. Now deposition was threatened. Like a barren tree, Berengar deserved to be uprooted and Innocent prepared to send a mission to the region.[46] As was usual in such missions, the Cistercians were chosen as his agents.[47] At last Berengar reacted, protesting that the legates were going far beyond their papal mandate, chiefly in the accusation of heresy.[48] Innocent's response was to concentrate on only two of the worst sins his archbishop had displayed, namely avarice and negligence.[49] At that Berengar came to Rome to see the Pope, full of excuses, promises, and biblical texts of his own. His favorite seems to have been "let him that is without sin cast the first stone."[50] Innocent, possibly glad to have provoked some sort of response

[41] Ibid., cols. 904–5.

[42] June 29, 1203. *PL* 215, cols. 83–84.

[43] *PL* 15., cols. 272–75. Cf. *PL* 217, Sermones XXVIII and XXIX, cols. 439–50 and esp. col. 450, "Tectum est charitas."

[44] Baumann, "Deadliest Sin," 9–11.

[45] May 28, 1204. *PL* 215, cols. 355–57.

[46] See May 29, 1204. *PL* 215, cols. 360–61 and 358–60.

[47] Led by Arnald Amaury, Abbot of Cîteaux, Peter of Castelnau and Raoul of Fonte-froide. C. Thouzellier, *Catharisme et Valdéisme en Languedoc à la fin du XIIe et au début du XIIIe siècle*, Faculté des lettres et sciences humaines de Paris, Recherches 27 (Paris, 1966); *PL* 215, cols. 360–61.

[48] On November 26, 1204, Berengar appealed against the papal legates. C. Devic and J. Vaissète, *Histoire de Languedoc*, 15 vols. (Toulouse, 1872–1892), 8 (1879): 509–11.

[49] December 6, 1204, *PL* 215, cols. 472–74.

[50] May 9, 1206, *PL* 215, cols. 883–85.

at last, excused Berenger. The pope must have taken into account Berengar's own need for charity. (He was, it seems, very elderly and debilitated). Innocent read him a much-needed homily. Profit should not be financial but measured in souls. Instead of illicit exactions and usurious transactions, generous acts of hospitality and kindness should be shown to pilgrims and the indigent alike.[51] Returning to Narbonne, Berengar's memory apparently failed him, and some eight or ten more fierce letters emanated from Rome until 1211.[52] So lax was the archbishop that his removal became vital for Innocent's program of clerical reform. Innocent's denunciations of Berengar have been called vitriolic by some.[53] Indeed, papal language may have been somewhat overstated to achieve a result. All to little effect. At various times, Innocent attempted more indirect approaches. He encouraged the Poor Catholics, the followers of Durand de Huesca, to carry out acts of charity and mercy in the area centered on the diocese of Elne.[54] Berengar was outraged at such activities within his province, but he did not mend his ways. Indeed, the problem was only finally solved on 12 March 1212 when he was replaced by the Cistercian Arnald Amaury, former abbot of Citeaux.[55] By 1213 the purge had been completed. Not only was Berengar's partner in crime, the Archbishop of Auch, deposed, but the bishops of Frejus Carcassonne, Beziers, Toulouse, Vence and Rodez had also been deprived.[56]

With such forcible stricture of his fellow bishops we must consider how far Innocent's own actions matched up to the need to care for the welfare of the flock. Before so doing, however, we need to see what provisions for charity were made by others, including works of charity and mercy, were an integral part of the Rule of St Benedict.[57] Indeed, Benedict had insisted that the poor and strangers should be received in his monastery "as though each one were Christ himself." The problem for each monastery was how it could continue to perform these functions of welfare and

---

[51] Sed ... peregrinis et indigentibus largus sit et benignus, ibid., col. 884.

[52] May 29, 1207, *PL* 215, 1164–65; July 5, 1209, *PL* 216, 73–4; ibid., cols. 283–84; ibid., cols. 408–9.

[53] See, e.g., Thouzellier, *Catharisme et Valdéisme*, 243.

[54] *PL* 216, cols. 601–02; P. Biller, "*Curate infirmos*: the Medieval Waldensian Practice of Medicine," *Studies in Church History* 19, (1982): 65–77. The hospital at Elne in Rousillon contained fifty beds where the distressed poor, the sick, orphaned and abandoned children and women in childbirth were tended by men and women observing the common life.

[55] Arnald Amaury, Bishop of Narbonne, March 12, 1212–d. September 29, 1225; C. Eubel, *Hierarchia Catholica Medii Aevi*, (Regensberg, 1893), 1:356.

[56]*PL* 214, cols. 374, 456–58; 215, cols. 272–73, 366–68; 216, cols. 283, 408–9; 217 cols. 159–60.

[57] J. McCann, ed., *The Rule of St. Benedict* (London: Burns & Oats, 1952) 26: 91; A. de Vogue, "Honorer tous les hommes. Le sens de l'hospitalité Bénédictine," in *Revue d'Ascétique et de Mystique* 40 (1964): 129–38.

hospitality without diminishing its practice of the contemplative life, as the numbers of the poor increased and their demands became more insistent.[58] By the twelfth century, the shift of emphasis had occurred, doing little to resolve this tension between contemplation and welfare. This new emphasis was increasingly symbolic, involving alms or maintenance of only a token number of selected poor.[59] The Abbey of Cluny, for example, fed eighteen pensioners, the descendants of the *matricularii*, within the monastery; in addition, it distributed food to seventy-two poor men and women at the gate.[60] On certain days, the Abbey provided one night's shelter to pilgrims and gave them bread and wine for their journey. Most symbolic of all was the ritual of the *mandatum*, the traditional washing by monks of the feet of a few chosen poor men, face to face, in a liturgical setting and especially in the ceremony of Holy Thursday. While monasteries may have ceased to function in the fullest sense as charitable institutions, they did nevertheless often provide houses for the poor and infirmaries for the sick and for lepers just outside their gates. These were regarded to all intents and purposes as part of the monastery, subject to the same liturgical provisions and under the control of the almoner acting there for the abbot. The almoner, *eleemosynarius*, was to be chosen for qualities of genuine compassion, ardent charity, mercy, piety, and sincere care for the welfare of orphans and the disinherited.[61]

This system could break down, especially under the strain of two particular conditions. In times of famine, great crowds of the poor and dispossessed could not be prevented from flocking to any monastery for assistance; for example, in 1197 at Val Saint-Pierre, fifteen hundred people crowded to the door of the almonry each day, queuing overnight before distributions of alms were to be made to ensure that they would be first amongst the beneficiaries.[62] Nor were these poor people all from the peasant classes. Nobles, too, were affected[63]—by the loss of vineyards or lands through the calling in of a mortgage or the exactions of a usurer—

---

[58] M. Mollat, "Les moines et les pauvres."

[59] M. Rouche, "La Matricule des Pauvres: Evolution d'une institution de charité du Bas Empire jusqu'à la fin du Haut Moyen Age,"*Etudes* 1: 83–110.

[60] W. Witters, "Pauvres et Pauvreté dans les coutumiers monastiques du Moyen Age,"*Etudes* 1:177–215, esp. 205–9; M. Plaudecerf, "La Pauvreté à l'Abbaye de Cluny d'après son cartulaire,"*Etudes* 1:217–27.

[61] *Rule of St. Benedict,* 53:119–23; W. Witters, "Pauvres et Pauvreté," in *Etudes* 1: 196–210.

[62] M. Mollat, "Le problème de la pauvreté au XIIe siècle," in *Cahiers de Fanjeaux,* 2 (1967): 23-63, esp. 26.

[63] G. Ricci, "Naissance du pauvres honteux: entre l'histoire des idées et l'histoire sociale," *Annales: Economies, Sociétés, Civilisations* (1983): 158–77; Idem, "Povertà, vergogna et povertà vergognosa," *Società e Storia* 2 , (1979): 305–37; J. C. Peristiany ed., *Honour and Shame: The Values of Mediterranean Society* (Chicago: University of Chicago Press, 1966).

and the increased presence of nobles or those from the upper levels of society now fallen on hard times seems to have been a particular feature of the 1190s which had to be treated with the utmost sensitivity.

The second condition that frequently placed an additional strain on the whole system of welfare was deeply rooted in the Benedictine Rule that allowed each monastery to have a considerable degree of autonomy.[64] This autonomy was a perpetual source of trouble, as Innocent knew to his cost.[65] In June 1208, in his capacity as Bishop of Rome and hence as local diocesan bishop, he visited the great Benedictine Abbey of Monte Cassino, which guarded the southern approaches to the Papal States.[66] Here he found a most unsatisfactory situation, partially caused by the local autonomy on the election of the abbot. Roffredo, Abbot of Cassino (1190–1209), had to be most seriously reprimanded for not fulfilling his duty of hospitality and almsgiving.[67] He was further accused of misappropriating revenues that should have been used for the benefit of the infirmary. On Roffredo's death his successor, Atenolfo, proved to be precisely in the mold of Archbishop Berengar and was deposed in 1215.[68] Innocent's letter to Cassino in September of that year reveals the chaotic state of monastic discipline and the collapse of all charitable functions.[69] Hospitality that had been withdrawn was to be restored so that the sick and the poor fleeing to this refuge for comfort should receive it there fully. Indeed, anyone who has struggled up this particular mountain (alt. 1,707 ft.) will sympathize with those who had been harshly sent away!

The truth of the matter was that while the numbers of the poor were increasing spectacularly, monasteries were becoming far less useful in providing charity than their more flexible rivals who did not feel the same need for withdrawal from the world. These rivals were Canons Regular

[64] M. Maccarrone, "Primato Romano e Monasteri dal Principio del Secolo XI ad Innocenzo III," in *Istituzioni Monastiche e Istituzioni Canonicali in Occidente (1123-1215)* (La-Mendola–Milan: Vita e Pensiero, 1980), 49–132.

[65] U. Berlière, "Innocent III et les monastères bénédictins," *Revue Bénédictine* 20-22 (1920): 22-59, 145-159; Bolton, "*Via Ascetica*,"161-191.

[66] *PL* 215, cols. 1593-1600; L. V. Delisle, "Itinéraire d'Innocent III dressé après les actes de ce pontife," in *Bibliothèque de l'Ecole des Chartres* (Paris, 1857), 500–34, esp. 509.

[67] *Rule of St. Benedict:*, chap. 64, pp. 145–49; D. Knowles, *From Pachomius to Ignatius: A Study in the Constitutional History of the Religious Orders* (Oxford; Clarendon, 1966), 6; *PL* 213, col. 168 "... gaudemus plurimum et electionis canonicae apostolicum libente impertimur assensum"; 215, cols. 1593–94; Berlière, "Innocent III et les monastères bénédictins," 149–51.

[68] *PL* 217, cols. 249–53; L. Tosti, *Storia della Badia di Monte Cassino*, 3 vols., (Naples, 1842–1843),2: 289–92.

[69] Tosti, *Badia di Monte Cassino*, 2:289.

living according to the Rule of St. Augustine.[70] One such was Jacques de Vitry, a canon from Liege. Trained in the school of Peter the Chanter in Paris, Jacques de Vitry was particularly well qualified to bring together academic theory and practical charitable activity.[71] This popular preacher and sensitive observer of contemporary religious phenomena chronicles in his *Historia Occidentalis* the quite remarkable expansion of works of charity and assistance on behalf of the sick, the poor, the homeless, travelers, pilgrims, and lepers around 1200.[72] In chapter 29, he describes those hospitals for the poor and leper houses founded in his own day by men and women alike, who had renounced the world and dedicated themselves to the care of the infirm. Indeed, his own spiritual mother, Mary of Oignies, the "new saint" of the diocese of Liege, had worked together with her husband in similar fashion in a leper colony at Willambroux on the River Sambre in Brabant.[73] Jacques de Vitry speaks generally of "hospital religious," who observed the Rule of St. Augustine, wore the religious habit, lived separately and chastely, and observed the canonical hours as often as their ministrations allowed. Clearly, those who organized such hospitals were well on the way to becoming full-fledged religious since they were also required to attend a chapter on faults to regulate discipline. Chaplains were to minister to the poor and sick while those too ill to leave their beds could hear the Divine Office, and be exhorted both to grace and to patience. Confessions were heard on death beds, and extreme unction was dispensed. After death, the poor were buried decently by the religious.[74]

Jacques de Vitry extols these hospital brothers and sisters for acting as the ministers of Christ. It requires, he says, a martyr's courage to overcome natural disgust in the face of the unbearable stench of the sick. These good people are sober and upright, dealing with all bodily needs and bearing filth and squalor in this world for spiritual reward in the next. Yet, realizing the weakness and fragility of human beings, Jacques de Vitry adds as a warning a chapter on the known abuses of certain of these hos-

[70] J. C. Dickinson, *The Origins of the Austin Canons and their Introduction into England* (London: SPCK, 1950); *La Vita Communi del clero nei secoli xi e xii, Miscellanea del Centro di Studi Medioevalii* III, 2 vols. (Milan: Pubblicazioni dell'Università Cattolica del Sacro Cuore, 1962); C. W. Bynum, *Docere Verbo et Exemplo: An Aspect of Twelfth Century Spirituality*, Harvard Theological Studies 31 (Missoula, Mont.: Scholars Press, 1979), and idem, *Jesus as Mother: Studies in the Spirituality of the High Middle Ages* (Berkeley: University of California Press, 1982).

[71] Baldwin, *Masters, Princes and Merchants*, 1:137–49. All his sermons are listed in J.B. Pitra, *Analecta Novissima Spicilegii Solesmensis Altera Continuatio* (Tusculum, 1888), 2:344–442.

[72] Hinnebusch, *Historia Occidentalis*, 29: 146–51.

[73] *Vita B. Mariae Oigniacensis*, ed. D. Papebroeck, *Acta Sanctorum*, June IV (Antwerp, 1707), 636–66; B.M. Bolton, "*Vitae Matrum*: A Further Aspect of the *Frauenfrage*," in *Medieval Women, Studies in Church History*, Subsidia I, ed. D. Baker (London: Blackwell, 1978), 253–273.

[74] Hinnebusch, *Historia Occidentalis*, 147.

pital congregations.[75] Under the cloak of hospitality and piety lurk extortion, deception, and lies. Sometimes those who should care do not do so. They collect alms from the faithful on the pretext of giving to the poor, but instead they profit greatly—rather like crafty merchants or cunning innkeepers. Often, those who themselves give little to the poor, receive much under the pretext of alms. So rich are they reputed to be that they grow richer than hunters. But even worse than that is what Jacques de Vitry identifies as external hypocrisy among those he calls *fratres barbati*, bearded brothers, as well as among hirelings and lying priests. All their charity is performed without faith, mercy or affection. They turn houses of hospitality and piety into robbers' dens, prostitutes' brothels, or synagogues of Jews!

In spite of his fierce criticism of those institutions that had gone astray, Jacques de Vitry could only praise certain other hospital foundations for the ardor of their charity, the unction of their piety, the rigor of their discipline, and their upright and honest dignity. And then he provides the names of the very best of his day: the Hospital of Santo Spirito in Rome, the Hospitals of St. Sampson in Constantinople and SS Anthony and Mary, both at Roncevalles in Navarre, the latter being particularly renowned for its special care of sick pilgrims. Paris and Noyon in the Kingdom of France, Provins in Champagne, Tournai in Flanders, and his own Liege in Lotharingia all deserve a mention.[76] Of these hospitals, that at the very top of this list was Innocent III's own foundation, Santo Spirito in Rome.

Innocent's own caritative works within Rome and the Patrimony are very much in the mainstream of what Jacques de Vitry considers important. While initiating new projects, Innocent never fails to make them relevant to past tradition and to his own obligations and duties as Bishop of Rome. From late antiquity the revenues of the Roman Church were divided into four parts, an arrangement known as the *quadripartitum*.[77] The pope retained one part for himself and distributed the second among his clergy, who in Innocent's case, were those canons who served the Basilica. A third part was assigned for the upkeep of the church and the fourth part for the relief of the poor. Just how much Innocent spent on almsgiving, says his biographer, only God himself knew.[78] Immedi-

---

[75] See ibid., 148–50 and 282–84, for an extensive bibliography. See also M. Revel, "Le rayonnement à Rome et en Italie de l'Ordre du Saint-Esprit de Montpellier,"*Cahiers de Fanjeaux* 13 (1978): 343–55; E. D. Howe, *The Hospital of Santo Spirito and Pope Sixtus IV* (New York: Garland, 1978).

[76] See Hinnebusch, *Historia Occidentalis*, 150, 279–284; PL 216, col. 217.

[77] A. H. M. Jones, "Church Finance in the Fifth and Sixth Centuries," *Journal of Theological Studies* 11 (1960), 84-94.

[78] *Gesta*, CXLV, cciv-ccv. Quantam vero pecuniam in hoc opus expenderit, novit ille qui nihil ignorat.

ately after his election he set aside as alms for the poor not only their traditional portion but also his own income from offerings made in St. Peter's. Besides this he had one-tenth of his total income set aside for charitable work while from what remained he frequently gave alms generously and secretly. All those alms coming to him as pope were received by the papal almoner for distribution according to "ancient custom." Hence, we are told that he fed the hungry, clothed the naked, found dowries for poor virgins, and cherished abandoned children. He frequently gave money to help monks and poor nuns, recluses and hermits, visiting them personally, and in the case of the nuns, freeing them from debt incurred through no fault of their own. His almoner was instructed to go around and diligently to search out the poor and weak (*pauperes et debiles*). In particular, he was to find the noble poor and give to them a special seal or sign so that those who carried and produced it should each week receive money for food. Again, this provision was in tune with the common attitude of the canonists that the church should mitigate the sense of shame felt by a nobleman who had fallen on hard times. Innocent often spent as much as fifteen pounds each week on the distribution of such alms, not counting those who received a daily dole in food, money, or clothing. Poor children were encouraged to come to the papal table when meals were over and were allowed to eat what remained. In commemoration of Christ himself and in imitation of monastic welfare, the Pope performed the *mandatum pauperum* each Sunday by washing, drying, and kissing the feet of twelve poor men. He then ensured that all were fed and cared for, paying 12 pence to each one.[79]

Innocent's great new hospital on the banks of the Tiber epitomized all the pope's aspirations for social welfare in Rome, linking past and present, tradition and innovation, care of body and of soul. All this was underpinned by the literal imitation of Christ's acts on earth, placing a new emphasis on love of one's neighbor and on the corporal acts of mercy.[80] Innocent's foundation of Santo Spirito brought together all these strands in his thinking on social welfare. Even the site was significant, for the hospital replaced or incorporated the Schola Saxonum or pilgrim hostel for the English nation and utilized the nearby Church of Santa Maria in Sassia (Saxia) where several kings of Wessex lay buried.[81] The hostel, or *zenodochium*, was the responsibility of the bishop of Rome, but by the twelfth

[79] See ibid., CXLIII, cciv–cc; B. M. Bolton, "Daughters of Rome: All One in Christ Jesus!" *Studies in Church History* 27 (1990): 101–15; cf. Witters, "Pauvres et pauvreté," in *Etudes* 1:177–215, esp. 198–205.

[80] R. Brentano, *Rome before Avignon: A Social History of Thirteenth-Century Rome* (London: Longman Group, 1974), 19–21.

century the number of English pilgrims was clearly in decline. In 1163, the deacon of the Saxon School wrote to complain that the income from offerings was falling while scarcely anyone from England, either cleric or layman, could be found to serve in it.[82] By 1200, the *zenodochium* was standing empty and derelict—but ripe for development!

The institutional model for Innocent's hospital came from France. In May 1198, he approved the hospitals of Saint-Esprit in Montpellier, Marseille, and Millau together with two small houses in Rome, one at Santa Maria in Trastevere and the other at S. Agatha to serve pilgrims and travelers entering the city.[83] The rector of the Hospital of Montpellier and the brethren were recognized as *religiosi* who observed the Rule of St. Augustine and were taken into papal protection as an *ordo*. Building may have begun as early as 1201 on the site of the abandoned English school, and it was certainly well under way by 1204.[84] From this association Innocent III found a pretext for inviting King John to contribute to his new hospital.[85] An annual payment of 100 marks was made from the English exchequer and the king was remembered in the necrology of the hospital. Yet alms and donations were collected not only from England but from Montpellier, Italy, Sicily, and Hungary, too.[86] To these donations, Innocent added 1,000 silver marks from his own private fortune. As he writes "the superfluity of wealth which is often gathered together for death can be better used to provide necessities for the poor in life—for it is not beneficial to lay up earthly treasure nor to allow mammon to make enemies out of friends." The Church of Santa Maria in Sassia, he adds, is a particularly suitable place for hospitality and almsgiving "for there, in future time, God willing, the poor and infirm will be received and restored to health and other works of piety made manifest." He and his successor popes witness in Christ Jesus "who is about to come to judge the living and the dead, that this hospital, founded with the goods of the Roman Church and amply endowed, ought to be given special care."[87]

---

[81] W. Levison, *England and the Continent in the Eighth Century* (Oxford: Clarendon Press, 1946), 39–44.

[82] *Materials for the History of Thomas Becket, Archbishop of Canterbury*, ed. J. C. Robertson, 7 vols., *Rolls Series* 67 (London, 1875-1885), 5 (1881), 64-65.

[83] April 22 and 23, 1198. *Register* 1:95, 97, 139–44; *PL* 214, cols. 83–86.

[84] June 19, 1204. *PL* 215, cols. 376–80.

[85] C.R. Cheney, *Pope Innocent III and England* (Stuttgart: Hiersemann, 1976), 237–38; *Rotuli Chartarum...* 1:1(1199-1216), ed. T. D. Hardy, Record Commission (London, 1837), 123.

[86] Tantum Italia, et Sicilia, et Anglia, et Ungaria. *PL* 215, col. 378. The bishop of Chartres was also prevailed upon to assign the third part of the income of a prebend to the hospital. Ibid., col. 1334.

[87] *Gesta*, CXLIV, cols. cc-cciii, CXLIX, col. ccxxvii, cols. 377, 380.

A fifteenth-century legend held that Innocent had been the victim of a terrible, punishing dream.[88] Fishermen in the River Tiber were catching in their nets, not fish but instead the bodies of babies unwanted by their sinful mothers. These they placed at Innocent's feet. There was perhaps a grain of truth in this legend for the hospital set out to care for unwanted babies and for orphaned children. A box placed next to the door of the hospital allowed for the depositing of infants at any hour of the day or night. It was clearly understood that no awkward questions would be asked and no names traced afterwards. The hospital also catered to female pilgrims in labor, even providing a series of cradles so that each pilgrim baby might sleep alone.[89] Destitute children were raised by the Sisters of the hospital. Boys were apprenticed to a suitable trade while the girls were provided with marriage dowries unless they proved to have a vocation. Female sinners, many of whom were prostitutes, were admitted during Holy and Easter weeks if they were truly penitent.[90] But this hospital was by no means designed solely for mothers and their babies or for women alone. Once a week, the Brothers of the hospital were instructed to go into the streets and were actively to seek out both male and female infirm paupers so that they might be brought back for nursing and care.

Nothing of Innocent's original hospital building stands today. Destroyed by fire in 1471, it was reconstructed and enlarged between 1473 and 1478 by Sixtus IV.[91] All that remains now is the series of frescoes in the Corsia Sistina of the hospital (nowadays a male geriatric ward) depicting its legendary history and its building, first by Innocent and then by Sixtus IV.

In the city of which he was bishop Innocent was able to care for his flock by direct intervention,[92] but he was well aware that care for bodies went hand-in-hand with care for souls, that there was no real difference between material and spiritual welfare. Nowhere is this more clearly demonstrated than in his Sermo VIII De tempore, composed for the first Sunday after Epiphany, when the text for the day is the marriage feast at Cana (John 2:1–11).[93] On this day, probably 3 January 1208, the image of

---

[88] P. De Angelis, L'Architetto e gli affreschi di Santo Spirito in Saxia (Rome, 1961), 130–134; Lowe, Hospital of Santo Spirito, 15–92.

[89] PL 217, 1129–58, esp. chap. LIX, De cunabulis puerorum, col. 1148.

[90] Ibid., chap. XLVI, De peccatricibus suscipiendis, col. 1146.

[91] Lowe, Hospital of Santa Spirito, 15–92.

[92] R. Ambrosi de Magistris, "Il viaggio d'Innocenzo III nel Lazio e il primo Ospedale in Anagni," Storia e Diritto 19 (1898): 365–78 provides evidence of a further hospital foundation on August 26, 1208, at Anagni, south of Rome.

[93] PL 217, cols. 345–50.

the veronica[94] was carried processionally in its special reliquary from its home in the Basilica of St. Peter's by the canons there to the hospital on the Tiber.[95] Not only did this dramatic representation of Christ signify his willingness to suffer for all people, but it also acknowledged the role of Veronica, who was herself poor, the servant and maid of the Virgin Mary.[96] While the hospital of Santo Spirito represented Innocent's practical concern for the sick and poor, for those who suffered and for pilgrims, so its association with this venerable and precious image was formalized by the creation of a new liturgical station in which the Pope himself was to play the central part, delivering this exhortatory sermon on works of piety and welfare.[97]

Innocent exhorts his audience to consider the threefold marriage of faith, youth, and sacrament, all of which were to be found in the care provided by his new hospital. As the marriage at Cana represented the joining of flesh and spirit, so zeal of charity is united with love of salvation, converting men from error to charity and from vice to virtue.The wine at the feast represents charity, flowing freely at first as does charity in the first flush of its enthusiasm. When the wine begins to run out, then charity grows cold and requires reawakening with a sermon of instruction and exhortation. The miracle of the best wine coming last shows that "charity never fails" (1 Cor. 13:8). The six jars at the feast represent the six corporal works of mercy commended by Christ: feeding the hungry, giving drink to those who thirst, caring for the guest or traveler or the sick or those in prison, and clothing the naked. The jars are made of stone to represent firmness and each jar may contain double or triple measure. Food and drink can be given in three ways: the material, as natural food; the sacramental, through the eucharist; and the doctrinal, through the writings of scripture. The sick may be tended to in two ways, in heart and in body; likewise, the prisoner and the guest. When charitable works are perfectly carried out, the jar is filled to the brim and water transformed into wine. At the marriage feast, continues Innocent, the bridegroom is the Holy Spirit; the bride is grace; Jesus, the Divine Sermon; his disciples, honest habits; the Mother of Jesus, the catholic faith; the master who presides at the feast is reason, which rules amongst the natural virtues of the spirit.

---

[94]Or Veronica's veil, a relic said to be a cloth that a woman used to wipe the face of Jesus on his way to Calvary, which retained the print of his face.

[95]S.J.P. Van Dijk and J. Hazelden Walker, *The Origins of the Modern Roman Liturgy* (London, 1960), 102–3, 460–61. See also my "Advertize the Message: Images in Rome at the Turn of the Twelfth Century,"*Studies in Church History* 28 (1991).

[96]E. Delaruelle, "Le problème de la pauvreté vu par les théologiens et les canonistes dans la deuxième moitié du xii siècle,"*Cahiers de Fanjeaux* 2 (Toulouse, 1967): 48–63, esp. 62.

[97]*Gesta* CXLIV, cols. cci-ccii.

Cana of Galilee is the conversion of sinners, and the third day is the time of grace. Water is mercy, wine is charity. The six jars are the corporal works of mercy and the ministers who administer these are liberality and happiness. Water becomes wine when the effect of mercy gives shape to the gift of charity. The heretic, too, begins with good wine that is sound doctrine or an honest way of life—but when he has made men drunk, then they are led astray by the disease of error or the ferment of evil in the poor wine.[98] This was the first miracle of Jesus in Cana of Galilee when he justified the impious, converted evil, and won back the sinner—and on account of this his disciples believed in him.

Innocent concludes his sermon by referring to the liturgical station which he has instituted at Santo Spirito, making his hospital just such a place as Cana, where vices are transformed into virtues, where the corporal works of mercy are performed in all their fullness, where the mother of Jesus is to be found, in whose honor the church is dedicated. At the Station of the Veronica the Virgin finds her son whose effigy is carried with reverence to the hospital so that the faithful may wonder at his glory, having come together to celebrate the marriage of piety and mercy. Lest any should leave hungry from the feast, all are to celebrate liberally, joyfully, and healthily, and shall receive one full year in remission of their sins.[99] As a spectacular gesture, one thousand poor pilgrims together with three hundred poor from the surrounding area were each to receive three pence taken from the papal treasury—one for bread, one for meat and the third for wine.

Innocent's vision of the *vita apostolica* included love of one's neighbor in every sense. He combined this with a traditional function of the bishop of Rome, that of arranging for the ransoming of captives from their enemies and their subsequent welfare. He was to give many reminders throughout his pontificate of those thousands of Christians held by the Saracens, in prison or in slavery on the galleys of the Mediterranean.[100] He made frequent exhortations that every possible effort should be made to liberate them. In Rome on December 17, 1198, Innocent had approved the Order of Trinitarians.[101] Its founder, John de Matha, had come from Marseille, where a similar organization already existed for the redemption

---

[98]*PL* 217, cols. 346–50.

[99]*Gesta*, CXLIV, cols. cc-cciii; Brentano, *Rome before Avignon*, 19–21.

[100]P. Deslandres, *L'Ordre des Trinitaires pour le rachat des Captifs*, 2 vols. (Toulouse-Paris, 1903); "Islam et chrétiens du Midi (XIIe-XIVe siècle),"*Cahiers de Fanjeaux* 18 (1983).

[101]*Register* I, 481, 703-708; *PL* 214, cols. 444–49.

of Christian slaves in Moslem captivity.[102] One-third of all the order's revenues was used to pay for suitable ransoms or exchanges of captured Christians. Another third was used in the order's hospitals for the rehabilitation and care of these former prisoners, while the last third was used to maintain the brothers of the order, who lived according to the Rule of St. Augustine. In 1199, Innocent wrote to Miramolino, the Almohad caliph of Morocco, to commend those Trinitarian brothers sent to ransom prisoners.[103] By 1209 he speaks of the Order's influence as extending "from sea to sea."[104] In that year, the founder of the Trinitarians, John de Matha, retired to become a hermit in the Claudian Aqueduct by the Arch of Dolabella on the Celian Hill, where he remained until his death in 1213.[105] Legend held that he had a vision—of Christ himself holding by his two hands a couple of slaves, one black and one white, both manacled and in fetters. A mosaic of this vision dated 1210 above the gateway of the monastery of San Tommaso in Formis and enclosing the hermit's cell must have arrested the attention of Romans and pilgrims alike. Here was another highly practical and valuable example of charity and welfare, the idea of ransom already well known to Gregory the Great, but updated by Innocent to the realities of the early thirteenth century. Now he turned the minds of all Christians towards the plight of captives and of fellow Christians suffering in the East, exhorting them to perform their charitable responsibilities. He did not seek a totally new system to relieve poverty and suffering; instead, he showed that he was prepared to go to great lengths to support orders like the Trinitarians who were so eager to share in the sufferings of others.

Yet, in spite of all this good work, Innocent himself was not immune from criticism. Indeed, he was frequently parodied in savage terms, quite similar to those he had used against Berengar of Narbonne. The avidity of many churchmen for power, honor, and riches was a constant theme of contemporary satirists. The Roman Church in particular was the object of bitter hatred and scandal on account of its alleged venality and voracious appetite for money. The *Gospel according to the Silver Mark*, a Goliard poem and a frightful—even blasphemous—parody of a sacred text, was an explicit denunciation of all popes up to this time.[106] A particular feature

---

[102] G. Cipollone, *Studi intorno a Cerefroid, prima casa dell'ordine trinitario (1198-1429)*, Ordinis Trinitatis Institutum Historicum, Series prior, I (Rome: Gregorian University, 1978); idem, *La Casa della Santa Trinità di Marsiglia (1202-1547)*, Series prior 2 (Vatican City: Typis polyglottis Vaticanis, 1981).

[103] March 8, 1199. *Der Register Innocenz III, 2 Jahrgang (1190-1200)*, O. Hagender, W. Maleczek and A. Strand, eds. (Rome-Vienna: Abteilung für Historische Studien des Österreichischen Kulturinstituts in Rom, 1979) 9, 16–17; *PL* 214, col. 544.

[104] June 21, 1209, Cipollone, *La Casa della Santa Trinità*, 206–7.

[105] Brentano, *Rome before Avignon*, 14-15.

[106] A. Hilka and O. Schumann, *Carmina Burana, Die Moralisch-Satirischen Dichtungen* (Heidelberg: Winter, 1930): 86.

of much of this satirical writing was its constant reference to biblical texts: the avarice of Gehazi, servant to the Prophet Elisha (2 Kings 4:17–37, 5:20–27) and of Simon Magus (Acts 8:9–24) were especially prominent.

One such anonymous satire, dating from the first quarter of the thirteenth century, Lombard in origin, accused Innocent of precisely those charges of avarice and negligence which he had levied against Berengar. Now, though, it is Innocent's turn to be portrayed as the hireling of the Gospels, who runs from the sheep only to allow the ravaging of the flock (in this case by the growth of heresy). This "new Solomon" reigns in evil times, when all is subordinated to venality. He is no better than the others; indeed, he is far worse precisely because of the position he holds. He rarely observes the Sabbath, caring more for the profit and glory of justice than for the welfare of his people. Such impiety is even more serious when it masquerades as piety. One who calls upon others to bark but does not do so himself is revealed as the shepherd caught out in crime while his sheep are massacred by ravaging wolves. Through his acts, Rome *caput mundi* is irreparably stained and blemished.[107] While established laws and principles have perished in the fire or are fused into the gold of avarice, the church has ceased to care for the faithful. Now it is openly said that Rome "bites the hand that feeds it." The Bishop of Rome is powerless, tossed around like an anchorless ship in a huge storm. When the sinner has sinned, money steps in to wipe away the crime and thus fills Innocent's own purse—although the satirist does not tell us in what part of the papal anatomy we might find this purse. (Innocent was far more specific about Berengar!) Peter, once the peaceful fisherman of souls, is now the predatory hunter, avid for their money.

Such satire is particularly biting as it cleverly echoes the words and phrases that Innocent himself often used. The pope's anonymous biographer was quick to retort to such criticism by showing how Innocent earnestly considered the best means by which avarice could be extirpated. We know from another source, the Collection of Vatican Bulls addressed to the Canons of St. Peter's, that in April 1212 Innocent seems to have been forced to make a quite unprecedented, deliberate, and very public denial of the appalling accusation that he, the pope, was appropriating for his own use those alms given at the high altar and at the tomb of St. Peter.[108] Clearly the criticism, however untrue, hit its mark. Characteristically, after explaining carefully where the money did go, Innocent's final reply

---

[107]M. T. d'Alverny, "Novus regnat Salomon in diebus malis: Un satire contre Innocent III" in *Festschrift Bernhard Bischoff*, ed. J. Autenrieth and F. Brunholz (Stuttgart:A. Hiersemann, 1971), 372–90; Bibliothèque Nationale, Paris, Ms. Lat. 3236A, fol. 84.

[108] April 24, 1212. *Bullarum Sacrosanctae Basilicae Vaticanae*, 1: 96–97.

to his critics was that God himself would "recognize the lies of these guilty men at the Day of Judgment."

In conclusion, it must be said that the pragmatic nature of Innocent's approach to problems—involving as it did the need for "realism"in achieving what was best for the Church—could often be misunderstood. More than a tinge of hypocrisy can always be found in an office which has to be both political and spiritual.[109] If we examine Innocent's approach to welfare, a series of apparent contradictions, consistent in their inconsistencies, might well appear to a casual or biased observer. This could have been a fatal flaw in his caritative program. But to those who have some understanding of the way of Christ in a fallen world where evil has to be faced, Innocent's approach to welfare may be appreciated as a most successful spiritual activity in a political office.

In considering some of these apparent contradictions, I mention first Innocent's support for the ideal of monastic poverty as the way to achieve salvation. This is matched by his insistence on the need for all such religious institutions to achieve solvency through financial competence.[110] Here, money and no money at all are used in the same breath. He does so because he knows from observation and personal experience that insolvency leads to spiritual decadence, with all that that entails. His decretal *Cum ad Monasterium* of February 1203, with its very firm statement, applauds the sound basis of communal property found in many monasteries but deplores an individual monk's possession of private property, utterly condemned by St. Benedict himself in his Rule and which, as Innocent says "not even the pope himself has the right to abrogate."[111] Innocent thus supported financial rectitude at all times and most especially in the monasteries.

Innocent presents a similar attitude about alms to the poor. We have already seen that in his first treatise Innocent considers the blessedness of almsgiving, yet he is quick to warn against what has been called "the false cloak of destitution,"which could mean that those in receipt of alms were content to live a life of perpetual comfort.

He is at pains to point out that the cry of the poor must always be heard but he is also insistent that any answer to such a cry must require that the gospel is preached to them so that they may be fed in spirit as well as in body. Further, he was equally aware that the message of salvation

[109]For a pertinent insight into this problem in a slightly earlier period see J. Anderson and E. T. Kennan, *Five Books on Consideration: Advice to a Pope* (Bernard of Clairvaux), Cistercian Fathers' Series 13 (Kalamazoo: Cistercian Publications, 1976), 16–17.

[110]Bolton, "Via Ascetica," 177–179.

[111]*Corpus Juris Canonici*, ed. A. Friedburg, 2 vols. (Leipzig, 1879), 2: Decretal of Gregory IX,3: *De statu monachorum et canonicorum regularum*, 35, 6, cols. 599–600; *PL* 214, cols. 1064–66; *Chronicon Sublacense 593-1369*, Muratori, 24, VI, ed. R. Morghen (Bologna, 1927), 34–37.

was a mission to individuals, which could become overenthusiastic and unrealistic in its demands. Innocent's solution was usually to form an order or to approve an existing institution of *religiosi* to protect such individuals from the wiles of the Devil. It was in just this spirit that he could enable the new mendicant orders to play their vital role in spite of the strong current of belief among the hierarchy that no such new orders were necessary. It is interesting to conjecture whether St. Francis, with his life of poverty and charity, and St. Dominic, with his immeasurable strengthening of the faith through teaching, would ever have achieved such prominence in the history of the Church without that significant oiling of the wheels on their behalf by Innocent. His pragmatic approach to the welfare of the flock within Christ's church was crucial for future development but it brought him considerable criticism. Like Berengar of Narbonne but with much less reason, he was charged with letting his purse distract him from his duty. Yet, in Innocent's far-reaching approach to social welfare, epitomized by that evocative Baby Box by the Tiber, there can be absolutely no doubt that his heart was in the correct part of his anatomy!

The Madonna and Brothers of the Confraternity of S. Maria della Morte,
Bologna. Miniature from frontispiece of the 1562 Statutes

CHAPTER 8

RELIGION, THE PROFIT ECONOMY, AND SAINT FRANCIS

LESTER K. LITTLE

> By the time of Innocent III, the biblical tension noted by Kee between material poverty (actual physical needs) and spiritual poverty (humility) was markedly increased by urban development and the rise of a profit economy. Up to this point the church's expression of divine protection for a vulnerable humankind took the form of rich liturgical ritual, with its opulent display of wealth. Now, however, the growth of urban poverty and economic vulnerability led to views that the proper index of an intense and true religious devotion was distribution of wealth to the poor. The problem of wealthy religious communities was solved by the Dominican and Franciscan Orders, which adopted a policy of corporate as well as individual poverty, and which focused their ministry on the issues of urban wealth and poverty. In their preaching and ministry the friars became intermediaries between the wealthy and the poor. In so doing they provided the rich with justification for their wealth and the poor with charity while at the same time maintaining the poor in their poverty. In all of this the friars stimulated alms to the poor without in any way challenging the social structures that benefited the wealthy. Indeed, the friars were so attractive to the wealthy that the mendicant development of the lay confraternity became a popular middle way between becoming a friar and just giving alms.

Three decades ago, I spoke with a Dominican scholar in Paris about the thesis I was just starting to formulate. He listened attentively and then said that while he feared he could not be of any help, he knew precisely the person who could: "A fellow Dominican, named Chenu," he said, "Marie-Dominique Chenu. He lives in our order's convent in Rouen and comes to Paris once a month for the day. Just write to him there (I'll give you the address), and he will set you an appointment on the day of his next visit to Paris." I wrote to Chenu and his immediate reply came exactly as predicted. The hour we spent together in that appointment was the most important of my career. In view of such a grandiose statement, it may seem odd that I cannot recall exactly what did and did not transpire during that hour that was so important. The problem is not that I don't remember what happened, it's rather that I remember much more happening than could possibly be squeezed into an hour, for it was only after meeting Chenu that I really started to read him. Over time, as I always had the image of him from that lone encounter in my mind as I read, I amalgamated all that I learned from him into that image, and thus, in a sense, into my recollection of that hour.[1]

The historical lesson I learned from Chenu was of a prolonged, stressful adjustment by the Latin church to extensive social and economic changes that came about, roughly, during the eleventh and twelfth centuries. Chenu had a view of the spiritual life that predominated in the time before these changes occurred, a spiritual life that was well suited to a traditional rural society. He then saw the development of an urban society and a commercial, monetary economy, which took place, however, without the commensurate development of new forms of spirituality and ministry in the church. After a series of critiques and reforms, which mostly raised pertinent questions but gave no adequate answers, he saw the nearly simultaneous foundations, at the start of the thirteenth century, of the Dominican and Franciscan Orders as a relevant and efficacious response to the religious exigencies of the new social situation. I will return to this interpretation shortly and expand upon it. Suffice it to say here that it was the kernel of much of the work I have done since. It taught me a way to combine intellectual history (in this period essentially theology) and institutional history (essentially that of the church) with both religious history and the history of social and economic developments.[2]

But why did Chenu live in Rouen and why did he spend only one day a month in Paris? Because in 1954 Chenu had been suspended from his position as a professor of theology by Pope Pius XII and exiled to Rouen, with the concession that, once a month, he could go, for just a day, to Paris. Anything he wrote and sought to publish was subjected to severe censorship. Chenu had been one of the leaders of the worker-priest movement, which sent priests, many of them Dominicans, into factories to minister to industrial workers. His exile was part of a general crackdown in which the movement was disbanded, and Chenu's equally famous confrere Yves Congar was also silenced and sent away. The French clergy, in Chenu's

---

[1]For a brief presentation of Chenu and selections from some of his writings, see Olivier de La Brosse, ed., *Le Père Chenu, la liberté dans la foi* (Paris: Cerf, 1969); for collections of articles, see his *La foi dans l'intelligence* and *L'Evangile dans le temps* (Paris: Cerf, 1963); for a bibliography of his writings from 1921 to 1965, prepared by A. Duval, see *Mélanges offerts à M.-D. Chenu, Maitre en Théologie* (Paris: J. Vrin, 1967).

[2]See especially Chenu's essays in *La théologie au 12ème siècle*, (Paris: J. Vrin, 1957), tr. J. Taylor and L. K. Little as *Nature, Man and Society in the Twelfth Century: Essays on New Theological Perspectives in the Latin West* (Chicago: University of Chicago Press, 1968, reprinted 1983).

analysis, kept to an antiquated structure that served the needs of the substantial middle class; it was strong in those vast nineteenth-century parishes of the right bank with their massive sanctuaries. At the same time the clergy was nowhere to be found among the spralling bidonvilles, the working-class slums filmed in the 1946 documentary "Aubervilliers."[3] The Roman papacy found Chenu and his friends dangerous: they dressed in ways and performed tasks considered to be below the dignity of the clergy. There are photographs that document the movement in action: of Dominican mine workers with their lamps and their blackened faces, of Chenu addressing a demonstration outside the Renault factory at Billancourt on behalf of the workers who had been laid off.[4]

Chenu was no first-time offender in 1954. Already in 1937 a weekly magazine he helped edit was closed down and its editors denounced for outspoken opposition to the Italian invasion of Ethiopia and to the civil war launched by General Franco against the Spanish Republic. Also in 1937, as head of the Dominican faculty of theology at Kain in Belgium, he had published a program that set out his vision of the discipline of the history of theology.[5] In 1942 that publication made it onto the Index of Prohibited Books and gained its author a long-term sabbatical, every professor's dream. The charge was that he had relativized theology, making of it a human science, explicable in historical, rather than mystical, terms. At Kain, where this curriculum had been worked out, Chenu developed his notion of combining the most scientifically rigorous study of medieval texts with the most exacting analysis of and participation in contemporary social issues. Medieval theology went hand in hand with the problems of low wages or unemployment, and the lack of proper housing, schooling, and medical care.[6] Learning and an active apostolate: it was the original Dominican program, but from the Rome of Pius XII it looked like Communism.

The lessons taught by Chenu were thus much broader than an interpretation of the adjustment of spirituality to socioeconomic change in the twelfth and thirteenth centuries, for he taught by demonstration a harmonious integration between theology and history, between scholarship and social action, between history and life. For Chenu, the Incarnation and the

---

[3] Georges Sadoul, *Le cinéma français (1890-1962)* (Paris: Flammarion, 1962).

[4] François Leprieur, *Quand Rome condamne: Dominicains et prêtres-ouvriers* (Paris: Cerf, 1989). This is a full account of the worker-priest movement told from the side of the Dominicans. The documentation includes photographs, texts, a glossary, a chronology of the movement, and a biographical guide to its participants.

[5] *Une école de théologie: Le Saulchoir* (Kain-les-Tournai and Etiolles, 1937; reprint Paris: Cerf, 1985).

[6] Leprieur, *Quand Rome condamne*, 16–24.

Gospels took on meaning and value precisely because of their insertion in time, in the life of humankind, in the world. Like Master Peter Abelard, whom Chenu so admired[7] and whose final days were so poignantly described by Abbot Peter the Venerable to Heloise, Père Chenu was widely known "for his unique mastery of knowledge," yet he remained "steadfast in his own gentleness and humility." Like Master Peter, Chenu remained studious to the end, his mind ever vigilant.[8] Chenu himself died February 11, 1990. These remarks then are dedicated—they couldn't *not* be dedicated—to his memory.

RELIGION IN PRE-COMMERCIAL EUROPE

The religious expression of Carolingian and post-Carolingian Europe, roughly from the eighth century to the eleventh, was fundamentally liturgical. Political legitimacy itself was established by liturgy, in particular by the ceremony of royal unction, and the making of both political agreements and judicial decisions had important liturgical dimensions. The extreme precariousness of life fostered a religion whose main component was ritual. In a world marked by unpredictable, sudden, deadly shifts of fortune, the only bastion of security and continuity, the only point of contact with eternity, was the monastery. The principal activity and responsibility of the monks of that period was the fulfillment of the *opera dei* (works of God); this consisted of the recitation of psalms and prayers during the eight services of the twenty-four hour monastic liturgical cycle. The number of psalms recited and hence the length of these services escalated considerably, especially in the tenth century. In some monasteries during the same period even the most banal parts of the daily routine, outside of the recitation of the Daily Office, acquired an obsessively ritualized manner.[9] Another basic characteristic of this liturgical religion was the dominant presence of the vocabulary, imagery, and thought patterns of a particular reading of the Bible.[10] God the judge was distant and stern; divine judgments were uncompromising, as were religious polemics and indeed all religious discourse.

In this early Europe, where the forces of nature remained an utter mystery to the small, poor, and widely scattered populace, a saint was an

---

[7]See for example Chenu's lecture *L'éveil de la conscience dans la civilisation médiévale* (Montreal, 1968), 17–32.

[8] Betty Radice, tr., *The Letters of Abelard and Heloise* (Harmondsworth: Penguin, 1974), 282–84.

[9]Barbara H. Rosenwein, "Feudal War and Monastic Peace: Cluniac Liturgy as Ritual Aggression," *Viator* 2 (1971): 132.

[10]Pierre Riché, "La Bible et la vie politique dans le haut Moyen Age," in P. Riché and Guy Lobrichon, eds., *Le Moyen Age et la Bible*, (Paris: Beauchesne, 1984), 391–95.

exceptional person who had been blessed. Holy people could resist the devil and cope with phenomena that defeated most others. The great majority of people, the "others," needed continually to be blessed. A continuing function of bishops and abbots and priests, in the meantime, was to bless. They blessed people and things and places and occasions; they called upon various agents, divine, saintly, or ecclesiastical, to impart their respective blessings.[11]

The divine protection provided by benediction was regarded by some as literally a protective shield, invisible in some cases, capable even, in others, of rendering the blessed person invisible. The Irish missionary-saint, Colomban, evaded captors in this way when he was under an order of expulsion from Frankish Gaul. Queen Brunhilda sent soldiers to the monastery where he was staying. Though he was seated in the vestibule of the church reading a book, they could not find him. Their clothes brushed against his clothes and a few soldiers even tripped over him. To his delight, Columban perceived that while he could see them, to them he was invisible.[12]

In a vision reported by St. Boniface, a monk who had come back to earth after death described the astonishing scenes he had observed. One involved the recently deceased Coelred, a king much despised by the clergy. When the monk first saw him, Coelred was protected by an angelic screen against the assault of demons. It looked like a huge open book suspended over his head. As the demons swirled about him they begged the angels protecting him to withdraw their protection. The demons brought up a long list of damning charges against the former king and threatened to shut him up in the deepest dungeon of hell and to torment him forever, as he deserved. (As we might imagine, the point of this letter was to terrify Coelred's successor.) Against this plea the angels had to admit that they could not build a strong case, that on account of his own demerits they could no longer protect him. "So they withdrew the shelter of the protecting screen, and the demons with triumphant rejoicing gathered together from every part of the universe ... and tormented the king with indescribable cruelties."[13] Thus the forces of evil were ever present in this world, and if one was momentarily off guard or found without the protection of a blessing, demons were ready to pounce.

The religious had an exclusive monopoly on both blessing and praying. They prayed for themselves but, we should note specially, for others

---

[11]*Dictionnaire d'achéologie chrétienne et de liturgie*, II: part 1, cols. 670–727, "Bénédition."

[12]Jonas, *Vita sancti Columbani*, 20, *Monumenta Germaniae* Historica (Hannover: Hannsche Buchhandlung, 1885–; henceforth cited as MGH), Scriptores rerum merovingicarum IV: 90.

[13]*Epistolae s. Bonifatii et Lulli*, 10, MGH, Epist., 3:252–57.

as well. They were vicarious holy people. Their monopoly upon spiritual power included exclusive access to divine authority and the only means of communication between the living and the dead. The religious blessed the dying and the dead. They buried the dead. And they prayed thereafter for the salvation of the dead. The living, in their desire to assist their departed relatives, had necessarily to rely upon the intervention of the religious. The names of those whom the religious undertook to pray for were inscribed in "books of life" (*libri vitae*). The earliest of these now extant dates from the year 784. Religious communities entered into agreements to pray for each other's members; they undertook to pray for ecclesiastical and secular authorities whom they wished to favor, and they prayed for their benefactors. The names were entered in groups, sometimes of entire monastic communities or of entire extended families. The *Liber memorialis* of Reichenau Abbey contained over forty thousand names. The persons named were to be recommended during the Eucharist. There was no way that all the names could be read out at each Mass; instead, the book was placed on the altar during the Mass and the monks prayed for all who were listed therein. The phrase "book of life" occurs frequently in the Bible, always figuratively; in the book of Revelation, it is said that those are not destined for salvation "whose names have not been written in the book of life" (Rev. 17:8), and that anyone whose name is not written in the book of life shall be cast into a pool of fire (Rev. 20:12,15). But in the Carolingian religious world such registers did exist; promises or menaces about names being inscribed in or excised from books did not conjure up imaginary registers floating in clouds, but real ledgers, kept among the liturgical paraphernalia of churches and, during Mass, placed in view on the altar.[14]

The manipulation of this power to list and pray for someone, or not to, as the case may be, is apparent in a letter sent in 1022 by the canons of St. Mary's of Chartres, the cathedral, to Herbert, bishop of Lisieux. St. Mary's had a number of dependent churches in the diocese of Lisieux and Herbert must have asked the mother church to pay for each of them a tax called "visitation dues." The reply of the canons points out that this exaction was contrary to custom: "The bishops of blessed memory in whose dioceses we have churches have always shown their loving and reverent devotion to our most holy lady by not exacting from us, her unworthy servants, the payment that you demand." Next the canons cautioned the bishop against bringing upon himself the blame for causing them to suffer, for, they assure him, they are inspired by concern for his welfare.

[14]N. Huyghebaert, *Les documents nécrologiques*. Typologie des sources du Moyen Âge occidental 4 (Turnhout: Brepols, 1972), 13-16.

Moreover, "we hope to see you listed in the list of benefactors of our blessed community, so that as we continually offer sacrifice to the Lord for them, and thus also for you, and recount in his presence your good works, we may declare that you, too, are worthy of being included in the book of heavenly life."[15]

The prayers, blessings, and psalms were said, all the colorful liturgy was played out in sanctuaries as resplendent as the materials, craftsmanship, and resources of the age permitted. The dense concentration of gold, silver, and precious gems in churches found justification in the prime function of all churches: worship. The best that society could afford was not too good for the sanctuaries in which the saints were honored and God worshipped. Western monasticism from the seventh century to the twelfth took great pride in the splendor and riches of its churches. Biblical support was lent by the description of the construction of the Temple of Solomon (1 Kings 5:7). Wealth was not opposed to religious devotion but was rather an index of its intensity and validity. The churches at York and Hexham were considered treasure houses in the bleak and poor landscape of seventh-century Northumbria.[16] When in the century following, Benedict of Aniane's new monastery was built at Inden, "He took great care to acquire precious ecclesiastical vestments, silver chalices, and whatever else he deemed necessary for the *opera dei*."[17] John of Salerno commented on Saint-Martin of Tours in the tenth century that it was "a place full of virtue, remarkable for miracles, overflowing with riches, excelling all in the practice of religion."[18] The massive churches of the great age of monasticism, for example Cluny III, built in the years on either side of 1100, were built on a larger scale than were these forerunners but on the same principle. Even as a new spirituality took shape in the twelfth century and leveled stinging attacks on the old, Abbot Suger gave voice to the old view with undiminished vigor as he formulated an aesthetic theology to justify the stupendous abbey church at Saint-Denis.[19] The religion of the age can thus without exaggeration be qualified as a liturgical spirituality founded on conspicuous consumption.

The caste that presided over these splendid palaces of prayer claimed to live in poverty. They considered themselves the "poor of Christ." How

[15]F. Behrends, ed. and tr., *The Letters and Poems of Fulbert of Chartres* (Oxford: Clarendon, 1976), 112–15.

[16]"Life of Wilfrid," in *Lives of the Saints*, ed. and tr. J. F. Webb (Baltimore: Penguin, 1965), 148–49, 154–55.

[17]Ardo, *Vita Benedicti Anianensis*, 17-18, MGH, SRG, XV, pt. 1, 206–07.

[18]*Vita sancti Odonis*, 1:16. *PL* 51, 133.

[19]E. Panofsky, ed. and tr., *Abbot Suger on the Abbey Church at Saint-Denis*, 2d ed. (Princeton: Princeton University Press, 1974).

are we to resolve the paradox of this claim to poverty by the guardians of a luxurious cult? Michel Mollat has made clear that the meaning of "poverty" and related terms is not the same in every historical context.[20] Poverty is relative. Abstract and absolute as it seems, it is instead concrete and relative. In the context of health, the sick are poor. In the context of civic rights, the disenfranchised are poor. In medieval society, the pilgrim was considered poor, a pilgrim even who was wealthy, because in the context of the security of home and of the warm company of family and friends, the traveler is poor. In Carolingian and post-Carolingian society, the principal meaning of "poor" was to be without power. Widows and orphans were considered poor, and from those cases in which such individuals were known to possess great wealth, modern scholars deduced that their poverty consisted in their being without power, the more so even as their wealth was inadequately protected. The religious of the age, as far as we are able to establish any notion of their social origins, came from the wealthiest, most powerful sector of society. What they surrendered as individuals when they entered the religious life was not so much their wealth (for their families sometimes sent them to monasteries accompanied by sizeable donations) but their power. They surrendered their horses and weapons, the means and symbols of power in their time.[21]

If such is our understanding of the voluntarily poor, what are we to make of the materially, involuntarily poor? How were they regarded and how were they treated? For material poverty surely existed at the time, given that life was based on an agricultural economy that operated barely at subsistence level. The organized charity of monasteries distributed food at designated gates and hours. These distributions were of excess or left-over material, not an equal, or proportional, sharing of everything available between monks and the poor assembled at their door. Charitable distributions were ritualized; an occasion was marked, for example the anniversary of the death of a donor, by inviting in and feeding the apostolic number of twelve paupers, ritually washing their feet and serving them a proper meal at table. The choice of the number of paupers and of the way to treat them was made on the basis not of the needs of the poor outside the monastery at that moment but of the internal, liturgical needs of the religious community. Thus before the development of a commercial economy in Europe, religion remained highly formal or liturgical; it was

[20]Michel Mollat, *The Poor in the Middle Ages: An Essay in Social History,* tr. Arthur Goldhammer, (New Haven: Yale University Press, 1986).

[21]For references on these matters and on what follows in the next few pages, see Lester K. Little, *Religious Poverty and the Profit Economy in Medieval Europe* (Ithaca: Cornell University Press, 1978).

monopolized by a caste of specialists who equated liturgical splendor with genuine religion.

THE PROFIT ECONOMY

The next major piece to put in place concerns the development of a profit economy, for there appeared a commercial, market economy, not so rapidly as is happening these days in eastern Europe, but rapidly nonetheless, from the later tenth century on, with Italy, by nearly every index, always in the lead. I will make only a rapid survey of the key elements in this development, which some historians have chosen to deal with as a single, long-term nexus of change extending over three centuries, to the time of the Great Plague (1348 on), and which some of these historians have chosen to call the Commercial Revolution. The term was taken over by way of conscious analogy to the Industrial Revolution, whose thoroughgoing reverberations through all sectors of modern life and culture are well known. The Commercial Revolution is inseparable from, unthinkable without, a threefold increase in the overall European population. This increase was possibly initiated by, in any case certainly abetted by, a series of marked improvements in agricultural production and diet. More significant than this general increase was the concentration of a small segment, a maximum of perhaps five percent, of this population in communities of more than a few thousand people, that is, in communities that we can define as urban. The growth of an urban society was fed by the development of commerce and of one major new industry, preindustrial of course, namely the manufacture of woolen cloth. The life blood of this new commercial activity, which was notably expanded by the cloth market, was a greatly increased supply of money and a much more vigorous circulation of money. This three-century period of economic development presents a textbook case of the division of labor, nowhere more so than in agriculture itself, by the way, as it became organized for the market, but also in the definitions of trades, in sorting out the competence of various kinds of artisans, and in developments within the professions. The handling of money, at one time by virtually all merchants, itself became a specialty, that of the money merchants, or bankers.

Such thoroughgoing social change was not without its strains and dislocations, not without, to be sure, new forms of poverty. In its wake came the urban poor, the precarious nature of the development at the lowest levels of the hierarchy of trades and jobs, and the day-to-day hiring (or not) of the sort that goes on every day, now, in Johannesburg or San Diego.

The urban pauper, like everyone and everything else urban, was new; so, too, was the urban mendicant. An awareness of their presence became generalized by the 1160s, and because these poor were begging, we know that their poverty was defined not so much by a lack of power as by a lack of food, clothing, and shelter; they were the poor as we have known them primarily ever since.

As testimony to these innovations we can point to the burst of popularity in the twelfth century for an old story, the *Life of Saint Alexis*.[22] The nucleus of this Greek story is the report of a spiritually heroic "man of God," born of wealthy parents in the fifth century at Constantinople, who left home on his wedding day and lived the rest of his life as a beggar in Edessa. Among the many alterations to appear in later versions of this story was the identification of the central figure with the name Alexis, the transposition of the parents' home from Constantinople to Rome, and most revealing, having the hero return from Edessa after a while to Rome, where for the final seventeen years of his life, he lives unrecognized as a beggar by the door of his parents' home. The Latin version well established by the start of the twelfth century in Rome was then translated into all the major vernacular languages of Europe. The relics of St. Alexis were found in Rome; a cult grew up that included church dedications throughout Europe.

The religious life recorded the same social changes in its own way as well. The standard form of monastic life, centered upon liturgical celebration, performed in a resplendent, theatrical setting, drew criticism from persons familiar with, if not actually steeped in, the new social setting. The first criticism came from northern Italy, the most precocious area of commercial development in Europe. From the new point of view, the old spirituality seemed excessively elaborate, needlessly luxuriant; the claim of monastic poverty seemed contradictory, even hypocritical. In place of the ancient temple of Jerusalem and the formalism of the Old Testament as the standards, reformers now brought to the fore the modest community of the Apostles at Jerusalem as a model. Against huge churches with densely decorated altars and disciplined choirs, new value was attributed to the hermit's cell, simple churches without the distraction of statuary, richly colored windows, or glittering ornaments. The Camoldolese, Vallombrosians, Cistercians, and Carthusians all perceived the old order as compromised by wealth and all tried to avoid the entanglements of urban life, the market economy, and the money nexus. Their analysis of the failures of the old monastic order was mostly on the mark, but their flight from the sources of the new problems prevented them from resolving the new social problems and eventually exposed them to the same dangers of compromise that so haunted the old monastic life.

---

[22]See Susan Ashbrook Harvey, "The Holy and the Poor: Models from Early Syriac Christianity ," beginning on p. 43 of this work.

THE ROLE OF THE FRIARS

To turn now to the third main part of the argument, we see that the advent of the friars came not entirely out of the blue, that is, not without the way having been prepared by others, yet its importance lies in its having resolved the problem of the formation of a spirituality properly suited to the new social conditions. The Dominican and Franciscan Orders resolved the problem of wealthy religious communities by adopting a policy of corporate as well as individual poverty. Moreover, they operated exclusively in cities, they ministered to an urban audience, and they demonstrated great sensitivity to urban problems, including that of poverty. Some historians saw the friars as ministering directly to the poor, as speaking to them and as offering material help to them. Modern research has not been able to sustain this agreeable notion, thus demoting it to romantic myth. Rather than try to survey the whole question of the friars and poverty, I confine my remaining comments to two topics that do, I think, offer insight into the approach of the friars to the issue of economic poverty: the sponsoring of confraternities and the role of St. Francis as intermediary.

THE SPONSORING OF CONFRATERNITIES

In the course of the thirteenth century the Dominicans organized convents in over seven hundred cities, and the Franciscans did the same in about twice that number of cities. The individual friar joined the order, and not an individual house the way a monk did, friars often traveled from one convent of their order to another, and hence from one city to another. They assumed posts of considerable importance in some of the leading courts of the time, thus gaining high visibility. They may have seemed omnipresent—"The whole earth is their cell and the ocean is their cloister," wrote one detractor—but it would be more accurate to say that they were present wherever the new market economy and urban society were to be found, hence in cities and on the roads connecting them.[23] Their visibility was greater because of the form their ministry took, namely preaching. They instructed the laity in the principal doctrines of the faith. They preached to them the fundamental lessons of the gospels. Their churches were designed not for dazzling performances of a mysterious rite, but as large halls suitable for the reading of scripture and the preaching of its message. Having neither fled from the world nor hidden themselves from its inhabitants, the friars were, in their world, in their own part of the

---

[23]Matthew Paris, *Chronica Majora*, ed. H. R. Luard, 7 vols., Rolls Series (London, 1872-1884), 2: 511; 4: 346; 5: 529.

world, everywhere to be seen. The figure of the friar in fourteenth century literature was not always favorable—think only of Boccaccio and Chaucer—but whether it was favorable or not is unimportant in this context; that the figure of the friar was by then so recognizable is important. The friars built churches and convents of impressive size, and on expensive urban real estate observed St. Bonaventure, and thus had to raise large sums of money. They raised this money for the "poor," meaning themselves; in this they resembled their monastic predecessors. But what we see little of is direct, material aid passing from friars to poor people.

For direct aid from the friars to the poor, we must look at their conception of the laity and at some of the lay confraternities the friars sponsored or helped organize. While the friars were prideful and at times defensive concerning their orders, some of their most articulate spokesmen saw their role as one of preparing the laity to lead spiritual lives. They inherited one of the most radical ideas of the twelfth-century reform movement (called by Chenu "the evangelical awakening"), which held that the only religious rule of true value was the gospel and that all those who professed it and lived by it were the truly religious.[24] Dante echoed this thought in saying that "good and true religion" is accessible to those who are married, and not just to those who follow St. Benedict, St. Augustine, St. Francis, and St. Dominic.[25]

Some of the more radical of the Franciscans fell heir to the prediction of Joachim of Fiore that a new, spiritual age was about to appear, with the friars as its harbingers, an age in which the priesthood would be superfluous. Yet even the impeccably orthodox Franciscan preacher Berthold of Regensberg allowed that of all the orders then in existence, considering especially the many orders of monks and friars, only one was necessary, namely, the order of married people. Society could get along without all the others, he said, but not without this one. Thus by the thirteenth century the idea had taken root that lay people could lead spiritual lives as worthy as those of any who professed religion. Indeed in that century the new saints of northern Italy emerged from the laity: merchants such as Omobono of Cremona, and artisans such as the goldsmith Faccio of Verona.

The same age that produced the lay saint produced also the lay confraternity. The new urban culture spawned numerous associations: political, economic, social, and so forth. Rarely, though, did such associations hold to one function only. Guilds that were formed, for example, to protect mutual economic interests exerted political influence and engaged in

[24]Chenu, *Nature, Man and Society*, 239–69.
[25]*Convivia*, 4:28.

corporate religious devotions. Here, in speaking of lay confraternities, I have in mind those associations whose primary purpose for being was religious. The friars were neither the inventors nor the exclusive founders of lay confraternities, but they soon became active founders and promoters of them. In their own churches and in some of the others they organized groups of lay people, wrote statutes for governing them, and maintained a privileged, guiding role for themselves in their operation. In a confraternity called the Misericordia, founded jointly by Dominicans and Franciscans in 1256 at Bergamo in northern Italy, the members, both men and women, elected their own officers. The rules governing elections and the particular tasks of the officers as well as the conduct of their meetings were most carefully spelled out in the statutes, which were written by a Dominican. At the same time any member of either the Franciscan or Dominican Order could attend and take part in a meeting of the Misericordia's governing council. A concrete example of the friars' view of the laity can be seen in the devotions of the Misericordia (and countless confraternities like it). The individual members had to learn the Pater Noster; they were to recite it several times, often on specified occasions. In the past, praying had been done by an elite caste of specialists in religion. The friars, themselves part of that caste, propagated the evangelical record of Jesus' attack on the spiritual monopoly of priests in which he taught his followers, when they prayed, to say, privately and simply, "Our Father." The full implication of this could be the eventual elimination of the exclusive social "order of those who pray."[26]

The friars got lay people not only to pray but also to make charitable donations. Charity held a special place in the spirituality of the mendicant orders. The friars themselves emulated the poverty of Jesus and the Apostles and thus adopted the spiritual ideal of itinerancy and begging. They also emulated the evangelical models of caring for the sick, sharing with the needy, and keeping company with those shunted to the margins of society. At the same time, there are abundant indications that the friars' religious messages were mostly directed to the dominant (and hence wealthier) elements of the urban society of the thirteenth and fourteenth centuries. The connection is that an essential part of that message reminded the relatively well-off of their continuing obligation to share their bounty with the poor.

---

[26]For the references on these paragraphs concerning confraternities and St. Francis, see Lester K. Little, *Liberrty, Charity, Fraternity: Lay Religious Confraternities at Bergamo in the Age of the Commune*, Smith College Studies in History 51 (Northampton, Mass.: Smith College, 1988).

While the sources give slight evidence, as already mentioned, of direct assistance to poor people by the friars, apparently the latter felt it was more efficacious to organize the very people who had command of material resources into associations largely devoted to assisting the poor. The treasurers of the Misericordia, not the friars, were to go through the city and suburbs in search of the poor and ill and imprisoned and others in need in order to distribute alms to them. In some confraternities any member who found something gave it to the treasurer, and if the owner was not located within a year it was distributed to the poor. A confraternity solely for assisting prisoners in one city had someone stationed at every Mass in every church of the city to seek alms. It is not unusual to find a confraternity that existed exclusively for the administration of assistance to the poor. Some asked their members to make weekly contributions; at Santa Caterina of Bergamo, also every Sunday the treasurer had to go with two members of the consortium throughout the neighborhood of Santa Caterina. They were to visit those in prison as well as the ill and poor and to distribute to them the alms as they deemed proper. And still every Sunday, the treasurer had to account to the general membership for all receipts and disbursements. Quite different is the consortium of another neighborhood, Saint Michael, where mention of money is present throughout the rule, mostly in connection with fines, but the poor are not mentioned until the very end. There, in what surely looks like an afterthought, it was ordered that whenever the treasury of the confraternity had over forty imperial shillings, provision having already been made for oil and wax, the treasurer, with the advice of the parish priest and the councilors, should give that leftover amount, "for the love of God," to the poor.

In yet another variant, at Astino just outside the walls of Bergamo, a charitable distribution used to take place on the Sunday of St. Lazarus (the fifth Sunday of Lent), which was for many a dreaded time of the year when winter reserves were exhausted. Yet all such redistribution took place within carefully set, even if implicit, boundaries. We never hear of it altering any individual's social standing: largesse made no rich person poor, charity made no poor person rich. In representations of confraternity members distributing alms to the poor, the latter are physically tiny by comparison to their benefactors; the handing over of goods did not diminish the wealthy or increase the poor in size. The intention, and the reality undoubtedly often achieved in such distributions, was amelioration of the extreme hardships imposed by poverty.

What the modern observer may look for impatiently, but is not likely to find before the middle of the fourteenth century, is an analysis and criticism of the structures of the time that fostered injustice and inequality. The most sensitive reactions remained moral, either by patronizing the poor (giving alms) or identifying with them (embracing voluntary poverty). The material effects on actual conditions were in either case necessarily modest. A middle way between just giving alms and becoming a friar was to join one of the confraternities; a lay person thereby assumed some of the responsibilities and some of the prerogatives of a friar. In some sense the confraternities also served to bridge the great social differences separating the poor from all the rest of society. Of course poor people did not belong to confraternities (they could not make weekly contributions of alms), but in the giving of alms and their subsequent redistribution, interaction between rich and poor, the illusion of generosity, took place. And this interaction, like all philanthropy, in turn both justified the rich in their wealth and helped maintain the poor in their poverty.

ST. FRANCIS AS INTERMEDIARY

And now we turn briefly to Francis, not the Francis who lived in central Italy and died in 1226 (not the son of the wealthy cloth merchant of Assisi, the one who abandoned his patrimony to live a life of poverty in imitation of Jesus and the Apostles, nor the one who towards the end of his life suffered the stigmata), but the Francis of memory, history, iconography, hagiography, and propaganda who took over in 1226 where the other one left off. Of this latter Francis, there are many versions. In one he is disheveled and ragged, while in another handsomely groomed. In one he is more subservient to the clergy, while in another more independent, and so on. The course of his life was made to seem parallel to that of Jesus; the two lives conformed, as was demonstrated in the *Liber de conformitate*. In this tradition, Francis is acknowledged as the second Christ, the other Christ: *Franciscus alter Christus*, the full embodiment of the *imitatio Christi*.

But this model could be, and was, turned around, for there are multiple versions of Jesus as well. The Italian Franciscan who wrote the *Meditations on the Life of Christ* in the late thirteenth century asserted that Mary and Jesus had not been really poor but chose voluntarily to become poor. In her strong desire for poverty, this author continued, Mary received the gifts of the Magi as if she were poor, and then she distributed them to poor people. Here the Franciscan model has been turned around and projected onto Jesus, a case of *imitatio Francisci*, or of *Christus alter Franciscus*. Francis is a saint for modern times (the thirteenth and fourteenth centuries) and Jesus has undergone *aggiornamento*. What do these images signify for the history of attitudes towards poverty?

Everywhere that there were conspicuous wealth and conspicuous poverty (the two extremes, in close proximity, are an inescapable characteristic of our cities), there were friars and representations of Francis. They were symbols of poverty to be sure, but by extension of wealth also, and similarly of weakness and power, and of both life and death. The friar reminded the wealthy of the transitory nature of their wealth, not just of the chance that riches could be lost but that, even if good fortune endured, human life itself would eventually be lost.

The poor could sometimes be placated and temporarily screened from view, but not the friars. Recruited from the dominant classes of the cities (Francis's mercantile background was not unusual), the friars did not stay out of sight nor did they shy away from calling the attention of the wealthy to their riches. They preached to, they ministered to, the rich. But they did not threaten the rich; instead they gave them comfort by justifying their ways of making money. The response of the wealthier class to the friars was explosive. They gave the friars shelter and sustenance when they arrived, and helped them build their churches and convents. They rushed to associate themselves with the friars in every way they could.

The way for the rich to keep the poor at bay was to support the friars and then, by extension, to imitate some aspects of their lives by joining the confraternities that these founded or inspired. The friars were not really the poor, but rich people dressed up as the poor; giving to them was a symbolic way of giving alms. Some donations to the confraternities went more directly to the involuntary poor.

In some representations of Francis, the voluntarily poor man is shown together with involuntarily poor people; these images depict the startling contrast between the conditions of voluntary and involuntary poverty.[27] Francis is healthy and handsome, and adequately dressed in his friar's robe. He makes a generous, inviting gesture. Meanwhile, the poor, as depicted in a fresco in Lombardy, are miserable; they are shown reduced to a wretched state, dehumanized by hunger, their gaunt faces filled only with submission, and their bony hands barely able to hold the bowls with which they beg for food.

But there is more to such a representation than the dyad between the two types of poor. There is the viewer to take into consideration; otherwise the image has no purpose. Francis, the poor, and the viewer form a triad. The viewer is drawn to Francis; the viewer is supposed to venerate Francis, and indeed if the image works properly the viewer identifies with Francis. Also the poor display a reverential attitude towards Francis, and thus a second side of the triad is connected. But the miserable pauper is repulsive to the viewer, who thus can establish no identification with him. The triangle is not complete; the third side of the triad is not closed in. No direct relationship between viewer and the poor is established, but only

[27]George Kaftal, *Iconography of the Saints in Tuscan Painting* (Florence: Sansoni, 1952), 407; cf. Little, *Liberty, Charity, Fraternity*, 96, 97.

an indirect one, which passes via Francis. The role of Francis is thereby that of an intermediary. The son of a wealthy cloth merchant, he embraced the dregs of society. He never became completely poor, however. He remained always a rich man, disguised as a pauper. He was, and is, the intermediary between rich and poor.

CONCLUSION

It is time now to review the main lessons that emerge from this historical material. The first is that poverty takes many forms and that it is relative. The second is that there is a continuing need for the study of social conditions, and particularly of social change or innovation, in order to be timely in identifying new forms of poverty and their causes. The third and final lesson is that there is a continuing need for articulate intermediaries with the poor, a need for sensitive and courageous individuals willing to risk antagonizing the Establishment by going where it fears to tread.

Marie-Dominique Chenu was one of these. When he first left to go into exile in Rouen, he had to comfort those of his friends who were more manifestly upset than he was. Here is what he told them: "There is not an example in history of a society that has been able to adjust to important innovations without first defending itself against them and opposing those who at the moment seem to be upsetting the existing equilibrium."[28]

---

[28]De La Brosse, *Le Père Chenu*, 146.

Shoemaker

Weaver

Hatter

Barber

Craft Guilds
From woodcust of the sixteenth century

CHAPTER 9

CONFRATERNITIES AND GUILDS
IN THE LATE MIDDLE AGES

ANDRÉ VAUCHEZ

The late medieval urban and economic developments brought in their wake new experiences of alienation as persons lost the web of relationships fostered by village life, and experiences of impersonalism as money and day-labor displaced barter and crafts. The late medieval confraternities met these social needs by providing new possibilities for association. The fundamental social welfare contribution of confraternities was to provide "belonging" in a world where freedom was defined by incorporation into a collective order and where that order alone protected the rights of its members. Confraternities also engaged in specific acts of charity for their members such as certain forms of assistance in times of need, funeral rites, and abundant intercessory prayers. By the late Middle Ages, "great confraternities" progressed from pious associations to powerful institutions of mutual aid that were able to influence a town's program for social assistance. Because these charitable activities were rooted in a worldview of a "religion of deeds" based on a theology of satisfaction and an "accountability in the next life," the Protestant Reformers reacted strongly against them. Such a ritualistic conception of charity seemed by the eve of the Reformation to have rendered the confraternities incapable of responding constructively to the new urban needs for social welfare.

This chapter does not aim to trace the whole history of the confraternal movement in the Middle Ages; a brief essay cannot deal with all the many documents and problems involved. At the same time, a synthesis of the subject would be doomed to failure in advance, for the history of the confraternities is to a great extent still to be written. The observations here are restricted to the work that has already been done in this area, especially the recent research, in order to show both the state of current scholarship and the areas yet to be explored. These observations concern only the area extending from Flanders to Tuscany via the Rhine Valley and Savoy, concentrating on France, Switzerland, northern and central Italy. This does not of course mean that confraternities did not exist elsewhere.

The study of medieval confraternities is not new, but has periodically been in fashion for different reasons.[1] The historiography of the confraternal movement began in Western Europe. From 1840 onwards, interest in the confraternities, as well as the various guilds and the so-called corporations, reflected a post-romantic climate characterized by the desire to return to a more or less idealized medieval Christianity. After 1870, the denunciation of the evils linked to the exploitation of workers and to modern individualism gave rise, particularly among the defenders of social Catholicism, to a nostalgia for a pre-capitalist society which protected the weak by enfolding them in hierarchical organic structures. This longing formed the basis of a variety of historical works of unequal worth. Above all it resulted in numerous publications of source material—statutes and registers of the confraternities—which, in France for example, still form the documentary basis of our research in this area.

The second period, extending from the interwar years to the 1950s, was characterized by the stimulating influence of sociology, especially German sociology. This was because neither Emil Durkheim nor Marcel Mauss, the fathers of French sociology, was particularly interested in the phenomenon of group associations. Max Weber, on the other hand, one of the founders of the new discipline, took up the task of studying the so-called social structures. These included structures that existed between the social structures (the state, the "commune," the church) and the natural community (the family). The application of this methodology to the sphere of history was the concern of Gabriel Le Bras, whose article dealing with the Christian confraternities, published in 1940–1941 and re-edited in 1956 in his *Studies in Religious Sociology*, should be noted here.[2] Starting from the viewpoint of the church as a conglomerate of religious groupings and as an organization based on a permanent dialogue between its grassroots and its hierarchy, Le Bras emphasized the importance of studying the confraternities precisely at a point of convergence between the requirements of the ecclesiastics and the aspirations of the laity. The pious associations of the laity, in the Middle Ages at least, provided a subtle counterbalance to the oppressive preponderance of priests within the church. It is with a similar perspective that Father Meersseman, a French-writing Flemish Dominican, undertook the study of the confraternities of devotion. He pointed out their crucial role with regard to positions of status and privilege within a secular religiosity. It is appropriate to pay

[1]In regard to this historiographical approach, see André Vauchez, "Jalons pour une historiographie de la sociabilité," in F. Thelamon, ed., *Sociabilités, pouvoirs et société. Actes du colloque de Rouen 1983* (Rouen: Université de Rouen, 1987), 7–15.
[2]Gabriel Le Bras, *Etudes de sociologie religieuse*, 2 vols. (Paris: Presses Universitaires de France, 1956).

him homage. His remarkable works, recently republished in Italian trans-lation under the title *Ordo Fraternitatis*, have outside of Italy not had the renown that they deserve.[3]

Since the 1960s, other approaches to the phenomenon of the confrater-nities, and more generally to the phenomenon of association, have been taken, and the works of Maurice Agulhon have been particularly influen-tial. His study of the progressive passage of Provençal aristocracy from the confraternities of the penitents to the Masonic lodges revealed the fun-damental importance of the social practice of associations in bringing together groups that on an ideological level appear to have nothing in common.[4] Agulhon and his followers have also emphasized the existence of regional variations in sociability. An example is the rise in Provence of the *chambrettes*, or informal clubs, meeting in specific locations and surviv-ing under a variety of names, depending on the period, while maintaining identical structures and objectives.[5]

This new area of inquiry, which was initially opened up by specialists in the modern period, encouraged medievalists from the 1970s onwards to take up the study of the confraternities once more. Without claiming to give an exhaustive list, and while restricting the list to France, Switzer-land, and Italy, I draw attention to the following scholarship: Jacques Chiffoleau on Avignon and the *Comtat* , Noël Coulet on Provence, Giusep-pina Gasparini on Venitia, Charles M. de la Roncière on Tuscany, and Lester K. Little on Bergamo and its surroundings.[6] Their works have con-tributed to the revival of research in an area where essential work is still to be done. In the past few years a number of young scholars have begun working along these same lines.[7]

The initial conclusions that emerge from these recent works point to the universality of the phenomenon of confraternities during the latter

---

[3]G. G. Meersseman, *Ordo Fraternitatis. Confraternite e pietà dei laici nel Medio Evo*, 3 vols. (Rome: Herder, 1977).

[4]Maurice Agulhon, *Pénitents et franc-maçons* (Paris: Fayard, 1968).

[5]Cf. L. Roubin, *Les chambrettes des provençaux* (Paris: Plon, 1970).

[6]Jacques Chiffoleau, "Les confréries, la mort et la religion en Comtat Venaisson à la fin du Moyen Age," *Mélanges de l'Ecole française de Rome, Moyen Age - Temps Modernes* 91 (1979): 785–815. N. Coulet, "Le mouvement confraternel en Provence et dans le Comtat Venaissin au Moyen Age," in Ch. M. de la Roncière, ed., *Le mouvement confraternel au Moyen Age. France, Italie, Suisse (Actes de la Table Ronde de Lausanne, 1985)*, Rome-Lausanne, 1988, 83-110. G. de Sandre Gasparini, *Statuti di confraternite religiose di Padova nel Medio Evo* (Padua: Istituto per la Storia Ecclesiastica Padovana, 1974); Ch. M. de la Roncière, "La place des confréries dans l'encadrement religieux du contado florentin," *Mélanges de l'Ecole française de Rome, Moyen Age —Temps Modernes* 85 (1973): 13–77, 633–77. Lester K. Little, *Liberty, Charity, Fraternity. Lay Religious Confraternities at Bergamo in the Age of the Commune* (Northampton: Smith College, 1988).

[7]A comprehensive, useful survey of these recent studies is in *Le mouvement confraternel. France, Italie, Suisse (Actes de la Table Ronde de Lausanne, 1985)* (Rome: Ecole Française de Rome, 1987); cf. also J. Henderson, "The Flagellant Movement and Flagellant Confraterni-ties," *Studies in Church History* 15 (1978): 147–80.

centuries of the Middle Ages, at least in the geographical area we are considering. For this period we cannot find any areas where confraternities are totally absent; there are, on the contrary, regions like Italy where the archives hold plenty of documentation, and others where there is less evidence. This last statement should, however, be qualified. In many cases the research undertaken and the questions asked have brought to light sources for the history of confraternities which were once believed to be nonexistent, for example in central Switzerland. We can now assert, without fear of contradiction, that the confraternal phenomenon assumed massive proportions in the West between the fourteenth and sixteenth centuries and not only in the Mediterranean regions.

While one finds at least one confraternity per parish in Provence around 1400, it is not unusual to count several per village in the diocese of Geneva during the same period. And towns as far apart as Florence and Berne each had several dozen which assembled hundreds if not thousands of people altogether. Women and young people were not excluded and sometimes even met in special associations, as Richard Trexler has shown for fifteenth-century Florence.[8] The social milieux involved were certainly diverse. The world of confraternities was largely composed of independent craftsmen and tradesmen, and there appears to have existed, in the towns at least, a sort of unwritten limit which left out the highest echelons of the nobility and excluded the salaried workers unable to afford the modest entrance fee. But—at least in a relative sense, in terms of the establishment and recruitment of the confraternities—this universality did not exclude regional dissimilarities and variations. The differences in density that can be noticed here and there are not linked solely to the chance preservation of source material. The example of Normandy reveals a centuries-old contrast between upper Normandy with its wealth of confraternities, especially near Rouen, Fécamp, and Evreux, and lower Normandy where, in the fifteenth century, they were markedly less widespread. It must be acknowledged that these are differences which to a large extent are not yet explained, and subsequent studies will have to attempt to account for them.

Mysteries also remain with regard to the chronology of the confraternal movement and the various stages of its evolution. In Italy as in England they came into being early on, as Meersseman has shown, and in England as in Flanders the original link with the guilds seems clear. In France, particularly in the twelfth century, they made an appearance in the form of associations and prayer unions in conjunction with the monastic

---

[8]Richard Trexler, "Ritual in Florence. Adolescence and Salvation in the Renaissance," in Charles Trinkaus and Heiko A. Oberman, eds., *The Pursuit of Holiness in Late Medieval and Renaissance Religion* (Leiden: Brill, 1974), 200–64.

communities, paralleling the rapid upsurge of trade associations and the communal movement. But the first half of the thirteenth century marks an undeniable break in the history of these groupings. No doubt because of their egalitarian aspects, they seem at that point to have come up against the hostility of the powers-that-be, secular as well as ecclesiastical. In Marseilles for instance, in about 1230, the confraternity of the Holy Spirit was the starting point and the spearhead of the riot against the bishop's power that eventually led to the founding of a free commune.[9] Then, channeled and purified of all elements that worried the authorities, the movement took off again after 1300 with great momentum, reaching its peak in the fifteenth century. At that time it extended to all social categories, for that was the period when confraternities of priests were multiplying and new types of confraternities of devotion were appearing. But the most usual type, especially to the north of the Alps, was still the funeral confraternity, which guaranteed its members dignified funeral rites and abundant intercessory prayers, as well as, on occasion, a certain assistance with the difficulties of life. However, one cannot, as has sometimes wrongly been done, speak of the confraternity as a sort of medieval forerunner of our modern social security or National Health Service.

One cannot help but wonder about the factors which were at the root of the confraternities' general success towards the end of the Middle Ages. Various explanations, all of which reveal part of the truth, have been proffered. One is the renewed outbreaks of epidemics, which led to a dramatic increase in mortality and which upset the normal order of the succession of generations. Children rather often died before their parents, who dreaded that nobody would survive to bury them and pray for their souls. People feared not only a lonely death and being forgotten, but also the weakening of the links of family solidarity. But perhaps there is a more important reason. Deprived of the contentious aspects which they had taken on here and there in the twelfth and thirteenth centuries, the confraternities during the years 1300 to 1500 constituted a means of integration into civil life and access to social standing for individuals as well as groups. Indeed, they basked in an aura of respectability. Especially in the towns their so-called bourgeois status made them attractive to people on the margins of society (the lesser professions, immigrants recently arrived from the country, resident foreigners) who regarded the confraternities as a convenient means of infiltration and admission into what we now call the Establishment. The same phenomenon obtained on a religious level as certain confraternities such as the St. James pilgrims allowed simple

---

[9] P. Amargier, "Mouvements populaires et confréries du Saint-Esprit à Marseille au seuil du XIIIe siècle," in *La religion populaire en Languedoc du XIIIe à la moitié du XIVe siècle*, Cahiers de Fanjeaux, 11 (Toulouse: E. Privat, 1976), 305–19.

believers to play a more active and more visible role in the life of the parish or the local church. In a world where freedom was defined by incorporation into a collective order and where the assertion of an individual's rights was regarded as that of the group of which he was a member, the main aim was to *faire corps*, to "belong to a body," and to use this as a means for achieving recognition.

These positive considerations on the universal and widespread confraternal phenomenon should nevertheless be qualified in a number of ways. It is true that there were countless confraternities, and research into the archives in areas where they were plentiful constantly leads to new discoveries that allow us to add to the list. But we know that all these associations did not function at the same time; that several of them, at a given moment, amalgamated with others or ceased to exist. Furthermore, it is usually not possible to discover the reasons for these mutations. There was a sort of Brownian movement, which the fascinated historian can observe without really understanding it. There was a sequence of creation, intermittent disappearance and reappearance, and final dissolution, which lends to the confraternal phenomenon a changeable character and yet at the same time reveals underlying social dynamics whose components remain hidden. In any case, this instability illustrates well the power and inexhaustible creativity of the medieval associative movement, while at the same time uncovering its institutional fragility.

In addition to the aspects so far considered, more recent research allows us to go beyond a purely quantitative approach. While it is interesting to know that there existed, at a given period, one or several confraternities per village in such and such a region, it is even more interesting to define exactly what membership in such a group meant to its members. In short, is there not a risk of magnifying the importance of the confraternity in social and religious life when it was merely the accepted form—being sometimes the only one recognized and permitted by authorities—of community sociability, whether in terms of district, village, or profession? If that was the case, then the entries in its registers would have meant little more to the men and women of the Middle Ages than our own participation in the many associations to which we pay dues. Everybody knows that the latter certainly does not imply the existence of an authentic internal associative life. Indeed the investigations carried out in regions as different as Normandy or the Germanic world seem to indicate that plurality of membership was common everywhere. Some individuals even belonged to a dozen or more confraternities simultaneously! Such multiple membership would preclude members' extensive involvement in these associations. These would, therefore, have exercised a less profound influence than has previously been thought, with the exception of those confraternities of devotion which required that their members participate actively or else face fines or expulsion. Confraternities of devotion were, however, in the minority.

Catherine Vincent's recent study of Norman charitable organizations sheds new light on this fundamental question of membership participation.[10] Her study of the confraternities of this region, using their statutes and a few registers, reveals participation at two levels. For most members it was simply a matter of securing, by payment of a moderate subscription, a proper funeral or sometimes even one with pomp and ceremony. This was the kind of funeral which, as Chiffoleau showed with reference to Avignon and the *Comtat,* was from the end of the fourteenth century onwards sought after as much by the inhabitants of the towns as by those of the neighboring countryside.[11] Only the permanent officials of the associations, variously termed trustees (syndics), sergeants, or priors, really gave a lot of their time and formed the nucleus of influential persons, who by exercising responsibilities and attending a large number of meetings and religious services were really impregnated by the esprit de corps and the communal ideology that inspired it. In the extreme, it might be more appropriate to regard the confraternity less as a structure of sociability—which it was but only for a small minority of leaders—than as a relatively commonplace and in any case not binding phenomenon.

This hypothesis, however stimulating it may be, should nevertheless not become a new dogma. It would be going too far, I think, both to try to see the confraternity as a mere casual meeting place and also to regard it, as was done sometimes in the past, as a sort of Sunday school for the laity. One of the contributions of recent research in this area has in fact been to accentuate the problems of typology and to discount the traditional distinctions between professional confraternities, confraternities of charity or funerals, and pious associations. Apart from the groups of Penitents or Flagellants and the Third Orders of the Friars, which one encounters mainly in the Mediterranean regions, the confraternities at the end of the Middle Ages were almost always mixed.

Without concurring on an *a priori* definition of the confraternity, the authors of the most recent works agree in their emphasis on its open recruitment as well as its strongly multifunctional character. There certainly existed confraternities of priests or professions "in a pure state," to use the language of chemists, but the vast majority of these groups encompassed, in varying proportions, clerics and laypersons, men and women, young and old. Similarly, over and above differences, the same elements can almost always be found in their statutes. As a general rule, these com-

---

[10]Catherine Vincent, *Des charités bien ordonnées. Les confréries normandes de la fin du XIII au début du XVIe siècle* (Paris: Ecole normale supérieure, 1988).

[11]Chiffoleau, "Les confréries, la mort et la religon."

bine a certain number of simple religious acts (perpetual burning of candles before the altar of the patron saint, community mass in a church or chapel), charitable practices for internal and occasional external use, as well as an associative life which involved at least attendance at the annual banquet, if nothing else. But this empirical approach, which has the advantage of transcending the rigid and often artificial divisions established between the different types of confraternities, must not allow us to lose sight of the fact that there existed within the area thus circumscribed, perceptible differences of emphasis. We cannot equate an association content with one mass per year on the day of its patron saint with another that required participation in a monthly mass or Sunday service. Here, too, we must not overlook the originality of Central and Northern Italy where the confraternities, contrary to a widely accepted notion, were no more linked to the mendicant orders than they were elsewhere and yet from the thirteenth century onward constituted one of the environments in which secular spirituality blossomed.[12] That is shown by the role played by the *Laudesi* confraternities in the creation and development of a religious poetry in the vernacular.[13] But elsewhere, secular and religious aspects remained closely intertwined with the associative life, at least until the appearance, in the fifteenth century, of pious confraternities such as those of the Rosary or St. Ursala, especially in the Germanic world, or of the Corpus Christi confraternities in France and England.[14]

If the traditional typologies emerge rather shaken from the most recent works, others appear whose relevance still needs to be verified by future research. They concern, in particular, the notion of a territorial confraternity, that is to say, groups which united all or certainly the majority of the inhabitants of a village, a small market town or, in Italy, a *pivier*. This was a widespread institution to be found in Provence and in Dauphiné in the confraternities of the Holy Spirit, as well as in Lombardy in the *consortia plebis*. It would be wrong to regard these broad associations, which sometimes ended up by identifying themselves with the community of the inhabitants, as a purely rural phenomenon. They had their equivalent in the towns with the great confraternities (*grandes confréries*), such as the confraternity of the Holy Spirit in Fribourg whose mutations are particularly interesting to study. In the period between the early fourteenth and later fifteenth centuries, it progressed from its role as a pious association to

---

[12]Christopher Black, *Italian Confraternities in the Sixteenth Century* (Cambridge: Cambridge University Press, 1989).

[13]Cf. André Vauchez, "La Bible dans les confréries et les mouvements de dévotion," in P. Riché and G. Lobrichon, eds., *Le Moyen Age et la Bible* (Paris: Beauchesne, 1984), 581–95.

[14]Y. Dossat, "Les confréries du Corpus Domini dans le monde rural pendant la première moitié du XIVe siècle," in *La religion populaire*, 357–86.

that of a powerful institution of mutual aid which was to have a strong say in the town's program for social assistance.[15]

Apart from these institutional problems, whose importance is far from negligible, a consideration of the confraternities inevitably leads to the question of the relationship between the social and the religious elements in the medieval period. Questions arise in this area to which it is not always possible to give definitive answers, yet the historian cannot easily avoid them. Why was this need to "belong to a body," to *faire corps*, that was so fundamental in fourteenth and fifteenth century society, essentially transferred to confraternities that were dedicated to a saint or to the Virgin Mary, located in a church and meeting at least once a year for a mass and a banquet? Was it simply a camouflage for a professional association or a society of mutual help in the face of ecclesiastical or civil authorities which tolerated the confraternities, as we see in Paris in 1382 after the riots of the Maillotins, while at the same time suppressing the craftsworkers' associations? The reference to God, to the Holy Spirit, to the celestial court, and to the various intercessors that were invoked would, seen in this light, only be an ideological superstructure which need merely be removed in order to uncover the reality of the social tensions. The problem should probably not be formulated in such simple terms. Yet, whatever the case may be, it leads to a more comprehensive question concerning the part and the place of religion within the medieval associative movement as a whole.

If the confraternities are viewed in this light, it cannot be said (omitting again the particular cases of Italy, Provence, and Aragon's crown countries) that they provided education and deepened faith. But is it justifiable for all that to align the pious confraternities, which in the Mediterranean regions practiced a certain religious pedagogy and watched over the spiritual progress of the members, with the "societies of gluttons and boozers" denounced by Luther and immediately suppressed by the Reformation wherever it gained authority? The antithesis is probably also somewhat excessive, since the pursuit of the saints' intercessions for the deceased and the souls in Purgatory, the distribution of alms in times of hardship and scarcity, and the occasional organizing of aid for the sick were also embedded in a religious perspective. But it was a form of the "religion of deeds" so typical of the Late Middle Ages in these countries, and was founded on a theology of satisfaction and an "accountability in the next life" which in the eyes of the Protestant Reformers was the most abominable aspect of what they called "papist idolatry." It can be seen

---

[15]N. Morard, "Une charité bien ordonnée: la confrérie du Saint-Esprit de Fribourg," in *Le mouvement confraternel*, 275–96.

that the discussion is not yet closed, but recent research has highlighted some real problems and pointed to their complexity. At least one can take for granted, as John Bossey recently upheld in his good book *Christianity and the West*,[16] that the confraternities, even if they played only second fiddle in spiritual education, were nevertheless useful in teaching the faithful the Christian funeral ritual and in unifying the practices and the beliefs about death and the next world.

Specific reference to the social action of the confraternities is provided by Catherine Vincent's work on the Norman confraternities between the thirteenth and sixteenth centuries, which allows us to perceive both their importance and their limitations. There is no doubt that the earliest confraternities directed charitable activity toward the world of the poor and the sick. Thus the statutes of the confraternity of weavers at St. Lo, founded in 1234, specified that each member, annually on All Saint's Day, must give 6 deniers to the town hospital. Likewise in the ancient association of jugglers of St. Martin de Fécamp, two-fifths of the dues was directed to the leper house and one-fifth to the poor, not to mention the distributions of bread and beer provided by various other texts.

But by the later centuries of the Middle Ages this openness of the confraternities to the outer world tended to become restricted and reduced by symbolic gestures: the distribution of some deniers or bread to the poor on the feast day of the patron saint or on the occasion of a member's funeral, the invitation of thirteen poor people to the annual banquet, and so forth. By the fourteenth century the confraternities tended more and more to limit their generosity to their own members and to practice a simple mutual assistance. Thus in the case of misfortune they generally granted to members in difficulty a subsidy that could go as high as 6 deniers a week in the country or 20 sous in a large city such as Rouen. On average such aide was between one-half and one sou per day in the towns—equivalent to about the price of one chicken in the fifteenth-century market—and 1 denier in the villages—enough to buy one or two eggs. Thus it was an assistance which may have been helpful but which by itself did not allow a family to ensure its existence when its head had become incapable of working.

If the Norman confraternities at the end of the Middle Ages appear to be fearful of fostering idleness in displaying generosity toward their disadvantaged members, they were more fearful when the latter fell ill. In this case monetary assistance was provided which went up to 5 deniers per day in the country and to 2 or 2 sous per day in the town. We note that

---

[16]John Bossey, *Christianity and the West, 1400–1700* (Oxford: Oxford University Press, 1985).

at Rouen the subsidy thus practiced was raised sometimes to 3 sous per day when the illness lasted more than forty days. Some statutes also made provision for visitation of the sick on Sunday by the able-bodied fellow members, as well as the celebration of masses for their benefit. Pregnant women were not able to claim to benefit from this assistance but often had the right to a reduction of half their dues to the confraternity during their pregnancy. Other subsidies were sometimes provided to aid confraternal victims of a fire or to permit members to dower their daughters when they did not have the means.

But the most spectacular form of this mutual charity was without doubt the special assistance provided by the statutes for the fellow-members participating in distant pilgrimages (to Rome, St. James of Compostella, Jerusalem, St. Giles, St. Nicholas de Bari) as well as for the lepers who received as much as 20 sous at the time of their departure for the leper house. On such an occasion, the fellow members would escort the unfortunates in convoy to the limits of their parish as if the latter were the dead.

On the whole, the role played by the confraternities in the domain of assistance was no doubt not worthless nor itself insignificant in the Middle Ages. Even so, it is well to note that the extent of this aid becomes more and more of a question. In accord with their statutory obligations, the confraternities provided their members limited aid for the essentials of life, but over time, the importance of death and funerals eclipses other aspects of the "mutual love" which bound the members of the *charité* (the common name of confraternities in Normandy) to one another. In Normandy, in the fifteenth century, how the faithful were looking for this mutual love was less in financial aid enabling them to face the difficulties of life than in solidarity for facing death: the organization of processions from the house of the deceased to the cemetery, provision of a funeral pall to cover the coffin of poor fellow members, redemption of the excommunicated, who would otherwise not be buried in "Christian ground." It is above all at this level that the confraternal solidarity was fully operative and that it was sought out and valued.

New research is still to be done on the crises of the confraternities at the end of the fifteenth and the beginning of the sixteenth centuries, which even before the Reformation point to the existence of an inherent malaise. Their accumulation of wealth, especially in the case of the urban great confraternities, their spontaneous aspect (particularly the intermittent, eclipse-like appearance and disappearance of many of them), and their ritualistic conception of charity seemed to have rendered them incapable of responding to the new social requirements, especially in the domain of aid. Around 1500, confraternities almost everywhere began to lose ground in this sphere in favor of the municipalities or the state whose demands for rationality in administration, regulation, and health care as well as centralization of resources with regard to aid to the sick, the poor, and vagrants were to become accepted. This did not bring about the disappearance of confraternities but by passing into the hands of the authorities and by being reduced to mere institutions of the church such as parish guilds, they lost what had lent them their originality, their character of free association.

Another area, which has until now hardly been touched upon and toward which new research should be directed, is the anthropological approach to the rituals of sociability, especially greeting, meeting, and eating together, which played such an important part in the life of the confraternities. The available documentation is not, unfortunately, prolific, but the few items of information to be found in the statutes should be carefully studied with this perspective in mind. It might be appropriate, for example, to examine the link between the periodical charitable distributions by the confraternities and certain dates in the liturgical as well as the agricultural calendar which were punctuated by communal practices. It would also be of interest to look at the position held by the economics of death, the exchange of temporal possessions for hoped-for spiritual advantages, the vertical and horizontal circulation of intercessions within the association; and finally, to consider the relationship between their objectives, mostly in terms of funerals, and the importance which the burning of church candles held in their lives. It can be seen that several themes still remain to be explored, and new discoveries are yet to be made. But it seems clear that the study of the medieval associative movement, revived by new approaches, should provide us with a key to this past civilization which still fascinates our contemporaries, a civilization in which the desire to become included and incorporated does not appear to have been in conflict with the recognition of the individual's rights.

CHAPTER 10

THE LITURGY AFTER THE LITURGY: WELFARE IN THE EARLY REFORMATION

CARTER LINDBERG

> The medieval worldview formed by a "piety of achievement" idealized poverty as the preferred path to salvation actualized by either voluntary poverty or by alms to the poor. As Little states in his essay: "The most sensitive reactions remained moral, either by patronizing the poor (giving alms) or identifying with them (embracing voluntary poverty). The material effects on actual conditions were in either case necessarily modest." Urban efforts to respond to widespread poverty were thus stymied by the religious endorsement of poverty. The early Reformation in Germany, exemplified by Luther, undercut the medieval religious legitimation of poverty when it displaced salvation as human achievement with salvation as a divine gift. Towns were now freed to engage in a new field of discourse regarding social issues such as poverty and, with the active cooperation of Reformers such as Luther, they developed and passed new legislative structures for social welfare.

Late medieval social welfare was marked by struggles between urban laity and clergy over the administration of funds, properties, and institutions for relief of the poor. Contemporary historians frequently describe these struggles as lay efforts to rationalize and secularize early modern social welfare. They attribute these developments to humanism, developing urban political acumen, and bourgeois desire for social control.

My argument is that these important late medieval social and political developments received a new framework for articulation and legitimation by the early Reformation work of Martin Luther. Luther was a major contributor to the theory and praxis of early modern poor relief and social welfare. His theology not only undercut the medieval idealization of poverty; it also provided a theological rationale for social welfare that was translated into legislation. In the words of Robert Wuthnow, Luther "created, as it were, a *discursive field* in which to bring together in imaginative ways the practical realities of institutional life on the one hand and the ideas evident in Scripture on the other." This constructive resource for the development of social welfare was rooted in worship.[1] As such, social welfare for Luther was a specific example of liturgy after the liturgy, a work of the people flowing from worship. In short, the reform of worship entailed the renewal of social life.[2] A brief synopsis of Luther's medieval context is necessary to my argument.

The late medieval reading of the Bible and tradition was largely in terms of "a piety of achievement" measured by a "mathematics of salvation."[3] The familial, social, and demographic ruptures brought about by late medieval epidemics and urban migration along with the ecclesial crises extending from the Babylonian Captivity of the papacy through the Renaissance papacy led to what has been termed a "crisis of symbols of security."[4] This is pointedly illustrated by the widely popular fifteenth-century catechism, *Mirror of a Christian Man* by Dietrich Kolde. Kolde, whose catechism "was probably the most widely used Catholic catechism before and during the early years of the Reformation," summed up the widespread uncertainty about salvation when he wrote: "There are three things I know to be true that frequently make my heart heavy. The first troubles my spirit, because I will have to die. The second troubles my heart more, because I do not know when. The third troubles me above all. I do not know where I will go."[5]

These elements gave rise to what I call the "Avis mentality of religion," that is, when you are insecure about the market, try harder.[6] The

---

[1]Robert Wuthnow, *Communities of Discourse: Ideology and Social Structure in the Reformation, the Enlightenment, and European Socialism* (Cambridge: Harvard University Press, 1989), 134. It is important to remember that for this period worship was still a communal activity. Wuthnow, p. 26, states, "To the modern mind, trained to think of religion in terms of individual piety, sincerity of intentions, and private devotion, religion in this period consisted to a much greater degree of liturgy, officially organized and sanctioned by the church, which united the entire community in corporate participation."

[2]Cf. Theodor Strohm, "'Theologie der Diakonie' in der Perspektive der Reformation," in Paul Philippi and Theodor Strohm, eds., *Theologie der Diakonie* (Heidelberg: Heidelberger Verlagsanstalt, 1989), 183.

[3]These colorful and apt descriptions of late medieval piety are from Jacques Chiffoleau, *La Comptabilité de l'Au-delà. Les Hommes, la Mort et la Religion dans la Région d'Avignon à la Fin du Moyen Age (vers 1320–vers 1480)* (Rome: École Française de Rome, 1980).

[4]See, for examp0le, Frantisek Graus, "The Crisis of the Middle Ages and the Hussites," in Steven Ozment, ed., *The Reformation in Medieval Perspective* (Chicago: Quadrangle Books, 1971), 76–103; Heiko A. Oberman, "The Shape of Late Medieval Thought: The Birthpangs of the Modern Era," *Archive for Reformation History* 64 (1973): 13–33; Carter Lindberg, "Luther and the Crises of the Late Medieval Era," *Africa Theological Journal* 13/2 (1984): 92–104; et al.

[5]Denis Jantz, ed., *Three Reformation Catechisms: Catholic, Anabaptist, Lutheran* (New York: Edwin Mellon Press, 1982), 8, 127.

[6]A play on the words of a popular TV ad of the 1980s in which the Avis Car Rental Co. proclaimed "We're number two, so we try harder."

"economy of salvation," under the impact of religious uncertainty and the developing profit economy, was understood literally. Worship and welfare were no longer the inseparable expression of the community that "holds all in common" (Acts 4:32), but became distinct avenues, paved by money, for the achievement of salvation.[7] The mass was no longer communion, but the easily multipliable means to meet the "price of passage" from this world to the next.[8] And welfare was likewise perceived under the much overworked rubric from Ecclesiasticus that "almsgiving atones for sin."[9] Thus bishops and theologians quoted approvingly the old rationale that "God could have made all persons rich but he willed that there be poor in the world so that the rich would have an opportunity to atone for their sins."[10] Medieval preachers did not hesitate to refer to this relationship as a commercial transaction—the poor carry the riches of the wealthy on their backs to heaven.[11] An early fourteenth-century vernacular sermon by the Italian Dominican, Giordano da Pisa, similarly explains the divine rationale behind inequality:

> God has ordered that there be rich and poor so that the rich may be served by the poor and the poor may be taken care of by the rich. And this is a common organization among all peoples. Why

[7] "... forms of piety gained ground in the course of the Middle Ages in which concern for personal salvation was very strongly tied to material contributions to ecclesial institutions [foundations, masses, brotherhoods, poor relief]." Michael Bayer, "Die Neuordnung des Kirchenguts," in Helmar Junghans, ed., *Das Jahrhundert der Reformation in Sachsen* (Berlin: Evangelische Verlagsanstalt, 1989), 91–112, esp. 92.

[8] Cf. Chiffoleau, *La Comptabilité*, 323ff. Chiffoleau argues that the most evident sign of change in religion and piety in the late Middle Ages is "without doubt the penetration of mathematics, numbers, bookkeeping and cumulative logic in devotional practices" 434. Cf. also Hans Bernhard Meyer, SJ, *Luther und die Messe* (Paderborn: Bonifacius Verlag, 1965), 131.

[9] Ecclus. 3:30, "Water extinguishes a blazing fire: so almsgiving atones for sin." For example, in his *Libellus de Eleemosyna*, Innocent III clearly stated that almsgiving removes the stain of sin, and justifies and saves. J. P. Migne, ed., *Patrologiae cursus completus, series latina*, 221 vols. (Paris: Migne, 1844-1855), 217: 747 (hereafter cited *PL*).

[10] See Michel Mollat, *Les Pauvres au Moyen Age* (Paris: Hachette, 1979), 61. This theme is articulated, e.g., by the fourth-century North African bishop Optatus, the seventh-century French bishop Eligius (*PL* 87: 533), and the thirteenth-century pope Innocent III (*PL* 217: 749f.).

[11] This had already been stated centuries earlier by *the* theologian of the medieval church, Augustine. "If our possessions are to be carried away, let us transfer them to a place where we shall not lose them. The poor to whom we give alms! With regard to us, what else are they but porters through whom we transfer our goods from earth to heaven? Give away your treasure. Give it to a porter. He will bear to heaven what you give him on earth." *The Fathers of the Christian Church* (Washington: Catholic University Press, 1963), 11:268.

are the poor given their station? So that the rich might earn eternal life through them.[12]

The ancient tradition of the poor as intercessors with God was supplemented by a theology that presented the poor as objects for good works and thereby a means to salvation. On the eve of the Reformation, the "piety of achievement" permeated all aspects of worship and welfare.

By the fifteenth century, however, poverty was no longer only a theological virtue and an opportunity for the salvatory works of the rich; it was also a major social problem comprising a complex of issues involved with the developing profit economy, work, idleness, begging, and poor relief. Statistical studies of the tax registers of the time indicate that in the cities the portion of the populace who were without property, the so-called *Habnichts*, ranged from 30 to 75 percent.[13] Furthermore, there were major fluctuations in this widespread poverty because large numbers of day laborers survived at a subsistence level without any reserves for times of crisis; thus they were always on the verge of mendicancy.[14] Practical efforts to restrain begging were frustrated by a theology that legitimated begging and valued almsgiving, and by a church whose own mendicants compounded the social problems of poverty by their own begging. Sermonic and literary exposés of false beggars such as the *Liber vagatorum* were not directed against poverty and begging as such. Rather, they were designed to assist the charitable citizen concerned about the "embezzlement of heaven" because alms given to frauds went to the devil instead of God.[15] Religiously, begging continued to be valued as a vocation; the poor had an important social as well as soteriological function as intercessors for almsgivers.

[12]Sermon of 1303/4 cited by Daniel Lesnick, *Preaching in Medieval Florence: The Social World of Franciscan Dominican Spirituality* (Athens: University of Georgia Press, (1989), 126. Cf. also 151: "The Franciscan encouraged charity for the benefits it brought to the giver." The Catholic renewal movement of the sixteenth and seventeenth centuries did not significantly alter this motivation for charity. "It was not the poor person himself who counted, but the act accomplished in the sight of God or for the good of the church." Louis Chatellier, *The Europe of the Devout: The Catholic Reformation and the Formation of a New Society* (Cambridge: Cambridge University Press; Paris: Editions de la Maison des Sciences de l'Homme, 1989), 133.

[13]See the tables in Wolfram Fischer, *Armut in der Geschichte* (Göttingen: Vandenhoeck & Ruprecht, 1982), 17–18.

[14] Carlo Cipolla, "Economic Fluctuations, The Poor, and Public Policy (Italy—16th and 17th Centuries)," in Thomas Riis, ed., *Aspects of Poverty in Early Modern Europe* (Stuttgart: Klett-Cotta, 1981), 65–78.

[15] Peter Assion, "Matthias Hütlin und sein Gaunerbüchlein, der 'Liber vagatorum,'" in *Alemannisches Jahrbuch* (1971/72): 74–92, 87f.; Hans Scherpner, *Theorie der Fürsorge* (Göttingen: Vandenhoeck & Ruprecht, 1962), 50, 203f.; Robert Jütte, *Abbild und Soziale Wirklichkeit Des Bettler—und Gaunertums zu Beginn der Neuzeit* (Cologne: Böhlau, 1988), 43.

Luther undercut this medieval religious ideology of poverty by his doctrine of justification by grace alone, apart from human works. Since righteousness before God is by grace alone, and since salvation is the source of life rather than the achievement of life, poverty and the plight of the poor could no longer be rationalized as a peculiar form of blessedness. There is no salvific value in being poor or in giving alms. This new theology de-ideologized the medieval approach to the poor, which had both obscured the social and economic problems of poverty, and obstructed the development of rational responses to poverty.[16] In other words: "The role of a clear discursive field such as that enunciated by the reformers was to alter the framework in which specific conflicts and grievances were expressed."[17]

We can see the beginnings of this process already in that document by which the Reformation is conventionally dated: the Ninety-Five Theses (1517). Luther's critique of the sacrament of penance was grounded in Jesus' words, "Repent and believe in the gospel" (Mk. 1:15; Thesis 1). which apply to "the entire life of believers."[18] This struck directly at the heart of the contemporary church's power because the priest, according to church doctrine, determined the steps and conditions of penance necessary for the sinner to obtain God's grace. The anxiety before death and God's judgment was met by the necessity of good works. Thus it may be argued that alms to begging cripples, hungry children, and the poor as well as to the mendicant monks appeared as welcome aids in the endeavors for eternal salvation, but did little to liberate the conscience of the almsgiver.[19]

Luther, however, understood the preaching office to be responsible for the liberation of consciences, and therefore also responsible for raising and commenting upon issues of worldly government such as poor relief.[20] Furthermore, not only was the preacher obligated to social-ethical instruction and action; so too was the Christian congregation

---

[16] On the doctrine of justification as the source for Luther's social ethics, see George W. Forell, *Faith Active in Love. An Investigation of the Principles Underlying Luther's Social Ethics* (Minneapolis: Augsburg, 1959); David Steinmetz, "Luther and the Two Kingdoms," in his *Luther in Context* (Bloomington: Indiana University Press, 1986); Theodor Strohm, "Martin Luthers Sozialethik und ihre Bedeutung für die Gegenwart," in Hans Süssmuth, ed., *Das Luther-Erbe in Deutschland* (Düsseldorf: Droste Vl., 1985), 68–91; et al.

[17] Wuthnow, *Communities of Discourse*, 138.

[18] Jaroslav Pelikan & Helmut Lehmann, general eds., *Luther's Works*, 55 vols. (Minneapolis: Fortress; St. Louis: Concordia, 1955-1986), 31: 25 (hereafter cited as LW).

[19] Gerta Scharffenorth, *Den Glauben ins Leben ziehen ...: Studien zu Luthers Theologie* (Munich: Chr. Kaiser, 1982), 46.

[20] Cf. Strohm, "Martin Luthers Sozialethik," 71–72; Scharffenorth, *Den Glauben ins Leben ziehen*, 46-47. (note cont'd. next page)

(*Gemeinde*). Its worship activity was the source and resource for service to the neighbor.[21] In the Ninety-Five Theses Luther stated: "Christians are to be taught that he who gives to the poor or lends to the needy does a better deed than he who buys indulgences" (Thesis 43). Also, "he who sees a needy man and passes him by, yet gives his money for indulgences, does not buy papal indulgences but God's wrath" (Thesis 45). Luther rejected the ancient idea that the poor are the treasure of the church: "St. Laurence said that the poor of the church were the treasures of the church, but he spoke according to the usage of the word in his own time" (Thesis 59).[22]

By 1519 Luther had amplified this connection between theology, worship, and social ethics in a number of tracts and sermons. In his "Short Sermon on Usury"[23] he contrasted God's command to serve the neighbor with the self-chosen "worship" that concentrated on building churches and endowing masses to the detriment of the needy. In his treatise "The Blessed Sacrament of the Holy and True Body of Christ, and the Brotherhoods," written in German and addressed to the laity because Luther was concerned that the people understand his sacramentally rooted ethics,[24] he specifically relates reform of the mass to social ethics.

Heiko A. Oberman makes this same point concerning Luther's understanding of the gospel: "(T)he Gospel's *primary* function is not—as assumed today, and was indeed the case in the City Reformation —to change *obvious* injustice by introducing social legislation to establish *biblical* justice, but to unmask *hidden* injustice, thus saving the souls of duped Christians and opening the eyes of the secular authorities for their mandate to establish *civil* justice." "Teufelsdreck: Eschatology and Scatology in the 'Old' Luther," *Sixteenth Century Journal* 19/3 (1988): 435-450, esp. 444.

[21] Junghans, "Sozialethisches Denken," 70. Cf. also Igor Kiss, "Luthers Bemühungen um eine sozial gerechtere Welt," *Zeichen der Zeit* (1985): 59-65, 61.

[22] LW 31: 29-31. According to an early church tradition, the Roman deacon and martyr, St. Laurence (†258), responded to the demand that he surrender the treasures of the church by assembling the poor to whom he had distributed the church's possessions, saying, "These are the treasure of the church." Cf. "Laurence, St." in F. L. Cross and E. A. Livingstone, eds., *The Oxford Dictionary of the Christian Church* (New York: Oxford University Press, 1984), 804.

[23] *D. Martin Luthers Werke: Kritische Gesamtausgabe*, Weimar Ausgabe, 1883ff., 6: 3-8; cf. 7: 15-20. Hereafter cited as WA. This sermon was greatly expanded into "The Long Sermon on Usury" in 1520 (WA 6: 36-60), which in turn was appended to his 1524 treatise on trade that is known as "Trade and Usury" (WA 15: 279-313, 321-322; LW 45: 233-310).

[24] Subtitled "Fur die Leyen," WA 2: 739. The tract is in WA 2: 738-758; LW 35: 47-73. (Although the term confraternity is frequently used for these associations, Luther uses the German equivalent, "Bruderschaft.") Cf. Gerhard Müller, "Zu Luthers Sozialethik," in Helmut Hesse and Gerhard Müller, eds., *Über Martin Luthers "Von Kauffshandlung und Wucher"* (Frankfurt a.M./Düsseldorf: Verlag Wirtschaft und Finanzen, 1987), 59–79, esp. 62f. Luther's concern to provide theological and ethical guidance for the laity is evident throughout his catechisms. See his exposition of the seventh commandment in his *Large Catechism* in Theodore Tappert, ed., *The Book of Concord* (Philadelphia: Muhlenberg, 1959), 395ff.

The *significance* or effect of this sacrament is fellowship of all the saints.... Hence it is that Christ and all saints are one spiritual body, just as the inhabitants of a city are one community and body, each citizen being a member of the other and of the entire city....

To carry out our homely figure, it [Christian fellowship] is like a city where every citizen shares with all the others the city's name, honor, freedom, trade, customs, usages, help, support, protection, and the like, while at the same time he shares all the dangers of fire and flood, enemies and death, losses, taxes, and the like.... Here we see that whoever injures one citizen injures an entire city and all its citizens; whoever benefits one [citizen] deserves favor and thanks from all the others. So also in our natural body, as St. Paul says in 1 Cor. 12[:25–26], where he gives this sacrament a spiritual explanation, "The members have [the same] care for one another; if one member suffers, all suffer together; if one member is honored, all rejoice together." This is obvious: if anyone's foot hurts him, yes, even the little toe, the eye at once looks at it, the fingers grasp it, the face puckers, the whole body bends over to it, and all are concerned with this small member; again, once it is cared for all the other members are benefited. This comparison must be noted well if one wishes to understand this sacrament, for Scripture uses it for the sake of the unlearned.[25]

Luther's analogy of the relationship of sacrament and social ethics to the benefits and responsibilities of citizenship is noteworthy with regard to the relationship of the Reformation and the cities. The right use of the sacrament builds up community.[26] Thus the person in need is enjoined to "go joyfully to the sacrament of the altar and lay down his woe in the midst of the community ... and seek help from the entire company" just as a citizen would ask the authorities and fellow citizens for help.[27]

In short, Luther argued, this is a sacrament of love that shares "the misfortunes of the fellowship." "As love and support are given you, you in turn must render love and support to Christ in his needy ones."

[25] LW 35, 50-52. For Luther the sacrament applies not only to one's personal affliction but also to the affliction of all the needy everywhere. Cf. Ursula Stock, *Die Bedeutung der Sakramente in Luthers Sermonen von 1519* (Leiden: Brill, 1982), 248f.

[26] Luther emphasized that every citizen is a "member of the authority" because he is co-responsible for right governance. Cf. his "Sermon on Keeping Children in School" (LW 46, 207-258), and "Zirkulardisputation über Matth. 19, 21" (WA 39 II, 39-51.); Strohm, "Martin Luthers Sozialethik," 71; and Stock, *Die Bedeutung der Sakramente.*

[27] LW 35, 53f. This point was recalled in the church orders. Cf. Scharffenorth, *Den Glauben*, 116–17.

Indeed, on the basis of the sacrament, the Christian "must fight, work, pray" for the needy.[28] From Luther's perspective the late medieval church had broken this connection between worship and welfare to the detriment of each. "So we at present see to our sorrow that many masses are held and yet the Christian fellowship which should be preached, practiced, and kept before us by Christ's example has virtually perished."[29] Referring to the early church, Luther continues, "But in times past this sacrament was so properly used, and the people were taught to understand this fellowship so well, that they even gathered food and material goods in the church, and there ... distributed among those who were in need."[30] To emphasize his point, Luther interprets the origin of the Collect in the mass as a general collection and fund gathered to be given to the poor.[31] On the other hand, Luther may have been aware of patristic sources that linked worship and welfare, and provided rudimental models for his development of the common chest concept of social welfare.[32]

[28]LW 35: 54.

[29]LW 35: 54. LW 35: 56. The medieval Franciscan desire for poverty was related to its usefulness for salvation and thus had little to do with the involuntary poverty of the needy. See Lesnick, *Preaching in Medieval Florence,* 148–49.

[30]LW 35: 57.

[31]LW 35: 57. See also his "A Treatise on the New Testament, That Is, the Holy Mass," 1520, LW 35:95: "... the priest elevates in the paten and offers to God the unconsecrated host at the same time that the offertory is being sung and the people are making their offering. This shows that what is being offered to God by us is not the sacrament, but only those 'collects' and offerings of food and goods that have been gathered, that God is being thanked for them, and they are being blessed for distribution to all the needy."

[32]Justin Martyr's "First Apology" in Cyril Richardson, ed., *Early Christian Fathers,* The Library of Christian Classics, 1 (Philadelphia: Westminster Press, 1953), 287: "What is collected is deposited with the president, and he takes care of orphans and widows, and those who are in want on account of sickness or any other cause, and those who are in bonds, and the strangers who are sojourners among [us], and, briefly, he is the protector of all those in need." Tertullian's "Apology" in A. Roberts & J. Donaldson, eds., *The Ante-Nicene Fathers,* 3 (Grand Rapids: Eerdmans, 1953), 46: "Though we have our treasure chest, it is not made up of purchase-money, as of a religion that has its price.... These gifts are, as it were, piety's deposit fund. For they are ... to support and bury poor people, to supply the wants of boys and girls destitute of means and parents, and of old persons confined now to the house; such, too, as have suffered shipwreck; and if there happen to be any in the mines, or banished to the islands, or shut up in the prisons.... [W]e do not hesitate to share our earthly goods with one another. All things are in common among us but our wives." The renaissance of patristic studies at Wittenberg was heralded by Melanchthon's 1518 inaugural lecture, "On the Reform of Studies." Cf. Peter Fraenkel, *Testimonia Patrum: The Function of the Patristic Argument in the Theology of Philip Melanchthon* (Geneva: Droz, 1961). On Luther's early acquaintance with patristics and humanist contributions to it, cf. Helmar Junghans, *Der junge Luther und die Humanisten* (Weimar: Böhlaus, 1984). See also Maria Grossmann, *Humanism in Wittenberg 1485-1517* (Nieuwkoop: de Graaf, 1975), 112: "As the [Wittenberg] library became more and more a place for students and scholars, the works of the humanists, of the classical writers and of the Church Fathers were collected in increasing numbers. That a library of such a humanistic character could be the best basis for the new movement originating at Wittenberg is borne out by Luther's own testimony."

The extent to which the mass has degenerated from this service to God in the neighbor to self-service is evident, Luther claims, in "the evil practices of the brotherhoods." By the sixteenth century, brotherhoods which had originally been lay associations for devotional and charitable purposes had largely devolved into vehicles for salvation.[33] Each brotherhood had its own priests, altars, chapels, and festivals. An example is the Brotherhood of 11,000 Virgins in Cologne that assured participants of the merits of 6,455 masses, 3,550 entire Psalters, 200,000 rosaries, 200,000 Te Deums, and so forth. The merits of one brotherhood were multiplied through "cartel" arrangements with other brotherhoods.[34] Thus the Electoral Saxon councilor Degenhard Pfeffinger by his death in 1519 belonged to eight brotherhoods in Wittenberg, and through them enjoyed the salvatory achievements of 27 foreign associations. In 1520 there were 21 such brotherhoods in Wittenberg.[35]

Since these brotherhoods were based upon the multiplication of masses and other religious practices to achieve merit for salvation, Luther's critique of them is linked to his exposition of the sacrament. These supposed convocations of good works have become occasions for debauchery.

> What have the names of Our Lady, St. Anne, St. Sebastian, or other saints to do with your brotherhoods, in which you have nothing but gluttony, drunkenness, useless squandering of money, howling, chattering, dancing, and wasting of time? If a sow were made the patron saint of such a brotherhood she would not consent.... Woe unto them who do this, and [unto them who] permit it![36]

Real Christian brotherhood, Luther argued, would serve the poor. His initial elaboration of this point foreshadowed the development of the common chest and its institutionalization of social welfare in the evangelical church orders.

[33]"If giving alms helped to wash away sin, then helping the poor was a way for the wealthy to gain salvation. Just as the confraternity was a mutual aid organization that provided insurance against a sudden plunge from affluence to poverty, so it was also, through the opportunity to give to the poor, a means of acquiring insurance for the life eternal.... that member who did his or her best to follow its statutes [was promised] the blessing of God in this world and everlasting life in the next. Under the circumstances, that was a handsome return upon a modest investment." Lester K. Little, *Liberty, Charity, Fraternity. Lay Religious Confraternities at Bergamo in the Age of the Commune* (Northampton: Smith College, 1988), 97.

[34]Brotherhoods were also by this time known as "societies" and "consortiums," which were terms with the new commercial significance of pooling investments for profit-seeking ventures. Little, *Liberty, Charity, Fraternity*, 68–69.

[35]See Lindberg, "No Beggars among Christians," 316 n. 12, and Stock, *Die Bedeutung der Sakramente*, 276.

[36]LW 35: 68.

If men desire to maintain a brotherhood, they should gather provisions and feed and serve a tableful or two of poor people, for the
sake of God…. Or they should gather the money which they
intend to squander for drink, and collect it into a common treasury, each craft for itself. Then in cases of hardship, needy fellow
workmen might be helped to get started, and be lent money, or a
young couple of the same craft might be fitted out respectably
from this common treasury.[37]

These suggestions are further elaborated in Luther's 1520 writings,
the "Long Sermon on Usury," the "Treatise on Good Works," and the
"Address to the Christian Nobility." The latter writing in particular presents an explicit and forceful expression of Luther's new conception of
social welfare and poor relief based upon his doctrine of justification.
Here he urged that every city and place should take care of its poor, and
that all begging be forbidden. He conceived of securing a minimal existence for those unable to work but also stressed that those who were able
had a responsibility to work.[38] By this time Luther was already arguing
that the source of contemporary impoverishment is not the feudal
system but the new profit economy. "Therefore, I beg and pray at this
point that everyone open his eyes and see the ruin of his children and
heirs. Ruin is not just at the door, it is already in the house. I pray and
beseech emperor, princes, lords, and city councilors to condemn this
trade as speedily as possible and prevent it from now on…. In this connection, we must put a bit in the mouth of the Fuggers and similar com-
panies."[39]

THE INSTITUTIONALIZATION OF SOCIAL WELFARE

The first effort to institutionalize welfare in Wittenberg, known as the *Beutelordnung,* was passed by the town council with Luther's assistance sometime in late 1520 or early 1521.[40] The next major step was the council's
Wittenberg Order of January 1522[41] influenced by both Luther and his colleague Andreas Karlstadt. The focus of this legislation was the reform of
worship and welfare. Of the seventeen articles in this legislation, all but

---

[37]LW 35: 68-69. This same point is repeated in the "Address to the Christian Nobility."
"But if there were a brotherhood which raised money to feed the poor or to help the needy,
that would be a good idea." LW 44:193.

[38]LW 44: 189–91.

[39]LW 44: 213.

[40]For the text of this "Common Purse" and relevant literature, see Ernst Koch, "Zusatz
zur Wittenberg Beutelordnung. 1520 oder 1521," WA 59:62–65.

[41]Hans Lietzmann, ed., *Die Wittenberger und Leisniger Kastenordnung* (Berlin: De Gruyter,
1935).

three are concerned with alleviating the plight of the poor. A common chest was established for poor relief, low interest loans were provided for workers and artisans, and education and training for children of the poor were subsidized. Funding was provided from the endowments of the discontinued religious institutions and church properties. If this funding was not sufficient, article eleven provided for a sort of graduated tax on the clergy and citizens "for the maintenance of the multitude of the poor." Begging, including that of monks and mendicants, was abolished. Artisans and craftsmen unable to repay loans would be excused from repayment for God's sake. Daughters of the poor would be provided with appropriate dowries and given in marriage.

The next major legislative expression of the relationship of the reform of worship and the institutionalization of welfare was the Leisnig Order of 1523. In his Preface, Luther explicitly tied worship and welfare together. "Now there is no greater service of God [*Gottes Dienst*, i.e., worship] than Christian love which helps and serves the needy, as Christ himself will judge and testify at the Last Day, Matthew 25[:31-46]."[42] This biblical passage portrays the separation of the sheep from the goats on the basis of their respective care and neglect of the poor and the oppressed.

In September 1522 Luther responded to the appeal of the Leisnig town council and spent a week there assisting the parish in developing a comprehensive evangelical church order which included a common chest for poor relief. In January 1523 the town council and the congregation sent two representatives to Wittenberg with a formal letter requesting his further advice on their proposed ordinance.[43] The letter notes the establishment of a common chest "to the honor of God and for the love of fellow Christians," and requests Luther to provide the community with a biblical rationale for the calling of evangelical pastors and an evangelical order of worship. Luther responded to the town council on 29 January 1523 with a letter expressing his great joy and pleasure over their ordinance. He hopes that their order "shall both honor God and present a good example of Christian faith and love to many people."[44] By early summer Luther responded in print to the request for biblical warrants for Leisnig's plans in the following writings: "Ordinance of a Common Chest: Preface. Suggestions on How to Deal with Ecclesiastical Property," "That a Christian Assembly or Congregation Has the Right and Power to Judge all Teaching and to Call, Appoint, Dismiss Teachers,

---

[42]LW 45:172. Cf. Junghans, "Sozialethisches Denken," 70; and WA 12: 13, 26f. This is the motif of Christian vocation as *Gottesdienst*. Cf Müller, "Zu Luthers Sozialethik," 64f.

[43]WA Br 3: 21–23. See also WA 12:3ff.; LW 45:163ff.

[44]WA Br 3: 23.

Established and Proven by Scripture," and "Concerning the Order of Public Worship."[45]

The Leisnig parish proceeded to reform the order of worship and to set up their common chest for social welfare on the basis of Luther's advice and his theological legitimation of their concern through his doctrine of the universal priesthood of all the baptized. The organization and principles of the common chest included the election of ten directors or trustees by the community every year on the first Sunday after January 13: "two from the nobility, two from the incumbent city council, three from among the common citizens of the town, and three from the rural peasantry." The three important and detailed record books were to be kept in the chest, itself locked with four locks, and kept in a secure place in the church. The different locks had keys assigned to the representatives of the groups involved. The directors were to give triennial reports to the whole community. The funds from the common chest were also to be used for maintenance of buildings, pastors' salaries, and schools—including a special school for girls. This inclusiveness proved to be a strain on resources. Thus Johann Bugenhagen, the great Wittenberg formulator of church orders, later separated the common chest funds from the funds for church maintenance and education.

The Leisnig Order like its predecessor in Wittenberg prohibited all begging. This was a departure from the late medieval begging orders whose purpose was to control rather than eliminate begging.[46] The Reformation church orders mandated that only the truly needy should be supported, all others must either leave or work—a theme to be repeated in countless later pamphlets under the overworked motto that he who does not work shall not eat [2 Thess. 3:6–13].[47]

The initial funding for the common chest came from the expropriated church properties and endowments that the medieval church had cultivated as works contributing to salvation. Luther hoped that as a result of the Leisnig example there would "be a great decline in the existing foundations, monastic houses, chapels, and those horrible dregs which have until now fattened on the wealth of the whole world under

---

[45]LW 45: 161–76; LW 39: 303–14; LW 53: 7–14.

[46]See G. Uhlhorn, Die christliche Liebestätigkeit (Stuttgart, 1890), 3: 543: "None of these [medieval] ordinances pursued the goal of eliminating begging by an ordered poor relief program providing for the needy....These orders were thus able to provide little help for they had the effect of, so to speak, legalizing and organizing begging, thereby strengthening it more than combatting it. The complaint became universal that begging was increasing in spite of the begging ordinances."

[47]See Adolf Laube, ed., Flugschriften der frühen Reformationsbewegung, II (Berlin: Akademie Verlag, 1983), 1008. The distinction between the worthy and the unworthy poor was, however, already being made in the Late Middle Ages.

the pretense of serving God."[48] But Luther was very concerned about the possibility of plundering the church. "[T]here is need of great care lest there be a mad scramble for the assets of such vacated foundations, and everyone makes off with whatever he can lay his hands on."[49] Luther's advice was to place all the ecclesial assets in the common chest after providing for those who wished to remain in the cloisters, giving transitional support to those who wished to leave the monastic life, and partially restoring funds to the needy families of donors. The remaining capital was still a major financial resource, but with foresight for potential insufficiency in the future, the community decreed that each person in the parish "according to his ability and means, [annually] remit in taxes" what the general assembly deems necessary.[50]

In terms of direct relief to the poor, the order regulated disbursements of loans and gifts to newcomers to help them get settled, to the house-poor to help them get established in a trade or occupation, and to orphans, dependents, the infirm, and the aged for daily support. The order concluded on behalf of all the inhabitants that all its articles and provisions "shall at all times be applied, used, and administered faithfully and without fraud by the parish here in Leisnig for no other purpose than the honor of God, the love of our fellow Christians, and hence for the common good...."[51]

In a remarkably short period of time these reforms of worship and welfare became models for similar efforts throughout the empire. Luther, of course, did not stand alone in this development. His Wittenberg colleague, Karlstadt, utilized Luther's early writings[52] to develop his own position. In late January 1522 Karlstadt published his own perception of the relationship of worship and social welfare: "Von abtuhung der Bylder und das keyn Bedtler unther den Christen seyn sollen."[53] However, Karlstadt's removal of himself from the Wittenberg scene, and his falling-out with Luther, precluded any further contributions he might have made to the translation of theology into social welfare legislation. One early Reformer who did not contribute to the development of early

[48]LW 45:169f.
[49]LW 45:170.
[50]LW 45:192.
[51]LW 45:194.
[52]See Lindberg, "No Beggars among Christians," 324ff.
[53]January 27, 1522, three days following the Wittenberg Order. The tract is edited by Hans Lietzmann in the series *Kleine Texte für Theologische und Philologische Vorlesungen und Übungen*, 74 (Bonn: A. Marcus & E. Weber, 1911). My English translation of the latter half, "No Beggars among Christians," is in C. Lindberg, ed., *Piety, Politics, and Ethics: Reformation Studies in Honor of George Wolfgang Forell* (Kirksville: Sixteenth Century Journal Publishers, 1984), 157–66.

modern social welfare was Thomas Müntzer. This is of interest because of the association of Müntzer with the Peasants' War and the claims that he was a forerunner in social concerns.[54] But Müntzer, like Karlstadt, focused on the inner regeneration of the believer. For Müntzer there could be no liturgy after the liturgy because he was not looking for better days but rather the end of all days. In spite of his positive press as the forerunner of socialism, his theological work was not translatable into the legislation of church orders.[55] Furthermore, Müntzer's attack upon feudalism may have been less a concern for social justice than it was an expression of his close ties to the developing merchant class.[56] In his "Highly Provoked Vindication," Müntzer rejected Luther's critique of merchants and business practices expressed in his 1524 tract "Trade and Usury."[57] In contrast to Müntzer's attacks on the old order, feudalism, Luther focused his prophetic criticism upon the new order, the developing profit economy.[58] Economic life itself no less than social welfare is to serve the needy neighbor.

To suggest that "the Reformation was neither as radical nor as successful a break with the past as traditional Reformation historiography has led us to believe," or that the Reformation "seemed to have little real impact among the masses"[59] is to miss the power of the liturgy to stimulate change.[60] To gainsay this is to ignore the contemporary role of the

[54]Müntzer is one of those historical personalities who are known more by the history of their reception than by their own works. Siegfried Bräuer, "Die Theologie Thomas Müntzers als Grundlage seiner sozialethischen Impulse," Standpunkt (Evangelische Monatsschrift) 70/3 (1989): 62–67, esp. 63. For review essays of the most recent Müntzer scholarship cf. C. Lindberg, "Müntzeriana," Lutheran Quarterly 4/2 (1990): 195–214; and James M. Stayer, "Thomas Müntzer in 1989: A Review Article," Sixteenth Century Journal 21/4 (1990): 655–70.

[55]The kind of practical advice that Luther sets forth, e.g., in "To the Christian Nobility," is totally missing in Müntzer. Bräuer, "Die Theologie Thomas Müntzers," 63.

[56]Ulrich Bubenheimer, Thomas Müntzer. Herkunft und Bildung (Leiden: Brill, 189), 128, 141–44. The claim that Müntzer changed congregations in Zwickau because he was the champion of the poor is a legend. See Helmar Junghans, "Der Wandel des Müntzerbildes in der DDR von 1951/52 bis 1989," Luther 3 (1989): 102–30, esp. 104f., 125.

[57]Bubenheimer, Thomas Müntzer: Herkunft und Bildung, 142f.

[58]Throughout his career Luther attacked the new capitalism as a major source of social injustice and suffering, going so far as to exhort pastors to excommunicate "usurers." See, inter alia, "Kleiner Sermon vom Wucher," 1519 (WA 6:3–8), "Grosser Sermon vom Wucher," 1520 (WA 6: 36–60), "Trade and Usury," 1524 (LW 45: 233–310), "An die Pfarrhern, wider den Wucher zu predigten," 1540 (WA 51, 331-424), et al. Scharffenorth, Den Glauben ins Leben ziehen, 316f., comments that it is surprising that so little research has been done on these writings and their impact for they stimulated broad public discussion.

[59]R. W. Scribner, Popular Culture and Popular Movements in Reformation Germany (London: Hambledon Press, 1987), 353.

[60]Evangelicals often paid a high price for their faith. Cf. Scharffenorth, Den Glauben ins Leben ziehen, 332; and Paula Fichtner, Protestantism and Primogeniture in Early Modern Germany (New Haven: Yale University Press, 1989).

church in the fall of the East German government. The recent liturgy in the streets of Leipzig, i.e., mass demonstration, was a consequence of the liturgy of the prayer group of Leipzig's St. Nicholas Church. Like Luther, this community understood the relationship of worship and social change. It was from this Reformation conviction that the widely effective church orders penned by Bugenhagen and others flowed.[61] The reform of worship included the renewal of community life.[62] In the words of the title of the 1523 tract by the Strassburg reformer Martin Bucer: *One Should Not Live for Oneself Alone But for Others, and How to Go About It.*[63] The attempt to resolve social problems in the cities was a constitutive component of the early Reformation, and the decisive theoretical break-through for it goes back to Luther.[64]

[61]Martin Brecht, "Luthertum als politische und soziale Kraft in den Städten," in Franz Petri, ed., *Kirche und gesellschaftlicher Wandel in deutschen und niederländischen Städten der werdenden Neuzeit* (Cologne: Böhlau, 1980), 10. See also Lindberg, "No Beggars among Christians," and idem, "La théologie et l'assistance publique: Le cas d'Ypres (1525-1531)," *Revue d'Histoire et de Philosophie Religieuses* 61 (1981): 23–36. Scharffenorth, *Den Glauben*, 113ff., cites examples from the Church Orders, cf. Emil Sehling, ed., *Die evangelischen Kirchenordnungen des XVI. Jahrhunderts*, Tübingen, 1902ff. IV: 543 (Stralsund); III: 407f. (Breslau); VI/1: 445f. (Braunschweig); et al.

[62]Wilhelm Maurer, *Historischer Kommentar zur Confessio Augustana*, II (Gütersloh: Mohn, 1978), 177ff.

[63]*Martin Bucers Deutsche Schriften* (Gütersloh: Mohn, 1960), I:50ff. Cf. Steven Ozment, *The Reformation in the Cities* (New Haven: Yale University Press, 1975), 64ff.; Carlos M. N. Eire, *War against the Idols: The Reformation of Worship from Erasmus to Calvin* (Cambridge: Cambridge University Press, 1986), 90ff.; and Robert Stupperich, "Brüderdienst und Nächstenhilfe in der deutschen Reformation," in Herbert Krimm, ed., *Das diakonische Amt der Kirche* (Stuttgart: Evangelischer Verlagswerk, 1953):156–92.

[64]Adolf Laube, "Martin Luther und die Anfänge der städtischen Sozialreformen," paper presented at the Sixth International Congress for Luther Research, Erfurt, 1983. Cf. also Adolf Laube, ed., *Flugschriften der frühen Reformationsbewegung*, 2:1003ff. The emphasis upon the liturgy after the liturgy is, of course, not exclusive to Luther. As I suggested above, Luther may well have been aware of the patristic expressions of this intimate relation of worship and welfare even as he believed this relationship had been broken in the late medieval church.

Church of St. Francis at Assisi

CHAPTER 11

RELIGION AND EARLY MODERN SOCIAL WELFARE

THOMAS RIIS

The obligation to work is sometimes explained in terms of the so-called Protestant ethic, but this obligation long predates the Reformation. In the wake of the severe reduction of the labor pool caused by the fourteenth-century plague, countries throughout Europe legislated bans on vagabondage and emphasized work as a civic duty. Medieval theologians and moralists also considered work a remedy for idleness and sin as well as both an office for God and a punishment for original sin. Nevertheless, the obligation to work was secondary to the quest for salvation that utilized frequent saints' days, more votive masses, and new holy days. The Reformation rejection of these ways to salvation led to the elimination of the late medieval proliferation of holy days. Consequently the work week increased by fifteen to twenty percent; and where the amount of work remained constant, unemployment and underemployment increased as well. In contrast to traditional almsgiving, the early modern civic response to increasing poverty was characterized by distinguishing the deserving from the undeserving poor in order to use resources more efficiently. The rationale was that the able-bodied poor must be idlers, unwilling to work. And since work was a divine and human good, the workhouse came to be seen as an ideal solution. Contemporaries rarely realized that people could work and still be underemployed and in poverty.

Both the twelfth-century Renaissance and that of the fifteenth and sixteenth centuries developed slowly, and it is difficult to find one single event which could be said to constitute the beginning or the end of these two periods. On the other hand, in the history of European mentality, the Black Death about 1350 meant the beginning of an epoch. The plague-induced traumas from widespread death and dislocation which initiated that epoch influenced subsequent attitudes to religion, work, poverty, and welfare.

Our generation grew up under the threat of nuclear war, which in the 1950s and 1960s was much more real than it is today. Similarly, late medieval Europeans lived with the permanent danger of a sudden outburst of plague or other infectious diseases. Today we can try to influence politicians to decrease nuclear threat, but our medieval ancestors could do little about the plague.

Obviously they could pray that God would spare their community, and they could implore the saints to intercede with God on behalf of their prayers. In this context, the popularity of St. Roch of Montpellier is illuminating. He voluntarily assumed poverty and went to Rome as a pilgrim, where he nursed plague victims until he himself contracted the plague. He then retired to a lonely forest where a dog brought him food. He recovered and returned to Montpellier, where he died about 1327.[1] The rapid spread of his cult to many parts of Europe indicates that his life met a spiritual need of the late Middle Ages. Here was a man who had freely assumed poverty and who had recovered from the plague. This connection was not lost in the mentality of the day.

The story of St. Roch also indicates that the Black Death was not the only outbreak of plague in the late Middle Ages. Between 1350 and 1450, Norway for example had eight outbreaks of plague and one of small-pox.[2] Thus people were always cognizant of the danger of infection, and even worse of the danger of dying without confession. The religious art of this time from Sicily to Scandinavia includes representations of the triumph of death and the dance of the dead, graphic expressions of the knowledge that death reaches everyone regardless of rank or wealth.

It was also during this period that there was increased concern to find ways to shorten the soul's stay in purgatory. Pilgrimages, quests for indulgences, foundations of votive masses, and distributions to the poor were believed to be effective responses to this concern. But the certainty that these intentions and efforts would be successful continued to elude people.

The sumptuousness of votive masses increased throughout the fifteenth century, and the effects of indulgences were expanded, yet these endeavors swelled like a bubble which finally had to burst. Late medieval theology had recognized faith and deeds of charity as complementary means to justification. But when the Lutheran churches stressed justification by faith alone, many devout Christians must have felt relieved for they now no longer had to worry about the sufficiency of their own efforts.[3]

A new attitude towards work also began to arise during this period that became characteristic of the late Middle Ages and subsequent centuries until today. According to scholastic theology, God was pure act,

---

[1] See *Lexikon für Theologie und Kirche* 8 (Freiburg: Herder, 1963), cols. 1347–48.

[2] *Kulturhistorisk leksikon for nordisk middelalder*, 13 (Copenhagen, 1968), col. 240.

[3] These observations are the preliminary results of my research into the religious mentality of late medieval Denmark which I hope to publish fairly soon.

Actus purissimus; consequently persons could imitate God. This idea was sometimes linked to the widespread opinion in medieval theology that God would call a person to the trade or profession in which he would be most useful; work would thus be considered an office for God. On the other hand, the effort and labor connected with work could also be seen as a punishment for original sin (cf. Gen. 3:17-19). Obviously, also in late medieval thought the principal aim of work was to earn one's daily bread, but work was also considered a remedy against idleness and concupiscence.[4]

The Florentine preacher Simone de Cascia (first half of the fourteenth century) truly represents this latter view when he states that if a rich layman wanted to give away his fortune to the poor, he had better pursue a trade than beg. He further stressed the salutary character of work by his point that a rich man who has no need to work ought to do so anyway, and give the money earned to the poor.[5]

No wonder then that in times of economic crisis work was considered a civic duty. The Swedish Urban Statute from about 1350 obliged every able-bodied adult to work unless that person owned enough to live on for a year.[6] In 1349 and again in 1351 England introduced a similar rule compelling every able-bodied person under sixty to work. Analogous laws are to be found in Castille since 1351 and in Portugal in 1375. Most of these statutes were passed shortly after the Black Death and reflect its consequences in the decline in the working population.

In 1423 the city government of Brussels introduced for those from ten to sixty years of age the obligation to work.[7] Perhaps the city government wanted to show its efficiency in dealing with the problem of begging, and to render itself more attractive so that Duke John IV of Brabant and his court would return to Brussels. Moreover, the intention of the duty to work could be to create more taxpayers, as the city was increasingly prevailed upon to help finance the Duke's activities.[8] We should not forget, however, that already St. Paul had bluntly written that whoever does not work shall not eat (2 Thess. 3:10).

---

[4]*Lexikon des Mittelalters,* I (Munich-Zurich: Artemis-Verlag, 1980), col. 871.

[5]Philip Gavitt, "Economy, Charity and Community in Florence, 1350–1450," in Thomas Riis, ed., *Aspects of Poverty in Early Modern Europe,* 1 (Stuttgart: Klett-Cotta, 1981), 106.

[6]Eino Jutikkala, "Labour Policy and Urban Proletariat in Sweden-Finland," in Thomas Riis, ed., *Aspects of Poverty in Early Modern Europe,* 2 (Odense: Odense University Press, 1986), 135–36.

[7]Bronislaw Geremek, *La potence ou la pitié. L'Europe et les pauvres du Moyen Age à nos jours* (Paris: Editions Gallimard, 1987), 96, 110–11.

[8]See C. Dickstein-Bernard, *La gestion financière d'une capitale à ses débuts: Bruxelles, 1334–1467* (Brussels, 1977), 113–33.

We might expect that the changing attitude towards work could be revealed by an increasing number of working days per week. For certain European towns the length of the working week can be calculated:

Table 1: Length of Work Week[a]

CITY	DATES	DAYS PER WEEK
Bremen	1405–1406	4.9–5.2
Antwerp/Lier	1437–1600	3.7–5.0
Lyons	1501–1502	5.0–5.1
Malmo	1517, 1519	3.6–4.2
Istanbul	1555	5.3
Copenhagen	1607–1608	5.7
Aberdeen	1699–1700	5.0–6.0
Berlin	1700–1750	5.8

a. Source: Thomas Riis, "Le temps du travail—une esquisse," *Diogène*, 149 (1990): Table 10, p. 77; used by permission.

The long period covered by the figures from Antwerp and Lier show certain fluctuations. Together with figures from other European towns those from Antwerp and Lier allow us to see some kind of trend (see Table 2). At the beginning of the fifteenth century the week had about five working days; by 1440 this had fallen to about four. With the exception of the Antwerp/Lier figures for the second decade of the sixteenth century and those for the construction of the bridge over the Rhone at Lyons in 1501–1502, the work week had only about four days until about 1540. The bricklayers and masons of Antwerp and Lier worked harder during the central decades of the sixteenth century when Antwerp's demographic and economic strength culminated and an entire quarter of the city was being constructed.[9]

For Catholic Europe the trend shows that the number of workdays per week fell from about five at the beginning of the fifteenth century to about four a generation later. With certain exceptions, it remained at this level until the end of the sixteenth century. This could mean that concern about the soul's salvation introduced new saints, more votive masses, and new holidays.[10] Apparently the obligation to work was felt to be secondary to the quest for salvation.

[9]Thomas Riis, "Some Types of Towns in the 14th-16th Century Netherlands," in P. W. Klein and J. H. P. Paelinck, eds., *The Rhine-Meuse-Scheldt Delta: Historical Perspectives, Present Situation and Future Prospects* (Rotterdam, 1979), 20–28.

[10]In 1425, the council of the ecclesiastical province of Denmark introduced St. Anne's day as an official holiday of the church. J. Langebek, ed., *Scriptores Rerum Danicarum* 6 (Copenhagen, 1786), 458.

In Protestant countries, however, the week had more work days. An obvious explanation is that with the Reformation these ways to salvation were considered superfluous, and thus these obstacles to the triumph of the obligation to work were removed. The abolition of holidays dedicated to the feasts of saints would have increased the working week by 15 to 20 percent. As a consequence, the obligation to work is often looked upon as a characteristic of the Protestant countries. But it should be remembered that the principle of work is much older than this, and that in pre-Reformation England, Sweden, Castille, Portugal, and Brussels work was as compelling a duty as it would become in the Protestant countries.

Table 2: Antwerp/Lier Fluctuations[a]

DATES	DAYS PER WEEK
1437–1440	4.0
1441–1450	4.0
1451–1460	4.0
1461–1470	3.0
1471–1480	4.3
1481–1490	3.9
1491–1500	3.9
1501–1510	4.1
1511–1520	4.6
1521–1530	4.3
1531–1540	4.1
1541–1550	4.7
1551–1560	4.8
1571–1580	4.6
1581–1590	4.1
1591–1600	4.0

a. Source: Herman van der Wee, *The Growth of the Antwerp Market and the European Economy, Fourteenth-Sixteenth Centuries*, vol. 1 (The Hague: Nijhoff, 1963), 540–44.

In 1528, one of the mayors of Copenhagen planned to establish a hospital. In order to study the matter he asked the advice of the Carmelite friar Poul Helgesen, who lectured in the University of Copenhagen. Helgesen belonged to the theological vanguard of his time, accepting much of the criticism of the church advanced by Luther and other reformers. However, unlike them he remained faithful to the church of Rome.

According to Helgesen there were three causes of poverty: calamities, idleness, and neglectfulness. While some are necessarily poor because they were born in misery and do not know how to improve their situation, he regarded idleness as well as industry as a disposition granted by God.[11] This statement is interesting in its suggestion that poverty can be hereditary.[12]

In other cases, Helgesen continued, poverty was caused by calamities like illness, exile, captivity, and vice. As a matter of principle, the community is bound to assist its members when necessary, but wealthy members of the same family ought to take care of their poor relatives. When this was not possible, the community had to help. Moreover, he found that able-bodied persons could earn their living if their demands remained modest.

Like many of his contemporaries, Helgesen did not realize the extent of the problems concerning underemployment and hidden poverty. On the other hand, he saw that hosts of nondeserving beggars, whose numbers increased at the end of the Middle Ages, created in the mind of the average citizen a certain hostility to poor relief.[13] Stressing that nursing in hospitals those suffering from infectious diseases was charitable, he refused to see any charity in the confinement of others to hospitals. Obviously, his criticism aimed at the practice of confining the poor in institutions, a practice that had been current in Italy for about a century when Helgesen wrote his treatise.[14] Moreover, he stressed the importance of education, as it would enable people to earn their bread by honest work. Finding a causal nexus between poverty and criminality, Helgesen preferred the prevention of poverty to its cure.

Let us now have a look at different reactions of the poor to their situation. These reactions included food riots, criminality, exposure and abandonment of babies, and begging. Bad harvests would cause grain prices to rise and lead eventually to famine. As a matter of principle, urban governments should provide grain supplies for towns by stockpiling for future need, fixing maximum prices, and banning exportation

[11]For a summary of Poul Helgesen's reply, see Thomas Riis, "L'assistance aux pauvres et la Réforme danoise," *Dacia* 52 (1986): 13. The text itself, "Huore krancke, mijslige, saare, arme og fattige menneskir schule tracteris oc besorges, een kort vnderwijsning aff Broder Paulo Helie" was published in Marius Kristensen, ed., *Skrifter af Paulus Helie* 3 (Copenhagen, 1933), 3–37; it was first printed in Copenhagen in 1528.

[12]Anne Marie Rabier and Guy Piquet, *Soleil interdit ou deux siècles de l'exclusion d'un peuple,* Collections Igloos no. 96 (Pierrelaye, 1977), passim.

[13]*Skrifter af Paulus Helie,* 25-27. Cf. Franz Irsigler, "Bettler und Dirnen in der städtischen Gesellschaft des 14.-16. Jahrhundert," in Riis, ed., *Aspects of Poverty,* 2: 182-184.

[14]Bronislaw Geremek, "Renfermement des pauvres en Italie (XIV-XVIIe siècle). Remarques préliminaires," *Mélanges en l'honneur de Fernand Braudel I: Histoire économique du monde méditerranéen 1450-1650* (Toulouse: E. Privat, 1973), 208–9.

of grain. Food riots whose aim was to ensure the supply of victuals in reasonable quantities and at reasonable prices would occur regularly in many European countries. Apparently their number increased in the second half of the eighteenth century. One of the causes could be that agricultural improvement was still too slow to catch up with the growing population since the mid-eighteenth century. This was especially true for England which became increasingly dependent on foreign grain. Another reason was the change from a regulative economic policy to a laisser faire one. In Spain the grain trade was deregulated in 1765, but the harvest that year proved bad so prices rose in the spring of 1766 with the consequence that there were a large number of riots over large parts of the country. Similarly, the grain trade in France was deregulated in September 1774, and riots broke out the following spring.

But bad harvests and inadequate agriculture were not the only causes of inflated food prices and famine. Very often, the deficient infrastructure aggravated the problems of supplying victuals to inland towns, whereas the towns on the coast generally had much easier access to imports from abroad.[15] Although several of the remedies for these contingencies had been known for centuries, for example the creation of grain stocks and the regulation of prices, the problems of transport were, and are even today in developing countries, a most serious obstacle to the provisioning of inland regions.

Criminality was another kind of reaction by the poor. Very often the first offense was slight, but societal reactions pushed the delinquent further and further into marginality. Medieval Canon Law admitted the pilfering of food and other necessities for immediate use as a pardonable offense.[16] There is an echo of this in the legislation of medieval Denmark.[17] The reality could, however, be much harsher. In 1425 an adolescent of the French province of Dauphiné had been engaged as a servant to a family of Lyons. He left service without notice and was re-engaged as a servant, this time not far from Lyons. Again he fled from service. But this time he stole some clothes and a knife which he used to kill a couple of ducks which he and the son of his former employer then ate. The offender was arrested, whipped, and banned for two years.[18] If he

---

[15]Yves-Marie Bercé, *Révoltes et Révolutions dans l'Europe moderne, XVIe-XVIIIe siècles* (Paris: Presses Universitaires de France, 1980), 117–18.

[16]Michel Mollat, *Les pauvres au Moyen Age* (Paris: Hachette, 1978), 139–40.

[17]Johs. Brondum-Nielsen & Sven Aakjaer, eds., *Danmarks gamle Landskabslove*, (the customary law of Scania) 1/1 (Copenhagen, 1933), pars. 193, 207; ibid., 1, 2 (customary law of Scania, redaction in Latin by Archbishop Anders Sunesen), pars. 115-16; ibid., 8 (customary law of Sjaelland, "Valdemars sjaellandske Lov," Yngre redaction, Erik Kroman, ed. (Copenhagen, 1941), par. 87.

[18]Michel Mollat, "Les réactions des pauvres à la pauvreté en France au bas Moyen Age," in Riis, *Aspects of Poverty,* 2: 80–81; Mollat, *Les pauvres,* 300.

returned after that it would be extremely difficult for him to reintegrate into society. He would have to choose between marginality and migration.

Another response to poverty related to large families was the exposure of newborn children. This was also a solution taken by poor unmarried mothers. In medieval Scandinavia it appears to have been at least tolerated before the Christianization of the region. However, Christian authorities fought against this custom and succeeded in having it considered a crime.[19] Abandonment of a child, for example to an institution, was however not viewed as a crime and was even sometimes intended to be temporary.[20] Infanticide was of course a crime, and, as with petty theft, the reactions of society would often push an unmarried mother into marginality. There is even a case from the 1760s in Denmark of an unmarried mother killing her child not only because of her own problems, but out of compassion for the child because she knew in advance that the child would have a difficult life.[21]

In some countries, such as Norway or Denmark, the discovery of fornication involved public confession in church and the payment of fines, which at least in eighteenth-century practice were more favorable to the man than to the woman.[22] In Scotland, the Godly Discipline introduced by the Kirk exposed the couple on the stool of repentance. The humiliation both here and in Norway and Denmark pushed unmarried mothers into vagrancy and even infanticide.[23]

Strangely enough, repression appeared the only reaction to fornication in Denmark and Norway as well as Scotland. Although an orphanage was created in Copenhagen in 1605, it did not accept newborn infants because its main concern was the training of children for a trade.[24] Institutions where infants could be brought up or even abandoned were only created in the eighteenth century.[25]

In France hospitals for foundlings were created in the seventeenth century, first by St. Vincent de Paul in 1640 at Paris,[26] and in Italy the first

[19]*Kulturhistorisk Leksikon for nordisk middelalder* 1 (Copenhagen: Rosenkilde og Bagger, 1956), cols. 347–49.

[20]François Lebrun, *La vie conjugale sous l'Ancien Régime* (Paris: A. Colin, 1975), 155.

[21]Inger Dübeck, "Poor Women's Criminality in 18th Century Denmark and Norway," in Riis, *Aspects of Poverty*, 2: 203.

[22]Dübeck, "Poor Women's Criminality," 198–99.

[23]Ibid., 203. T. C. Smout, *A History of the Scottish People 1560-1830* (Glasgow: Fontana/ Collins Paperback, 1972), 74-77.

[24]Olaf Olsen, *Christian IVs tugt- og bornehus*, 2d ed. (Aarhus: Wormianum, 1978), 57–71.

[25]See Harald Jorgensen, "L'assistance aux pauvres au Danemark jusqu' à la fin du XVIIIe siècle," in Riis, ed., *Aspects of Poverty in Early Modern Europe*, 3 (Odense: Odense University Press, 1990), 26-27.

[26]Lebrun, *La vie conjugale* , 54.

hospital of this kind was opened in 1168 at Milan.[27] In France, the very existence of a hospital for foundlings which treated the abandonment of a child with discretion and tact had good effects: Almost all children admitted about 1700 had been exposed, whereas in the 1770s they had been abandoned at the hospital itself.[28]

The late creation of institutions for foundlings, and the repressive measures of Protestant society regarding fornication that eventually pushed unmarried mothers into marginality or crime consititute a clear difference between early modern Protestant and Catholic attitudes. Why did the Protestants concentrate upon the prosecution of sexual offenders? Smout suggests that a sexual offence was more easily discovered than "the deadly sins of greed, pride, untruthfulness, self-righteousness and hypocrisy." A long term effect can be seen in the popular association of the idea of immorality with sexual permissiveness, to the neglect of other forms of sin.[29]

Begging was obviously the classical answer to the question of poverty if you could only overcome your reluctance to stretch out your hand. Those eager to maintain a certain respectability could not. This group of "hidden poor" (*pauvres honteux, poveri vergognosi*) had become recognized by the mid-thirteenth century. The earliest known institution concerned for their relief was that mentioned at Modena in 1248. Similar initiatives were undertaken in thirteenth-century Flanders.[30]

One of the most ancient confraternities founded in order to assist the *poveri vergognosi* was that dedicated to the Virgin. Already active in Arezzo in 1257, its statutes of 1262 exempted its beneficiaries from the humiliation of begging; its brethren, who belonged to the leading strata of the city, would beg on their behalf.[31] Similarly, the weekly aid offered by the Florentine *Buonomini di S. Martino*, at best a supplement to the family's fare, allowed its recipients to have white bread regularly and thus to maintain their social status. When in 1470 the *Buonomini* began to

[27]Mollat, *Les pauvres*, 128; Luisa Dodi Osnaghi, "Ruota e infanzia abbandonata a Milano nella prima metà dell' Ottocento," in *Timore e carità. I poveri nell' Italia moderna* (Annali della Biblioteca Statale e Libreria Civica di Cremona XXVII-XXX, 1976-1979) (Cremona, 1982), 427; Edoardo Grendi, "Ideologia della carità e società indisciplinata: La costruzione del sistema assistenziale genovese (1470-1670)," ibid., 66; Daniela Lombardi, "Poveri a Firenze. Programmi e realizzazioni della politica assistenziale dei Medici tra Cinque e Seicento," ibid., 166-167. Christ's Hospital in London, established about 1550, did admit foundlings, but it must be considered a unique case in England. Cf. Paul Slack, *Poverty and Policy in Tudor and Stuart England* (London: Longman, 1988), 69, 119.
[28]Lebrun, *La vie conjugale* , 154–55.
[29]Smout, *History of the Scottish People*, 77.
[30]Giovanni Ricci, "Povertà vergogna e povertà vergognosa," *Società e Storia* 5 (1979): 305, 316.
[31]Ibid., 318.

give assistance to women in childbed, it often added confectionary, a capon, and a *fiasco* (flask) of wine to the usual swaddling clothes and diapers. This was what Florentine women in childbed used to eat, and the aid thus enabled the recipients to keep up with other respectable families.[32]

The group of *pauvres honteux* was difficult to discover because of its respectability. On the other hand, as the moral status of its members was beyond suspicion, their obvious claim to help was recognized by everybody. It is, however, my impression (which may be wrong) that at least in northern Europe pious foundations aiming expressly at this group appear rather late, namely in the course of the eighteenth century. The relief of the *pauvres honteux* seems fairly identical as far as aims and means were concerned in Catholic and Protestant countries; only the begging by the rich on behalf of the poor in Arezzo and elsewhere[33] could be seen as a symbolic assumption of poverty and/or as a penance.

It was more difficult to deal with other kinds of begging. Some cases were privileged, as the need for help was universally recognized. Old age, widowhood, physical or mental handicaps entitled a person to assistance; the same was true of orphans and the victims of calamities ranging from fire or natural catastrophes to Turkish captivity.[34]

Apparently, the cost of living rose drastically in many parts of sixteenth-century Europe, whereas wages increased at a much slower pace. Two factors, at least, were active in this development: agricultural stagnation and demographic pressure.[35] Obviously, the number of beggars rose as well. Since the medieval principle of giving alms to everybody declaring need was not adequate to this new situation, local authorities were faced with the alternative of reducing the number of grants in order to preserve their value or of giving a mere symbolic alms to everybody in need. The authorities opted for the former solution. The details of the individual schemes of poor relief may vary as may the time of their introduction, but in the general trend there is little, if any, differ-

---

[32] Amleto Spicciani, "The 'Poveri Vergognosi' in Fifteenth-Century Florence," in Riis, *Aspects of Poverty*, 1:131–32, 157.

[33] E.g., at Bologna in 1496; see Ricci, "Povertà vergogna e povertà vergognosa," 332–33.

[34] On the latter, see Sergij Vilfan, "Die fahrenden Mendikanten und ihre Struktur am Ende des 16. und in der ersten Hälfte des 17. Jhs. (Nach den Rechnungsbüchern von Ljubljana)," in Riis, *Aspects of Poverty*, 2:159–78.

[35] Geremek, *La potence ou la pitié*, 2:118–23.

ence between Catholic and Protestant countries.[36] The abolition of chantries and the gradual secularization of monasteries in Protestant countries provided funds for a more systematic poor relief. And in Catholic countries, authorities endeavored to make poor relief more efficient by consolidation of resources, for example, by merging small hospitals.

What actually characterizes early modern poor relief in contrast to traditional almsgiving was the fact that authorities now distinguished between the deserving poor and the others. The same categories as mentioned above still entitled aid, but with the important qualification that the recipients should be natives of the community or at least have lived there for a certain number of years.

Able-bodied beggars were considered idlers, and were ordered either to leave the community or to find work. However, this was difficult to enforce because of the many migrants in quest of work[37] who had to beg during their wanderings.[38] The discrimination against able-bodied migrants and beggars had several roots: the principle of the obligation to work emphasized in certain countries in the wake of the Black Death, and which spread to the rest of Europe; the need to do something efficient in order to cope with the serious social problems of the sixteenth century; the proto-mercantilist belief that begging by able-bodied persons was a waste of resources; and, the recognition that begging and vagrancy were incompatible with a well-governed polity, not least because of the fear of the spread of disease.

In this light, the workhouse was seen to be the ideal solution. If it seldom had economic success the reasons included lack of skilled labor, insufficient knowledge of the market conditions (such as engaging the poor in spinning to remedy the unemployment in the textile industry

---

[36]See the survey of major European countries in Geremek, ibid., 230–290. Cf. also, Elsie McKee, *John Calvin on the Diaconate and Liturgical Almsgiving* (Geneva: Travaux d'humanisme et renaissance, 1984), 96–106. For Scandinavia cf. Riis, *Aspects of Poverty,* 3: passim. On the special kind of poor relief of the so-called *Monti di Pietà*, which gave loans at a low rate of interest in late fourteenth and fifteenth-century Italy, see Riis, "Poverty and Urban Development in Early Modern Europe," in *Aspects of Poverty,* 1:16. Cheap loans were made available at Wittenberg by the 1522 statute regulating the church and the administration of poor relief. Cf. Carter Lindberg, "'There Should Be No Beggars among Christians': Karlstadt, Luther, and the Origins of Protestant Poor Relief," *Church History* 46 (1977): 322. In general, however, cheap credit as an instrument of poor relief seems to belong to a much later period in Northern Europe. Cf. Slack, *Poverty and Policy,* 206.

[37]Slack, *Poverty and Policy,* 94–95.

[38]Cf. Slack, and Jean-Pierre Gutton, "Les pauvres face à leur pauvreté: le cas francais 1500-1800," in Riis, *Aspects of Poverty,* 2: 94–95. Very often the reaction of the authorities pushed people further into marginality, thus making their reinsertion into society virtually impossible; cf. Slack, *Poverty and Policy* , 99–100.

caused by lack of demand!), and a lack of guaranteed sale of the goods produced by the poor. The Renaissance humanist Juan Luis Vives was aware of this last point and wanted to guarantee the sale of a certain quantity of the goods produced by the poor.[39] When less traditional solutions removed some of the obstacles mentioned, the workhouse would manage to make both ends meet. The brewery that the municipality of Salisbury opened in 1623 was run according to normal business practices, but had to contribute to poor relief from its income. It was much admired in its day, but its returns were insufficient to cover the large debt contracted when the enterprise was begun.[40] In Norwegian Bergen, the workhouse did fairly well in the eighteenth century when it sold cloth to the army. The production was run by a private entrepreneur who paid a fixed amount to the workhouse for his use of the poor. When in 1726 the army decided to buy its clothes elsewhere, the economic foundation of the workhouse was sapped, and it had to cease its activities.[41]

Very often, unfortunately, authorities did not achieve an efficient system of poor relief, and this not only because of insufficient resources. There were other reasons. Above all, contemporaries seldom recognized that people could work and yet be underemployed. Leading thinkers, such as St. Antonino of Florence in the fifteenth century, were aware of this problem,[42] but they had few successors[43] until the eighteenth century, when Montesquieu recognized that "a man is not poor because he

[39]Cf. Marcel Bataillon, "J. L. Vivès, réformateur de la bienfaisance," *Bibliothèque d'humanisme et renaissance. Travaux et documents* 14 (1952): 149. The Florentine hospital or workhouse created in 1621 was much concerned with the reinsertion of its inmates into society, perhaps more so than similar institutions elsewhere. Cf. Lodovico Branca, "Pauperismo, assistenza e controllo sociale a Firenze (1621-1623): materiali e richerche," *Archivio Storico Italiano* 141 (1983): 433. For late seventeenth and eighteenth-century England a chronology of attitudes can be established: 1660-1700, creation of work for the poor; 1700-1750, determent of the poor by means of the work-house, hiring out of the poor as manpower; 1750ff., more sympathetic attitudes including creation of work for the poor as a public responsibility, and outdoor relief. Cf. A. W. Coats, "The Relief of Poverty, Attitudes to Labour, and Economic Change in England, 1660-1782," *International Review of Social History* 21 (1976): 106-110.

[40]Paul Slack, "Poverty and Politics in Salisbury 1597-1666," in Peter Clark and Paul Slack, eds., *Crisis and Order in English Towns 1500-1700. Essays in Urban History* (London: Routledge & Kegan Paul, 1972), 182-83, 190-91.

[41]Stale Dyrvik, "Avgjerdsprosessen og aktorane bak det offentlege fattigstellet i Norge 1720-1760," in Stale Dyrvik, ed., *Oppdaginga av fattigdomen. Sosial lovgiving i Norden pa 1700-talet* (Oslo: Universitetsforl., 1983), 158.

[42]Philip Gavet, "Economy, Charity, and Community in Florence, 1350-1450," in Riis, *Aspects of Poverty*, 1:108.

[43]See John Hadwin, "The Problem of Poverty in Early Modern England," in Riis, *Aspects of Poverty*, 1:228, 230-33. One of the few exceptions was Sir Matthew Hale about 1600; see Slack, *Poverty and Policy*, 192.

owns nothing, but because he does not work.'[44] Thus, if the diagnosis — that unemployment was caused by idleness and bad will—was wrong, the cure was likely to be so as well.

Unemployment and underemployment had various sources. The Reformation abolition of a great number of holidays increased working time by 15 to 20 percent. If the amount of work remained stable, it would be finished earlier, thus leaving the workers with longer periods of unemployment or underemployment. Also, the use of hired armies would expose the mercenary, who had often enrolled in order to avoid poverty, not only to the enemy's fire but to poverty in a foreign country when the unit was disbanded. Even in a country such as Sweden with a conscript army, privates, noncommissioned officers, and their relatives constituted an astonishingly high share of the poor in eighteenth-century Stockholm.[45] Obviously, as a group they were more vulnerable than others.

From different centuries there are some hints in the documentation of a tendency towards falling social status if the family had to rely upon only one income. In other words, poverty could be hereditary. Speaking of a French case extending over the last two centuries, Anne-Marie Rabier and Guy Piquet discovered in a certain family "a cumulation of handicaps for generations."[46] I have found the same tendency during the sixteenth and seventeenth centuries for a couple of Danish families (or rather Scots established at Elsinore and their descendants).[47] Their only possiblity for breaking the cycle of poverty was to acquire a second income of sufficient size. If other examples from other periods and places will show the same tendency, we may see it as a general feature. Perhaps we shall have to revise our concept of contemporary poor relief. The dole is at best a substitute for the money earned by work, but it will not enable the recipient to break the vicious circle of poverty and unemployment. A second income for the family may be required!

---

[44]*De l'Esprit des Lois* (1748), 23: 29.

[45]Johan Söderberg, "La pauvreté en Suède 1500-1800," in Riis, *Aspects of Poverty*, 3: 114–15.

[46]Rabier and Piquet, *Soleil interdit ou deux siècles*, passim.

[47]Cf. Riis' "Les mouvements de longue durée: le déclin économique et les causes de la pauvreté," to appear in the proceedings of the symposium held at Caen, October 1989: "De Quatrième Ordre au Quart Monde. Les plus pauvres dans la démocratie hier, aujourd'hui et demain."

CHAPTER 12

THE LONG-TERM INHERITANCE OF POVERTY

THOMAS RIIS

The previous essay pointed to the suggestion by the sixteenth-century Danish friar Helgesen that poverty might be hereditary. The present essay explores the validity of this suggestion by an analysis of the records of a group of sixteenth-century Scottish immigrants in the Danish town of Elsinore. The research suggests that it is probable to posit a tendency to economic decline existing from one generation to another. The profound causes of such economic decline require further research, but the preliminary results suggest that social welfare which only replaces income lost by unemployment or underemployment is not sufficient to break the vicious circle of poverty and unemployment. But the revision of social welfare to meet this challenge depends not only on economic conditions but on a society's worldview and values concerning human worth and work—issues integral to the religious roots of social welfare from the Bible to the early modern eve of the present.

In spite of the recognition that a poor childhood is a wretched beginning for material success in life, scholars have traditionally viewed poverty as a phenomenon touching only a generation. Thus short-term fluctuations of personal poverty are known, but the long-term effects of poverty have hardly been studied at all.[1] Anne-Marie Rabier and Guy Piquet, utilizing the methodology of oral history, were able to establish the gradual changes in the material conditions of a family from the eighteenth century. Thus they were able to discover "an accumulation of disadvantages which last for generations," or which in a particular marginal family exist for more than a century; in short, they discovered that poverty can be hereditary.[2]

---

[1]Translation by Carter Lindberg of "Les movements de longue duré: le déclin économique et les causes de la pauvreté." The original French version appeared in the proceedings of the symposium held at Caen in October, 1989: "Du Quatrième Ordre au Quart Monde. Les plus pauvres dans la démocratie hier, aujourd'hui et demain." We are grateful for permission to translate and print this article.—Eds.

[2]*Soleil interdit ou deux siècles de l'exclusion d'un peuple*, Igloos no. 96 (Pierrelaye, 1977), and esp. 90, 129.

If this discovery has a general validity it will have staggering consequences for social welfare: The situation of the individual is perhaps only the result of an accumulation of disadvantages, each of which alone is not sufficient to cause destitution. Thus, if the nature of the disadvantages is known, it will be easier to discover the process leading to poverty.

My goal to see if the discovery of hereditary poverty is valid is based on old, non-French documentation from sixteenth- and seventeenth-century Denmark. Professor Felix-Paul Codaccioni, speaking of Lille, showed the usefulness of probate records. We shall use the same type of sources, but for the Danish town of Elsinore. We shall study a particular social group, namely Scottish immigrants whose total number culminates toward the end of the sixteenth century.[3]

The choice of this category of immigrants allows us to eliminate several causes of interference. As immigrants, at least during the first generation, they had to shift for themselves; and as Scots they were so far from their native land that the possibility of assistance from home was insignificant.[4]

It may appear strange that poor persons shall be mentioned hardly at all. This is because it is easier to trace wealthy families through many generations and to establish the phases of long-term processes, for example economic decline among well-to-do people.

A young Scotsman, Alexander Lyall, established himself in Elsinore, marrying no later than 1528 the daughter of the town mayor. His business prospered, and at his death in 1560 he was the wealthiest merchant in the town. He owned a manor house and a village; moreover, after 1548 he was the director of the Sund custom house. When he wrote his will in 1549, his fortune was at least 10,000 daler. He probably envisaged that one of his three sons would continue his business since another would be employed in farming the estate, and that the third would find employment in the church. One part of this plan was prevented by the king's purchase of the family's country estate.[5]

We do not have sources to permit the evaluation of the size of the fortune of Frederick, Alexander's eldest son, but everything suggests that he inherited his father's wealth since he succeeded him in his capacities as merchant, mayor, and director of the Sund custom house.[6] His son, David,

---

[3]Felix-Paul Codaccioni, "Approches de l'histoire du sous-prolétariat Lillois à la fin du XIXème et au début du XXème siècle," *Le Quart Monde: Partenaire de l'Histoire*, Dossiers et documents de la revue *Quart Monde* 1 (Pierrelaye, 1988), 29–60.

[4]Thomas Riis, *Should Auld Acquaintance Be Forgot ... Scottish-Danish Relations c. 1450–1707* (Odense: Odense University Press, 1989), 1:156.

[5]Ibid., 1: 162–70.

[6]Ibid., 1: 170–76.

upon his death in 1589, left a fortune of 2,925 daler, which was a considerable sum but probably much less than that of his brother.

The descendants of Frederick and David did not have the same material success. Frederick's son, Alexander (II), left at least 9,820 daler, whereas David's son, David (II), left no more than 425 daler.[7]

If we calculate the index of the family legacy, taking as a base the fortune of Alexander (I)—about 10,000 daler—we will arrive at the following numbers:

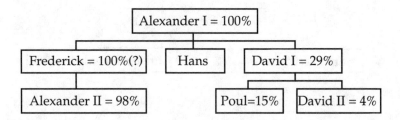

Thus one sees that Frederick's branch maintained its social level whereas David's did not reach it without running into debt.

What were the causes for this? Of course, individual factors cannot be excluded because not all the sons of the great merchant had his mettle. Also, the prosperity of Alexander (II) was at least in part due to the inheritance from his brother Frederick (II), who died a year before Alexander.[8] Aside from these causes, we find that the difference between the two branches goes back to the children of Alexander (I). Among them, Frederick was already assisting his father in the administration of the Sund custom house and succeeded him in this work as in business. Hans pursued an intellectual career whereas David was probably engaged with the rural property. But when the king bought the country property David must have had to find something else. Of course, he had his part of the inheritance and he was in business with his brother, but he did not have the same possibilities for profit as the latter, whose earnings would increase during the following generation.

Another notable family was allied to the Lyalls because the town councilor Hans Davidsen (I) was the brother-in-law of Alexander Lyall (I). We do not know the exact fortune of Hans Davidsen, but there is reason to

---

[7]Ibid., 1: 194, table 6.11. The 425 daler of David Lyall (II) corresponds to 638 daler in 64 skilling. At that time the Danes had two or three kinds of daler: the rigsdaler, based on the imperial standard of 96 skilling; the sletdaler (lit., bad daler) of 64 skilling; and the kwantdaler, of 80 skilling.

[8]Ibid., 2: 232.

believe that it was not paltry. His son David Hansen (I), merchant, town councilor, and assistant custom house officer at Sund, had a fortune in 1589 of 21,305 daler. His sons, Hans Davidsen (V), town councilor, and Christen Davidsen, mayor and assistant custom house officer, left respectively 9,060 daler in 1610 and 3,652 daler in 1659 whereas the fortune of Hans Hansen, the son of Hans Davidsen (V), did not exceed 850 daler.[9] Taking as the base the fortune of David Hansen (I) in 1589, we arrive at the following index:

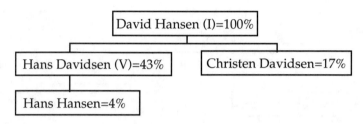

The figures indicate the same tendency that we have observed for the Lyalls, even if Hans Hansen's early death did not give him the time to make his fortune. The situation of Christen Davidsen was perhaps due to the fact that his tasks as mayor and assistant custom house officer left him little time for business; at the same time, his work assured him of a regular income that protected him from excessive indebtedness.

We have established the tendency to economic decline for two families even if it was not followed by a loss of social standing. One can recognize the tendency in the noble families from which the founder emigrated from Scotland.[10] Some would try to make good the loss of the family fortune by pushing their children toward reliable employment in the church, civil bureaucracy, or the armed forces, thus restraining the descending mobility of the family.

Thus it appears necessary to recognize the economic decline of a family over the course of generations as a long-term factor causing or aggravating poverty. Why it was so remains to be discovered. It is true that the fortunes were diminishing through division among the heirs, but on the other hand the immigrants probably had fewer resources when they settled in Denmark. The generational successions thus are probably not the reason for the long-term economic decline.

---

[9]Ibid., 1:192–94, tables 6.10 C and 6.11. Since the sum relative to Christen Davidsen is given in daler of 64 skilling, we have calculated in rigsdaler of 96 skilling for purposes of comparison.

[10]Ibid., 1:111–12 (the Sinclairs) and 1:114–20 (the MacAlpines or Machabaeus).

Sometimes these latter successions and statements of accounts enable us to detect certain short-term reasons for poverty. In this regard, the case of the tavern owner Samuel Gordon of Copenhagen is revealing. At his death in 1699 he left a debt of 53 daler, 36 of which was for his funeral and 4 was for medical assistance.[11] The following figures indicate the importance of funerals (daler of 64 skilling):[12]

Table 3: Funeral Allocations from Estates[a]

Date	Name	Funerals	Surplus/ Deficit
1626	David Lyall (II)	64	638+
1643	James Greenwood	90	120+
1651	Wife of Hans Jack	28	11–
1652	Wife of Hans Hansen	9	2–
1652	Widow of James Black	44	68–
1654	Alexander Glen	22	168–
1656	Hans Adamsen and wife	73	88–
1659	James Kerse	39	89–
1659	Wife of Albert Skraedder	28	4+
1663	William Jack	172	275–

a. Source: Landsarkivet for Sjaelland m.v. (Regional archives of Sjaelland, Copenhagen) Helsingor Byfoged, Skifteretsprotokoller E 42 fol. 88r–94v; E 46 fol. 375r; E 49 fol. 142r–143r, 262v–263r, 265r–269r; E 52 fol. 223r–226r; E 52b fol. 920v–922r; E 55 fol. 30v–32r, 257r–258v; E 58 fol. 169 (206)r–175(214)v.

The figures indicate strongly that the case of Gordon was not unique; much to the contrary, because one clearly sees the family's preoccupation with the departure of the deceased, which must be properly observed and seen as such by neighbors and friends.

The great funerals would mean an economic sacrifice that would aggravate a precarious situation or itself cause the deficit. A prolonged illness could have a similar effect, as the case of the tailor Hans Sandersen (V) indicates. At his death he left a deficit of 6 daler, but among his debts 39 daler were to go to the hospital where he had been nursed for thirty-nine weeks.[13]

[11]Ibid., 1:235–36.
[12]We omit a comparable example from the table: The surplus was 9 daler, but one of the children demanded 72 daler for the funeral, which was reduced to 55 to obtain equality between creditors and debtors. Landsarkivet for Sjaelland m.v. Helsingor Byfoged, Skifteretsprotokoler E 72 fol. 512r–513v of 6 July 1699.
[13]Ibid., E 51 fol. 472r–473v of 27 February 1655.

That a prolonged illness could cause poverty is not a novelty; to the contrary. However, the role of funerals seems to have been underestimated by historians, but not by contemporaries. The statutes of confraternities, guilds, or corporations nearly always contain clauses regulating members' behavior with respect to the death of a fellow member.

Nevertheless, our studies appear to confirm the hypothesis of Rabier and Piquet, cited at the beginning, which seems to open new perspectives and to invite researchers to specific work. To begin with, we do not have enough specific temporal and geographical analyses to allow us to say with certitude that a tendency to economic decline exists from one generation to the next. Today we can only say that it is probable.

Yet—and it is this that makes our research more than just an intellectual pastime—we must also and already now begin to research the profound causes of economic decline. Can the preceding generation's level of life only be maintained if there are supplementary resources, that is to say, alongside the principal income a sure compensation such as that of custom house inspector in several of the examples cited or the money earned from the work of the spouse? If so, it is understandable why social welfare, even today, does not suffice: It replaces a person's salary in case of unemployment, but it does not provide that double guarantee that will perhaps permit the poor person to break the vicious circle of economic decline.

CONTRIBUTORS

Brenda M. Bolton is Professor of Medieval History in the University of London, Westfield College. She has published a wide range of studies on medieval church history with special attention to monasticism and the pontificate of Innocent III. Her book *The Medieval Reformation* (N.Y. Holmes & Meier / London: E. Arnold, 1983) has been translated into Portuguese and Italian. Her study of Innocent III is in press.

Emily Albu Hanawalt is Associate Professor of Classical Studies and Religious Studies at Boston University. She contributed six chapters on late antique and early medieval Christendom in Howard Clark Kee, ed., *Christianity: A Social and Cultural History* (New York: Macmillan, 1991).

Paul D. Hanson is Florence Corliss Lamont Professor of Divinity and Professor of Old Testament in the Divinity School, Harvard University. His many books include *The Dawn of Apocalyptic: The Historical and Sociological Roots of Jewish Apocalyptic Eschatology* (Philadelphia: Fortress, 1975, rev. ed., 1979, 1984); *The Diversity of Scripture: A Theological Interpretation* (Philadelphia: Fortress, 1982; French translation, 1985); and *The People Called: The Growth of Community in the Bible* (San Francisco: Harper & Row, 1986).

Susan Ashbrook Harvey is Associate Professor of Religious Studies at Brown University. Her major work is in the area of early Syrian Christianity, and includes the editing and translating, with Sebastian Brock, of *Holy Women of the Syrian Orient* (Berkeley: University of California Press, 1987). Her most recent work is *Asceticism and Society in Crisis: John of Ephesus and The Lives of the Eastern Saints* (Berkeley: University of California Press, 1990).

Alexander Kazhdan is Senior Research Associate in Byzantine Studies at Dumbarton Oaks. His recent books include *People and Power in Byzantium: An Introduction to Modern Byzantine Studies* (Washington, D.C.: Dumbarton Oaks, 1982; with Giles Constable) and *Change in Byzantine Culture in the Eleventh and Twelfth Centuries* (Berkeley: University of California Press, 1985; with Ann Wharton Epstein). He is Editor in Chief of the *Oxford Dictionary of Byzantium*.

Howard Clark Kee is Aurelio Professor of the Bible emeritus at Boston University. He is known to thousands of undergraduate students through his text *Understanding the New Testament*. He is equally well known to biblical scholars for his studies on the social context of the early Christian community, including *Miracle in the Early Christian World: A Study in Sociohistorical Method* (New Haven and London: Yale University Press, 1983).

Carter Lindberg is Professor of Church History in the School of Theology at Boston University. He has written a history of renewal movements, *The Third Reformation?* (Macon: Mercer, 1983) and edited and contributed to *Luther's Ecumen-*

ical Significance (Philadelphia: Fortress, 1984) and *Piety, Politics, and Ethics: Reformation Studies in Honor of George W. Forell* (Kirksville: Sixteenth Century Journal Publishers, 1984). He contributed the chapters on Christianity in the Middle Ages and the Reformation in Howard Clark Kee, ed., *Christianity: A Social and Cultural History* (New York: Macmillan, 1991).

Lester K. Little is Dwight W. Morrow Professor of History at Smith College. His particular interest in the social history of religious movements is expressed in many of his publications including *Religious Poverty and the Profit Economy in Medieval Europe* (London: Paul Elek, 1978; Ithaca: Cornell University Press, 1979; paperback edition 1983; Spanish translation, Madrid: Taurus Ediciones, 1983) and *Liberty, Charity, Fraternity: Lay Religious Confraternities at Bergamo in the Age of the Commune* (Northampton, Mass.: Smith College, 1988; Italian edition, Bergamo: Lubrina Editore, 1988).

Timothy S. Miller is Associate Professor in the Department of History at Salisbury State University. He has written *The Birth of the Hospital in the Byzantine Empire* (Baltimore and London: The Johns Hopkins University Press, 1985) and is now researching Byzantine orphanages.

Thomas Riis has taught at the University of Copenhagen and the European University Institute in Florence. He is now President of the Danish Committee for Urban History in Copenhagen. He has edited and contributed to *Aspects of Poverty in Early Modern Europe* (Volume I, Stuttgart: Klett-Cotta, 1981; Volume II, Odense: Odense University Press, 1986; Volume III, Odense: Odense University Press, 1990) as well as various studies on early modern cities.

Alice-Mary Talbot is Executive Editor of the *Oxford Dictionary of Byzantium*. She edited and translated *The Correspondence of Athanasius I, Patriarch of Constantinople: Letters to the Emperor Andronicus II, Members of the Imperial Family and Officials* (Washington, D.C.: Dumbarton Oaks, 1975) and *Faith Healing in Late Byzantium: The Posthumous Miracles of the Patriarch Athanasios I of Constantinople by Theoktistos the Stoudite* (Brookline, Massachusetts: Holy Cross Orthodox Press, 1983.

André Vauchez is Professor of Medieval History at the University of Paris X, Nanterre. Many of his studies on the poor in the Middle Ages are included in his *Religion et Société dans l'occident médiéval* (Turin, 1980) which is being translated for English publication. Other books include *La spiritualité du moyen âge occidental* (Paris, 1975) and *La sainteté en occident aux derniers siècles du moyen âge* (Rome, 1981). His present research concerns images in the Middle Ages.

BIBLIOGRAPHY

This list is suggestive not exhaustive! Our topic is a particular concern for certain organizations (the World Council of Churches, the Lutheran World Federation), orientations, and disciplines (Marxist historical studies, Biblical studies, Reformation studies, Liberation theology), and related journals (*Ecumenical Review, International Review of Mission*). Entries in one section may also be relevant to another section. This bibliography is primarily of secondary sources but each entry will have references to the primary sources and to further literature.

BIBLIOGRAPHIC AIDS

Bauer, Gerhard, *Towards a Theology of Development. An Annotated Bibliography.* Geneva: World Council of Churches, 1970.

Candille, M. "Bibliographie d'Histoire des Hôpitaux," *Société Française d'Histoire des Hôpitaux* 33 (1976): 31–44.

Mollat, Michel, "Eléments de bibliographie sur l'histoire des pauvres et de la pauvreté au Moyen Age," in idem, *Etudes sur l'Histoire de la Pauvreté.* 2 vols. Paris: Publications de la Sorbonne, 1974. 2: 825–33.

Münsterberg, Emil. *Bibliographie des Armenwesens.* Berlin: Carl Heymanns, 1900/06.

Peterson, Paul, ed. *Poverty, hunger and religion: A Bibliography Selected from the ATLA Religion Database,* 2nd rev. ed. Chicago: American Theological Library Association, 1984.

Riis, Thomas. *Pauvreté et Développement urbain en Europe XVe–XVIIIe/XIXe siècles: Une Bibliographie.* Odense: Odense Universitet, 1981.

Soly, Hugo, "Economische ontwikkeling en sociale politiek in Europa tijdens de overgang van middeleeuwen naar nieuwe tijden." *Tijdschrift voor Geschiedenis* 88 (1975): 584–97. (N.B.: This entire issue is devoted to the subject of poverty and poor relief.)

Tawney, R. H. "Studies in Bibliography: 2, Modern Capitalism," *Economic History Review* 4 (1933): 336–356.

WORKS OF COMPREHENSIVE INTENT
AND/OR THEORETICAL ORIENTATION

Encyclopedias are very helpful orientations. One of the best is the *Theologische Realenzyklopädie* which is still in process. Cf. the entries "Armenfürsorge," "Armut," and "Eigentum," among others. The older *Religion in Geschichte und Gegenwart* is also useful.

Balz, Heinrich, ed. *Besitz und Armut*, Göttingen: Vandenhoeck & Ruprecht, 1986.

Boswell, John. *The Kindness of Strangers: The Abandonment of Children in Western Europe from Late Antiquity to the Renaissance.* New York: Vintage Books, 1990.

Daedalus. 1987. Issue devoted to philanthropy.

De Santa Ana, Julio. *Good News to the Poor: The Challenge of the Poor in the History of the Church.* Geneva: World Council of Churches, 1977.

—————————. *Separation without Hope.* Geneva: World Council of Churches, 1978.

—————————. *Towards a Church Care of the Poor.* Geneva: World Council of Churches, 1979.

Ehrle, Franz. *Beiträge zur Geschichte und Reform der Armenpflege.* Freiburg i. Br.: Herder, 1881.

Emminghaus, A., ed. *Das Armenwesen und die Armengesetzgebung im Europäischen Staaten.* Berlin: Herbig, 1870. (English trans.: *Poor Relief in Different Parts of Europe*, London, 1873.)

Fischer, Wolfram, *Armut in der Geschichte.* Göttingen: Vandenhoeck & Ruprecht, 1982.

Garraty, John. *Unemployment in History.* New York: Harper Colophon, 1978.

Geremek, Bronislaw. *La potence ou la pitié. l'Europe et les pauvres du Moyen Age à nos jours.* Paris: Gallimard, 1987.

Greinacher, Norbert, and Alois Müller. *The Poor and the Church.* New York: Seabury Press, 1978.

Harmati, Béla, ed. *Christian Ethics —Property and Poverty.* Geneva: Lutheran World Federation, 1985.

Harnack, Adolf von. "The Evangelical Social Mission in the Light of the History of the Church." In A. Harnack and W. Herrmann, *Essays on the Social Gospel.* New York: G. P. Putnam's Sons, 1907.

Hník, Frank M. *The Philanthropic Motive in Christianity: An Analysis of the Relations between Theology and Social Service.* Oxford: Blackwell, 1938.

Hunecke, Volker. "Überlegungen zur Geschichte der Armut im vorindustriellen Europa." *Geschichte und Gesellschaft* 9:4 (1983): 480–512.

Kantzenbach, F. W. *Christentum in der Gesellschaft*. 2 vols. Hamburg: Siebenstern, 1975.

Krimm, Herbert, ed. *Quellen zur Geschichte der Diakonie*. 3 vols. Stuttgart: Evangelisches Verlagswerk, 1960ff.

_____, ed.*Das Diakonische Amt der Kirche*. Stuttgart: Evangelisches Verlagswerk, 1965.

Lallemand, Léon. *Histoire de la Charité*. 4 vols. Paris: A. Picard, 1902–12.

Liese, Wilhelm. *Geschichte der Caritas*. 2 vols. Freiburg i. Br.: Caritasverlag, 1922.

Lindberg, Carter. "Through a Glass Darkly: A History of the Church's Vision of the Poor and Poverty." *The Ecumenical Review* 33:1 (1981): 37–52.

_____. "Property and Poverty in the History of the Church," in Béla Harmati, ed. *Christian Ethics —Property and Poverty*. Geneva: Lutheran World Federation, 1985, 36–55.

Lis, Caterina, and Hugo Soly. *Poverty and Capitalism in Pre–Industrial Europe*. Brighton,England: Harvester, 1982.

McCord, J., and T. H. I. Parker, ed. *Service in Christ: Essays to Karl Barth*. Grand Rapids: Eerdmans,1966.

Mollat, Michel, ed. *Études sur l'Histoire de la Pauvreté*. 2 vols. Paris: Publications de la Sorbonne, 1974.

Mullin, Redmond. *The Wealth of Christians*. Maryknoll, N. Y.: Orbis Books, 1984.

Nelson, B.N. *The Idea of Usury: From Tribal Brotherhood to Universal Otherhood*. Princeton, 1949; 2nd ed. Chicago: University of Chicago Press, 1969.

Ratzinger, G. *Geschichte der kirchlichen Armenpflege*. 2nd ed. Freiburg i. Br.: Herder Verlagshandlung, 1884.

Revue d'Histoire de l'Eglise de France 52 (1966).

Sachsse, Christoph, and Florian Tennstedt, eds. *Bettler, Gauner, und Proleten: Armut und Armenfürsorge in der deutschen Geschichte*. Hamburg: Rowohlt, 1983.

_____. *Geschichte der Armenfürsorge im Deutschland: Vom Spätmittelalter bis zum 1. Weltkrieg*. Stuttgart: Kohlhammer, 1980.

Scherpner, Hans. *Theorie der Fürsorge*. Göttingen: Vandenhoeck & Ruprecht, 1962.

Shewring, Walter, *Rich and Poor in Christian Tradition*, London: Burns & Oates, 1948.

Tawney, R. *Religion and the Rise of Capitalism: A Historical Study*. Gloucester, Mass., P. Smith, 1962 <c1926>

Townsend, P. *The Concept of Poverty*. London: Heinemann Educational, 1970.

Troeltsch, E. *The Social Teaching of the Christian Churches*. New York: Harper & Row, 1960.

Uhlhorn, Gerhard. *Die christliche Liebstätigkeit*, 3 vols. Stuttgart: D. Gundert, 1881–90, 1882–95. Reprinted Neukirchen, 1959.

_____. *Schriften zur Sozialethik und Diakonie.* Hannover: Lutherisches Verlagshaus, 1990.

Viner, J. *Religious Thought and Economic Society.* Durham, N.C.: Duke University Press, 1978.

PRE-BIBLICAL

Austin, M. , and P. Vidal–Naquet. *Economic and Social History of Ancient Greece.* Berkeley: University of California Press, 1979.

Bolkestein, H. *Wohltätigkeit und Armenpflege im vorchristlichen Altertum*, Utrecht, 1939; reprint Groningen: Bouma's Boekhuis, 1967.

Driesch, Johannes von der. *Geschichte der Wohltätigkeit: Die Wohltätigkeit im alten Ägypten.* Paderborn: Schöningh, 1959.

Finley, Moses. *The Ancient Economy.* Berkeley: University of California Press, 1973.

Hands, A. R. *Charities and Social Aid in Greece and Rome.* Ithaca: Cornell University Press, 1968.

Rostovtzeff, M. *The Social and Economic History of the Hellenistic World.* 3 vols. Oxford: Clarendon, 1941.

_____. *The Social and Economic History of the Roman Empire.* 2 vols. Oxford: Clarendon, 1957.

ISRAEL AND THE OLD TESTAMENT

Baudissin, W. "Die alttestamentliche Religion und die Armen." *Preussische Jahrbücher* 149 (1912): 193–231.

Birch, Bruce, and Larry Rasmussen. *The Predicament of the Prosperous.* Philadelphia: Westminster Press, 1978.

Epzstein, Leon. *Social Justice in the Ancient Near East and the People of the Bible..* London: SCM, 1986.

Fendler, M. "Zur Sozialkritik des Amos." *Evangelische Theologie* 33 (1973): 32–53.

Gelin, A. *Les Pauvres de Jahvé.* Paris: Cerf, 1953.

George, A. "La Pauvreté dans l'Ancien Testament," in *La Pauvreté Evangélique.* Paris: Cerf, 1971.

Gottwald, Norman K. *A Sociology of the Religion of Liberated Israel, 1250–1000 B.C.* Maryknoll, N. Y.: Orbis Books, 1976.

Kandler, H. J. "Die Bedeutung der Armut im Schrifttum von Chirbet Qumran." *Judaica* 13 (1957): 193–209.

Kuschke, A. "Arm und Reich im AT mit besonderer Berücksichtigung der nachexilischen Zeit." *Zeitschrift für Alttestamentliche Wissenschaft* 57 (1939): 31–57.

Liano, J. M. "Los pobres en el Antiguo Testamento." *Estudios Bíblicos* 25 (1966): 117–167.

Neusner, Jacob. *The Economics of Mishnah.* Chicago: University of Chicago Press, 1990.

Pastor, J. A. "Justicia social y defensa del pobre en el Antiguo Testamento." *Progección* (Granada) 13 (1966): 9–17.

Peters, N. *Die Soziale Fürsorge im Alten Testament.* Paderborn: Bonifacius–Druckerei, 1936.

Pleins, J. David. *Biblical Ethics and the Poor: The Language and Structures of Poverty in the Writings of the Hebrew Prophets,* Ph.D. diss., University of Michigan, 1986.

Ploeg, J. van der. "Les pauvres d'Israel et leur piété." *Oudtestamentische Studien* 7 (1950): 236–270.

Schottroff, Willy, and Wolfgang Stegemann, eds. *God of the Lowly: Socio–Historical Interpretation of the Bible* (Part 1–OT, Part 2–NT), Maryknoll, N. Y.: Orbis Books, 1984.

Wright, Christopher. *God's People in God's Land: Family, Land, and Property in the Old Testament.* Grand Rapids: Eerdmans, 1990.

NEW TESTAMENT

Aicher, G. "Kamel und Nadelöhr." *Neutestamentliche Abhandlungen* 1 (1908).

Augustin, George, et al. *Gospel Poverty: Essays in Biblical Theology.* Chicago: Franciscan Herald Press, 1977.

Batey, Richard. *Jesus and the Poor: The Poverty Program of the First Christians.* New York: Harper & Row, 1972.

Best, E. "Matthew 5:3," *New Testament Studies* 7 (1960/61), 255–258.

Collins, John. *Diakonia. The Sources and Their Interpretation.* Oxford: Oxford University Press, 1990.

Degenhardt, H. J. *Lukas, Evangelist der Armen, Besitz und Besitzverzicht in den lukanischen Schriften.* Stuttgart: Katholisches Bibelwerk, 1965.

Derrett, J. D. M. "Dives and Lazarus and the Preceding Sayings." *New Testament Studies* 7 (1960/61), 198–219.

Dombois, Hans. *Evangelium und soziale Strukturen.* Witten: Luther Verlag, 1967.

Feuillet, A. "Les riches intendants du Christ (Lk. 16:1–13)." *Recherches de Science Religieuse* 34 (1947): 30–54.

Gnuse, R. K. *You Shall not Steal: Community and Property in the Biblical Tradition.* Maryknoll, N. Y.: Orbis Books, 1985.

Gonzalez, Ruiz, and José Maria. *Pobreza Evangélica y Promoción Christiana*. Barcelona: Nova Terra, 1966.

Grant, F. C. *The Economic Background of the Gospels*. Oxford: Oxford University Press, 1926.

Grant, R. M. "Private Property," and "The Organization of Alms," in his *EarlyChristianity and Society*. New York: Harper & Row, 1977.

Gressmann, H. "Vom reichen Mann und armen Lazarus." *Abhandlungen der preussischen Akademie der Wissenschaften, phil.–hist. Klasse No. 7*. Berlin, 1918.

Heiligenthal, R. "Werke der Barmherzigkeit oder Almosen: Zur Bedeutung von Eleemosyne." *Novum Testamentum* 25 (Oct . 1983): 289–301.

Hiers, Richard. "Friends by Unrighteous Mammon: The Eschatological Proletariat (Lk 16:9)." *Journal of the American Academy of Religion* 38:1 (1970): 30–36.

Johnson, Luke. *The Literary Function of Possessions in Luke–Acts*. Missoula: Scholars Press, 1977.

Keck, L. A. "The Poor among the Saints in the New Testament." *Zeitschrift für die neutestamentliche Wissenschaft* 56 (1965): 100–129.

_____. "The Poor among the Saints in Jewish Christianity and Qumran." *Zeitschrift für die neutestamentliche Wissenschaft* 57 (1966): 54–78.

Kidd, Reggie. *Wealth and Beneficence in the Pastoral Epistles*. Atlanta: Scholars Press, 1990.

Kümmel, W. G. "Der Begriff des Eigentums im Neuen Testament," in *Heilsgeschehen und Geschichte* (Marburger theologische Studien) 3 (1965): 271–277.

Maynard–Reid, P. U. *Poverty and Wealth in James*. Maryknoll, N. Y.: Orbis, 1987.

Mealand, David. *Poverty and Expectation in the Gospels*. London: SPCK, 1980.

Mottu, Henri. "Exegesis with Key Marxian Categories of Lk. 189–114." *Union Seminary Quarterly Review* 29:3–4 (1974): 195–213.

Moxnes, Halvor. *The Economy of the Kingdom: Social Conflicts and Economic Relations in Luke 's Gospel*. Philadelphia: Fortress Press, 1988.

Pilgrim, Walter. *Good News to the Poor*. Minneapolis: Augsburg Publishing House, 1982.

Sattler, W. "Die Anawim im Zeitalter Jesu Christi." In *Festgabe für H. Jülicher*. Tübingen, 1927, 1–15.

Schäfer, Gerhard, and T. Strohm, eds. *Diakonie-biblische Grundlage und Orientierungen*. Heidelberg: Heidelberger Verlagsanstalt, 1990.

Schottroff, Luise, and W. Stegemann. *Jesus and the Hope of the Poor*. Maryknoll, N. Y.: Orbis, 1986.

Seidensticker, A. "St. Paul et la pauvreté." In *La Pauvreté Evangélique*. Paris: Cerf, 1971.

EARLY CHURCH

Amantos, K. "Zu den Wohltätigen Stiftungen von Byzanz." *Orientalia Christiana Periodica* 21 (1955): 15–20.

Avila, Charles. *Ownership: Early Christian Teaching*. Maryknoll, N. Y.: Orbis Books, 1983.

Banks, Robert. "The Early Church as a Caring Community." *Evangelical Review of Theology* 7/2 (Oct 1983): 310–327.

Bauer, C. "Diskussionen um die Zins- und Wucherfrage auf dem Konstanzer Konzil." In A. Franzen and W. Müller, ed. *Das Konzil von Konstanz*, Freiburg i. B.: Herder, 1964.

Beyschlag, K. "Christentum und Veränderung in der alten Kirche." *Kerygma und Dogma* 18 (1972): 26–55.

Bornkamm, G. "Christus und die Welt in der urchristliches Botschaft." In *Zeitschrift für Theologie und Kirche* 47 (1950): 212–226.

Bravo, R. Sierra. *Doctrina social y económica de los padres de la Iglesia*. Madrid: COMPI, 1976.

Campenhausen, H. "Early Christian Asceticism." In his *Tradition and Life in The Church*. Philadelphia: Fortress Press, 1968.

Christophe, P. *L'Usage Chrétién du droit de Propriété dans l'Ecriture et la Tradition Patristique*. Paris: Lethielleux, 1964.

Constantelos, Demetrios. *Byzantine Philanthropy and Social Welfare*. New Brunswick, N.J.: Rutgers University Press,1968.

_____. "Basil the Great's Social Thought and Involvement." *Greek Orthodox Theological Review* 26 (Spr/Sum 1981): 81–86.

Countryman, L. William. *The Rich Christian in the Church of the Early Empire*. New York: Mellen, 1980.

_____. "Welfare in the Churches of Asia Minor under the Early Roman Empire." *Society of Biblical Literature Seminar Papers* 16 (1979): 131–146.

Gager, John. *Kingdom and Community: The Social World of Early Christianity*. Englewood Cliffs, N.J.: Prentice–Hall, 1975.

Giet, Stanislaus. *Les Idées et l'Action sociale de Saint Basile*. Paris, 1941.

Giordani, Igino. *The Social Message of the Early Church Fathers*. Boston: St. Paul Editions, 1977.

Gonzales, Justo. *Faith and Wealth: A History of Early Christian Ideas on the Origin, Significance, and Use of Money*. San Francisco: Harper & Row, 1990.

Groh, Dennis. "Tertullian 's Polemic against Social Co–optation." *Church History* 40/1 (1971): 7–15.

Hamman, A., ed. *Riches et pauvres dans l'Eglise ancienne*. Paris: Grasset, 1962.

Harnack, Adolf. "Das urchristentum und die soziale Frage." *Preussische Jahrbücher* 131 (1908): 443–459.

Harvey, Susan A. *Asceticism and Society in Crisis. John of Ephesus and the Lives of the Eastern Saints*. Berkeley: University of California Press, 1990.

Hauschild, W. D. "Christentum und Eigentum: Zum Problem eines altkirchlichen 'Sozialismus.'" *Zeitschrift für Evangelische Ethik* 16 (1972): 34–49.

Hengel, Martin. *Property and Riches in the Early Church: Aspects of a Social History of Early Christianity*. John Bowden, trans. Philadelphia: Fortress Press, 1974.

Hermann, E. "Die Regelung den Armut in den byzantinischen Klöstern." *Orientalia Christiana Periodica* 7 (1941): 406–60.

Kretschmar, G. "Ein Beitrag zur Frage nach dem Ursprung der frühchristlichen Askese." *Zeitschrift für Theologie und Kirche* 61 (1964): 27–67.

Langen, John P. "Augustine on the Unity and the Interconnection of the Virtues." *Harvard Theological Review* 72 (Jan/Apr 1979): 81–95.

Leipoldt, J. *Der Soziale Gedanke in der altchristlichen Kirche*. Leipzig: Koehler & Amelang, 1952.

Miller, Timothy. *The Birth of the Hospital in the Byzantine Empire*. Baltimore: Johns Hopkins University Press, 1985.

Niederer, Frances. "Early Medieval Charity (Pope Gregory the Great)." *Church History* 21 (Dec. 1952): 285–295.

Osiek, C. *Rich and Poor in the Shepherd of Hermas*. Washington, D.C.: Catholic Biblical Association of America, 1983.

Patlagean, Evelyn. *Pauvreté économique et pauvreté sociale*. Paris: Mouton, 1977.

Poirier, M. "Charité individuelle et action sociale...." *Studia Patristica* 12/1 (1975): 254–260.

Ramsey. "Almsgiving in the Latin Church: The Late Fourth and Early Fifth Centuries." *Theological Studies* 43 (June 1982): 226–259.

Ritter, Adolf. "Christentum und Eigentum bei Klemens von Alexandria auf dem Hintergrund der frühchristlichen Armenfrömmigkeit und der Ethik der Kaiserzeit Stoa." *Zeitschrift für Kirchengeschichte* 86/1 (1975): 1–25.

_____. "Frühes Christentum—des Beispiel der Eigentumsfrage." In Stephen Pfürtner, ed. *Ethik in der europäischen Geschichte* 1. Stuttgart, 1988, 116–33.

Saint Croix, G. "Early Christian Attitudes to Poverty and Slavery." *Studies in*

Church History 12. Oxford: Blackwell, 1975.

Schilling, Otto. *Reichtum und Eigentum in der altkirchlichen Literatur: Ein Beitrag zur Sozialen Frage.* Freiburg: Herder, 1908.

Seipel, I. *Die wirtschaftsethischen Lehren der Kirchenväter* (Theologische Studien der Leo–Gesellschaft 18). Vienna, 1907.

Sherwood, M. M. *Sermon on Alms by St. John Chrysostom.* New York: New York School of Philanthropy, 1917.

Staats, Reinhardt. "Deposita pietatis — Die Alte Kirche und ihr Geld." *Zeitschrift für Theologie und Kirche* 76 (1979): 1–29.

Uhlhorn, G. *Christian Charity in the Ancient Church.* New York: Scribners, 1883.

Wagner, Walter H. "Lubricating the Camel: Clement of Alexandria on Wealth and the Wealthy." In Walter Freitag, ed. *Festschrift: A Tribute to Dr. William Horderin.* Saskatoon: University of Saskatchewan, 1985, 64–77.

Winslow, D. F. "Gregory of Nazianzus and Love for the Poor." *Anglican Theological Review* 47 (1965): 348–359.

MIDDLE AGES

Abel, W. *Massenarmut und Hungerkrisen im vorindustriellen Deutschland.* Göttingen: Vandenhoeck & Ruprecht, 1972.

Aers, D. "Piers Plowman and Problems in the Perception of Poverty: A Culture in Transition." *Leeds Studies in English* 14 (1983): 5–25.

Arduini, M. "Biblische Katagorien und Mittelalterliche Gesellschaft: Potens und Pauper bei Rupert von Deutz und Hildegaard von Bingen." *Soziale Ordnungen* 2 (1980): 467–97.

Baron, Hans. "Franciscan Poverty and Civic Wealth as Factors in the Rise of Humanistic Thought." *Speculum* 13/1 (1938): 1–37.

Baumann, Priscilla. "The Deadliest Sin: Warnings against Avarice and Usury on Romanesque Capitals in Auvergne." *Church History* 59 (1990): 7–18.

Bernard, Matthaus. "Nudus nudum Christum sequi." *Wissenschaft und Weisheit* 14 (1951): 148–151.

Bezold, Friedrich von, "Die Armen Leute und die deutsche Literatur des späteren Mittelalters." *Historische Zeitschrift* 41 (1879): 1–37.

Bienvenu, J. M. "Pauvreté, misères et charité en Anjou aux XIe et XIIe siècle." *Moyen Age* 72 (1966): 389–424; 73 (1967): 5–34, 189–216.

Bligny, N. B. "Les Premiers Chartreux et la pauvreté." *Le Moyen Age* 22 (1951): 27–60.

Bolton, Brenda. "Mulieres sanctae." *Studies in Church History* 10 (1973): 77–95.

_____. "Sources for the Early History of the Humiliati." *Studies in Church History* 11 (1975): 125–133.

_____. "'Paupertas Christi': Old Wealth and New Poverty in the Twelfth Century." *Studies in Church History* 14 (1977).

_____. "Poverty as Protest: Some Inspirational Groups at the Turn of the Twelfth Century," in S. Goransson, et al. *The Church in a Changing Society.* Uppsala: Almquist & Wiksell, 1978, 28–32.

Bosl, Karl. "Armut, Arbeit, Emanzipation (Zu den Hintergründen der geistigen und literarischen Bewegung vom 11. bis 13. Jahrhundert)," in Knut Schultz, ed. *Beiträge zur Wirtschafts– und Sozialgeschichte des Mittelalters.* Cologne: Böhlau, 1976.

_____. "Potens und Pauper: Begriffsgeschichtliche Studien zur gesellschaftlichen differenzierung im frühen Mittelalter und zum 'Pauperismus' des Hochmittelalters." In his *Frühformen der Gesellschaft im mittelalterlichen Europa.* Munich: Oldenbourg, 1964, 106–134.

_____. *Die Grundlagen der modernen Gesellschaft im Mittelalter.* 2 vols. Stuttgart: A. Hiersemann, 1972.

_____. *Das Problem der Armut in der hochmittelalterlichen Gesellschaft.* Österreichische Akademie der Wissenschaften, Philosophisch–Historische Klasse. Bd. 294. Vienna, 1974.

Brandt, A. von. "Mittelalterliche Bürgertestamente. Neuerschlossene Quellen zur Geschichte der materiellen und geistigen Kultur." *Vortrag* (8/7/72), Heidelberg: Carl Winter–Universitätsverlag, 1973.

Burke, P., ed. *Economy and Society in Early Modern Europe: Essays from Annales.* New York,: Harper & Row, 1972.

Chiffoleau, Jacques. *La Comptabilité de l'au–delà: Les Hommes, la Mort et la Religion d'Avignon à la Fin du Moyen Age (vers 1320–vers 1480).* Rome: École Française de Rome, 1980.

Chatillon, J. "Nudum Christum Nudus Sequere: Theme de la nudité spirituelle dans les ecrits Spirituels de St. Bonaventure," in W. Dettloff, et al. *S. Bonaventura 1274–1974.* 4 (1974): 719–772.

Cipolla, C. *Before the Industrial Revolution: European Society and Economy, 1000–1700.* New York: Norton, 1976.

Clasen, S. "Franziskus von Assisi und die Soziale Frage." *Wissenschaft und Weisheit* 19 (1952): 109–121.

Clay, R. M. *The Medieval Hospitals of England.* London: Methuen, 1909; London: Cass, 1966.

Courtney, William J. "Token Coinage and the Administration of Poor Relief during the Late Middle Ages." *Traditio* 3/2 (1972): 275–295.

Couvreur, G. *Les Pauvres ont–ils des droits? Recherches sur le vol en cas d'extrême nécessité depuis la 'Concordia' de Gratian (1140)*. Rome: Gregorian University, 1961.

Curschmann, F. *Hungersnöte im Mittelalter*. Leipzig: Teubner, 1900.

Daniel, E. Rapphy. "Spirituality and Poverty: Angelo da Clareno and Ubertino da Casale." *Mediaevalia et Humanistica* n.s. 4 (1973): 89–98.

Devisse, Jean. " 'Pauperes ' et 'Pauperta ' dans le monde carolingien: ce qu 'en dit Hincmar de Reims." *Revue du Nord* 48 (1966): 273–287.

Diehl, A. "Gemeiner Nutzen im Mittelalter." *Zeitschrift für Wurttembergische Landesgeschichte* 1 (1937): 296–315.

Duplessis, Robert S. "From Demesne to World System: A Critical Review of the Literature on the Transition from Feudalism to Capitalism." *Radical History Review* 4/1 (Winter 1977): 3–41.

Eklund, O. P. "Charity Tokens of the Netherlands." *The Numismatist* 60 (1947): 867–876; 61 (1948): 19–28.

Epperlin, S. "Zur weltlichen und kirchlichen Armenfürsorge im karolingischen Imperium: Ein Beitrag zur Wirtschaftsgeschichte im Frankreich." *Jahrbuch für Wirtschaftsgeschichte* (1963): 41ff.

Erbstösser, Martin. *Sozialreligiöse Strömungen im späten Mittelalter; Geissler, Freigeister, und Waldenser im 14. Jahrhundert*. Berlin: Akademie Verlag, 1970.

Esser, Cajetan. *Origins of the Franciscan Order*. Trans A. Daly and I. Lynch. Chicago: Franciscan Herald Press, 1970.

—————————. "Die Religiösen Bewegungen des Hochmittelalters und Franziskus von Assisi," in *Festgabe Joseph Lortz*. Baden–Baden, 1958. 2:287–315.

—————————. "Franziskus von Assisi und die Katharer seiner Zeit." *Archivum Franciscanum Historicum* 51 (1958): 225–264.

Flood, David, ed. *Poverty in the Middle Ages*. Werl–Westfallen: Dietrich–Coelde–Verlag,1975.

—————————, and T. Matura. *The Birth of a Movement: A Study of the First Rule of St. Francis*. Chicago: Franciscan Herald Press, 1975.

Foster, K. "A Note on St. Thomas' Teaching on Charity." *Downside Review* 77:249 (1958–59): 271–76.

Friedberger, Walter. *Der Reichtumserwerb im Urteil des Thomas von Aquinas und der Theologen im Zeitalter des Frühkapitalismus*. Passau, 1967.

Freyhan, R. "The Evolution of the Charitas Figure in the 13th and 14th Centuries," *Journal of the Warburg and Courtald Institute* 11 (1948): 68–86.

Gavitt, Philip. *Charity and Children in Renaissance Florence: The Ospedale degli Innocenti, 1410–1536*. Ann Arbor: University of Michigan Press, 1990.

Genicot, L. "Sur le nombre des pauvres dan les champagnes médiévales." *Revue*

Historique 52 (1977): 273–288.

Geremek, Bronislaw. *The Margins of Society in Late Medieval Paris.* Jean Bimrell, trans. Cambridge: Cambridge University Press, 1987.

Gilchrist, J. T. I. *The Church and Economic Activity in the Middle Ages.* London: Macmillan, 1969.

Gonnet, J., and K. V. Selge. "Vaudois Languedociens et Pauvres Catholiques." *Cahiers de Fanjeaux* 2 (Toulouse, 1967).

Gonthier, Nicole. *Lyon et ses Pauvres au Moyen Age (1350–1500).* Lyon: Hermes, 1978.

_____. "Les Hôpitaux et les Pauvres à la fin du Moyen Age: l'Exemple de Lyon." *Le Moyen–Age* 84 (1978): 279–308.

Graus, F. "Social Utopias of the Middle Ages." *Past and Present* 38 (1967): 3–19.

_____. "The Late Medieval Poor in Town and Countryside." Sylvia Thrupp, ed. *Change in Medieval Society: Europe North of the Alps, 1050–1500.* New York: Appleton–Century–Crofts, 1964, 314–324.

Grégoire, Reginald. "L'Adage ascetique 'Nudus nudum Christum sequi.'" *Studi Storici in Onore de Ottorino Bertolini.* 2 vols. Pisa: Pacini, 1972. 1: 395–409.

_____. "La place de la pauvreté dans la conception et la pratique de la vie monastique médiéval latine." *Il Monochesmo e la riforma ecclesiastica.* Milan: Publicazioni dell' Università cattolica del Sacro Cuore, 1971, 173–192.

Grosso, Anna Lazzarino del. *Armut und Reichtum im Denken Gerhohs von Reichersberg.* Munich, 1973.

Grundmann, Herbert. *Religiöse Bewegungen im Mittelalter: Untersuchungen über die geschichtlichen zusammenhänge zwischen der Ketzerei den Bettelorden und der religiösen Frauenbewegung im 12. und 13. Jahrhundert….* Hildesheim: Olms, 1961.

Herlihy, David. *Medieval and Renaissance Pistoria: The Social History of the Italian Town, 1200–1430.* New Haven: Yale University Press, 1967.

Holzapfel, H. *Die Anfänge der Montes Pietatis, 1462–1515.* Munich, 1903.

Irsigler, F. "Divites and Paupers in der Vita Meinwerci." *Vierteljahresschrift für Soziale und Wirtschaftsgeschichte* 57 (1970): 449–499.

Jaher, F., ed. *The Rich, the Well–Born and the Powerful.* Urbana: University of Illinois Press, 1973.

Jetter, D. *Geschichte des Hospitals, Band 1: Westdeutschland von den Anfängen bis 1850.* Wiesbaden: F. Steiner, 1966.

Kirshner, Julius, ed. *Raymond de Roover: Business, Banking and Economic Thought in Late Medieval and Early Modern Europe.* Chicago: University of Chicago Press, 1976.

Kölmel, Wilhelm. "Apologia Pauperum: Die Armutslehre Bonaventuras da Bagnoregio als soziale Theorie." *Historisches Jahrbuch* 94 (1974): 46–68.

Lambert, M. D. *Franciscan Poverty: A Doctrine of the Absolute Poverty of Christ and the Apostles in the Franciscan Order 1210–1323.* London: SPCK, 1961.

Lamothe, M. S. de Nuce de. "Piété et charité publique à Toulouse de la fin du XIIIe au milieu du XVe siècle, d'apres les testaments." *Annales du Midi* 76 (1964): 5–39.

LeGoff, Jacques. *Your Money or Your Life: Economy and Religion in the Middle Ages.* New York: Zone Books, 1988.

Lesnick, Daniel. "Dominican Preaching and the Creation of Capitalist Ideology in Late–Medieval Florence." *Memorie domenicane* n.s. 8–9 (1977–1978): 199–247.

_____. *Preaching in Medieval Florence: The Social World of Franciscan and Dominican Spirituality.* Athens, Ga.: University of Georgia Press, 1989.

Lindgren, Uta. "Europas Armut, Probleme, Methoden, Ergebnisse einer Untersuchungsserie." *Saeculum* 28 (1977): 396–418.

_____. *Frühformen abendländischen Hospitäler und Fürsorge im Lichte einiger Bedingungen ihrer Entstehung, 'Historia Hospitalium.'* Munster, 1978.

_____. *Bedürftigkeit–Armut–Not. Studien zur spätmittelalterlicher Sozialgeschichte Barcelonas.* Spanische Forschungen der Görriesgesellschaft, Zweite Reihe, Bd. 18. Münster: Aschendorff, 1980.

Linge, David. "Mysticism, Poverty, and Reason in the Thought of Meister Eckhart." *Journal of the American Academy of Religion* 46 (Dec 1978): 465–488.

Little, Lester K. *Religious Poverty and the Profit Economy in Medieval Europe.* Ithaca: Cornell University Press, 1978.

_____. *Liberty, Charity, Fraternity. Lay Relgious Confraternities at ergamo in the Age of the Commune.* Northampton: Smith College Studies in History, 51, 1988.

_____. "Pride Goes Before Avarice: Social Change and the Vices in Latin Christendom." *American Historical Review* 76:1 (1971): 16–49.

McDonnell, E.W. *The Beguines and Beghards in Medieval Culture, with Special Emphasis on the Belgian Scene.* New Brunswick, N.J.: Rutgers University Press, 1954.

McGovern, John F. "The Rise of New Economic Attitudes: Economic Humanism, Economic Nationalism during the Late Middle Ages and the Renaissance A.D. 1200–1550." *Traditio* 26 (1970): 217–253.

McLaughlin, T.P. "The Teaching of the Canonists on Usury (XII, XIII, XIV centuries)." *Medieval Studies* 1 (1939): 81–147; 2 (1940): 1–22.

Marthaler, B. "Forerunners of the Franciscans: The Waldenses." *Franciscan Studies,* n.s., 18 (1958): 133–142.

Martin, J. L. "La pobreza y los pobres en los textos literarios del siglo XIV." In *A Pobreza e a Assisténcia aos Pobres na Península Ibérica durante a Idade Média: Actas das 1as Jornadas Lusa–Espanholas de Historia Medieval Lisboa 25–30 Setembro de 1972*. 2 vols. Lisbon, 1973. 587–635.

Marx, W. J. *The Development of Charity in Medieval Louvain*. New York, 1936.

Maschke, Erich. *Gesellschaftliche Unterschichten in den südwest–deutschen Städten*, Stuttgart: Kohlhammer, 1967.

Menning, Carol. "Loans and Favors, Kin and Clients: Cosimo I de Medici and the Monte di Pietà." *Journal of Modern History* (Sept. 1989).

_____. "The Monte's 'Monte': The Early Supporters of Florence's Monte di Pieta." *Sixteenth Century Journal* 23 (1992): 661-676.

Miller, Timothy. "The Knights of St. John and the Hospitals of the Latin West." *Speculum* 53 (1978): 709–733.

Moisa, M. "Fourteenth Century Preachers' Views of the Poor: Class or Status Group?" In R. Samuel and G. S. Jones, eds. *Culture, Ideology and Politics*. London: Routledge & Kegan Paul, 1983, 160–175.

Mollat, Michel. *Les Pauvres au Moyen Age*. Paris: Hachette, 1978. (English trans.: *The Poor in the Middle Ages*. New Haven: Yale University Press, 1986).

_____."La Notion de pauvreté au moyen âge: Positiones de Problèmes." *Revue d'Histoire de l'Eglise de France* 52 (1966): 5–23.

_____."Les Moines et les pauvres, XIe–XIIe siècles." *Il Monachesimo e la riforma ecclesiastica (1049–1122)*. Milan, 1971, 193–215.

_____. "Die Armut der Franziskus: Eine christliche und gesellschaftliche Grundentscheidung." *Concilium* 17 (1981): 706ff.

Mone, F. J. "Armenpflege vom 13. bis 16. Jahrhundert." *Zeitschrift für Geschichte des Oberrheins* 1 (1850): 129ff.

Monteuffel, T. *Naissance d'une heresie: Les Adeptes de la Pauvreté voluntaire au Moyen Age*. Paris: La Haye, 1970.

Moorman, John. *A History of the Franciscan Order from its Origins to the Year 1517*. Oxford: Oxford University Press, 1968.

Mueller, Reinhold C. "Charitable Institutions, the Jewish Community, and Venetian Society: A Discussion of the Recent Volume By Brian Pullan." *Studi Veneziani* 14 (1972): 37–82.

Müller, W. "Die 'armen Leute ' in ostfrankischen Urbaren." *Archiv für Geschichte von Oberfranken* 39 (1959): 29ff.

Mundy, J. H. "Charity and Social Work In Toulouse, 1100–1250." *Traditio* 22 (1966): 203–287.

Murray, A. "Religion Among the Poor in Thirteenth Century France: The Testimony of Humbert de Romans." *Traditio* 30 (1974): 285–324.

Niederer, F. J. "Early Medieval Charity." *Church History* (1952): 285–295.

Nimmo, D. "Poverty to Politics: The Motivation of Fourteenth Century Franciscan Reform in Italy." *Studies in Church History* 15 (1978).

Noonan, John T. *The Scholastic Analysis of Usury.* Cambridge, Mass.: Harvard University Press, 1957.

Parsons, Anscar. "The Economic Significance of the Montes Pietatis." *Franciscan Studies* n. s. 1:3 (1941).

Peters, Marygrace. "Early Dominican Poverty''s Influence on Twelfth and Thirteenth-Century Social Structures." *Dominican Ashram* 8/3 (1989): 127–140.

Petry, Ray. "Social Responsibility and the Late Medieval Mystics." *Church History* 21 (1952): 3–19.

Pope, Stephen. "Aquinas on Almsgiving, Justice and Charity: An Interpretation and Reassessment." *Heythrop Journal* 32 (1991): 167–191.

Poston, M. M. *The Medieval Economy and Society.* London: Weidenfeld & Nicolson, 1972.

Rapp, F. "L'Eglise et les pauvres a la fin du Moyen Age: l'exemple de Geiler de Kaisersberg." *Revue d'histoire de l'eglise de France* 52 (1966): 39–46.

Reicke, Siegfried. *Das deutsche Spital und sein Recht im Mittelalter.* 2 vols. Stuttgart: Enke, 1932.

Ricci, G. "Naissance du pauvre honteux: entre l'histoire des idées et l'histoire sociale." *Annales E.S.C.* 38 (1983): 158–177.

Roover, Raymon de. "The Scholastic Attitude toward Trade and Entrepeneurship." In *Business, Banking, and Economic Thought in Late Medieval and Early Modern Europe, Selected Studies of Raymond de Roover.* J. Kirschner, ed. Chicago: University of Chicago Press, 1974, 336–345.

Rosenwein, Barbara, and Lester K. Little. "Social Meaning in the Monastic and Mendicant Spiritualities." *Past and Present* 63 (1974).

Rubin, Miri. *Charity and Community in Medieval Cambridge.* Cambridge: Cambridge University Press, 1987.

Salter, F. R. "The Jews in Fifteenth-Century Florence and Savanarola 's Establishment of a Mons Pietatis." *Cambridge Historical Journal* 5 (1936): 193–211.

Schneider, J. "Die Darstellung der Pauperes in den Historiae Gregor von Tours." *Jahrbuch für Geschichtswissenschaft* 4 (1966): 57–74.

Selge, K.V. *Die Ersten Waldenser.* 2 vols. Arbeiten zur Kirchengeschichte 37. Berlin: DeGruyter, 1967.

_____. "Die Erforschung der mittelalterlichen Waldensergeschichte." *Theologische Rundschau* 33:4 (1968): 281–343.

Tierney, Brian. *Medieval Poor Law: A Sketch of Canonical Theory and its Application in England*. Berkeley: University of California Press, 1959.

_____. "The Decretists and the 'Deserving Poor.'" *Comparative Studies in Society and History* 1 (1958–1959).

Tits–Dieuaide, M.-J. "Les Tables des Pauvres dans les anciennes principalités belges au Moyen Age." *Tijdschrift voor geschiedenis* 88 (1975): 562–583.

Uhlhorn Gerhard. "Vorstudien zu einer Geschichte der Liebestätigkeit im Mittelalter." *Zeitschrift für Kirchengeschichte* 4:1 (1880/81): 44–76.

_____. "Der Einfluss der wirtschaftlichen Verhältnisse auf die Entwickelung des Mönchtums im Mittelalter." *Zeitschrift für Kirchengeschichte* 14 (1894): 374–403.

Ullmann, W. "Public Welfare and Social Legislation in the Early Medieval Councils." *Studies in Church History* 7 (1971).

Vauchez, André. *Religion et Société dans l'Occident Médiéval*. Torino: Bottega d'Erasmus, 1980.

Vignes, Bernard Joseph Maurice. "Les Doctrines Économiques et Morales de Saint Bernard sur la Richesse et le Travail." *Revue d'Histoire Economique et Sociale* 16 (1928): 547–85.

Weber, Maurice. *Les Origines des Monts–de–Piété*. Rixheim, 1920.

Werner, Ernst. *Pauperes Christi: Studien zu Sozial–Religiösen Bewegungen im Zeitalter des Reformpapsttums*. Leipzig: Koehler & Amelang, 1956.

_____. "Ideologische Aspekte des deutsch–österreichen Waldensertums im 14. Jahrhundert." *Studi Medievali* 3rd Series, 4 (1963): 218–237.

Wilks, M. "Predestination, Property and Power: Wyclif's Theory of Dominion and Grace." *Studies in Church History* 2 (1965).

RENAISSANCE AND REFORMATION

Ackels, Maria. "Das Trierer Städtische Almosenamt im 16. und 17. Jahrhunderts: Ein Beitrag zur Analyze Soziale Unterschichten." *Kurtrierisches Jahrbuch* 24 (1984): 75–103.

Alves, Abel. "The Christian Social Organism and Social Welfare: The Case of Vives, Calvin and Loyola." *Sixteenth Century Journal* 20 (Winter 1989): 3–21.

Antonio, Armas Rumeu de. *Historia de la Previsión Social en España*. Madrid, 1944.

Ashley, William James. *An Introduction to English Economic History and Theory*. London: Longmans, Green & Co., 1920.

Baker, J. Wayne. "Heinrich Bullinger and the Idea of Usury." *Sixteenth Century Journal* 5 (1974): 49–70.

Barge, H. *Luther und der Frühkapitalismus.* Gütersloh: Bertelsmann, 1951.

_____. "Die Älteste Evangelische Armenordnung." *Historische Vierteljahrschrift* 11 (1908): 193–225.

_____. "Die Entstehung der Wittenberger Beutelordnung," *Theologische Studien und Kritiken* (1913): 461ff.

Batori, Ingrid, ed. *Städtische Gesellschaft und Reformation.* Stuttgart: Klett–Cotta, 1980.

Bauer, Clemens. "Conrad Peutingers Gutachten zur Monopolfrage: Eine Untersuching zur Wandlung der Wirtschaftsanschauungen im Zeitalter der Reformation." *Archiv für Reformationsgeschichte* 45 (1954): 1–43, 45–196.

_____. "Melanchthons Wirtschaftsethik." *Archiv für Reformationsgeschichte* 49 (1958): 115–160.

Behr, H. J. "Stephen Kempe und die erste Lutherische Kirchenordnung der Stadt Lüneburg." *Jahrbuch der Gesellschaft für Niedersächsische Kirchengeschichte* 64 (1966): 70–87.

Beier, A. L. *The Problem of the Poor in Tudor and Early Stuart England.* London: Methuen, 1983.

_____. *Masterless Men: The Vagrancy Problem in England, 1560–1640.* London: Methuen, 1985.

_____. "Vagrants and the Social Order in Elizabethan England." *Past and Present* 64 (1974): 3–29.

Beintker, Horst. "Aspekte zu Art und Gemeinde in Bugenhagens und Luthers Kirchenordnungensprogramm." *Evangelische Theologie* 47/2 (1987): 120–137.

Bell, Susan. "Johann … Günzburg 's Wolfaria: The First Protestant Utopia." *Church History* 36 (1967): 122–139.

Bergier, Jean François. "La Pensée économique et sociale de Calvin." *Annales economies, sociétés, civilizations* 17/2 (1962): 348–355.

Beyer, Michael. "Die Neuordnung des Kirchengutes." In Helmar Junghans, ed. *Das Jahrhundert der Reformation in Sachsen.* Berlin: Evangelische Verlagsanstatt, 1989.

Biéler, André. "Calvin and Capitalism." *Reformed and Presbyterian World* 26 (1960): 151–162.

_____. *La Pensée economique et sociale de Calvin.* Geneva: Libraire de l'université, 1961.

_____. *The Social Humanism of Calvin.* Richmond: John Knox Press, 1964.

Bisle, M. *Die Öffentliche Armenpflege der Reichstadt Augsburg mit Berücksichtigung der Einschlägigen Verhältnis in anderen Reichsstädten Süddeutschlands.* Paderborn: Schöningh, 1904.

Blaug, M. "The Myth of the Old Poor Law and the Making of the New." *Journal of Economic History* 23/2 (June 1963): 151–185.

Blockmans, W. P., and W. Prevenier. "Poverty in Flanders and Brabant from the Fourteenth to the Mid–Sixteenth Century: Sources and Problems." *Acta Historiae Neerlandicae* (1977): 20–57.

Bog, Ingomar. "Über Arme und Armenfürsorge in Oberdeutschland und in der Eidgenossenschaft im 15. und 16. Jahrhundert." In his *Oberdeutschland: Das Heilige Romische Reich des 16. bis 18. Jahrhunderts in Funktion.* Idstein: Schalz–Kirchen Verlag, 1986, 56–72.

Böhmer, Wolfgang, and Friedrich Kirsten. "Der Gemeine Kasten und seine Bedeutung für das Kommunale Gesundheitswesen Wittenbergs" in *Wissenschaftliche Zeitschrift Martin Luther Univ. Halle–Wittenberg: Mathematisch–naturwissenschaftliche Reihe* 34 (1985): 49–56.

Bonenfant, Paul. *Le Problème du Paupérisme en Belgique à la fin de l'Ancien Règime.* Brussels: Palais de Académies, 1934.

_____. "Un Aspect du Régime Calviniste à Bruxelles, La Bienfaisance," *Bulletin de la Commission Royale d'Histoire de Belgique* 84 (1925): 265–292.

_____. "Les Origines et le Caractère de la Réforme de la Bienfaisance Publique aux Pays–Bas sous le Règne de Charles–Quint." *Revue Belge de Philologie et d'Histoire* (1926–27), 5: 887–904; 6: 207–230.

_____. "Hôpitaux et Bienfaisance Publique dans les Anciens Pays–Bas des Origines à la fin du XVIIIe Siècle." *Annales de la Société Belge de l'Histoire des Hôpitaux* Special Vol. 3, Brussels, 1965.

Brecht, Martin. "Luthertum als Politische und Soziale Kraft in den Städten." In Franz Petri, ed. *Kirche und Gesellschaftlichen Wandel in Deutschen und Niederländischen Städten der Werdenden Neuzeit.* Cologne: Böhlau, 1980.

Brigden, S. "Religion and Social Obligation in Early Sixteenth Century London." *Past and Present* 103 (1984): 67–112.

Brummel, (Bonnie) Lee. "Luther and the Biblical Language of Poverty." *The Ecumenical Review* 32/1 (1980): 40–58.

Burke, Peter, ed. *Economy and Society in Early Modern Europe: Essays from Annales.* New York: Harper & Row, 1972.

Burrell, Sidney. "Calvinism, Capitalism, and the Middle Class: Some Afterthoughts on an Old Problem." *Journal of Modern History* 32 (1960): 129–141.

Caprivi, Leopold von. "Mit Scharfem Ökonomischen Blick: Luthers Schrift vom Kaufhandel und Wucher Bleibt Aktuell." *Lutherische Monatshefte* 21 (1982):

382–385.

Carriazo, José Marciá. *Las Ideas Sociales de Juan Luis Vives.* Madrid, 1927.

Caspari, Fritz. *Humanism and the Social Order in Tudor England.* Chicago: University of Chicago Press, 1954; reprinted New York: Teachers College Press, 1968.

Chill, Emmanuel. "Religion and Mendicity in Seventeenth Century France." *International Review of Social History* 7 (1962): 400–425.

Chrisman, Miriam Usher. "Lucas Hackfürt, Welfare Administrator, and the Problems of the Urban Poor." In *Social Groups and Religious Ideas in the Sixteenth Century: Studies in Medieval Culture XIII.* Kalamazoo, Mich.: The Medieval Institute, 1978.

Clasen, Claus Peter. *Anabaptism: A Social History, 1525–1618.* Ithaca: Cornell University Press, 1972.

Cuvelier, J. ed. *Documents Concernant la Réforme de la Bienfaisance à Louvain au XVIe Siècle.* Bulletin, Commission Royale d'Histoire 105 (1940): 101–115.

Daniel, Charles E. "Hard Work, Good Work, and School Work: An Analysis of Wenzeslaus Linck 's Conception of Civic Responsibility." In L. P. Buck and J. W. Zophy, eds. *The Social History of the Reformation: In Honor of H. J. Grimm.* Columbus: Ohio State University Press, 1972, 41–51.

Davis, Kenneth. *Anabaptism and Asceticism: A Study in Intellectual Origins.* Scottdale, Pa.: Herald Press, 1974.

Davis, Natalie Zemon "Gregory Nanzianzen in the Service of Humanist Social Reform." *Renaissance Quarterly* 20 (1967): 455–4464.

_____. "Poor Relief, Humanism and Heresy: The Case of Lyon." *Studies in Medieval and Renaissance History* 5 (1968): 216–276.

Delmonte, Carlos. "Revisión del pensamiento social de Calvino." *Christianisma y sociedad* 3:8, 96–114.

Demandt, Dieter. "Zur Wirtschaftsethik Huldrich Zwinglis." Knut Schultz, ed. *Beiträge zur Wirtschafts– und Sozialgeschichte des Mittelalters: Festschrift für Herbert Helbig.* Cologne: Böhlau, 1976, 306–321.

Dueringer, Karl. *Probleme der Caritas in der Schule von Salamanca.* Freiburg: Freiburger Theologische Studien, 75, 1959

Dummler, Karl. "Die Leisniger Kastenordnung von 1523." *Zeitschrift für Evangelisches Kirchenrecht* 29 (1984): 337–353.

Duplessis, Robert Saint–Cyr. "Charité Municipale et Autorité Publique au XVIe Siècle: l'Example de Lille." *Revue du Nord* 59 (1977): 193–219.

Durnbaugh, D. *Every Need Supplied: Mutual Aid and Christian Community in the Free Churches, 1525–1675.* Philadelphia: Temple University Press, 1974.

Ehrle, Franz. "Die Armenordnung von Nürnberg (1522) und Ypern (1525)." *His-*

torische Jahrbuch der Görresgeshellschafts 9 (1888): 450ff.

Elert, Werner. *Morphologie des Luthertums*, vol. 2: *Soziallehren und Sozialwirkungen des Luthertums*, 3rd ed. Munich: C.H. Beck, 1965.

Elton, G. R. "An Early Tudor Poor Law." *Economic History Review*, 2nd Series 6 (1953–1954): 55–67.

Fabiunke, Günther. *Martin Luther als Nationalökonom*. Berlin: Akademie Verlag, 1963.

Ferdinand, Elsener. "Der Arme Mann, Pauper im Prozessrecht der Grafen und Herzoge von Savoyen." *Revue d'Histoire du Droit* 44 (1976): 93–113.

Feuchtwanger, L. "Geschichte des sozialen Politik und des Armenwesens im Zeitalter der Reformation." *Schmollers Jahrbuch* 32 (1908): 167–204; 33 (1909): 191–228.

Fédon, R. "De Valdo à Luther: Les 'Pauvres de Lyon ' vus par un Humaniste Lyonnais." In *Mélanges A. Latreille* . Collection de Centre d'Histoire du Catholicisme, Université de Lyon II. Lyon, 1972.

Fideler, Paul. "Christian Humanism and Poor Law Reform in Early Tudor England." *Societas: A Review of Social History* 4 (1974): 269–285.

Fischer, Thomas. "Der Beginn der Frühmodernen Sozialpolitik in Deutschen Städten des 16. Jahrhunderts." In *Arbeitspapiere des Forschungs schwerpunktes Reproduktionsrisiken, Soziale Bewegungen und Sozialpolitik* 3. Bremen: Universität Bremen, 1980.

_____. *Städtische Armut und Armenfürsorge ins 15. und 16. Jahrhundert*. Göttingen: Verlag Otto Schwarz, 1979.

Flynn, Maureen M. *Sacred Charity: Confraternities and Social Welfare in Spain, 1400–1700*. Ithaca: Cornell University Press, 1989.

_____. "Charitable Ritual in Late Medieval and Early Modern Spain." *Sixteenth Century Journal* 16 no. 3 (1985): 335–348.

Forster, Wilhelm. "Thomas Müntzer, Vertreter einer politische Utopie?" *Franziskanische Studien* 67 (1985): 134–144.

Fosseyeux, Marcel. "La Taxe des Pauvres au XVIe Siècle." *Revue d'Histoire del'Eglise de France* 20 (1934).

Galpern, A. N. *The Religions of the People of Sixteenth Century Champagne*. Cambridge, Mass.: Harvard University Press, 1976.

Geremek, Bronislaw. "Criminalité, Vagabondage, Pauperisme: La Marginalité à l'Aube des Temps Modernes." *Revue d'Histoire Moderne et Contemporaire* 21 (1974): 337–375.

Goertz, Hans–Jürgen. *Alles gehört Allen: das Experiment Gütergemeinschaft vom 16. Jahrhundert bis heute*. Munich: C. H. Beck, 1984.

Graham, W. Fred. *The Constructive Revolutionary: John Calvin and His Socio–Economic Impact.* Richmond: John Knox Press, 1971.

Greaves, Richard L. *Society and Religion in Elizabethan England.* Minneapolis: University of Minnesota Press, 1981.

Grimm, Harold J. "Luther 's Contributions to Sixteenth–Century Organization of Poor Relief." *Archiv für Reformationsgeschichte* 61 (1970): 222–234.

Gutton, J. *La Société et les Pauvres en Europe (XVIe–XVIIIe siècles).* Paris: Presses Universitaires de France, 1974.

Harvey, Richard. "Recent Research on Poverty in Tudor–Stuart England: Review and Commentary," *International Review of Social History* 24 (1979): 237–252.

Heller, Henry. *The Concept of Poverty: The Calvinist Revolt in Sixteenth Century France.* Leiden: Brill, 1986.

Hendel, Kurt. "The Care of the Poor: An Evangelical Perspective." *Currents in Theology and Mission* 15/6 (1988): 526–532.

Henderson, R. "Sixteenth Century Community Benevolence: An Attempt to Resacralize the Secular." *Church History* 38/4 (1969).

Hering. "Die Liebestätigkeit der deutschen Reformation," *Theologische Studien und Kritiken* 56 (1883): 661–729; 57 (1884): 207–275; 58 (1885): 195–263.

Herlihy, David. *Medieval and Renaissance Pistoia: The Social History of an Italian Town, 1200–1430.* New Haven: Yale University Press, 1967.

Hill, Christopher. "Puritans and the Poor." *Past and Present* 2 (1952): 32–50.

Hordern, Richard. "Luther's Attitude towards Poverty." In Walter Freitag, ed. *Festschrift: A Tribute to Dr. William Hordern.* Saskatoon: University of Saskatchewan Press, 1985, 94–108.

Hotton, John. *Liber Vagatorum: The Book of Vagabonds and Beggars.* London: Penguin Press, 1932.

Imbert, Jean. *Les Hôpitaux en Droit Canonique.* Paris: J. Vrin, 1947.

_____. *Les Hôpitaux en France.* Paris: Presses Univ. de France, 1958.

Irsigler, F., and A. Lassotta. *Bettler und Gaukler, Dirnen und Henker.* Cologne: Greven Verlag, 1984.

Jordan, W. K. *Philanthropy in England, 1480–1660.* London: Allen & Unwin, 1959.

_____. *The Charities of London 1480–1660.* London: Allen & Unwin, 1960.

_____. *The Charities of Rural England, 1480–1660.* New York: Russell Sage Foundation, 1961.

Jütte, Robert. *Obrigkeitliche Armenfürsorge in Deutschen Reichsstädten der Frühen Neuzeit.* Vienna: Böhlau, 1984.

_____. *Abbild und soziale Wirklichkeit des Bettler– und Gaunertums zu Beginn der Neuzeit.* Cologne: Böhlau, 1988.

_____. "Vagantentum und Bettlerwesen bei Hans Jakob Christoffel von Grimmelshausen." *Daphnis* 9 (1980): 109–131.

_____. "Poor Relief and Social Discipline in Sixteenth Century Europe." *European Studies Review* 11 (1981): 25–52.

_____. "Der Prototyp eines Vaganten– Haus von Strassburg," in Heiner Boehnecke und Rolf Johannsmeier, eds. *Das Buch der Vaganten:Spieler– Huren–Leutbetrüger.* Cologne: Prometh Verlag, 1987.

_____. "Die 'düche der Armen' in der Frühen Neuzeit am Beispiel von Armenspeisungen in deutschen und westeuropäischen Städten." In *Jahrbuch des Instituts für deutsche Geschichte* 16 (1987).

_____. "Diets in Welfare Institutions and in Outdoor Poor Relief in Early Modern Western Europe." *Ethnologia Europaea* 16 (1987).

Kahl, Gisela. "Martin Luther, 'Der Älteste Deutsche Nationalökonom. '" *Wissenschaftliche Zeitschrift der Friedrich Schiller Universität* 33/3 (1984): 315–326.

Kalberlah, Gerhard. "Der Soziale Gedanke in Bugenhagens Braunschweiger Kirchordnung." *Jahrbuch der Gesellschaft für Niedersächsische Kirchengeschichte* 51 (1953): 113–117.

Kelly, J. T. *Thorns on the Tudor Rose: Monks, Rogues, Vagabonds, and Sturdy Beggars.* Jackson, Missippi: University Press of Mississippi, 1977.

Kiernan, V. "Puritanism and the Poor." *Past and Present* 3 (1953): 45–51.

Kingdon, Robert M.. "Social Welfare in Calvin's Geneva." *American Historical Review* 76:1 (1971): 50–69.

_____. "Calvinism and Social Welfare." *Calvinist Theological Journal* 17 (Nov 1982): 212–230.

_____. "Calvin 's Ideas About the Diaconate: Social or Theological in Origin?" In C. Lindberg, ed. *Piety, Politics, and Ethics.* Kirksville, Mo.: Sixteenth Century Journal Publishers,1984.

Kiss, Igor. "Luthers Bemühungen um eine Sozial Gerechtere Welt." *Zeichen der Zeit* (1985): 59–65.

Klassen, P. J. *The Economics of Anabaptism, 1525–60.* The Hague: Mouton, 1964.

Knight, David. "Saint Ignatius ' Ideal of Poverty." *Studies in the Spirituality of the Jesuits* 4/1 (1972).

Kohls, E . W. *Evangelische Bewegung und Kirchenordnung.* Lahr: Schauenburg, 1966.

Kunst, Hermann. *Evangelischer Glaube und politischer Verantwortung, Martin Luther als politischer Berater seiner Landesherrn und seine Teilnahme an den Fragen des öffentlichen Lebens.* Stuttgart: Evangelisches Verlagswerk, 1976.

Lane, Frank P. "Poverty and Poor Relief in the German Church Orders of Johann Bugenhagen, 1485–1558." Ph.D. diss., Ohio State University, 1973.

_____, "Johannes Bugenhagen und die Armenfürsorge der Reformationszeit." *Braunschweigisches Jahrbuch* 64 (1983): 147–156.

Lange, Hermann. *Geschichte der Christlichen Liebestätigkeit in der Stadt Bremen im Mittelalter.* Münster: Münsterische Beiträge zur Theologie, Heft 5, 1925.

Laube, Adolf. "Social Arguments in early Reformation Pamphlets and Their Significance for the German Peasant 's War." *Social History* 12 (1987).

_____, ed. *Flugschriften der frühen Reformationsbewegung.* 2 vols. Vaduz: Topos Verlag, 1983.

Leclère, François. "Recherches sur la charité des bourgeois envers les Pauvres au XIVe siècle à Douai." *Revue du Nord* 48 (1966): 139–154.

Lehmann, Hermann. "Luthers Platz in der Geschichte der Politischen Ökonomie." In Günter Vogler, S. Hoyer, and A. Laube. *Martin Luther: Leben, Werk, Wirkung.* Berlin: Akademie–Verlag, 1968, 279–294.

Leonard, E. M. *The Early History of English Poor Relief.* Cambridge: Cambridge University Press, 1900.

Lindberg, Carter. "There Should Be No Beggars Among Christians: Karlstadt, Luther, and the Origins of Protestant Poor Relief." *Church History* 46 (1977): 313–334.

_____. "La Théologie et l'Assistance Publique, le cas d'Ypres." *Revue d'Histoire et de Philosophie Religieuses* 61 (1981): 23–36.

_____. "There Should be No Beggars among Christians: An Early Reformation Tract on Social Welfare." In C. Lindberg, ed. *Piety, Politics, and Ethics.* Kirksville, Mo.: Sixteenth Century Journal Publishers, 1984

_____. "Reformation Initiatives for Social Welfare: Luther 's Influence at Leisnig." In Diane Yeager, ed. *The Annual of the Society of Christian Ethics.* Washington, D.C.: Georgetown University Press, 1987, 79–99.

Lorz, Jürgen. *Das reformatorische Wirken Dr. Wenzelaus Lincks in Altenburg und Nürnberg (1523–1547).* Nürnberg: Korn & Berg, 1978.

Marshall, Gordon. *Presbyteries and Profits: Calvinism and the Development of Capitalism in Scotland, 1560–1707.* Oxford: Oxford University Press, 1980.

Martz, Linda M. *Poverty and Welfare in Hapsburg Spain.* Cambridge: Cambridge University Press, 1983.

Maschke, E. "Die Unterschichten der Mittelalterlichen Städte Deutschlands." In Erich Maschke and Jürgen Sydow, eds. *Gesellschaftliche Unterschichten in den Südwestdeutschen Städten.* Stuttgart: Kohlhammer, 1967, 1–74.

McKee, Elsie. *John Calvin on the Diaconate and Liturgical Almsgiving*. Geneva: Librairie Droz, 1984.

Moeller, Bernd. "Imperial Cities and the Reformation." In *Imperial Cities and the Reformation: Three Essays*, H. C. Erik Midelfort and Mark Edwards, eds. and trans. Philadelphia: Fortress Press, 1972, 41–115.

Muralt, Leonhard von. "Zwingli als Sozialpolitiker." *Zwingliana* 5 (1929–1933): 276–296.

Müller, Gerhard. "Johannes Bugenhagen." *Zeitschrift der Savigny Stiftung für Rechtsgeschichte* 72 (1986): 277–303.

Müller, Lydia. *Der Kommunismus der mährischen Widertäufer*. Leipzig, 1927.

Nitti, F. S. "Poor Relief in Italy." *The Economic Review* 2 (1892).

Nobbe, H. "Die Regelung der Armenpflege im 16. Jahrhundert nach den evangelischen Kirchenordnungen." *Zeitschrift für Kirchengeschichte* 10 (1889): 569–617.

Nolf, J. *La Réforme de la Bienfaisance à Ypres au XVIe Siècle*. Ghent: E. Van Goethem, 1915.

Olson, Jeannine. *Calvin and Social Welfare*. Selinsgrove: Susquehanna University Press, 1989.

Park, Katherine. *Doctors and Medicine in Early Renaissance Florence*. Princeton: Princeton University Press, 1985.

Parsons, Anscar. "Bernardine of Feltre and the Montes Pietatis." *Franciscan Studies* 1:1 (1941).

Parsons, Anscar. "The Economic Significance of the Montes Pietatis." *Franciscan Studies* 1:3 (1941).

Pelling, M. "Healing the Sick Poor: Social Policy and Disability in Norwich, 1550–1640." *Medical History* 29 (1985), 115–137.

Petri, Franz, ed. *Kirche und Gesellschaftlicher Wandel in Deutschen und Niederländischen Städten der Werdenden Neuzeit*. Cologne: Böhlau, 1980.

Pischel, Felix. "Die ersten Armenordnung der Reformationszeit." *Deutsche Geschichtsblätter* 17 (1916): 317–330.

Postel, Rainer. "Zur Bedeutung der Reformation für Religiöse und soziale Verhalten des Bürgertums in Hamburg." In Bernd Moeller, ed. *Stadt und Kirche im 16. Jahrhundert*. Gütersloh: Gerd Mohn, 1978, 168–176.

Pound, John F. *Poverty and Vagrancy in Tudor England*. London: Longman Group Ltd., 1971.

Press, Volker. "Martin Luther und die Sozialen Kräfte Seiner Zeit." In Erwin Iserloh and Gerhard Müller, eds. *Luther und die Politische Welt*. Stuttgart: Franz Steiner Verlag, 1984, 189–227.

Pugh, W. J. "Social Welfare and the Edict of Nantes: Lyon and Nîmes." *French Historical Studies* 8/3 (1974): 349–376.

Pullan, Brian. *Rich and Poor in Renaissance Venice: The Social Institutions of a Catholic State to 1620.* Cambridge, Mass.: Harvard University Press, 1971.

_____. "Poverty, Charity, and the Reason of State." *Bollettino Istituto di Storia della Societa et dello Stato Veneziano* 2 (1960): 17–61.

_____. "The Famine in Venice and the New Poor Law, 1527–1529." *Bolletino dell'Istituto di Storia della Societa e dello Stato Veneziano* 5–6 (1963–1964): 141–202.

_____. "Catholics and the Poor in Early Modern Europe." *Transactions of the Royal Historical Society* 26 (1976): 15–34.

_____. "The Old Catholicism , The New Catholicism, and the Poor." In Giorgio Politi, et. al., eds. *Timore e Carita I Poveri Nele ' Italica Moderna.* Cremona, 1982, 13–25.

Rau, V., and E. Saez, eds. *A Pobreza e a Assisténcia aos Pobres na Peninsula Ibérica durante a Idade Média.* Lisbon, 1973.

Rauls, Wilhelm. "Die Fürsorge für die Armen in der Geschichte der Braunschweigischen Landeskirche." *Jahrbuch der Gesellschaft für Niedersachsische Kirchengeschichte* 66 (1968): 178–209.

Rich, Arthur. "Zwingli als Sozialpolitischer Denker." *Zwingliana* 13 (1969–1973): 67–89.

Riis, Thomas, ed. *Aspects of Poverty in Early Modern Europe.* 3 vols. Stuttgart: Klett–Cotta, 1981; Odense: Odense University Press, 1986 and 1990

Rowntree, B. S. *Poverty: A Study of Town Life.* New York: Garland, 1980.

Rublack, Hans–Christoph. "Martin Luther and the Urban Social Experience." *Sixteenth Century Journal* 16/1 (1985): 15–32.

Rudolph, Günther. "Thomas Müntzers sozialökonomische Konzeption und das Traditionsbewusstsein der sozialistischen Arbeiterbewegung." *Deutsche Zeitschrift für Philosophie* 23 (1975): 558–569.

Rüger, Willi. "Mittelalteriches Almosenwesen. Die Almonenordnung der Reichsstadt Nürnberg." *Nürnberger Beiträge zu den Wirtschafts– und Sozialwissenschaften* 31 (1932).

Salas, Maria Jiménez. *Historia de la Assistencia social en España en la Edad Moderna.* Madrid, 1958.

Salter, F. R. *Some Early Tracts on Poor Relief.* London: Methuen, 1926.

Scharffenorth, Gerta. *Den Glauben ins Leben ziehen ... Studien zu Luthers Theologie.* Munich: Chr. Kaiser Verlag, 1982.

Scholl, H. "The Church and the Poor in the Reformed Tradition." *The Ecumenical Review* 32 (1980): 236–256.

Sommer, Donald. "Peter Rideman and Menno Simons on Economics." *Mennonite Quarterly Review* 28 (July 1954): 205–223.

Stauffenegger, R. "Réforme, richesse et pauvreté." *Revue d'Histoire de l'Eglise de France* 52 (1966): 52–58.

Strohm, Theodor. "Luthers Wirtschafts und Sozialethik." In Helmar Junghans, ed. *Leben und Werk Martin Luthers von 1526 bis 1546*. Vol. 1. Berlin: Evangelische Verlagsanstalt, 1983, 205–223.

Stupperich, Robert. "Das Problem der Armenfürsorge bei Juan Luis Vives." In August Buck, ed. *Juan Luis Vives: Arbeitsgespräch in der Herzog August Bibliothek Wolfenbüttel vom 6 bis 8 November 1980*. Hamburg: Hauswedell, 1981, 49–62.

Süssmuth, Hans. *Studien zur Utopia des Thomas Morus: Ein Beitrag zur Geistesgeschichte des 16. Jahrhunderts*. (Reformationsgeschichtliche Studien und Texte, 95) Münster: Aschendorff, 1967.

Sydow, Jürgen. *Städtische Versorgung und Entsorgung im Wandel der Geschichte*. Sigmarinan: Thorbecke Verlag, 1981.

Tawney, R. H., and E .E. Power, eds. *Tudor Economic Documents*. 3 vols. London: Longmans, Green & Co., 1924.

Thomson, J. A. F. "Piety and Charity in Late Medieval London." *Journal of Ecclesiastical History* 16 (1965): 178–195.

Tobringer, Alice. *A Sixteenth Century Urban Report* (1. Intro and Commentary, 2. Translation of Vives 'On Assistance to the Poor'). Chicago: University of Chicago, School of Social Service Administration, 1971.

Todd, Margo. *Christian Humanism and Puritan Social Order*. Cambridge: Cambridge University Press, 1987.

Trexler, Richard. "Charity and the Defense of Urban Elites in the Italian Communes." In F. Jaher, ed. *The Rich, The Well–Born, and The Powerful*. Urbana: University of Illinois Press, 1974.

Tronrud, Thorald J. "Dispelling the Gloom. The Extent of Poverty in Tudor and Early Stuart Towns." *Canadian Journal of History* 20 (1985): 1–21.

Valla, F. del. "La Mendicidad y el paro en el 'Socorro de los Pobres' de J. L. Vives." *Razón y Fé* 125 (1942): 78–95.

Van Cleve, John Walter. *The Problem of Wealth in the Literature of Luther's Germany*. Columbia, S.C.: Camden House, 1991.

Vogler, Günter. "Gemeinnutz und Eigennutz bei Thomas Müntzer," in S. Bräuer, and H. Junghans, eds. *Der Theologe Thomas Müntzer*. Berlin: Evangelische Verlagsanstalt, 1989.

Wandel, Lee Palmer. *Always Among Us: Images of the Poor in Zwingli 's Zurich.* Cambridge: Cambridge University Press, 1990.

Webb, Beatrice, and Sidney Webb. *English Poor Law History,* Part I: *The Old Poor Law.* London: Longmans, Green & Co., 1927.

Wee, H. van der. "Les Archives Hospitalières et l'Étude da la Pauvreté aux Pays–Bas du XVe au XVIIIe siècle." *Revue du Nord* 48 (1966): 5–16.

Weitzmann, Wilhelm. *Die Soziale Bedeutung des Humanisten Vives: Eine Analyse und Würdigung seiner Schrift, 'De Subventione Pauperum."* Borna–Leipzig: Noske, 1905.

Winckelmann, Otto. *Das Fürsorgewesen der Stadt Strassburg vor und nach der Reformation.* Leipzig: Heinsius, 1922.

_____. "Die Armenordnungen von Nürnberg (1522), Kitzingen (1523), Regensburg (1523), und Ypern (1525)." *Archiv für Reformationsgeschichte* 10 (1912–13): 242–80; 11 (1914): 1–18.

Wolf, E. "Die Sozialtheologie Zwinglis." In *Festschrift Guido Kisch.* Stuttgart: Kohlhammer, 1955, 167–188.

Wright, J. William. *Capitalism, the State, and the Lutheran Reformation: Sixteenth Century Hesse.* Athens: Ohio University Press, 1988.

_____. "Reformation Contributions to the Development of Public Welfare Policy in Hesse." *Journal of Modern History* (on demand supplement, D1145–D1179). Abstract in Vol. 49/2 (June 1977).

_____. "A Closer Look at House Poor Relief through the Common Chest and Indigence in 16th Century Hesse." *Archiv für Reformationsgeschichte* 70 (1979): 225–238.

Wunsch, Georg. "Luthers Beurteilung des Wuchers: ein Beitrag zur Reformatorischen Ethik." *Die Christliche Welt* 29 (1915): 26–31, 66–69, 86–91, 127–131.

MODERN PERIOD

Adams, Thomas. *Bureaucrats and Beggars: French Social Policy in the Age of the Enlightenment.* Oxford: Oxford University Press, 1990.

Alrutz, K., et al. *Poverty and Wealth.* Washington, D.C.: University Press of America, 1982.

Bindemann, W. "Zwischen Utopie und Realität: Kirche in Solidarität mit den Armen," *Die Zeichen der Zeit* 6 (1981): 201–213.

Bremner, R. H. "Modern Attitudes towards Charity and Relief." *Comparative Studies in Society and History* 1 (1958–1959).

Chatellier, Louis. *The Europe of the Devout: The Catholic Reformation and the Formation of a New Society.* Cambridge: Cambridge University Press, 1989.

Clouse, Robert G. *Wealth and Poverty.* Downers Grove: InterVarsity Press, 1984.

Colson, E. "Weber Revisited: The Reformation and Economic Development Today." *Fides et Historica* 4:2 (1972): 73–85.

De Swaan, Abram. *In Care of the State: . . . Welfare in Europe and the USA in the Modern Era.* New York: Oxford University Press, 1988.

Dickenson, R. *Poor, Yet Making Many Rich: The Poor as Agents of Creative Justice.* Geneva: World Council of Churches, 1983.

Dinges, Martin. *Stadtarmut in Bordeaux 1525–1675. Alltag, Politik, Mentalitäten.* Bonn: Bouvier Verlag, 1988.

Dorr, Donal. *Option for the Poor, A Hundred Years of Vatican Social Teaching.* Maryknoll, N. Y.: Orbis Books, 1983.

Dorwart, R. A. *The Prussian Welfare State before 1740.* Cambridge, Mass.: Harvard University Press, 1971.

Duchrow, Ulrich. *Global Economy: A Confessional Issue for the Churches?* Geneva: World Council of Churches, 1987.

Eisenstadt, S. N., ed. *The Protestant Ethic and Modernization.* New York: Basic Books, 1968.

Ellwood, David. *Poverty in the American Family.* New York: Basic Books, 1989.

Fairchilds, Cissie. *Poverty and Charity in Aix–en–Provence, 1640–1789.* Baltimore: Johns Hopkins University Press, 1976.

Gannon, Thomas, ed. *The Catholic Challenge to the American Economy.* New York: Macmillan, 1987.

Ginzberg, Lori. *Women and the Work of Benevolence: Morality, Politics, and Class in the Nineteenth–Century United States.* New Haven: Yale University Press, 1990.

Gollwitzer, Helmut. *Die reichen Christen und den arme Lazarus: Die Konsequenzen von Uppsala.* Munich: Chr. Kaiser, 1969.

Graham, Gordon. *The Idea of Christian Charity: A Critique of Some Contemporary Conceptions.* Notre Dame: University of Notre Dame Press, 1990.

Grün, Willi. *Speners soziale Leistungen und Gedanken.* Würzburg, 1934.

Gutierrez, G. *The Power of the Poor in History.* Maryknoll, N.Y: Orbis Books, 1983.

Harnack, A., and W. Hermann. *Essays on the Social Gospel.* New York: G.P. Putnam's Sons, 1907.

Henslin, James. *Homelessness: An Annotated Bibliography.* New York: Garland, 1991.

Higginson, R. "From Carl Schmitt to Dorothea Sölle: Has Political Theology Turned Full Circle?" *Churchman* 97/2 (1983): 132–140.

Hilton, Boyd. *The Age of Atonement: The Influence of Evangelicalism on Social and Economic Thought 1785–1865.* New York: Oxford University Press, 1988.

Himmelfarb, Gertrude. *The Idea of Poverty: England in the Early Industrial Age*. New York: Knopf, 1984.

Huften, Oliver. *The Poor of Eighteenth–Century France, 1750–1789*. Oxford: Oxford University Press, 1974.

Husock, Howard. "Fighting Poverty the Old–Fashioned Way." *The Wilson Quarterly* 14/2 (1990): 78–91.

Jennings, Theodore. *Good News to the Poor: John Wesley's Evangelical Economics*. Nashville: Abingdon Press, 1990.

Jeremy, David. *Capitalists and Christians: Business Leaders and the Churches in Britain 1900–1960*. Oxford: Oxford University Press, 1990.

Jones, C. *Charity and "bienfaisance": The Treatment of the Poor in the Montpellier Region 1740–1815*. Cambridge: Cambridge University Press, 1982.

Katz, Michael. *In the Shadow of the Poorhouse: A Social History of Welfare in America*. Basic Books: New York, 1986.

_____. *The Undeserving Poor: From the War on Poverty to the War on Welfare*. New York: Pantheon Books, 1989.

Krieger, Leonard. "The Idea of the Welfare State in Europe and the United States." *Journal of the History of Ideas* 24 (1963): 553–568.

Levi, Werner. *From Alms to Liberation: The Catholic Church, the Theologians, Poverty and Politics*. New York: Praeger, 1989.

Lindemann, Mary. *Patriots and Paupers: Hamburg, 1712–1830*. New York: Oxford University Press, 1990.

Lutz, Charles, ed. *God, Goods, and the Common Good*. Minneapolis: Augsburg, 1987.

Magnuson, Norris. *Salvation in the Slums: Evangelical Social Work, 1865–1920*. Grand Rapids: Baker Book House, 1990.

Mandler, Peter. *The User of Charity: The Poor on Relief in the Nineteenth–Century Metropolis*. Philadelphia: University of Pennsylvania Press, 1990.

Marsden, George. "The Gospel of Wealth, the Social Gospel, and the Salvation of Souls in 19th–Century America." *Fides Historica* 5 (1973): 10–21.

Mathews, Shailer. *Jesus on Social Institutions*. New York: Macmillan, 1928.

Mathias, Peter. "Adam's Burden: Diagnosis of Poverty in Post–Medieval Europe and in the Third World Now." *Tijdschrift voor Geschiedenis* 89 (1976): 149–160.

McKee, Elsie. *Diakonia in the Classical Reformed Tradition and Today*. Grand Rapids: Eerdmans, 1989.

Meeks, M. Douglas. *God the Economist: The Doctrine of God and Political Economy*. Minneapolis: Fortress Press, 1989.

Miguez, N. "Solidarity with the Poor: A Test of Ecclesial Renewal." *The Ecumenical Review* 31 (1979): 261–272.

Mommsen, Wolfgang. *The Emergence of the Welfare State in Britain and Germany, 1850–1950.* London: Helm, 1981.

Muelder, Walter. *Religion and Economic Responsibility.* New York: Scribners, 1953.

Murray, Charles. *Losing Ground: American Social Policy 1950–1980.* New York: Basic Books, 1984.

Nürnberger, Klaus, ed. *Affluence, Poverty, and the Word of God.* Durban, S. A., Lutheran Publishing House, 1978.

Odendahl, Teresa. *Charity Begins at Home: Generosity and Self–Interest Among the Philanthropic Elite.* New York: Basic Books, 1990.

Ohl, J. F. *The Inner Mission.* Philadelphia, 1911.

"On Becoming Poor: A Symposium on Evangelical Poverty." *Studies in the Spirituality of Jesuits* 8 (1976).

Owen, David. *English Philanthropy, 1660–1960.* Cambridge, Mass.: Harvard University Press, 1964.

Philippi, Paul, and Theodor Strohm, eds. *Theologie der Diakonie. Ein europäischer Forschungsaustausch.* Heidelberg: Heidelberger Verlagsanstalt, 1989.

Piven, F. F., and R. A. Cloward. *Poor People's Movements.* New York: Vintage Books, 1977.

——————————. *Regulating the Poor: The Functions of Public Welfare.* New York: Vintage Books, 1971.

Pollard, Sidney. *Wealth and Poverty: An Economic History of the Twentieth Century.* Oxford: Oxford University Press, 1990.

Rauschenbusch, Walter. *Christianity and the Social Crisis.* New York: Macmillan, 1920.

——————————. *Christianizing the Social Order.* New York: Macmillan, 1921.

Rossi, Peter H. *Down and Out in America: The Origins of Homelessness.* Chicago: University of Chicago Press, 1989.

Sachsse, C., and F. Tennstedt. *Geschichte der Armenfürsorge in Deutschland.* Stuttgart: Kohlhammer, 1980.

Sattler, Gary. *God's Glory, Neighbor's Good: A Brief Introduction to the Life and Writings of A. H. Francke.* Chicago: Covenant Press, 1982.

Schiff, Jerald. *Charitable Giving and Government Policy: An Economic Analysis.* New York: Greenwood Press, 1990.

Schiller, J. *The American Poor.* Minneapolis: Augsburg Press, 1982.

Scholtz, Harald. *Evangelischer Utopianismus bei Johann Valentin Andreae.* Stuttgart: Kohlhammer, 1957.

Smith, Timothy. *Revivalism and Social Reform.* New York: Harper & Row, 1957.

Solomon, Howard. *Public Welfare, Science, and Propaganda in Seventeenth Century France.* Princeton: Princeton University Press, 1972.

Taylor, G. *The Problem of Poverty 1660-1834.* London: Longman House, 1969.

Trattner, Walter, ed. *Social Welfare or Social Control? Some Historical Reflections on "Regulating the Poor."* Knoxville: University of Tennessee Press, 1983.

Wresinski, Joseph, et al. "Grande Pauvreté et Précarité Economique et Sociale." *Journal Officiel de la République Française* 6 (1987).

Index of Scripture References

Old Testament 1
Genesis
    book of 16
    3:17-19 195
    38 27
Exodus
    12:38 18
    20–24 19
    21:1-22 19
    21:28-32 19
    23:10-11 20
Leviticus
    19:35-36 20
Deuteronomy
    book of 24
    6:24 34
    14:28-29 25
    15:11 24
    16:20 26
    23:24-25 25
    24:17-28 25
    24:19-22 24
    30:15-20 24
Judges
    book of 20
    8:23 21
1 Kings 5:7 153
2 Kings
    4:17-37 143
    5:20-27 143
Nehemiah 5:1-13 27
Psalms
    book of 22
    45:4 22
    45:6-7 21
Proverbs, book of 93
Isaiah
    1:10-17 23
    5:8-23 23
    5:8-9 22
    7 23
    8 23
    11:3-4 23
    36 23
    39 23
    40 through 50 26
    61:1-2 2
Jeremiah 31:31-34 26

Amos
    2:6-8, ...22
    5:21-24 23
Sirach 4
Ecclesiasticus
    book of 179
    3:30 4

New Testament 30
New Testament (Syriac) 47
Q source 32-37, 40

Matthew
    3:1 36
    5 through 7 74
    5:3ff. 36
    6:2 34
    6:2-4 81
    6:3 36
    9:9 32
    10:1 40
Mark
    gospel of 32-35
    1:15 181
    1:19-20 31
    2:1 30
    2:14 32
    6:3 31
    10:17-31 34
    10:25 ....1, 29
    10:30 73
    12:1-12 31
    19:21 4
Luke
    1 through 17 38
    1:51-53 37
    4:18-19 2
    4:25-27 38
    4:7:1-17 38
    6:20 36-37
    6:20-21 33
    6:21 36
    6:22 33
    6:24-35 37
    6:29-30 33
    6:35 34

Luke (*continued*)

6:38 ....34, 37
6:45 37
7:34 33
8:1-3 39
9:3 34
10:4 34
10:7 40
10:9 34
12:22-31 34
12:31 35
14:21 66
23:55-56 39
24:1-9 39
John 2:1-11 139
Acts

2:44-45 39
4:32 179
4:32-35 39
5 39
8:9-24 143
18:3 35
Romans

15:24 35
15:25-27 35
16:23 40
1 Corinthians

4:10 63
9:6 35
13:8 140
16:1-14 35
16:29 35
2 Cornithians

8:2 35
8:9 74
8:13-14 35
9:7 128
Philippians 4:15-19 35
1 Thessalonians

2:9 35
4:17 36
2 Thessalonians 3:10 195
1 Timothy 5:18 40
1 Peter 2:12 72
Revelation

17:8 152
20:12 ....15, 152

Extra-Biblical Literature

Didache

1:4-6 40
13:1-7 40
2:6 40
3:5 40
4:5 40
Barnabas 19:8 40
Shepherd of Hermas

(Sim. 9.20.1-4) 41
(Vis. 3) 41
Diatessaron of Tatian 47

Subject Index

Abuse, spousal, 111, 113-14, 120
"Acres of Diamonds," by Conwell, 2-3
Acropolis of Constantinople, 85-86
Agape, and charity, 74
Agulhon, Maurice, 167
Akakios (priest), 83, 90
Akkadia, 9
Alexios I Komnenos, 86, 94
Alexis, St., 156
Almsgiving
    by confraternities, 159-60
    by Innocent III, 127, 136-37
    meanings of, 54-55, 58-59
    reforms of Rabbula, 50-51
    symbolic, to friars, 162
Amiaud, Arthur, 63
Amorites, 16-17
Amos (prophet), 23
Andrew of Crete, 84, 91, 98
Andrew the Fool, St., 79
Anna (abbess), 121
Anna Komnene, 77, 86, 94, 108, 115-16
Antecessor, Julian, 70
Antony of Egypt, 59
Antwerp, work week in, 196
Aquila and Priscilla (early Christians), 35
Arezzo, 201
Arianism, of urban ascetics, 89
Aristenos, Alexios, 102-3
Ascalon, city of, 31
Asceticism
    Life of the Man of God, 59-61
    models of, 57-58
    and social welfare, 54
    in Syrian Christianity, 55
    terminology of, 64-65
    urban, 8-898
    and wealth, 52
Ascetics
    Athanasia of Aegina, 113
    Mary the Younger, 111
    Rabulla, 48-66
    Simeon the Stylite, 55-66
    Theophano, 107
    Thomais of Lesbos, 112
Ashbrook Harvey, Susan, 4, 213
Ashdod, city of, 31
Athanasia of Aegina, 113

Athanasios, 1
Athenais-Eudokia, 107
Atonement, and good works, 179
Attaleiates, Michael, 77
Augustine of Hippo, 5
Auxentios, St., 89

Babylon, 26, 10-11
Balsamon, Theodore, 102
Basil of Caesarea, 51, 92
Basil of Cappadocia, 78
Begging, 201
    in Byzantium, 78-79
    discrimination against, 203
    and reformation of worship, 188
    as salvatory work, 179
Belissareotis, John, 102-3
Benedictine Rule, and social welfare, 134
Benevolence, as *philanthropia*, 69
Berengar II, 129-31
Bergen, Norway, 204
Berthold of Regensberg, 158
Bethsaida-Julias, city of, 31
Bible. *See* Scripture Index
Black Death. *See* Plague
Bolton, Brenda M., 4, 213
Boniface (monk), 151
Book of Alms by Innocent III, 127-29
Bossey, John, 174
Boston University Humanities Foundation,
    viii
Botaneiates, Nikephoros III, 77
Brotherhoods, 184-85
Browning, Robert, 96
Brunhilda (queen), 151
Brussels, work week in, 197
Bryennios, Nikephoros, 77
Bucer, Martin, 191

Caesarea, city of, 30
Camoldolese Order, 156
Canaan, 1, 9-16
Canons of Rabbula, 52-53, 61-62
Canons Regular, 134
Capernaum, city of, 30-31
Carthusian Order, 156
Cascia, Simone de, 195
Castile, work week in, 197

Catechetical instruction, 95-96, 178
Catholics, and work week, 196-97
Charity
    Innocent III's treatises on, 127
    of Rabbula, 48-55
    ritualized, in middle ages, 154
    shift in meaning of, 44
    taxation for, in Israel, 25
    as women's ministry, 104-22
Chenu, Marie-Dominique , 147-50, 158, 163
Chiffoleau, Jacques, 167, 171
Children, 92-93, 200
Choniates, Niketas, 103
Choumnaina, Irene, 109
Christ. See under Jesus Christ
Christ Philanthropos monastery, 109
Christian tradition, and almsgiving, 81
Christianity, Byzantine and Syrian,43-82
Chrysostom, John, 51, 76, 81, 114-15
Church(es)
    at Astino, 160
    Church of the Resurrection, 91
    Constantinople, 87
    Jerusalem, 87
    Narbonne, 130-31
    St. Michael, 160
    St. Paul, 98, 114-15
    Santa Caterina of Bergamo, 160
    Santa Maria in Sassia, 137-38
    as welfare agent, 71-72, 125-26, 129-45
Church-state relations
    and ecclesiastical charity, 80
    and Orphanotropheion, 84, 98-99
    and social welfare, 54, 72, 79
Cistercian Order, 131-32, 156
Cities, in early Palestine, 30-31
Clemency, as philanthropia, 69
Clement of Alexandria, 4
Clientage, in early Palestine, 32-35
Cluny, abbey of, 133
Cluny III, abbey of, 153
Codaccioni, Felix-Paul, 208
Colomban (Irish missionary), 151
Commercial Revolution, 155-57, 186
Comnéne, Anne. See under Anna Kom-nene
Comnenoi (Komnenoi) emperors. See under
    individual forenames
Confraternities.
    earliest, 201
    establishment of, 125
    historiography of, 165-76

Confraternities (continued)
    sponsored by friars, 157-61
Congar, Yves, 148
Constantelos, Demetrios, 67-68, 70, 83
Constantinople, 83-104
Convents. See Monasteries/Convents
Conwell, Russell H., 2-3
Copenhagen, 200
Corinth, 40
Coulet, Noumlautel, 167
Criminality, and poverty, 199-200
Cyprian of Carthage, 58
Cyril of Alexandria, 47
Cyril Phileotis (ascetic), 94

Danel (legendary Canaanite), 15
Daniel of Sketis (abba), 79
Davidsen, Hans, 209ff.
De Cascia, Simone, 195
De Courson, Robert, 124, 126
De Huesca, Durand, 132
De Matha, John, 141-42
De Paul, St. Vincent, 20
De Vitry, Jacques, 126, 134-36
Deaconesses, 114-115
Deacons, in Edessa, 49-50
Death, in medieval theology, 194
Debtors, and Israelite law, 19
Demark,200, 205
Didache, 40
Disaster relief, 129
Disease, medieval understanding of, 194
Divorce, from mad spouse, 68-69
Dominican Order, 147-50
Dor, city of, 31
Doukaina, Irene, 108-9, 119
Durkheim, Emil, 166

East Roman Empire, 83ff.
Ecology. See Land management
Economy
    decline, and hereditary poverty, 208-12
    development of, and Commercial
        Revolution, 155-57
    and food supply, 199
Edessa, 45, 156
Education
    under Alexios I, 94-95
    catechetical instruction, 94-96
    of children, 92-93

co-educational, 93
Education (*continued*)
    within confraternities, 173-74
    law school, 102
    music, 89-92
    at Orphanotropheion, 85
    teaching methods, 93-95
Egypt, 1, 9-16
Elijah (prophet), 23, 56
Elsinore, Denmark, 205, 207-8
Emancipation, in Mesopotamia, 13
England, 137-38, 197
Epic and myth, 7, 11, 19
Eschatology,
    and almsgiving, 81
    and materialism, 35
Eshnunna, law code of, 10
Ethical behavior, and Scriptures, 93
Ethics. *See* Social ethics
Etymology
    of almsgiving, 54-55
    of asceticism, 64-65
    of philanthropy, 67-70
Eudokia (widow), 121
Eugenios Diakonia, 91
Europe
    profit economy in , 155-57
    religion in Middle Ages, 150-55
    work week in, 194ff.
Eustathios of Sebasteia, 93
Eustathios of Thessalonike, 79-81
Exodus, of Israelites, 17-18
"Eye of needle" saying, 1-2, 29.
Ezra (prophet), 26

Flaccilla (wife of emperor), 108
Florence, 201
Food distribution, 118-19
Food riots, and economic policy, 198-99
Foundling institutions, 200-201
France136, 138, 200, 208
Francis, St., popular views of, 161-62
Franciscan Order, and urban ministry, 148
Friars
    Poul Helgeson, 197-98, 207
    and lay confraternities, 158-61
    and urban poverty, 157
Fulk of Neuilly, 126
Funerals, as socioeconomic indicators, 211-12

Galata Hill, leprosarium on, 90
Gasparini, Giuseppina, 167
Genesios, Joseph, 85-86
Gennadios, 90
Gentleness, as *philanthropia*, 69
Giordano da Pisa, 179
Gleaning, and social reforms, 24-25
Gordon, Samuel, and economic decline, 211
Gospel according to the Silver Mark, 142
Gospel tradition, and materialism, 33-34
Grace, and social justice, 18
Gregory of Nazianz, 89
Gregory the Great, 126-27
Guilds, 158-59, 165-76

Hagia Sophia, 84, 90-91
Hagiography, and attitudes to charity, 73
Hammurabi Code, 10-13
Hanawalt, Emily Albu, 213
Hanson, Paul D. , 1, 6, 213
Haremheb (Pharaoh), 14-15
Harvey, Susan Ashbrook, 4, 213
Health care, in Edessa, 49
Hebdomon monatery, 80
Hebrews, emergence of, 17-18
Helgesen, Poul (friar), 197-98
Herakleios (emperor), 71, 87
Herbert (bishop of Lisieux), 152
Hereditary poverty. *See under* Poverty
Historiography,
    of confraternities, 165-76
    and funeral records, 211-12
    and oral history, 207
    of Orphanotropheion, 84-85, 87-88
    of social welfare, 148, 177
    of women, 105-6
History of theology, 149
Hofheinz, Fred L., viii
Holidays, and work week, 194-96, 205
Holobolos (instructor, orator), 97
Holy man. *See* Ascetic
Hosea (prophet), 2323
Hospices, 83
Hospitals, 83, 115-17
    establishment by Innocent III, 137-38
    in France, 136, 138
    history, 84-85
    and "hospital religious," 135-36
    maternity, 116, 139
    Pantokrator monastery, 83-116
    staff, 117

SS Anthony and Mary, 136
Hospitals (*continued*)
    of St. Sampson in Constantinople, 136
    of Sampson Xenon, 96, 100
    of Santo Spirito in Rome, 136
Hostels, in Rome, 137
Humanitas, and *philanthropy,* 2
Humility, and asceticism, 63-66
Hymns, Akkadian, 9-10

Ibas, bishop of Edessa, 48, 51
In Praise of Charity, by Innocent III, 128-29
Imitation of Christ, in asceticism, 65-66
Infanticide, 200
Innocent III, 126-45
Isaiah (prophet), 23
Isin, law code of, 10
Israel, 16-21, 26-27
Italy, 200-201

James (disciple of Jesus), 31
Janin, Raymond, 83
Jeremiah (prophet), 26
Jericho, city of, 30
Jesus Christ
    "eye of needle" saying, 1-2
    parables
        Good Samaritan, 38
        Great Supper, 38
        Rich Fool, 38
        Wicked Tenants, 31
    socionomic status, 32-33
    as *tekton* (craftsman), 31
    wedding at Cana, 139-41
Joachim of Fiore, 158
Joanna (wife of Chuza), 39
John (disciple of Jesus), 31
John II Komnenos, 84, 116
John of Salerno, 153
John the Almsgiver, 116
John the Almsgiver of Alexandria, 51
John the Merciful (Patriarch), 78, 81
John the Paphlagonian, 84, 99, 103
John the Theologian, St., 80
Joppa, city of, 31
Juan Luis Vives, 203
Judical powers, of orphanage director, 85, 97
Julian (361-363), 71
Julian of Cuenca, 125
Justin II (emperor), 77, 87, 98
Justinian (emperor), and Orphanotropheion,

100
Justinian I (d. 565), 71
Kain (Belgian univeristy), 149
Kantakouzenos, John, 69
Karlstadt, Andreas, 186, 189
Kataskepenos, Nicholas, 74, 95
Kazhdan, Alexander, 4, 213
Kee, Howard C., 4, 213
Kekaumenos (11th c. figure), 77
Keret (Canaanite king), 16
Kingship. *See* Monarchy
Knoerle, Sr. Jeanne, SP, viii
Kolde, Dietrich, *Mirror of a Christian Man,*
    178
Komnene, Anna. *See under* Anna Kom-nene
Komnenoi emperors. *See under* individual
    forenames

Laity, religious life of, 158-59
Land management, and Deuteronomic re-
    form, 20, 24-25
Langton, Stephen, 124
Law codes, 10-14
    Canon, 199
    Eshnunna, 10
    of Hammurabi, 10
    Basilika, 71
    Ecloga, 101
    Ekloge, 68
    Epanagoge, 76
    Justinian, 101
    Lipit-Ishtar of Isin, 10
    Maat, 10-14
    Palestinian, 30
    and*philanthropia,* 68
    Roman, 85
    reforms of, 101
Le Bras, Gabriel, 166
Leisnig Order, and social welfare, 187
Lekapenos, Romanos I, 76
Leo I, 83-84, 86, 92
    and Orphanotropheion, 99-100
Leo III, and Orphanotropheion, 101
Leo V, 86
Leo VI, 68
Leontios of Neapolis, 78
Leprosariums, 90, 116
Levi (Matthew; disciple of Jesus), 32
Lier, work week in, 196
Life of Rabbula, 46-55
Lille, France, 208

Lilly Endowment Foundation, viii
Lindberg, Carter, 6, 214
Lipit-Ishtar, code of, 10
Literature, in educational curriculum, 93
Little, Lester K., 4, 167, 214
Liturgy
    in Middle Ages, 150
    and Innocent III's charity, 140
    and preaching, 157
Luther, Martin
    sermons on social welfare, 186
    and social welfare, 177-78, 181-82
Lutheranism, 194
Lyall, Alexander, 208ff.

Maat (law and custom), 14
Macedonia, 35
Macedonians (so-called), and social welfare, 89
Madness, as grounds for divorce, 68-69
Makedonios (bishop), 88, 90
Makrembolites, Alexios, 69, 75
Maleinos, Michael (monk), 72
Mango, Cyril, 81, 86
Marathonios (deacon), 88
Marduk (Babylonian god), 11
Mary of Egypt, 74
Mary of Oignies, 135
Mary the Younger of Bizye, 110-11
Materialism, and morality, 80
Matthew (Levi; disciple of Jesus), 32
Mauss, Marcel, 166
Medieval theology, and social welfare, 149
Meersseman, G.G., 166-168
Mental illness, 121-22. *See also* Miracles
Mercy, and *philanthropia*, 69
Mesopotamia, social welfare in, 9-16
Michael IV, 84
Michael VIII, 97
Miller, Gregory, viii
Miller, Timothy S., 5, 214
Miracles
    of Jesus Christ, 139-41
    of Mary the Younger, 111
    of Thomais of Lesbos, 112
Miramolino, 142
Misericordia Confraternity, 159
Modena, 201
Mollat, Michel, 154
Monarchy
    in Ancient Near East, 21-27

Monasteries/Convents
    of Lips, 117
    of Theotokos Kecharitomene, 119
        economic restrictions, 52
    and materialism, 79-81
    in Middle Ages, 150
    philanthropy of, 117-18
    San Tommaso in Formis, 142
    social services within, 119-22
    and social welfare, 132-33
    and urban friars, 157-58
Monasticism, 88, 156
Monte Cassino, abbey of, 134
Morality, and materialism, 80
Muelder, Walter, viii
Müntzer, Thomas, 190
Music, of Orphanotropheion, 89-92
Mystikos, Nicholas, 69
Myth and epic, 7, 11, 19

Nazareth, 30
Near East, and roots of social welfare, 7-28
Nehemiah (prophet), 26
Nicea, 83
Nicean orthodoxy, and Arian heresy, 89
Nikephoritzes (monastery owner), 80
Nikephoros, 84
Nikephrous I, 71, 98-99
Nikephoros I Phokas, 79
Nikephoros III Botaneiates, 77
Niketas, 92
Nikon (priest), 86
Norway, 200, 204

Occupational groups
    craftsmen, 32
    financial/property manager, 39
    goldsmiths, 50
    money lenders, 33
    moneychangers, 33
    priests, 33
    tax collectors, 33
    tent makers, 35
Old-age home, 83, 102, 116
Olympias, St. (deaconess), 76, 114-15
Orphanage director, powers of, 97-98

Orphanotropheions
  of Constantinople, 83-104
  of Rome, 92
Orphans, 19, 139

Pachymeres, George (historian), 97
Palaeologina, Theodora, 117
Palaeologos, Michael, 96-97
Palestine, socioeconomic conditions, 30-32
Pantokrator Monastery, 84-85
Parker, Simon, viii
Patlagean, Evelyne, 53-54
Paul the Apostle, attitude toward wealth, 35-36
Peter Abelard, 150
Peter the Chanter, 124, 126, 134
Peter the Venerable, 150
Pfeffinger, Degenhard, 185
Philanthropy, 4-5.
  of women of means, 109-14
  as clemency, 69, 81
  concept/etymology of, 67-70, 103
  of deaconesses, 114
  of empresses, 106-9
  of institutions, 115-22
  as means of sanctification, 110
  as religious act, 109
  and social class, 77-78
Philanthropy, contrasted with humanitas, 2
Phileotes, Cyril, 74
Philistines, and early Israel, 21
Philology, and social class, 1
Photios, 69
Pickel, Bill, viii
Piquet, Guy, 205, 207, 212
Plague, 193-94
Poor Catholics Order, 132
Pope Gregory I, 4
Portugal, work week in, 197
Poverty. See also Wealth
  and asceticism, 49
  and begging, 180
  attitudes toward, 161ff.
  Byzantine understanding of, 76
  definitions of, 78-79
  and "deserving poor," 203
  and European Commercial Revolution, 155-57
  and Great Plague, 194
  hereditary, 205, 207-12
  "hidden poor," 201

Poverty (continued)
  in historical context, 154
  in Late Antiquity, 44-45, 53
  material vs. spiritual, 36-40
  in Reformation, 197-98
  shelters for the poor, 83
  terminology for, 74-75
  urban, 155-56, 180
  urban mendicancy, 155-56
Pragmatism, in Innocent III's program, 144-45
Prayer, by laity, 159
Preaching
  by friars, 157
  as social-ethical instruction, 181-82
Priscilla and Aquila (early Christians), 35
Prodromos, Theodore (poet), 1-3, 76, 96
Prokopios of Caesarea (historian), 107
Prophets
  Amos, 23
  Elijah, 23, 56
  Ezra, 26
  Hosea, 23
  Isaiah, 23
  Jeremiah, 26
  Nehemiah, 26
  office of, 22-23
  Samuel, 21-22
  Simeon the Stylite, 55-66
  and social reforms, 24
Prostitutes, reformatory for, 107
Protestants, and work week, 197
Psellos, Michael, 81
Pseudo-Prodromos (poet), 76
Ptochoprodromos (poet), 73, 76
Ptolemais, city of, 31
Pulcheria (regent), 107
Purgatory, medieval views of, 194

Qenneshrin, city of, 46

Rabbula (bishop of Edessa), 44-55
Rabier, Anne-Marie, 205, 207, 212
Reformation
  attitude to confraternities, 173-74
  attitude towards work, 194-95
Religion, in pre-commercial Europe, 150-55
Religious, activities of, in Middle Ages, 152
Rest homes, 83, 102, 116
Riis, Thomas, 6, 214
Ritual, importance of, 150-51

Roch of Montpelier, St., 194
Roffredo, Abbot of Cassino, 134
Romaios, Eustathios, 101-2
Roman law, in Constantinople, 85
Romanos I Lekapenos, 76
Rome
    and concept of poverty, 76
    East Roman culture, 83-85
    social class in, 1
    socioeconomic conditions, 30-32
Roncigraveere, Charles M. de la, 167

Sadducees, in early Palestine, 33
St. Andrew the Fool, 79
St. Alexis, 156
St. Roch of Montpelier, 194
St. Vincent de Paul, 20
Sainthood, marriage no bar to, 113
Saldarini, Anthony, 30-31
Salisbury, 204
Salvation, "economy" of, 178-79
Sampson Xenon institution, 96, 100
Samuel (prophet), 21
Scandinava, infanticide in, 200
Schumann, Reinhold, viii
Scottish immigrants, in Denmark, 205, 207-8
Scriptures. *See also* Index of Scripture refer-
    ences
    in educational curriculum, 93
    Hebrew, and social welfare, 7
    and social reform, 24
Scythopolis, city of, 30
Sepphoris, city of, 30
Sexual offenses, and poverty, 200-201
Shalom, 18, 23
Shamash, Akkadian god of justice, 9-10
Shepherd of Hermas. See under Index of Scrip-
    ture References
Simdat Sarrim (royal decree), 13
Simeon Salos of Emesa, 64
Simeon the Stylite (Syrian ascetic), 55-66
Simokatta, Theophylactus, 69, 77
Singing, song. *See under* music
Sixtus IV (pope), 139
Smith, Abraham, viii
Social ethics
    in Ancient Egypt, 14
    and Deuteronomic reforms, 26-27
    and Israelite law codes, 20-21
    of Martin Luther, 181-83
Social integration, and confraternities, 169f

Social justice
    in Ancient East, 9-10
    Deuteronomic, 25
    and the Hebrew Exodus, 17-18
Social reforms, and Israelite prophets, 24
Social services, of convents, 119-20
Social status
    and social welfare, 201-2
    vocabulary for, 1
    and worldview, 8
Social theory, and Israelite law codes, 20
Social values and worldview, 7-28
Social welfare
    in Byzantium, 70-82
    in Byzantium, 67-83
    in Canaan, 9-16
    and church-state relations, 54
    by confraternities, 174-75
    in Constantinople, 90
    vs. contemplative life, 133
    cultural roots of, 2-6
    and Deuternonmic reforms, 24-26
    in Israel, 18-19, 22
    epitomized in Santo Spirito hospital,
        137-38
    in Egypt, 9-16
    and Hammurabi Code, 12-13
    and hereditary poverty, 208
    Innocent III's attitude to, 123-45
    institutionalization of, 115-22, 186-91,
        201
    intellectual debate on, 124-25
    in Israel, 16-21
    legislation for, 186-91
    Luther's sermons on, 177-78, 186
    of "Macedonians," 89
    medieval motivations for, 81
    in Mesopotamia, 9-16
    in Palestine, 76
    vs. *philanthropia*, 70
    private, 72
    and Reformation, 177-91, 198
    as responsibility of the church, 126-45
    Roman, 76
    and social-political tension, 53-54
    and social status, 77-78,, 201-2
    in Sumeria, 9
    systematization of, 202-3
    and tithing, 25
    urban, 88-89
    and worship/liturgy, 178, 183-84

Socioeconomic status
    and confraternities, 169-70
    early Christian, 32, 35-36, 39
    in Palestine, 31-35
    and family decline, 208-12
    in Rome, 30-32
    in Syriac Christianity, 43-44
    of women, 106
Sociology, 166
Sons and Daughters of the Covenant, 49, 53
Soomenos (historian), 88
Sophia (wife of emperor), 87
State, as welfare agent, 70-72
State-church relations. See Church-state relations
Stilbes, Constantine (teacher), 96
Stoicism, 2
Sumeria, 9
Sweden, work week in, 197
Symeon the Theologian, 73
Synedrion (city council), 30-31, 33
Syriac Christianity, and asceticism, 43-66

Talbot, Alice-Mary, 4, 214
Tamar, story of, 27
Taxation, in Byzantium, 78
Themistios (rhetorician), 68
Theodora (empress), 107
Theodora of Thessalonike, 120-21
Theodore of Edessa (monk), 72-73
Theodotos, 86
Theology See Worship and social welfare
Theophanes (chronicler), 77, 87, 98
Theophano (empress), 107, 113-14
Thessalonica, 83
Thomais of Lesbos, 73, 110, 112-13
Thomas the Apostle, 45
Tiamat (Babylonian god), 11
Tiberias, city of, 31
Timokletos (hymnist), 90
Tithing, and social social welfare, 24-25
Tomb inscriptions, 14
Torah tradition, 26-27
Trexler, Richard, 168
Trinitarian Brethren, 141-42

Ugaritic texts, 15-16
Under/Unemployment, and medieval theology, 149, 204-5
United States social welfare, 27-28
Universitary of Paris, 124, 126
Ur, 10

Ur-Nammu (dynastic founder of Ur) 10
Urban asceticism, 88-89
Urbanization, 148ff., 155-57
Urukagina, ruler of Lagash, 10
Utu, Sumerian god of justice, 9

Val St.-Pierre, 133
Vallombrosian Order, 156
Vauchez, André, 4, 6, 140
Veronica, St., 140
Vincent, Catherine, 171, 174
Vincent de Paul, St. 20
Vives, Juan Luis, 203
Vocation, religious. See Ascetics; Friars, Prophets

Wealth
    as almsgiving, 58-59
    Franciscan attitudes toweard, 162
    in gospel tradition, 32-40
    Roman views, 1-2
    in first-century church, 37-40
    in second-century church, 40-41
    and support of clergy, 40
    and support of Jesus, 39
Weber, Max, 166
Widows, 19, 120
    jurisdiction over, 85
    and philanthropy, 72-73
Wittenberg Order, and social welfare, 186-87
Wolf, Robert, 83
Women
    as financial/property manager, 39
    and personal ministry, 104-22
    physicians, 116
    who support Jesus, 39
    worship practices of, 111-12
Work
    as civic duty, 195
    and medieval theology, 149, 193
    theology of, 194-95
Work week, length of, Table 1-Table 2, 196-97
Worker-priest movement, 148-50
Workhouses, 203-4
Worldview, 7-9, 13, 17
Worship, and social welfare, 178, 183-84, 188
Wuthnow, Robert, 177-78

Zachariah of Mitylene, 90
Zonaras, John, 94-95
Zotikos orphanage founder), 86-88